Shouting Down the Silence

Shouting Down the Silence

 A Biography of Stanley Elkin

David C. Dougherty

UNIVERSITY OF ILLINOIS PRESS

Urbana, Chicago, and Springfield

Frontispiece: painting by Joan Elkin, photograph
by the author. Used by permission of Joan Elkin and
Marilyn and Steve Teitelbaum.

Publication of this volume was assisted by
a grant from the Center for the Humanities,
Loyola University Maryland, Baltimore.

Library of Congress Cataloging-in-Publication Data
Dougherty, David C.
Shouting down the silence : a biography of
Stanley Elkin / David C. Dougherty.
p.   cm.
Includes bibliographical references and index.
ISBN 978-0-252-03508-1 (cloth : alk. paper)
1. Elkin, Stanley, 1930–1995.
2. Authors, American—20th century—Biography.
I. Title.
PS3555.L47Z63   2010
813'.54—dc22   2009024341
[B]

Shouting Down the Silence
is for Stanley's muse, Joan, and mine, Barbara.

Contents

ᘘ Acknowledgments ᘘ

Correspondence from or to Stanley Elkin, unless otherwise noted, is from the two Elkin Collections at the Olin Library, Washington University, or from diskettes from Elkin's personal computer that were supplied by Molly Elkin, Esq., and by the Olin Library. Special thanks to Chatham Ewing, then Olin Library Special Collections librarian, for transforming the documents from a Lexitron format to one that is accessible via standard word processing programs. Other archives cited include the Albert and Naomi Lebowitz and the William H. Gass archives in the Olin Library Special Collections, as well as the Anne and Georges Borchardt archives at Columbia University.

Citations to and quotations from Elkin's novels, stories, and novellas, unless otherwise noted, refer to the Dalkey Archive series of Elkin texts. Because Elkin often used ellipses in his works and his letters to emphasize a point or guide the sentence's rhythm, I've used bracketed ellipses [. . .] to indicate that I'm omitting content from quotations.

Portions of some chapters have appeared, in substantially different form, in other publications. The author thanks the editors for permission to incorporate revised versions in this book.

Portions of chapter 6 appeared in the following publications: *New England Review* 27 (2006); "Meeting Bad Men," the foreword to *A Bad Man* (Normal, Ill.: Dalkey Archive, 2003); and *Dictionary of Literary Biography: American Short Story Writers since World War II*, edited by Patrick Meanor and Gwen Davis (Detroit: Bruccoli-Clark, 1998).

Portions of chapter 7 appeared in "Listening In on America," the introduction to *A Casebook on Stanley Elkin's* The Dick Gibson Show, series editor Robert McLaughlin (Normal, Ill.: Center for Book Culture, Dalkey Archive Press, 2006).

A portion of chapter 10 appeared in "Mr. Elkin and the Movies," in *New England Review* 60 (2009).

Portions of chapter 11 appeared in "'Because Everything Has a Reasonable Explanation: Our Ticket to *The Magic Kingdom*," the introduction to *A Casebook on Stanley Elkin's* The Magic Kingdom, series editor Robert McLaughlin (Normal, Ill.: Center for Book Culture, Dalkey Archive Press, 2006).

I take this opportunity to thank the Elkin family, especially Joan, for help, information, and encouragement in the research for this project. My gratitude also goes out to the many individuals who have agreed to personal interviews and to those who have communicated with me by telephone, letter, or email during the past six years. The cordial assistance of the Special Collections staff at the Olin Library of Washington University is gratefully acknowledged, as is a James Merrill Library fellowship for research at the Olin. Travel funding from Chancellor Danforth and Loyola University Maryland, and hospitality at Sewanee University, helped to make the journey possible. Summer research assistants Michael Weineke and Jonathan Weedon, funded by the Center for the Humanities at Loyola, helped me to manage and coordinate ever-expanding file drawers. The interlibrary loan staff of the Loyola–Notre Dame Library ably and graciously located and supplied access to rare published items.

 Shouting Down the Silence

🎛 1 🎛 "A Sum of Private Frequencies"

> [I]t is still his—uniquely inflected, Gibson-timbered, a sum of
> private frequencies and personal resonances, as marked as his
> thumbs—because the show must go on and he must be on it.
>
> —*The Dick Gibson Show*

More than a decade after his death in 1995, Stanley Elkin's
place in twentieth-century literary history appears to be even more in question
than it was during the final decade of his life. He emerged from the cultural and
literary revolutions of the 1960s as a prominent Young Turk, a radical innovator
in both style and theme, whose influence among the literary community was by
1980 almost universally acknowledged. One could confidently have predicted
that he would be recognized by future generations as a leading figure in the
literary history of his time. He won many major awards; in his roles as mentor,
university teacher, presenter and leader at a variety of influential writers' conferences, and extraordinarily successful reader on the lecture circuit, he impressed
his force and example on an entire generation of younger writers. He was arguably by 1980 among the dozen most influential fiction writers in North America.
As his work matured and his themes took on a greater seriousness during the
1980s, however, Elkin watched in disappointment as his sales plummeted and
as other writers emerged as the era's leading stylists. As his health deteriorated,
his novels were remaindered and shortly after his death a posthumous national
Book Critics Circle Award was more a recognition of the value of Elkin's oeuvre
than of his final novel's individual merits. Elkin's novels and collections of stories
eased out of print, to be issued by Dalkey Archive Press in an effort to keep the
work available long enough for readers to catch up with the talent of this truly
extraordinary, and brilliant, literary innovator.

Although he was a generous mentor to many younger writers, Elkin may have
contributed to the decrease in his works' popularity both in the general reading
public and the literary community by insisting on the absolute uniqueness of his
art. Much as he resisted in his personal life the "myth of the American Artist," he
maintained, consistently and sometimes stubbornly, that his work should not be
approached via the context of the many literary movements that emerged out of
the 1960s. Although Elkin was a true original, an eccentric and often outrageous

creative person, he lived a life that was quite unlike the prevailing myth of the American artist. Unlike Ernest Hemingway and Norman Mailer, who lusted after adventure and the public spotlight, often projecting their own thinly described experiences as the source of their work, Elkin lived a quiet upper-middle class life in University City, Missouri. His protagonists often reflect elements of Elkin's personality, although he insisted that his characters weren't autobiographical—a claim this biography contests. The flamboyant antisocial behavior of his protagonists originated in Stanley's imagination, not in his experience. Moreover, he took an interest in politics and is believed by friends and associates to have voted generally Democratic and progressive, but he was largely uninterested in policy issues and only occasionally supported specific candidates or platforms. Overall, politics didn't occupy center stage in his life. He invented a famous telephone call from President Nixon to end his masterpiece about communication and radio, *The Dick Gibson Show* (1971), in which Nixon's frustrations about his inability to end the Vietnam War mirror on a national scale the personal anxieties of those persons who stay up all night to listen to and participate in the comparatively new entertainment phenomenon of talk radio. And one of his final essays, unfortunately never published, was about the theatricality of the 1992 Democratic Convention, recalling, perhaps, Mailer's journalistic innovations in *Miami and the Siege of Chicago* and *St. George and the Godfather*. But his closest friends agree that for Elkin politics was more a spectator sport than a serious preoccupation.

Moreover, in an age that chronicled author affairs in the tabloids and in which the serial marriages of such writers as Hemingway, John Updike, Saul Bellow, and Philip Roth rated gossip column notice, very little scandal ever wafted near Elkin. He married Joan Jacobsen on January 17, 1953, and they remained together for the rest of his life. He dedicated most of his books to her, and her art—she's a gifted painter—adorns several of his book jackets. One of his final novellas, "Her Sense of Timing," is a thinly disguised tribute to their love and his dependence on Joan as his health deteriorated during the 1980s. He and his family lived in University City, Missouri, about which he wrote the charming essay "Why I Live Where I Live" (1980). There were few hints, except for his recreational and subsequently medicinal use of marijuana, of personal scandal. He was, however, a gregarious man who needed very much to be the center of any gathering, and his behavior was often innocently and sometimes deliberately outrageous. But his skills as a raconteur and wit were so compelling that his colleagues and acquaintances eagerly accommodated him. I want to make public my gratitude to Joan for the patient and supportive help she has provided in piecing together this life history. She has offered leads, anecdotes, encouragement, wise counsel, and inspiration.

My goal is to guide the reader through the life history of an extraordinarily talented, complex, and original creator whose life and work were driven by a paradox central to the American artistic experience of his era. From the publication of his second novel, *A Bad Man* (1967), to his death, Elkin was driven by the desire for both commercial and artistic success. These two goals contained the seeds of their inevitable contradictions and therefore propelled him in conflicting directions. Although materially and professionally successful by middle-class measures, even by standards for university faculty, Elkin felt that he never received the recognition and rewards his art deserved. From the 1970s forward, he often expressed regret about, and occasionally even resentment of, his lack of popularity with general readers. Here's a version he shared in 1989: "All things being equal, I'd rather be me than Stephen King. But I wouldn't mind having a small percentage of King's sales. He wouldn't even miss them."[1] Among the shrewdest observers of American culture during the second half of his century, Elkin understood the artistic and ethical costs of fame and material success. He eloquently exemplified the compromises that can lead to material success and its discontents in many of his characters, particularly Dick Gibson, Ben Flesh of *The Franchiser* (1976), and Bobbo Druff of *The MacGuffin* (1991), without the condescension and even condemnation characteristic of many serious American writers. Moreover, his several brushes with Hollywood showed him another variation on what it takes to achieve success and fame. Much of his creative life was consumed by a desire to capture the Horatio Alger version of the American dream, a goal undoubtedly fueled by his excruciatingly complicated relationship with his immigrant father, who became a well-to-do salesman and a manifestation for his son of the possibility that one can through hard work and talent obtain wealth, comfort, material well-being, and power. This overwhelming need, with both practical and psychological ramifications, inevitably affected Elkin's relationships with other writers, whose success he from time to time envied, though he generally remained in cordial relationships with the individuals. Although it would be a facile generalization to propose that this paradox is true of all writers of Elkin's time and place, the temptation of ready wealth and instant success was especially powerful during a half-century when the authority of the written word was increasingly challenged by that of the visual image, and during which the film industry eagerly converted narratives—excellent, good, mediocre, and wretched—into box office enterprises. The artist in Elkin, however, always recognized the compromises this definition of success would involve.

On the other hand, Elkin was trained in the professional study of literature as an historical and formalist critic. He was subsequently affiliated with two distinct but related artistic communities, the university creative writing program and the writer's conference or workshop environment. He was therefore influenced by the vocation, widespread in American universities at mid-century, of the artist as one whose principal obligations are remaining true to his vision and resisting both the pernicious influences of materialism and the pressures of even the literary community to influence one's unique vision. Elkin's close reading of William Faulkner for his doctoral thesis and many seminars he subsequently taught reinforced this view. In Faulkner he found a mentor and an intimidating role model—a truly major writer negotiating his own careful path between his gregarious nature as both artist and raconteur, and the need to isolate himself to discover and shape his vision. This is a literary debt Elkin often acknowledged. In 1989 he confirmed that several sections of his favorite among his novels, *George Mills* (1982), contained deliberate adaptations of Faulknerian techniques, specifically those of *Absalom, Absalom!* Moreover, the technique of his masterwork, *Stanley Elkin's The Magic Kingdom*, owes much to that of Faulkner's masterpiece of the macabre, *As I Lay Dying.* After completing his dissertation, as a member of the English Department at Washington University Elkin participated in what can be called a regional center of artistic renewal. He had grown up in Chicago, during the decade that Theodore Dreiser and James T. Farrell played leading roles in the creation of a new, distinctly midwestern, fiction. When he moved to St. Louis he joined a creative writing faculty on the verge of achieving international literary prominence. Elkin's early successes were instrumental in establishing the university's English Department as a center of creative excellence, able subsequently to draw established writers like Howard Nemerov and William Gass to join Elkin, Jarvis Thurston, Mona van Duyn, and John Morris. His reputation helped the university to bring many established writers to campus for shorter-term Hurst fellowships. As a mentor at Bread Loaf and later Sewanee, and as a teacher of creative writing at Washington University and a visiting professor at several universities, Elkin participated, occasionally abrasively, in the nurturing of American creative writing during the second half of the twentieth century.

In spite of the support system for his creativity these networks of colleagues provided, Elkin became increasingly insistent on the uniqueness of his art. As his fame spread in literary communities in the United States, France, England, Germany, and Japan, he adamantly denied that his work was allied with, or should be read in the context of, such literary groups as "Jewish American writers"; although born Jewish, and although the characters in most of his early stories are Jews, Elkin was an atheist and most of his later characters' religious affiliations are ambiguous, though several were born in Jewish communities. He once maintained that the only "legitimate" Jewish American writer was not Joseph Heller, Bellow, Roth, or Elkin, but Isaac Bashevis Singer, who "writes out of an essentially Jewish tradition—almost a Hebraic tradition. He knows the rules; he knows the forks; and therefore he is a Jewish writer." He even more vigorously disassociated himself from the black humor movement of the 1960s. He reacted very strongly to this "label" when it was used to describe the temper and tone of his early successes, notably *Criers and Kibitzers, Kibitzers and Criers* (1966) and *A Bad Man.* He once snapped that "black humor is a term invented by

Time Magazine" and consistently maintained that he simply didn't understand what the term meant. He also defended his position by pointing out that black humorists paint a generally pessimistic picture of life by presenting disease, deformity, stupidity, or depravity as objects of humor, whereas he maintained that, despite the preoccupation of his fiction with disease, defeat, disappointment, and suffering, his work was optimistic. He once told an interviewer, "A writer has only two things to say. He says 'yes' or he says 'no.' To anything. He approves or he disapproves. It's of no matter, it's absolutely of no consequence whether he approves or disapproves. The important thing is the writer's style, the writer's invention."[2] And, like his contemporary John Updike, Elkin consistently chose "yes," despite his eloquent rendering of life's risks and disappointments.

He also responded even more aggressively to claims that he was a satirist. He maintained that satirists have political agendas, a desire to change or improve the world by mocking a person, organization, or institution. He claimed that despite, for example, his emphasis on the standardizing effects of consumer culture in *The Franchiser,* his goal was aesthetic rather than political—and that the artist who succumbs to the temptation to "change the world" risks trivializing the aesthetic goals of serious writing. Late in his life Elkin maintained equally stubbornly that he didn't consider himself a "metafictionist," a writer who creates works in which the philosophical creation of a system of reality is analogous to the artist's creating a narrative. He did, however, defer to interpretations claiming that *The Living End* (1979), a "triptych" of novellas, plays with the notion of the artist as creator/God, which is a tenet of much metafictional theory. Another paradox in the life of this uniquely creative personality asserts itself: he thrived on interaction with his fellow artists, and was a notoriously stern taskmaster in his creative writing classes, often reducing male and female students to tears with his merciless comments on their stories; his cabin at Bread Loaf was called the "Dragon's Den." By contrast, he was unusually generous to young writers by reading their work and providing book jacket comments about their materials when they were published. Although he cultivated his image as a tough, hardnosed critic, he was often a resource for struggling writers—but only if they were serious about the work they were doing. Despite his need for and generous participation in the wide variety of literary communities, however, Elkin insisted, perhaps wrong-headedly and surely stubbornly, that he was absolutely unique as a creative artist. He represented himself as one who cannot be read in the light of literary movements, but thereby isolated himself as a writer who refused to be affiliated with any literary context.

His life story, moreover, is an inspiring chapter in the human drama of overcoming obstacles. His adult life would bring far more than anyone's fair share of health problems, which he eventually faced with courage and which transformed his writing toward seriocomic contemplation of our mortal condition. He suffered his first heart attack at age thirty-eight, and then was diagnosed with multiple sclerosis four years later, although undiagnosed symptoms had presented earlier. As one close friend from graduate school put it, Stanley's diagnosis transformed him from a hypochondriac in his youth to a near-stoic contemplator of the universal human fate that we inevitably suffer our broken bodies[3]—as well as broken dreams. In response to one symptom of his disease, a loss of function in his hands, he became one of the first important American writers to use a word processor. During a time when many artists and cultural observers lamented the depersonalization of writing through this technology, Washington University invested in a word processor for a writer whose handwriting had become un-decipherable. Using what he subsequently referred to not only as a "dedicated" (that is, an early computer whose sole application was text creation) but also a "devoted" word processor, Elkin completed five important novels. He also used it to write his third book of novellas and an impressive number of essays, cul-minating in the collection *Pieces of Soap* (1992). Despite—and because of—his illnesses and their many related complications, his writing continued to grow in aesthetic richness and philosophical depth.

The title of this biography is a phrase Elkin created to describe his novel-in-copyediting, *The Dick Gibson Show,* a study in alienation, paranoia, and the possibility of communicating. When his editor asked for jacket copy, Elkin responded, in his own handwriting,

> Dick Gibson is an itinerant radio man who has been in radio since the begin-nings. This is the story of his apprenticeship, an apprenticeship as long as life. As fatal and roundabout as evolution. Using radio as a metaphor, the novel is about the human voice, which is, as Gibson finds out, the sound that the soul makes. The Dick Gibson Show shows us something important, whether it is laughing in one register or crying out in another, shouting down the silence. Also, it is very dirty.[4]

This is a good description of many Elkin protagonists, and of their creator's life as well. His characters, and Elkin, both as a novelist and personality, are LOUD. They talk and talk, asserting themselves against the eternal silence that surrounds us. As his life progressed, especially after his father's death in 1958, his heart attack, and then his diagnosis of multiple sclerosis, Elkin was increasingly preoccupied by human mortality. And it didn't take a heart attack to get the message across to him—the very first line of his first published novel, *Boswell: A Modern Comedy* (1964), reads, "Everybody dies, everybody. Sure." But as the message of nature became increasingly personal, Elkin became persuaded that artistic, strategic, and ornate language is our best and only response to the silence that surrounds and awaits us. As the literary work and character to which he alludes more often than any other single literary source puts it, "the rest is silence." Hamlet doesn't want to stop talking. Neither does Elkin. Neither do his characters. As Faulkner, his role model, said in his Nobel Prize address, "I believe that man will not merely endure: he will prevail. He is immortal, not because he alone among creatures has an inexhaustible voice, but because he has a soul, a spirit capable of compassion and sacrifice and endurance." As the squire Jöns in Ingmar Bergman's great film *The Seventh Seal* (1957) puts it when told to "be silent" by the knight as they await Death's final assault, "I shall, soon enough. But under protest." Elkin became silent "under protest" in 1995, but his artistic voice remains to show us how to do what Dylan Thomas exhorted his father and all of us to do: "rage, rage against the dying of the light." His friend Dan Shea captured this theme beautifully while introducing Elkin at his final Washington University appearance:

> His characters spiel on in order to outlast silence, which had a head start, which will have the last word. They know that so long as they speak, mortality bides its time. Death and the artist are cobra and flutist, but with this difference: Stanley Elkin taunts the cobra so that he will not himself be charmed into a vague dreaminess.

2 # When Stanley Elkin Was a Little Boy
New York and Chicago, 1930–48

When Dick Gibson was a little boy he was not Dick Gibson.
And he could get Omaha, could get Detroit, could get
Memphis.

   —*The Dick Gibson Show*

The child is father to the man.

   —William Wordsworth, "My Heart Looks Up"
   and "Ode: Intimations of Immortality"

About Elkin's early life we only have sketchy details. There are documented facts, such as his education in Chicago public schools, and friends recall trips they took together. But most stories of Elkin's childhood are exactly that—stories, many told by Elkin, or secondhand anecdotes by friends and relatives. This dependence on oral history compounds the biographical challenge for three obvious reasons: first, the majority of people who actually knew Elkin as a child are deceased; parents, uncles and aunts, teachers, rabbis, and other supporting adults are long gone, so the anecdotes are for the most part secondhand. Close childhood friend Harry Richman, mentioned as an offstage character in *The Rabbi of Lud*, lapsed into a terminal coma less than a month before I wrote him to arrange an interview, and we will never know how much valuable information was forever lost. The narratives that remain are subject to the embellishing that goes naturally with recalling our shared lives with someone who has gone on to become a celebrity. My recollection of playing against a baseball player who later starred in the major leagues has become embellished by his success, and I suspect that his fastball wasn't quite as lethal as I recall it, and I probably hit fewer line drives against him than I remember. Second, most people who became central to Elkin's adult life didn't know him as a child. His widow Joan met him in college, so her anecdotes about his childhood are secondhand. Similarly, Stanley's sister Diane was twelve years younger, so by the time she was six he was off to college, and she remembers a brother who was rapidly becoming an adult with a life away from home. She has fond memories of him as protector and playmate, a "great older brother," but "then he went away and I felt abandoned."[1] Finally, all of Stanley's friends—*all of them*—believe, suspect, or know beyond doubt that Stanley's stories about his youth, the source for most of the anecdotes they can share, were enriched, sharpened, and edged for mirth and humor by a master storyteller, so their literal veracity can never be assumed. As the hero of "The State of the Art" explains, "Because it makes a better story is why."

Although his fiction from time to time retold stories about his friends and associates, his work is also not a reliable source for inferring his childhood history. The names of childhood associates figure prominently in his early fiction, most frequently his mother's maiden name. He often expressed distaste for James Joyce's novels, and Elkin never wrote a "Portrait of Stanley as a Young Man." He did, however, from time to time fictionalize personal experiences he never had, like "Three Meetings," a memoir/essay recalling encounters with Vladimir Nabokov, whom Elkin never met.[2] On the other hand, some of his very early unpublished stories seem to draw upon his and his family's experiences. The challenge, then, is to sort fact from fable in order to construct a picture of the childhood that prepared Stanley to become Elkin.

Stanley Lawrence Elkin was born May 11, 1930, in New York City. His father Philip had emigrated from Russia as a toddler and became a salesman for the Coro-Cohn Jewelry Company, then the largest manufacturer of costume jewelry in the United States. About his grandparents little is known; Elkin told a relative in 1991 that his maternal grandfather's name was David Bloom. Philip married Zelda Feldman, who remained a housewife. The family lived in New York for three years after Stanley's birth, until Philip was transferred to Chicago to take over a territory that included much of the Midwest. As Stanley would say in a moving tribute, "He looked like a man of the forties. The shaped fedora and the fresh haircut and the shined shoes. He was handsome, I mean. Like an actor in a diplomat's part, a star-crossed secretary of state, say. Phil *looked* romantic. [. . .] He was a traveling salesman, a rhinestone merchant, a purveyor of costume jewelry to the trade. [. . .] He was no Willy Loman. I never asked him, 'What happened in Philly, Philly?'"

As this excerpt suggests, Elkin was in awe of his father, a man who in even Stanley's adult mind maintained mythic proportions. Certainly this powerful, wiry, handsome, driven, authoritarian, successful man was the single most forceful influence in his life, even after he became Elkin—he recalled with great pride that his father earned $50,000 a year in the 1940s. As he eloquently put it in 1987, "Some golden age of the personal we shared through his stories, his actor's resonances, all those anecdotes of self-dramatizing exigency, of strut and shuffle and leap and roll. In those days it was his America."[3] Yet being the son of a mythic figure, even if the son may have elaborated the myth, is a mixed blessing. There are few healthy father-child relationships in Elkin's work—as late as *The Rabbi of Lud* the protagonist reluctantly learns that his selfish parenting is the cause of his daughter's hoax about visits from the Virgin Mary, and a central conflict of *The MacGuffin* concerns Druff's failures as a father. Arguably the most autobiographical father-son conflict occurs in *The Dick Gibson Show*. The protagonist recalls his father's taking him to a pioneer radio event in Pittsburgh, as a result feeling "a special sense of his own destiny" (13). But when Gibson revisits his home during his "apprenticeship," he profoundly feels the impossibility of persuading his father of the value or importance of his commitment to perfecting his craft as a radio voice: "A pantomime of solid misunderstanding" (82). Gibson also finds his father mercurial, even protean, in his second return home. Many of Stanley's friends believe that he remained intimidated by Phil well into adulthood and literary fame. Marilyn and Steve Teitelbaum feel that the Stanley they knew, by then an acclaimed writer, was intimidated by Phil and felt his own mortality all the more keenly because of Phil's several heart attacks and early death: they "never got the flavor of love for his father, but of awe toward him." Other St. Louis friends, Naomi and Al Lebowitz, agree. Naomi was Elkin's colleague for more than three decades, and Al, a lawyer who handled the Elkins' taxes for many years, is also a novelist:

> NAOMI: His father was a hard-assed operator, who would demean Stanley by saying "What kind of a present is that for Father's Day" or something like that. Phil would want to teach Stanley some kind of economic lesson by showing him how stupid his gift choice was. He was also a wonderful storyteller, and a very charismatic man. Although Stanley told many stories about how tough his father was, he was in awe of him, he really worshipped him. He never really got to the stage of adolescent rebellion.
>
> AL: His father was, from all reports, a very domineering, egocentric human being, but Stanley never once spoke ill of him.[4]

Elkin's younger son Bernard, who was born after his grandfather died and knew him only by reputation, tells it more succinctly: "He was an ass, a very strict man, who always made Stanley go to bed early"—but Bernard also recalls that his father didn't tell the children much about Phil. Elkin's brother-in-law, Marshall Jacobsen, who met Phil after Joan began to date Stanley in 1950, remembers the elder Elkin as a "fine tenor voice, loved to sing," but also as a "tough guy"—stubborn, intense, with a bad temper: "When Phil came into a room, he was the center." And after reading his friend and colleague John Morris's memoir, Elkin was moved to express empathy with Morris's discussion of his father's insanity: "My father, while never committed, was just a bit of a madman himself, and, in important ways, my Muse. For one, he never talked down, for two, he was a better storyteller than I'll ever be, for three [. . .] he taught me to be a pretty fair country Ping-Pong player in my day." A story Stanley loved to tell about his father captures his toughness, his intensity, and his ability to intimidate people. After a lengthy hospital stay, his doctors cautioned Phil against driving home. The cause of the hospitalization was a heart attack he suffered while on the road, later to be the core narrative of Elkin's first, unpublished novel. Driving along the North Side, he was animatedly telling Stanley a story when he lightly bumped the car ahead, stopped at a red light. The driver, "an immense guy, nineteen feet tall," charged back shouting, "'Hey, you sonofabitch, what the fuck do you think you're doing driving like that? Why the hell don't you pay—" and Phil "without batting an eyelash, puts his hand into the inside pocket of his jacket, pretending he's got a gun in there. And he says, cool as hell, 'Get back into your car, and I want to see you drive through that red light.' And the guy just turned white and got into

Phil and Zelda "Tootsie" Elkin during the 1940s. By permission of Diane Brandwein.

the car, zipped off, went through the red light, and my father laughed his ass off. That story typifies my father to me. He was a very overpowering man."[5]

Phil supported his son's going to college and graduate school, and somewhat reluctantly his choice of a career as a writer. He had a copy of Stanley's recently published story in the New York hotel room in which he died. But Phil could be a tough critic when it came to writing about business. Elkin recalled giving his father a copy of "A Sound of Distant Thunder," published during the final year of Phil's life, but when Phil got to the part where the shopkeeper buys twelve gross of an unspecified item, he said, "'This is shit. Nobody would ever buy twelve gross of this particular item.' . . . That was his criticism of the story." The year before, Donald Feine of *Views* magazine sent his regrets that publication of an issue containing "The Party" had been delayed because of financial problems at the magazine. Feine dangled the carrot that the cover illustration would relate directly to "The Party" if Elkin could provide the artwork gratis: "[I]n the interest of promoting Stan Elkin, you might have one of your artist friends whip up a red hot illustration of your story, suitable for cover design." In red ink across the top, Phil looked out for his son's interests: "Stanley [t]his is a pitch if I've ever seen one. Dad"[6]

While or just after he was in the army, Stanley apparently asked for his father's life story and Phil wrote about emigrating to America:

> My place of birth is Russia. I truthfully don't know the city as I came over to this country when I was about 1 yr.–1½ yrs. old. The port of entry was New York. I can only guess as to the date that I entered this country and by a simple matter of arithmetic, today being my birthday and being 53 years old, I would say that I arrived here sometime during the year of 1904 or 1905.
>
> I don't know what you mean when you ask for my alien registration number. However, my father became a naturalized American citizen on February 4th, 1914.[7]

Almost thirty years after Phil's death Elkin succinctly summarized his impact. Both available facts and anecdotes by friends and family members suggest that this is a candid and accurate self-analysis: "Well, maybe there was a conflict between myself and my father. I always wanted to please him, and I never seemed quite able to do it. Although I think that if he had lived long enough, he might have been pleased. My father was a remarkable man. [. . .] He was always an impeccably enthusiastic man who would come home and tell us the things that had happened to him on the road. He was a marvelous story teller. Quite the most interesting man I've ever known. And maybe that I'll ever know. He was one hell of a man. But he was so special that he scared me. I tried to *be* him."[8]

By contrast his relationship with his mother was more uniformly nurturing. Zelda Feldman was a New Yorker, the only one of three sisters ever to marry. Her sisters Rose and Frances figure in several of Elkin's early stories. Zelda met the dashing Phil at a camp in Oakland, New Jersey, where her grandmother either managed or worked at a resort restaurant. Groups of New York young people went to "the Camp" to relax in the foothills of the Catskills, roughly thirty miles northwest; Zelda's group called themselves the "Blues Chasers." There she met Phil, who had gotten away from the city with some friends, and a courtship followed. For many years after their marriage and his transfer to Chicago, Zelda took Stanley and later Diane to Oakland for extended summer vacations, often while Phil worked at Coro-Cohn's New York office, spending weekends at the Camp. Elkin nostalgically recalled some of those summers in the final section of his first, incomplete, novel, when the point of view shifts from Stephen Feldman, based on Phil, to David, Stanley's alter ego. Like many of the families who vacationed there, the Elkins eventually replaced the tent they erected each summer with a small bungalow. After *The Living End* came out, Elkin received a letter from a childhood friend recalling their days in Oakland, their emerging testosterone, and Stanley's combativeness: "For several winters we went our ways, only to meet during July and August on a few acres surrounded by the Ramapo River and the now-defunct Susquehanna RR. Days were taken up by softball, swimming by the falls, and evenings exploring the darkness and the blossoming girls . . . I can't remember which was more productive." Now "most of the homes along the river have changed hands and it's now a haven for young married people to

Stanley and Diane at "the Camp," Oakland, N.J. By permission of Diane Brandwein.

set up homesteads. The ball field is unkempt, the old restaurant is unkempt, the old restaurant on the corner is a burnt out ruin, but there are still a lot of kids doing the things we did. Remember Sandy, Jay, Larry, Sheila, Ruth (of the heavy chest), and my favorite Marlene . . . and of course Bob of the bad teeth and bad manners, who you as champion and largest protector had to annually rearrange his features."[9]

"Tootsie," as Mrs. Elkin was known by her friends, was an outgoing, amusing person, who smoked too much and loved playing cards, betting on the ponies, traveling, entertaining friends, and caring for her family. Poet Barry Spacks remembers his mother's first cousin as lively, vivacious, someone who represented "a notch higher in the social scale" for Jewish immigrant families, someone more worldly and sophisticated than his Philadelphia neighbors. In fact, visiting the Elkins' Forest Park house, where they moved in the 1940s, was one of his first intimations of a higher social order. By contrast, Joan Elkin remembers Tootsie as a forceful ally who always took Joan's side when she and Stanley argued. High school classmate Bud Siegel was impressed by Tootsie's accent. When teased about it, Stanley retorted, "[M]y mother speaks with such a New Jersey accent that if a bird flew into the toilet, she'd say a boid flew into the terlet." Tootsie played cards with Bud's mother at least once a week, and he recalls especially the pride Stanley took in showing him pictures of Tootsie as a girl, before she put on weight: "[B] oy, was she gorgeous!" Tootsie's honor was the impetus for one of Stanley's more chivalric-aggressive Boy Scout moments. He and Herb Gold were denmates, and after one troop meeting Herb "cast disparaging remarks" about Stanley's mom, "followed by a knuckle sandwich, delivered by you unto my dad."[10]

The move to the South Side of Chicago was perhaps more traumatic for Tootsie than for Phil, who immersed himself in work, spending a good portion of every year on the road. They settled in a predominately Jewish neighborhood near the intersection of Seventy-fourth and Chappell streets. The South Side Hebrew Congregation dominated that corner. The Elkins attended, but they were casual rather than dedicated members. Although she made many friends on Chappell Street, where they lived in a second-floor apartment, Tootsie missed the east and looked forward to summer trips to Oakland in Phil's Oldsmobile. Micki Avedon, born Maxine Hackman, knew Stanley in elementary school and as a playmate among the large gang of kids who liked to hang out near their apartments. She recalls that Tootsie once confided in Mrs. Hackman that she hoped for a daughter to complement Stanley. Phil's and especially Tootsie's New York accents impressed Micki, and Stanley stood out among their playmates because of his own. Ruth Becker Buell also recalls that when Stanley first came to school his classmates thought he had a speech disorder. And they had plentiful opportunities to hear his accent. He "talked a lot" and "was the brightest kid in the class. He always had a long, involved answer to every question that came up in school." She recalls that

Stanley and Tootsie
Elkin. By permission
of Diane Brandwein.

his assignment papers were regularly read to the class, either by the teacher or by Stanley, accent notwithstanding, at the teacher's bidding, as models of excellence. They went to Bryn Mawr elementary school for grades 1–8, where Ms. Avedon remembers a "nice mix" of Jewish and gentile kids, with few tensions. She has nostalgic memories of the block: "We were children of that [the Depression] generation. Our block was like a little village." She remembers Stanley as having a "strong core" and being "very amusing, and he chose whether to get himself into something or not." But he wasn't unusually mischievous. He had a great sense of humor and a completely original way of looking at the other kids and their pranks. He and his buddy Morty Haberman were "very sophisticated for kids." "I liked Stanley. Not a crush, but I really liked him." According to "Uncle Ruthie" Buell, he was a smart but not a naughty child. He was a vocal presence, always talking about things the other kids had never heard of. But she doesn't recall his ever being called to the principal's office for misbehaving—and she's pretty sure she would remember if he had been there, because she spent a lot of time in detention. Outside the classroom, she does not recall Stanley's being conspicuous at recess. She is, however, pretty sure he did not get teased much at school, as many kids did. In addition to his being intimidatingly smart, he gave the impression that he didn't really care about others' opinions, and that kept the teasers and bullies off balance. Stanley made a physical impression not as a handsome lad, but as a "serious-looking boy." Ms. Buell can't recall the schoolgirls giggling over or teasing one another about Stanley. Then again, many years later, he was one of three childhood acquaintances she commemorated in a song she wrote about first childhood loves.[11] And Bud Siegel's daughter Gail recalls her dad's stories about Stanley's hypnotizing Dianne Schramm, who later married Haberman, in an automobile parked near Seventy-first Street during the mid-1940s. This was his first successful attempt at hypnosis, but the problem was, he couldn't figure out how to bring her back. Eventually Dianne woke on her own with a splitting headache, and as far as the Siegels know, Stanley never again tried hypnosis with anything except a pen, a typewriter, or a word processor.[12]

Not all of Stanley's childhood memories were pleasant, however. His first serious illness kept him out of school for most of first grade. He recalled this decades later: "I spent first grade in a hospital room in Chicago, did a year in bed in the Michael Reese Hospital for a deep strep throat in the pre-penicillin dark ages when the treatment for strep was high dosages of radium delivered two or three times weekly for a year."[13] Although neither Ms. Avedon nor Ms. Buell recalls ethnic trouble in the community or at school, Elkin told his sister and spouse stories about fighting with Irish kids nearby, sometimes on the way to or from school. He told Joan about a fight involving his friend Bill Guggenheim: probably in high school, they entered a bowling alley on Seventy-first Street, where a retarded boy was being picked on by some Irish youths with whom Stanley and Bill had had prior confrontations. They intervened, but several more boys joined the fray against them; Stanley and Bill took off. He told Diane about fights with other Irish kids as well—she's confident that he wouldn't have started the fights, but she suspects that he'd have responded forcefully to a comment or a gesture.

Most of those who knew him in childhood recall Stanley as thoughtful, smart, verbal, and committed to being a writer, even in the early grades. Like most boys of his generation, he also enjoyed sports, and he especially loved to play baseball and softball. Well into his adult life he played softball regularly, with a reputation as a good hitter and a lackadaisical fielder. His bar mitzvah, however, shows a different side of the thoughtful youth, who at age thirteen was by his own admission a terrible student of Hebrew:

> If I had been Bar Mitzvahed on my thirteenth birthday, the Haftorah portion [reading from the Books of the Prophets] was a massive one. I couldn't do it.

I never opened a book. I was terrible. Rabbi Barker, who was in charge of the Hebrew School, knew I was worthless, and he found a very short Haftorah portion for me. That's why I was Bar Mitzvahed on July 17, although my birthday is May 11. You see, July 17 was a passage that I could handle. This was OK because my parents decided that it would be nice to Bar Mitzvah the kid in New York. That way, my grandmother and all my aunts and other relatives could come. Then we had the problem that we went to New Jersey at the end of June, as we always did, and my mother had to find a synagogue where I could be Bar Mitzvahed, on July 17. This is true. My grandmother lived in Brooklyn, not far from Eastern Parkway, at that time a very Jewish neighborhood. We must have gone into three temples, and the rabbi would interview me, then say, "Get out of here." So finally we got one who was willing to do the job, and I still had to read it from a kind of crib.[14]

About this time Stanley also got into some trouble with his parents. He was after all a lively and imaginative youth with a lifelong love of gadgets. The quotation from *The Dick Gibson Show* introducing this chapter mentions the young "Gibson's" affection for radios, and throughout his life Stanley purchased nearly every new radio technology that hit the market. He told Joan the story of his parents' buying a record player, one of the first in the neighborhood. Because Phil and Tootsie weren't home when it was delivered, Stanley and Guggenheim opened it right away, but they couldn't get it to work. They figured the problem was some packing inside the unit, so they pulled it out. It was a baffle, and they'd destroyed the speaker. Later, in high school, he got into more serious trouble. He had recently acquired his driver's license, and Phil and Tootsie were on a trip. Stanley had a date and took the family auto without permission. He hadn't driven more than three blocks when he crashed into either a parked car or a post—versions of the story differ. Terrified, he told a neighbor he needed to get the car fixed before his parents came home, and the neighbor agreed to help him. The repair was arranged, but it cost $800, depleting Stanley's savings from his bar mitzvah, odd jobs, and allowances. Before his parents returned to Chicago, the repaired automobile was back in its garage. The neighbor told Phil about this in praise of Stanley's industry when the family returned. Phil chastised his son about taking the car without permission and the subsequent deception, but he also secretly replaced the money in Stanley's account.[15]

Of course he dated during high school. A few of his dates wrote him after he became famous, and he admits in "My Shirt Tale" that he had the annoying habit of singing—not lip-synching—to them on the dance floor, perhaps emulating the way Phil's fine tenor voice commanded the attention and affection of his peers. He mimicked Perry Como, Frank Sinatra, Dick Haymes, and Bing Crosby into the ears of his dancing partners: "It was, I thought, the way the sexes spoke to each other, pure mating ritual." Late in his life he told Saul Bellow an amusing

story about ruining a good thing by not writing, throughout the family's summer trip to New Jersey, to a girl who'd agreed to go steady with him "because I
couldn't figure out [. . .] how to sign the letter, thinking that if I signed it 'Stanley'
she might not know who it was, but if I signed it 'Stanley Elkin' it would have
seemed ridiculous in case she did." Shortly after high school was done, he lost
his virginity along with three friends in a Kankakee bar-whorehouse, "the girls
old, most of them, as our mothers, politely hustling sex like a box of candy."[16]

South Shore High School classmate and neighbor Bud Siegel also found Stanley
"verbally very bright, very funny, very abusive, very profane. What was on the
tip of his brain was on the tip of his tongue," so he was "always on the verge of
having a fistfight with somebody" in school. They played sandlot sports together.
They enjoyed softball at the schoolyard, or in the street if older athletes claimed
the diamond. A neighbor and varsity basketball player at Northwestern, Jake
Findley, joined them while he was home from school, and it wasn't long before
Stanley insulted him during an argument over some minor matter relating to
the game. He challenged Jake to fight, and within seconds he was in a headlock,
with Jake pummeling his face mercilessly. No one made an effort to break it up,
and eventually Jake simply shoved him away. The beating was the talk of the
neighborhood for more than two weeks, the consensus being that Stanley had it
coming, that he'd shot off his mouth once too often, this time to the wrong guy.
He also showed some adolescent pettiness when Morty Haberman made the high
school football team and was showing off the equipment he'd been assigned.
Stanley became jealous. He grabbed the helmet, ran to the toilet, and tried to
flush it down. Morty rescued the helmet, then demonstrated conclusively that he
was the better athlete via the time-honored ritual of fisticuffs. Rather than bitterness over the pounding or shame over the pettiness of trying to flush his friend's
helmet, Stanley told the story on himself with the expectation that everyone at
school would think it was as funny as he did.

He excelled, of course, in high school classes, especially English. He had the
first wire recorder anyone in the neighborhood had ever seen, and for English assignments he'd write skits that he and his friend Bill Garrett would act out. He'd
play the recording as his book report. One afternoon they invited Bud Siegel to
perform, but "I wasn't very talented, so they let me work the recorder" thereafter. Shortly after his fortieth high school reunion, which he traveled to Chicago
to attend, however, Elkin told his daughter Molly that he had few memories
of high school because he didn't "really think I was all that interested in other
people." The Elkins were the first family on the block to own a television set. The
neighborhood boys congregated at their apartment to watch baseball and hockey
games. Phil welcomed the boys to the living room, but at the time he suffered
from a breathing disorder that caused him to snore the moment he lay down on
the couch, even while wide awake. Bud recalls that he and Stanley had this in

common, which differentiated them from the other kids: each was at ease with
and proud of his affection for his father; each kissed his father good morning
and good night, although they were both was as tall as their dads by the time
they completed high school.[17]

Although Stanley's fretting over sports, cameras, record players, automobiles,
dating, and sex are fairly typical adolescent experiences, he was thinking as well
about more ominous matters. Shortly after publishing *The Magic Kingdom*, a
novel that at many levels challenges the notion of a god who permits wholesale
suffering among children, Elkin explained to a reporter from *The Catholic Review*
how he "dropped Judaism as a boy." Throughout his adult life, although his fiction ruminated increasingly on the nature of a deity and creation, he remained
an atheist. He sprained his ankle during the High Holy Days. At the temple there
was much standing and sitting. "In the end I said, '[W]hat does he want from me?
I'm a 12-year-old kid. It's killing me.' [. . .] I just thought it was crazy. If I were
God I wouldn't want worship. [. . .] God is supposed to be above all that."[18] In
graduate school Elkin combined this experience with an adolescent's maturing to
create "The Fall," an unpublished initiation story that emulates Joyce's "Araby."
The narrator-protagonist is becoming aware of his separation from the world
around him, as a Jew on the South Side who dresses up for High Holy Days and
gets off from school, two things that separate him from his gentile classmates:
"It may have been that on those days I felt I must officially declare my apartness
from them, let them know tacitly that though I could be friendly with them, play
with them, joke with them, and even fight with them, I was a Jew." His alienation
increases when his gentile friend Morty (Elkin's friend Morty Haberman was
Jewish) looks at the mysterious paraphernalia of "your church" and in return
shares his secret, a pornographic book. The protagonist responds with righteous
indignation, although the adult narrator, like Joyce's, judges his adolescent pos-
turing: "That I may not really have been angry is important too. But anger, I
had somehow determined, was to be my official stand in the eye of the world. I
cultivated it; I brandished it." While rushing to the synagogue as a refuge from
both the pornographic initiation and the intuitive realization that his insulting
Morty changes their relationship forever, he trips, spraining an ankle. Inside, he
sits by a woman he doesn't know, and the combination of confusion from his
encounter with Morty, his attraction/revulsion about the book, and the rising
pain in his ankle lead him to another adolescent transference. When she supports
him because his ankle pains him visibly and responds to a prayer incorrectly by
apologizing for "the sins we have committed before thee by unchastity," the youth
becomes aroused and his secular fall, witnessing the pornography, is compounded
by directed lust and blasphemy: "[A] high holiday which I had single-handedly
and with something like dedicated purpose defiled inexorably." His epiphany,
while not quite as dramatic as Joyce's, or for that matter as the autobiographical

occasion on which it is based, is that while all these transformations are taking place, the world continues as if nothing at all were happening.[19]

This questioning of religion took place in the context of Stanley's increasing anxiety about human mortality, perhaps occasioned by heart problems that were beginning to present with both parents. Decades later he told this story about 1944, his fourteenth year. Some neighborhood adolescents were fooling with a Ouija board. When Stanley's turn came, he asked, "When will I die?" The answer was 1956, so for the next dozen years he was "running scared." When 1956 came and went, he "breathed a massive sigh of relief. Now I figure it means I'm gonna die when *I'm* 56." From that time forward, he continued to observe a substantial "rigmarole of incredible superstitions," such as pulling his ear when someone sneezed or when death was mentioned. Many close friends corroborate his superstitious habits: he had several exercises to ward off death when someone talked about it. He'd spit over his shoulder when someone said something he associated with bad luck. There was an additional, very complicated, series of exercises, "and of course I [Steve Teitelbaum] knew exactly what was going on, so I'd keep on talking about death to make him go through this series of exercises over and over." Naomi Lebowitz once asked him, "Stanley, why do you spit over your shoulder?" He replied, "Because it keeps bad luck away, that's why." Naomi stared at his cane and said, "Look at the things that have happened to you. Has it *helped?* MS and a heart attack. How could it get any worse, Stanley? You had to give up cigarettes, now you're going to have to give up grass." So he stopped spitting over his shoulder, at least around the Lebowitzes and Teitelbaums.[20]

The 1948 South Shore High School yearbook lists Stanley's activities as Movie Operator (he was throughout college interested in making home movies), Discussion, Commencement Committee, Clean-Up Committee, and Shore Line Staff—not exactly quarterback or student government president—but his most educational experiences in high school may have come outside the classroom, fueling his lifetime fascination with travel and commerce. His parents were avid travelers, and the annual journeys to New Jersey were supplemented by auto trips covering much of the northeast during his childhood and adolescence. His sister has photographs of herself at age six, Stanley at eighteen, and Tootsie in Washington, D.C., possibly a side trip relating to his high school graduation. But the most important trip he made, for his future as a writer, happened one summer when he accompanied Phil on a two-week business trip to Indiana. Later Stanley would recall, "The buyers were just delighted to see him. And he called them 'dear' and he called them 'honey' and they called him 'Phil.' I suspect, and maybe I didn't suspect until later on, a kind of intimacy there that may have ultimately been a sexual intimacy. I mean, you get awfully lonely in those, doing those one-night stands that he did." Another interview tells the same story with a slightly different twist: "I was with him in small Indiana towns where he would take the jewelry out of the telescopes, which are salesman's cases, and actually put the earrings on his ears, the bracelets about his wrists, and the necklaces about his throat. This wasn't drag, but the prose passionate and stage business of his spiel. The man believed in costume jewelry, in rhinestones and beads, and sang junk jewelry's meteorological condition—its Fall line and Spring."[21] This trip impressed on the high schooler the awesome force of rhetoric, the capacity to self-dramatize and exert the will, the sheer fun of power that so profoundly animates his fictional heroes, from Push the Bully ("A Poetics for Bullies") and Leo Feldman (*A Bad Man*) to Nate Lace and Ben Flesh (*The Franchiser*), as well as the non-entrepreneurs who depend on rhetoric to assert their individuality. It also taught him, or reinforced the theme of tales Phil brought home from the road, a respect for money, business, and what these things represented that most serious novelists of his generation never really understood; many of them treated business and businesspersons with condescension and contempt. By contrast, Elkin, seeing humor in any enterprise, remained fascinated by what he called "the shop-talk of personality": "the language of myth and risk and men sizing each other up. It's steely-eyed-appraisal talk, I-like-the-cut-of-your-jib speech, and maybe that's not the way it happened. But that's the way my father told it and it became The Story of How They Gave Him the Central Standard Time Zone."[22]

After high school his cousin Barry Spacks spent a portion of the summer of 1948 in the Forest Park home Phil had acquired. Someone, perhaps Stanley or Harry Richman, came up with the idea of taking a road trip. After Harry borrowed a relative's auto, they journeyed through Wisconsin and Minnesota into Canada: "One afternoon we napped in a field and damned if the farmer didn't wake us with a pitchfork." Spacks felt genuinely threatened by the farmer's belligerence. Although they both learned much from the trip, Spacks recalls that their relationship was becoming competitive by age eighteen. Both had already focused their ambitions on becoming writers. Barry was writing poetry and Stanley had his eye on writing fiction. One late afternoon, Harry, feeling drowsy as he drove, made an innovative use of their bickering about writers and the relative virtues of poetry and fiction. Years later, Barry wrote a poem about it:

> He must have figured our babble
> Would keep him awake down the moonless highway.
>
> And so we talked on and on, me and Stanley,
> Miles and miles. Who knows what we said.
> Words. Harry declared it a tie."[23]

Shouting down the darkness. Two aspiring writers who were cousins, arguing about who was better, or whose preferred genre was greater. And they would be competitors for many years. But before either could launch a writing career, there would be college, a military obligation, marriage, and graduate school.

Young writers, it turns out, aren't that much different from the rest of us in this respect—when we go away to college, twists and turns in the road that we never anticipated change our lives in ways that remind us of Robert Frost's poem "The Road Not Taken." The road Stanley took led him to Champaign-Urbana and the University of Illinois.

☯ 3 ☯ College, Graduate School, and the Army, 1948–57

[A]n awful soldier, a clown in khaki. There was, I think,
something woeful and deficient in me and it was good I
served in what was merely the Quartermaster Corps in what
was only the Cold War in what was simply Virginia. Otherwise I could have done real harm to myself and others instead
of my just dumb vaud-evillainy and bungling sad-sackery on
KP, my stints of let's-pretend guard duty in the funky watches
of those southern nights. I don't know why I think of this
now, why I truly regret I was not a better soldier.

—Elkin to Saul Bellow, August 18, 1992

As a youth Elkin had traveled extensively in the United States.
The family made annual trips to New Jersey and visited relatives in Brooklyn
and New York. His sister has photographs of Stanley in the Rockies, the Grand
Tetons, the nation's capital, and the Alleghenies. But it was a short journey, from
Forest Park to Champaign-Urbana, that would make the most profound change
in his young life. Although the distance was merely 130 miles, he would undergo
profound personal and intellectual transformations. As the first member of his
immediate family to go to college, Stanley enacted the American dream of immigrant families since the nineteenth century. And, as is often the case when a
firstborn goes off to school, adjustments in behavior and attitude accompanied this
change of address. Within four brief years, Stan, as he now called himself, would
confirm his life's vocation and begin to write seriously, would change his sartorial
habits, and would find the girl who would share his life and be the true muse of
his fiction. He would also experience a lifetime passion, radio, from the inside.
He would serve in the military. And he would be the defendant in a lawsuit.

Although he was by age eighteen a veteran traveler, he was homesick during his entire first year at Illinois. Two decades later he admitted, "I went from
Champaign to my home in Chicago every weekend. That's how much of a baby I
was. My parents had a beautiful home." He entered college with the intention of
studying journalism, though he'd made up his mind to be a fiction writer while in
high school. Freshman composition teacher William Stringfellow persuaded him
that "while there is certainly fiction in newspapers, a prospective fiction writer

should major in English."[1] There were probably several conversations over the Elkins' kitchen table about the relation between higher education and preparation for a vocation. He could, if he went on to graduate school, have the safety net of a university teaching career.

> I pretended to write when I was in grammar and high schools, and once I got into college I took all the writing courses I could—I was very lucky, I had very good writing instructors: George Scouffas, Jerry Beaty who is a professor at Emory University now, and Randall Jarrell, the poet and novelist. I learned a great deal from these people. I don't feel I'm anywhere near as good a teacher of writing as they were. I walked into the "Ph.D. trap," not so much as a trap as a way of postponing my life. When I became an English major, I did not know that I was going on for a master's degree. When I went on for a master's degree, I did not know that I was going to pursue the Ph.D. When I started to pursue the Ph.D., I didn't think then that I would ever finish it.[2]

In one of Scouffas's (Elkin borrowed his name for a minor character in *The MacGuffin*) classes, Stanley met a writer who hadn't changed his mind about becoming a journalist. Robert Novak, a syndicated columnist and one of two members of the class of 1952 to be later awarded an honorary doctorate by the university (the other was Elkin), recalls something special about his classmate during their first creative writing seminar. Because Scouffas encouraged workshop practices, there was intense interaction among the students, and Novak found Elkin's writing challenging, often brilliant. As they critiqued each other's original compositions and those of their classmates, it became clear that this was an "interesting fellow" and during the next few months "we became friendly." They soon found that their intellectual ambitions reached somewhat higher than those of their classmates, so they began to study for exams together, usually far outpacing their peers as a result. They often talked well into the night, frequently going "far off the subject," during the week or so leading up to exams. And one night during their junior year they jointly concocted a fantasy about an eight-foot Hawthorne apparition in Elkin's closet, to be placated only by their answering questions about his novels and stories.

Their friendship was, however, principally confined to the pursuit of academic excellence. They discussed their ambitions to write for a living. Elkin insisted that he wanted to be a novelist, and if he couldn't make a living doing that, he'd be a professor and write as an avocation. Novak suspects that their association may have frustrated whatever ambitions he secretly harbored toward becoming a novelist. "Stanley was clearly the smartest guy in any of the classes we took together—and he was such a gifted writer that it was intimidating."

Their study sessions usually took place in Elkin's room in the Men's Residence Hall, where GDIs (independents, or those unaffiliated with any fraternity) lived on campus. Novak lived down the street at Alpha Epsilon Pi, but the few times they tried to study there, the distractions of frat life interfered with their work. Elkin and his roommate anticipated the "Odd Couple" of Neil Simon's Broadway and later television hit. Bill Lynch was older than his classmates, having served in the army before attending college, and he maintained many vestiges of military discipline. On campus Lynch was conspicuous in his military camouflage: "[A]n odd fellow, but a really neat person." Novak knew him from ROTC as well. Lynch was fastidious, keeping his side of the room in the precise fashion of a proud ex-soldier, the prequel to Felix Unger. Stanley was, by contrast, "a slob. He wore sandals, and his feet usually weren't very clean. I'm not at all sure he was a daily bather"—an Oscar Madison in the making. Although Stanley berated Lynch and Novak about ROTC, the roommates were synergetic. As different as they were, they seemed genuinely to like each other, and Novak often felt a kind of seriousness about college life in their room that he missed in the frat house—even if the most striking thing about the room was the symmetrical and formal division between the tidy "Lynch" and the messy "Elkin" sides.

Novak also recalls Elkin as less social during college than one might, based on the gregariousness of his adult life, suspect. When they studied together, often for several hours, he doesn't recall anyone stopping by to chat or telephoning. When Novak steered the conversation to the preferred topics of frat house conversation, sports and women, Stanley often lost interest, unless to psychoanalyze Novak's passion for basketball. They never double-dated and Novak doesn't recall a single time Elkin talked about girls in whom he was interested: "As far as I could see, he had no friends and no social life" at the university except for himself and Lynch. But they often shared their anxieties about whether they would be able to succeed as writers. Although each tried to project confidence in his talent, both were aware that the odds against success in journalism and novel writing were great, and each felt some support from knowing a fellow-aspirant felt anxiety about the path that lay ahead. These sessions persisted until their senior year, when Novak took a job with the *Courier* as a sportswriter; having launched the profession he had by now decided on as his future, he and Elkin somewhat drifted apart.[3]

While Novak was progressing toward a great job as a sportswriter, his study buddy was moving away too. The defining moment of the Illinois years took place when his childhood pal Bill Guggenheim introduced Stan to a coed Bill had himself dated, but who "didn't really like him all that much." Two years younger than Stanley and the daughter of an immigrant butcher from the South Side, Joan Jacobsen was instantly smitten with the unorthodox aspiring writer. She never dated Bill again, and soon she and Stanley were keeping regular company. On their first date he escorted her to a sound booth at the campus radio station WILL, where he was appearing as Heathcliff in a broadcast of *Wuthering Heights*. She recalls his acting frequently in radio drama, both as an undergraduate and in graduate school, but she doesn't recall his ever performing on stage in college.[4] He didn't know it then, but he was preparing for his third novel, *The Dick Gibson Show,* a spectacular picaresque about a man who felt "marked, historically attached to radio" (12). Almost a decade after *Gibson* he wrote a play for National Public Radio, *The Coffee Room,* based loosely on the personalities of his colleagues in the Washington University English Department. Shortly after, he played the semiautobiographical role of Leon Mingus in a broadcast of that play. But before that happened, there was one more eventful trip; soon there would be wedding bells and a profound change in Stanley's life.

When Yash Snider moved into the South Side neighborhood, he was already a student at the University of Illinois. He recalls Stanley, just out of high school, as a bit of an "oddball" with a newfangled wire recorder, who insisted on recording conversations and events. During the summer of 1951, Snider joined the "gruesome threesome" for a trip out west. Harry Richman, Guggenheim, Stanley, and Yash borrowed Harry's uncle's Frazier automobile. Most of the time they slept in the car to save money, but occasionally they treated themselves to a motel "on the cheap." They toured the Black Hills and Yellowstone, and Yash recalls that things got a little scary while Stan was driving in the Black Hills. Unaccustomed to a standard transmission, he reached for the brake but hit the clutch at a most inopportune moment while climbing a steep hill. Fortunately he was able to recover the car from its backward freewheeling. On the way home, Yash too narrowly avoided a mishap. While he was looking at the side road and talking with his friends, the road surface suddenly changed from asphalt to gravel just as he entered a turn too fast. Once more, fortune smiled on the travelers as the car fishtailed to a stop with nothing harmed but Yash's pride. The high point of the trip was a mule ride down the Grand Canyon, which Snider recalls vividly and cherishes the photo. Guggenheim also told his wife about riding donkeys into the canyon. Although the trip was exciting, Stanley was preoccupied with his father's illness. The first thing he looked for when they stopped for an evening meal or fuel was a pay phone to check in with the family. This may have been Stanley's final bachelor trip.[5]

Stanley and Joan were married on January 1, 1953, in Chicago. The county clerk who signed the marriage license was Richard J. Daley, later Chicago's notorious mayor and the figure of repression during the 1968 Democratic Convention in his city. Coincidentally, Elkin got the inspiration for "The Bailbondsman" while reading *Boss,* Mike Royko's biography of Daley. In 1953, however, his future as a professional writer looked anything but certain. He'd completed his bachelor's degree in 1952, having acquitted himself with distinction as a scholar. A couple of collaborations with his fellow undergraduates Ron Hansen and "A. Jones" deserve special mention.

Of course he wrote undergraduate term papers, most of them judged "outstanding" by the professors, on topics relating to American literature, but also on

Faust, Ruskin, Machiavelli, the Old English "Dream of the Rood," and Samuel Johnson. Additionally, he and "A. Jones" submitted a five-page verse dialogue called "The Romance of Rosalynde: The World's Last Eclogue" for Professor Milligan. This lengthy dialogue between "Polyglot" and "Billy" is in rhymed couplets, with several obvious poetic effects, including personification and sticho-mythia, reflecting the undergraduates' learning pastoral conventions. As the authors profess, it was "written in imitation to that of Theocritus, and, in more recent times, of the eighth eclogue" of Spenser. Professor Milligan supported the A grade succinctly, calling it "a thing of beauty." For another class Stanley and Ron Hansen teamed up to write "Blooming Idiot: Conspiracy by Hansen and Elkin." This is quickly explained, "Greek expressions [. . .] by Hansen. Paper by Elkin." What follows is a clever seven-page dialogue between "Hansen" and "Elkin" about the aesthetic and thematic properties of Katherine Anne Porter's "Flowering Judas" (1930). They debate the story's artistry in subtle detail and the issues of revolutionary ideology versus Marxist commitment in the story. Hansen recalled after Elkin became famous that Professor Beaty reduced both semester grades to A- because the "collaboration was unauthorized." Beaty also told Hansen privately that they were the only promising writers in the class: "He was obviously partially accurate." Hansen dedicated his own story "Ma-lingering" to this former collaborator.[6] These two efforts tell us conclusively that Elkin was thinking in subtle, creative ways, well beyond the obligations to complete class assignments.

By January 1953, Stanley was in the M.A. program at Illinois, and Joan expedited her college education to three and a half years so they could marry. She'd completed high school in 1950 and had gone to Champaign to study art. Because of family issues, she spent her sophomore year at the University of Illinois–Chicago, then returned to Champaign for her third year, during which she met Stanley. Her brother Marshall recalls meeting Stanley for the first time: "He was a very impressive guy to a ten-year old!" In Joan's painting of Marshall's bar mitzvah, Stanley, age twenty-six, stands very tall at six feet among those present.[7] For the first years of their marriage, they enacted the life of many a newly married graduate student before and since. They rented a tiny apartment on South Gregory Place in Urbana where they lived hand to mouth, often having as little as five dollars in the checking account to get through the final week of the month. Undeterred, Stanley often said, "Let's go out to eat and see a movie." At those times it was all Joan could do to stretch the budget to the next payday. Her parents often brought food from her father's shop when they visited, and the young couple lived on cash wedding gifts during the first years. Phil and Tootsie also provided an allowance. Stanley took several temporary jobs, including sell-ing Jell-O door to door and tearing the covers off remaindered magazines for a local newsstand.[8] His most memorable job was as a watchman for the Labor

The happy couple, 1952. From the Elkins' wedding album.
By permission of Joan Elkin.

Day weekend in 1953. In 1983 he elaborated the summer job story, after telling
it in a more cryptic form in "Where I Read What I Read" (1982).

> I was taking a summer class at Northwestern. And [the professor] asked us
> to read *Ulysses*. I had never read any Joyce at all before that. I had a job at
> the Peacock cleaners in Chicago, where I worked literally ten minutes a day.
> It was an eight-hour day, but I only worked ten minutes. It was an incredible
> job. I think it made me what I am today. I think as a matter of fact it poi-
> soned me. I had to store fur coats people would bring in from time to time
> during the day. I had to go down into the vault. There were no gas masks or
> anything. I couldn't smoke. Now that's bad when you can't smoke. I don't
> mean that something would explode though probably all the fur coats would
> have exploded. I mean it just destroyed my taste buds. It destroyed everything.

Towards the end of the summer they asked me if I would be night watchman for 48 hours. And that's when I read *Ulysses* in one fell swoop, lying on a dry cleaning table, the smell of this garbage giving me multiple sclerosis. I just did not have any sense of the book and frankly I've not gone back to it. So Joyce was not an influence.

As he put it in the essay, "I had a headache that would last for days, an olfactory hyperesthesia that would actually return full blown when I visited Dublin sixteen years later. Hey, I was like Bloom in Nighttown, like Proust in the cookie jar, the disparate impressions of laundry and literature like things bonded in genes." This became the central experience of an unpublished novella from graduate school, "The Outlander," in which the narrator becomes erotically involved with the dry cleaners' angry outcast, a tall Amazon named Levoiser.[9] Somehow, they managed to make it through Stanley's M.A. And he was writing with an eye toward publication during this time.

He sent a story, "The Sound of Distant Thunder," to his cousin for possible publication. Barry Spacks's reply wasn't encouraging: not all the editors had read the story, but those who did weren't enthusiastic: "[H]ere's my suggestion: get a heavier motivation for the threat of a smashed store at the end (either by particularizing your negro point of view at the end, or make the threat more general by dropping these three reappearing brothers and letting the color mass sort of seethe; cut the opening detail way down; build up the relationship between the two brothers, and start it earlier in the story; have Feldman wonder about the street's decay, veiled but in the story's terms, from the very beginning; make the heat more oppressive—dramatize a growing malaise more heavily to smooth out the movement toward your ending violence. . . . I think you have a good story here but it definitely needs work."[10] *Epoch Magazine,* however, accepted it for the 1957 winter edition. Although we can never ascertain what changes Elkin made after receiving Spacks's comments, many of the issues, especially the sense of malaise and the motif of oppressive heat, seem to have been addressed in the final version. It would be Elkin's first story to appear in a substantial publication, but not his first story. That was "The Dying," published in *Illini Writers,* a student journal, in 1950. Despite his many professions that he neither liked nor was influenced by Joyce, the brief author's note to his first publication announces that the writer, a junior, "likes Joyce."[11] And "The Dying" is clearly an imitation of Joyce's masterwork "The Dead"—if one is going to imitate, why not the best? The plot is a series of vignettes developing two old maids, named for and modeled on Elkin's aunts Rose and Frances Feldman, as they separately mourn their aunt's death. As they prepare to sit shivah with their cousin, they come to terms with the different path, including marriage and removal to Chicago, their sister Zelda (Elkin's mother's name) has chosen. Zelda hints broadly that she'd like to move back to New York if her husband could arrange a transfer. Nothing's resolved; like the masterpiece on which it's modeled, "The Dying" paints a picture of the living dead, who survive in the shadow of past family warmth and love, something that can be no more. His first publication, like many of his graduate school efforts, was a near-successful effort to transform family folklore to art.

Among the few dated manuscripts in Elkin's archives is a twelve-page verse play called "A Cup for God" (June 12, 1954) that clearly belongs to his M.A. days. It can mercifully be classified as "juvenilia," the kind of thing most of us have written, then destroyed. But it provides insight into a stage in Elkin's artistic growth. It's intensely political, something the mature artist generally eschewed in his work. Part free verse, part iambic pentameter, "A Cup" is set in ancient Athens, and is for the most part a dialogue between "Political Prisoner," sentenced to death for speaking out against a state that "like superstitious sluts does seek / Advice and counsel from those pimps who eagerly / Supply some puerile panacea to our wounds,"[12] and his protégé, Christie, who conspires to arrange his escape. After several pompous discussions of duty and political expedience, the prisoner refuses on the ground of conscience to escape. It ends with the news that an omen portending the prisoner's death is imminent, and the prisoner, his protégé, and the prisoner's son agree to the necessity of his sacrifice, chanting "A Cup for God." It seems as if Elkin were unconsciously grafting T. S. Eliot's *Murder in the Cathedral* onto Plato's *Symposium*, with a mix of Shakespearean bombast from his more political plays. Not surprisingly, he never mentioned it in letters or interviews, and there's no record of its ever having been offered for publication.

Although he never wavered in his gratitude to Scouffas, Beaty, and Dan Curley among his creative writing teachers, Elkin considered Randall Jarrell his most brilliant mentor. His final conference with the poet, who told his students on the first day of class that he'd have nothing to say about their stories until the final conference, was as traumatic as Elkin's conferences with his students would eventually be—much like a 1983 conference with Erin McGraw, a student in a writer's conference at Indiana University. His reputation for gruffness had of course preceded him and he didn't disappoint. During the session, he skewered McGraw's story, telling her and the rest of the participants that it lacked promise. In fact, he said it had no redeeming qualities. Later in the individual conference, which she approached with considerable trepidation after having been hauled over the coals in the general session, McGraw was amazed at how deftly he pointed out many problems with the story—and how closely he had read it. By the time he finished quizzing her, she was painfully aware of its shortcomings. But his insistence that she write about something she really cared about led to "the first decent story I ever wrote, 'Striking Balance.'" Elkin's own conference with Jarrell was in late April, and he went to Jarrell's office ahead of time, but Jarrell didn't show up. Twenty minutes after the appointment, "I did what no one did in those days." He called the poet's home and it was obvious that the call awakened Jarrell, who replied that he'd pick Elkin up in his convertible:

Well, when he showed up he was still in his pajamas. He was wearing carpet slippers. He told me [. . .] we'd do the conference in the car. The stories I'd written were on the seat between us. We drove around Urbana for two hours. He knew my stories at least as well as he knew Chekhov's [readings Jarrell had assigned throughout the semester]. He knew them so well he could tell me the page numbers he wanted me to turn to. It was devastating. His observations about my stories were shrewd and cruel and withering. When he let me out I was at once incredibly depressed and incredibly exhilarated. Depressed because what he had to say was so annihilating, exhilarated because no one had ever taken me so seriously before.

He was amazed when he received one of only two As in that class and later confronted Jarrell in the hall, but had to remind the poet who he was: "'I was in your writing class, Professor Jarrell. My name is Stanley Elkin? You gave me an A.' 'Yes?' Jarrell said. 'Well,' I said, 'it's just that there were 25 people in that class, only two A's.' 'Yes?' 'My name is Stanley Elkin? You gave me an A.'" Elkin told Jarrell again and again how important it was for him to become a writer, but Jarrell still couldn't place him:

> "Well, just if I do all that, the perseverance, the practice, the sacrifice and will and dedication, do you think, if I live long enough and get better,—I was in your class, you gave me an A, you only gave two, my name is Stanley Elkin— I'll publish even one story before I die?"
> He looked at me and shrugged. He said, "I don't know."[13]

By the time he received his M.A., Elkin probably wasn't sure either. He received at least three more rejections in 1954. Arabel Porter wrote in April that "The Sound of Distant Thunder" "doesn't seem quite right" for *New World Writing* and *The American Hebrew* rejected an unspecified story that "has great merit" but the journal was not "in the market for new material." To round out the year, *The Jewish Horizon* gently rejected "The Party" because of its length, although the editors were unanimous in their praise, and asked, "Could you please relieve our gloom by submitting some stories of shorter length?"[14] Although editor William Herskowitz let him down kindly, Elkin may have begun to suspect that Jarrell was right.

Just after Christmas 1954, Jack and Jeanette Mulligan wrote from Paris, "I'm sorry for all your troubles with the lawsuit. You should have hit him harder. Think how seldom people like us hit someone and look what happens. I can't count that high in dollars, Stan. I'd probably try to claim that he tried to goose Joan with a straw." Al Lebowitz also heard about a lawsuit from Stanley's graduate school days—Stanley got into a fight at a drive-in theater and tried to punch a guy out, and a lawsuit followed. Jack Mulligan was a friend from Illinois. Joan believes Jack and Stan briefly roomed with a fellow named Johnson. She recalls that Mulligan "spooked" Stanley, who saw Jack as a Hemingway bohemian, very smart, stunningly handsome, a small dark Irishman, and a fierce drinker. Marshall Jacobsen also recalls Stanley's introducing him to Mulligan in Greenwich Village during the 1950s as a bohemian artist friend whom he obviously admired. Stan was convinced that Jack was the first true genius he'd encountered. Although enrolled in graduate school, Jack often skipped the classes he was scheduled to attend in order to visit others that interested him, based on his friends' reports of the teacher's delivery or the topic for the class. He and Jack took Jarrell's creative writing class. One evening, the Mulligans invited the Elkins to a party at their apartment. When they arrived they were amazed to discover that Jarrell was the guest of honor. Stan was astonished by and a little in awe of Jack's chutzpah. Shortly after, the Mulligans shocked their friends by selling everything they owned that wasn't moveable and relocating to Paris, writing to Stanley, "Grad school is certainly a waste of electricity if you are still interested in creative literature." Joan: "We thought this was the most romantic thing we could imagine. Of course, we couldn't imagine doing anything like that ourselves." Jack was planning to be a writer, and this was what a true creative genius appeared to be at this point in Elkin's life.

The lawsuit Mulligan mentioned: Stanley didn't like going to dentists, and throughout his life he avoided preventive appointments, only appearing in a dentist's chair when he was in pain. In Urbana he developed a terrible toothache that finally drove him to a dentist who prescribed codeine. That night, the Elkins had plans to go to a movie with the daughter of one of Tootsie's friends, who was at the university, and her date. Stanley tried to beg off because his tooth was aching, but the friend and her date suggested a drive-in instead. Early in the evening it became apparent that the pain was getting worse and the narcotic was wearing off. But the friend wanted to stay for the second feature. His discomfort and impatience grew in parallel courses, so during the credits after the second feature, he drove forward, not backward as is usual at drive-in theaters. As a result he ended up in a diagonal position while other drivers made for the exits. An attendant was letting all the drivers in orthodox lanes leave the theater, while staring from time to time at the Elkin vehicle struggling to squeeze into the exit lane. All this time, Stanley's irritation that they hadn't left between features was being fueled by his growing discomfort, and eventually he got out the car and shouted, "When the hell are you going to let us out?" Joan talked him back into the car, warning, "Now he's never going to let us out, Stanley."

After nearly all the other patrons had departed, the sixteen-year-old attendant signaled for the Elkin auto to right itself and exit. As the car passed, the attendant muttered, "Motherfucker." Stan slammed on the brakes, jumped out of the car, stormed back, and took a roundhouse swing. The attendant raised his flashlight to protect himself, and the blow aimed at his face caught the hand holding the flashlight at exactly the angle to break his thumb. As the youth howled in agony and his thumb dangled at a grotesque angle, Elkin's anger, pain, and codeine disappeared instantly. He began to stammer apologies and drove the youth to an emergency room. While treatment was administered they exchanged apologies— Stanley contrite about losing his temper and the attendant acknowledging that he was in the wrong for denying Elkin access to the exit and calling him a vulgar name. He assured Stanley that his insurance would cover the hospital visit, that he would not expect restitution over a provoked attack. After he drove the attendant home, Stanley and he were, in Joan's recollection, "best friends forever"; they actually embraced on the doorstep.

A few days later the Elkins were served with formal papers indicating that they were being sued for $5,000, an immense sum for struggling graduate students in those or any days. Shocked and afraid, he called his father. Phil, anything but happy about his son's problems but probably secretly rejoicing in this manifestation of Stan's being a tough guy, recommended a lawyer, who wouldn't even listen to their case without a $150 retainer. Phil sent a check to cover the consultation. The newlyweds' troubles were anything but over, however. The Champaign newspaper carried a story about a university teacher sued for assault and Elkin became fearful that this would cost him his new job as a teaching assistant. Joan finally persuaded him to see the department chairman, who assured him that he had nothing to worry about on that front. With his father's check and this assurance he met with the lawyer, who listened impatiently to his account of the events, then snapped, "You don't have a leg to stand on. He's local, you're university." As Stan began to protest, the lawyer added, "Anyway, you're in the wrong. His right to say something to you is protected by the First Amendment and you don't get to hit him for saying it. We've got to get this settled." Stanley was convinced that he had no chance to prevail when his friend stated that she hadn't heard the attendant say anything, and Joan's corroboration was inadmissible as spousal testimony. Somehow, the lawyer was able to negotiate a settlement for $250, which Phil paid.[15]

When Elkin completed his M.A. in 1954, the United States was emerging from the Korean War, and the House Un-American Activities Committee hearings manifested the Cold War mentality that prevailed throughout the decade. The House Committee investigated subversive elements in the arts, particularly film, and government agencies—tactics Senator Joseph McCarthy would refine as chair of the Committee on Government Operations until his 1954 censure.[16] In this climate with the Cold War in full force and bomb shelters constructed in the suburbs, young men in good health lived with anxiety about the draft. One way to minimize one's service obligation was to "volunteer for the draft," thereby reducing the service obligation from three to two years. In 1954 Stanley volunteered and entered the unhappiest phase of his young life. As his character Dick Gibson would discover when he was drafted in the 1971 novel, "There he experienced the total collapse of civilization" (88). Assigned to basic training at Fort Carson, Colorado, he claims to have lost sixteen pounds, weighing 176 and "in strictly the best physical condition of my life." He recalls reading Thomas Mann during December, when he had connived to get out of orders to France "only because I'd heard that you pulled two weeks of KP on the ship going over" and volunteered to help set up a bivouac in the mountains in a goldbricking strategy common among draftees. While "the guys were chinning themselves up and down the Rockies" on a nine-mile hike, Stanley and a few others accompanied Sergeant Turner by truck up the mountain to set up camp. After setting up a few mess tents, the recruits thought they had it made until Turner ordered them to dig a hole "the size of a boy's bedroom" and bury the ammunition. This task took until about four A.M., and the men were permitted to sleep until ten, then rewarded with a good breakfast and some free time. Stanley carried his book and an air mattress a few hundred feet away to a glorious overlook on "the most beautiful day in the history of weather," convinced that he'd beaten the odds of a nine-mile hike. Suddenly his rapture with "Mario the Magician" was interrupted by shouts that Turner was dissatisfied with the ammunition concealment, and Stanley found himself running down the mountain: "Perhaps that day I invented hang-gliding, broken field, Rockies running, the encumbered downhill, downforest dash," only to be caught and confronted by Turner, who reminded him how much trouble he'd be in for being AWOL and stealing an air mattress, then startled him by asking, "Don't you want to dig?" He offered trainee Elkin the option to guard the site after the others completed the task to Turner's satisfaction. Before his ten-hour guard duty began, however, he learned that all Turner demanded was that they spread a tarpaulin over the hole, but at least he was able to finish "Mario the Magician" while guarding a hole in the Rockies.[17]

Upon completing his basic training he was assigned to Fort Lee, Virginia, where he was even unhappier than in Colorado. Living in a barracks, he wrote and called family members, complaining frequently about the boredom, drudgery, and rigidity of army discipline. In August he wrote, "Today, honey, they started giving us the muscle business. We had to run around an area slightly larger than the state of Rhode Island. Well I ran about 300 miles and had to drop out. This is called physical training. It builds you up." Speaking of the increasing number of chin-ups the recruits were forced to complete, he groused, "Why do you know that in a week you can drop dead of a heart attack." By November he was convinced that advanced training was going to be even more rigorous than basic: "Today was our first day of classes and we, the khaki student princes, the khaki collegians, the olive drab kids, started our somewhat less than rugged intellection considered advanced training by the United Stated Army, an institution of learning somewhere between the gutter and kindergarten. If today's lectures were any indication, these eight weeks are going to make the most strenuous

P.T. endured at Ft. Carson seem like a peasant recess. This goes on for ten hours a day, and the most strenuous thing I do all day is trying to keep my eyes open." By mid-November he became concerned that his calls were irritating the family: "I had the uneasy feeling, first of all, that my father was annoyed at my call, and that you [Joan], too, were somewhat disturbed." There was some consolation because he got the "writing job," a manual about the use of forklift trucks, which he thought was his greatest goldbricking achievement while in the army. Perhaps the perceived annoyance was precursor to an audacious proposal he made on November 15—that Joan give up her job in Chicago and move to Petersburg, Virginia. But by the end of November she'd apparently agreed, because he begged almost paternalistically for her to drive carefully, promising that for the first time they would really be alone together: "We can get a hell of a lot done, from babies to books, and that's all I think about."[18] They set up housekeeping in Colonial Heights while Stanley continued advanced training in Quartermaster School, which he completed in December. They were close friends with Robert and Jean Kipniss—he later became a prominent New York artist—with whom they kept up an intermittent correspondence over the years. Joan recalls that Robert was mysterious, whereas Stanley was open and gregarious. They spent pleasant evenings in their tiny apartment, where they entertained the Kipnisses in the bedroom, which was approached by walking through the kitchen and the bathroom. They were also friends with Sherman and Lerida Hermberger of Oklahoma.[19]

Stanley had volunteered for the draft and Robert had been drafted, so they expected to remain privates, whereas many enlisted men wanted to advance in the army. Stanley helped Robert pass this bad time because "he was entertaining and Joan was charming." Both felt "like fish out of water" in the army and in the South: "It was terrible." But they were fortunate enough to have spouses there, so they could treat the quartermaster corps pretty much like an ordinary job. They could arrive on base at 8 A.M. and leave at 4 P.M. Monday through Friday, whereas unmarried enlistees were constantly on base except for leaves, and had to live in a barracks: "It was a pretty lousy time for most of us. We resented being there in a way the regular army guys could never understand. We loved Stanley's humor because without it we would have fallen apart. Being in the army in Richmond was too terrible and Stanley helped us through it." Novak considered Stanley a sartorial disaster in college, and he was a natural mocker of army decorum as well: "He could put on a freshly ironed khaki uniform, and within five minutes it would look as if he had slept in it."

What really shocked both was being among Southerners for the first time. In his duty assignment, illustrating army manuals, Robert encountered quite a few locals: "And every white guy, sooner or later, would take out his wallet and show you pictures of his car, his boat, his kids, and a black man hanging from a tree. As a New Yorker, I'd never encountered the Klan before. Neither had Stanley. We were shocked and a little scared." Elkin also reacted to undisguised prejudice in a November 1955 letter to Joan:

> The old south is old. It, at least this part of it, feeds on the memory of the past. It institutionalizes the past, makes of it a product. And sells itself on street corners like an old whore. Virginia was one of the 13 original colonies and don't you forget it. The motels are all colonial, but they are neat, and their restaurants are chromed and the paint is fresh. . . . In front of each home is the inevitable Jockey Club hitching post. The smiling Negro stands in frozen elegance and proffers the ring that is not taken. He is a symbol of tradition. What Virginia has not learned is that tradition cannot *be* symbolized. It is not something that WAS, but something that *is.*"

A frightening instance of being outsiders occurred one evening in a Petersburg movie theater. The Kipnisses, the Elkins, and another couple were seeing a "perfectly awful" movie and Stanley was entertaining everyone with his comments when a huge guy in front stood up, turned, and showed them his handgun and badge, saying "'I'm a lawman here. You people shut up right now.' And we did. But we didn't stay for the second feature."

Robert had also been an English major in college, so they talked about books they'd read or planned to read, as well as their resentments of Uncle Sam. Elkin could find humor in any situation, and "I was kind of surprised when he became a professor and a novelist. I fully expected him to become a comic on the nightclub circuit. And he'd have been a great success."[20] With Joan in Colonial Heights, Stanley became less unhappy, if not reconciled to army life. One distraction was participation in an amateur theater group in nearby Richmond. Joan recalls his acting in several amateur productions there, and one of Stanley's anecdotes illustrates his talent for self-dramatization. It concerned an improvisation during a play in which he acted with Roger Mudd, later an anchor for CBS News. In Elkin's version, Mudd stumbled as he came onto the stage, dropping the gun he carried as a prop. Stanley picked it up and handed it to him, improvising "I don't know anything about guns." Many years later, however, Molly Elkin met the newsman in Washington and recounted the story. Mudd quipped, "That never happened." Shortly before Elkin died he told William Gaddis about the compound name of Charles Mudd-Gaddis, a character in *The Magic Kingdom*: "I often use the names of friends [. . .] because of the sound their names make on the page." He acknowledged that he joined William's name with that of "a very impressive guy I used to know" during six weeks of rehearsals and performance while he was stationed in Virginia. He didn't, however, mention the anecdote about improvising.

Kipniss doesn't recall seeing Elkin on stage, but he remembers several trips the couples made to Richmond to enjoy movies. These trips sometimes provoked ill feelings because Stanley had a car and his bad driving habits were already well

Rehearsing *The Petrified Forest* with the director, about 1955.
By permission of Joan Elkin.

established. He would engage in an animated conversation with Kipniss in the rear seat, sometimes tuning around to make his point while driving at seventy miles per hour. One evening the Kipnisses were getting nervous as one near-collision followed another. Finally Robert snapped, "For Christ's sake, Stanley, shut up and keep your eyes on the road." For a while Stanley would desist and drive, but soon he'd be looking back over the seat until a passenger reprimanded him again.[21] To this day Robert can't understand why Stanley never had an accident on the way to or back from Richmond. But the friendship flourished because of his humor and the danger was offset by laughter.

Whether the Mudd improvisation did or didn't happen, Stanley found some relief from the drudgery of military life acting on the stage, writing about forklifts, and mainly having Joan in Virginia. In August the family got a scare when

Tootsie underwent a serious operation, joining Phil as a heart patient. And he told Bill Guggenheim in a January 1957 letter congratulating them on their first child, "With us, nothing is new. So what's old? So what is old is that I hate the Army. I'm on K.P. next week, the insurance on my car is due, we are eating meatloaf, and for two cents I'd desert."[22] He was looking forward to civilian life and resuming his efforts to get published. In October *Virginia Quarterly Review* rejected two articles about William Makepeace Thackeray, "Thackeray and the Well of Experience" and "Acquiescence and Renunciation," both revisions of M.A. papers. The second is of special interest as it foreshadows Elkin's adult insistence on the autonomy of the work of art, which manifests intentionalities of which only the author can be aware: "I maintain that Thackeray was, after all, at least as well aware of his own life as I am, and that his own work was a conscientious justification of his own actions." He continues, "Essentially what happens is that Thackeray injects a spirit into the facts before he disposes of them artistically, so that we are given a *reason* for their being, a justification for their tragedy." He also submitted "The Party" to *Views* magazine and received this encouraging rejection in November: "Our final opinion is that we like the manner but believe there's just a little too much matter. Will you do us a favor; reappraise PARTY yourself and see if you can't do a little cutting; tighten it a little. Chances are your rewrite will be accepted." Finally, the handwritten letter he had been waiting for showed up in the Gilbert Cottages mailbox: Baxter Hathaway of *Epoch* advised him that "A Sound of Distant Thunder" would be out in the 1957 winter or spring issue.[23] Stanley was becoming Elkin.

Although several magazines had refused it, "A Sound of Distant Thunder" is a surprisingly mature story, one that foreshadows "Criers and Kibitzers, Kibitzers and Criers." It moreover resembles the subgenre of the Jewish American shopkeeper story Bernard Malamud, whose path often crossed Elkin's, perfected in *The Assistant,* also published in 1957. This is not to suggest any kind of influence— Elkin had submitted "Distant Thunder" for publication two years before—but rather an evolving motif in Jewish American fiction, one that would become central to Elkin's early work. In the story, shopkeeper Meyer Feldman reluctantly confronts social and economic change in his South Side neighborhood, with the thunder of the title literally prefiguring a storm and symbolically suggesting the violence that accompanies major social and economic changes. While he sees the street on which his china shop stands changing before his eyes, his barber friend complains that he has to cut "a schvartze's hair" and a photographer gripes that he has to work a "schvartze's wedding" to survive economically.[24] Although Feldman professes economic and cultural loyalty to the street and the Jewish community, his closest friend is selling his toy store and moving to a larger location in a gentile district where he can "put up a stage for Santa Claus at Christmas time" (25).

But for Feldman the street represents a cultural tradition he can't imagine surviving without, even if business is bad. During the day on which the story takes place, he meets only two customers, one sent by his brother-in-law in search of a discount. Still, the neighborhood means something to him: "Jews had to stick together, Feldman knew. They couldn't be happy unless they were with each other" (18). The central conflict is, however, between Feldman and three unnamed African American youths who represent the changes taking place on the South Side and the resentment of Jews by the new population. He encounters them three times, and each episode is more confrontational. In the second meeting, they enter his store, inquiring about the price of a china set, and then ask, "How much is it if a Jew buys it for us?" establishing multiple levels of racial animosity. The final time he sees them from his apartment window, with more youths, moving along the street with threatening paraphernalia; intuitively, he knows their destination. He resigns himself to the destruction of his store and the beauty its stock represents, taking no action to prevent the young men from acting out their resentment of the more affluent shopkeeper class. In this respect, the story represents a path Elkin's fiction might have taken, a meditation on ethnicity and the forces of social change, and it is likely that he would have rivaled Malamud and Philip Roth as masters of serious Jewish American fiction had he done so.

A trip to New York in late 1956 or early 1957 produced one bad and one very good result. He wrangled leave to attend a nephew's bris, or Brit Milah, in New Jersey. When they arrived, the wealthier Bloom family, some of whom had Ivy League educations, treated them shabbily. But they never got to the actual bris. Stanley wore his army-issue khakis, largely because he couldn't afford a new suit. An aunt of the baby to be circumcised said, "You're not going to my nephew's bris in those pants, are you?" Stanley replied, "No, I guess we aren't" and they immediately returned to Virginia. Stanley frankly envied their wealth and opportunities, and he was profoundly hurt by their condescending attitude. He recalled this put-down a few months before he died:

> [Y]ou said, "Stanley, couldn't you have found an entire pair of pants to wear to my nephew's bris?" and I rose from the sofa where we were sitting, announced to my wife, "Come on, we're getting out of here," and stormed into—a closet. I found my way back to the living room and, pulling a stunned Joan behind me, stormed out again, climbed into my car, and sped back down the road the 100 miles [really about 370] to Fort Lee and the relative safety of the U.S. Army. Naming names, I've used that anecdote a thousand times in my fiction classes to illustrate the impossibility of trying to write a story (which, unsuccessfully, I worked on for about two years) when you're too close to the material. That was too complicated a weekend for me. Thinking about it now, all these years later, it still is.

When she learned about an unpublished story called "Bris" in the archive, Joan suspected that he wrote the story as a way of getting revenge on the Bloom clan. But he remained fond of Ben Bloom, who had sent money so they could buy gas to come to New Jersey, and who was really happy to see them and sorry when they left.[25]

But the trip had an unexpected benefit. The inspiration for *The Dick Gibson Show* occurred while he was in the army, probably on that journey. During a stop at a New Jersey Turnpike rest area, Elkin chanced upon a distinctive radio voice he never identified. He began to muse upon the ways in which radio personalities formed a new class of American celebrity and upon the connections among the audience listening to the program, as well as the needs these connections serve. If the announcer sounded lonely, it occurred to Stanley that the audience must be lonely as well: "[W]e were invisible and yet his voice was a link between all of us, and it struck me that this is a strange, a very, very strange job."[26] This experience stayed with him for nearly a decade before he could convert it to high art.

In 1957, Stanley's army ordeal ended on August 17, with an honorable discharge from "Co B 1st Bn QMSR, Ft. Lee, Va.[27] His reserves obligation would be in force until 1961, but for all practical proposes, he was ready for the next stage of his life. The problem was, what would that be? He wasn't ready to launch a career as a writer, and he had barely enough degrees to earn a living as a professor. With two ailing parents and an increasing desire for children of their own, Stanley and Joan decided to do what many of us do when the path is uncertain: they headed back to graduate school.

⚙ 4 ⚙ Family Crises, Graduate School, and a Literary Career, 1957–60

(I was a graduate student, protected up to my ass in ivy.)
My daddy's rich and my mamma's good lookin'.

—Introduction to the 1990 edition of
Criers and Kibitzers, Kibitzers and Criers

For many academics, graduate school is a hard time. Teaching assistants are notoriously underpaid. There are papers to be written, research, intense reading assignments, and seminar preparation. Then there's always the looming specter of comprehensive exams, seemingly designed to remind the student how little he or she actually knows about the discipline, and the challenge of learning to teach undergraduates and the real mastery of material that university teachers need. And of course there are inexhaustible but exhausting reams of undergraduate papers to read, mark, return, and cope with disappointment and griping. Finally, there's long-term anxiety about the doctoral thesis, selecting a topic, and recruiting a mentor. Yet a surprising number of us look back at these as the happiest years of our lives. For Elkin, anything in Urbana probably seemed wonderful after the army years, but his graduate school challenges were compounded by volunteer work on a literary magazine, essays and reviews for college publications, struggles to publish professionally, a profound family sorrow, and enlarged family responsibilities. He also had increasing hypochondriac symptoms to contend with, and two friends believe his first, undiagnosed, symptoms of multiple sclerosis presented during this time.

As a youth Stanley had been persuaded by the Ouija board that he'd die in 1956, but that date came and went while he was in the army, so he began the Ph.D. with anxiety about his general health, a state of mind compounded by worry about both parents' heart disease. Probably this concern, combined with the fact that many of his childhood friends, notably Bill Guggenheim, had started families, led the Elkins to consider enlarging their family despite the financial uncertainties of graduate school. After they found that conception wasn't happening, they adopted their infant son and named him for Stanley's father, in 1958.[1] But Phil was denied the blessing of holding his namesake. The stress of several heart attacks had caught up with him; he died in New York, still at work, in January, in his mid-fifties. He was originally buried in Chicago, but later Tootsie had the body moved to New Jersey. Stanley was profoundly touched to learn that Phil had his published story on a hotel nightstand when he died. Undoubtedly, Irwin Gold's note of February 14, 1958, brought some consolation:

> One day last spring [. . . y]our father phoned, excited that the story had been published, wanting to tell what his son had done. Fifteen minutes later he phoned again; in his initial excitement he had forgotten to ask where the magazine could be purchased. I think there were two or three calls after that in the next hour, calls reporting which stores had stocked the magazine, calls indignant that not every store *did* stock the magazine, calls fierce with pride that his son was in the magazine.

Months before his own death, Elkin recalled learning about Phil's passing, driving back to Chicago, and sitting shivah: "I still miss my father and am puzzled every month or so when he returns in my dreams."[2] The most important figure in his life, certainly the one he strove to please and emulate, was gone. Stanley directed his energy toward rearing his son and advancing his life's work as a writer, something of which Phil had become proud.

While developing several stories for publication and learning the craft of teaching, Elkin continued to write for university outlets, especially the magazine *Coffee*. Among his surviving efforts, three essays command particular interest, especially his review of the film *Porgy and Bess* (1959). Like his M.A. period verse play "A Cup for God," this review exhibits a profound social consciousness. He takes the film, and Hollywood in general, to task for contributing to the myth of happy, poor, African American life during the Jim Crow era: "[A]ll the pictures about Negroes that I know of [. . .] have been musicals. It's almost as if Hollywood is in some kind of conspiracy to perpetuate the folk myth (the white-folk) that the Negro, if he doesn't have anything else, a decent job, money in the bank, civil rights, has rhythm." Citing James Baldwin's censure of the film, Elkin complains that Dorothy Dandridge, the widely admired jazz singer who played Bess, was dubbed over by a "heavily voiced opera singer" (African American Adele Addison) with the effect that Dandridge is "well, beautiful, but she can't act and they don't *let her sing*. [. . .]" His assessment of Sidney Poitier's performance is scathing: "paralyzed in more than just the legs" and a "white man's Porgy." He caps his condemnation by making a well-intentioned if inaccurate assessment of discrimination in the arts, concluding that there was a shortage of experienced African American actors: "There is no real Negro theater, and parts for Negroes have simply not been written into white men's plays. This is one of the peculiarly oblique results of discrimination." Although the twenty-nine-year-old was wrong in assuming that competent African American actors didn't exist, he was sympathetic and perceptive about institutional discrimination in the

popular arts. Readers offended by the overt racism of some of Elkin's characters
or the occasional use of racially insensitive language by the narrators of certain
novels will find something to ponder in this sympathetic portrayal of the plight
of African Americans in the theater and films.

In a slightly less serious vein Elkin reviewed *The Immoral Mr. Teas* (Russ
Meyer, 1959), a soft-core pornographic movie that showed at the Illini Theater.
Some film historians consider this the first commercially viable blue movie. To
Coffee's readers he confesses sneaking in after the movie had been in town for
three weeks, but discovering an overall sadness to the whole business, a "consciousness of deep loneliness and great guilt, and one feels a terrible pity for the
solitary airmen from Chanute [Air Force Base], for dateless college boys, for aging,
graying men, invariably transients, salesmen perhaps, and for oneself." While he
admits to enjoying stag flicks as a high school boy, the "professionalization" of
pornography leads him to contemplate the social implications of a blue movie
outgrossing commercial films in Urbana. Its appeal, he concludes, is "ultimately
to the losers, the outsiders, the ragtag corps of the spiritually maimed, and all
the layers of sophistication heaped upon this picture like coats of whitewash
come finally to nothing." Elkin waxes prophetic, anticipating Robert Coover's
The Adventures of Lucky Pierre (2002), which explores the premise that in the
near future pornographic movies will be treated with the kind of seriousness that
characterizes film study in many universities: "[W]e may be letting ourselves in
for a whole new approach to public pornography. I see the day where films may
vie on the open market for the business of discriminating customers." Somewhat
more ponderously, his review of Ingmar Bergman's *The Magician* challenges "high
seriousness" in film study and criticism. He questions the ethos of "film studies,"
with its emphasis on art for art's sake, saying the only film worth watching among
the thirteen sessions since he joined the Film Studies Club was *The Maltese Falcon;*
in the others, "once in a while one of us runs across a recognizable emotion."
Overall he challenges the "major premise of film historians, that pictures stand
or fall on the basis of their photography, cuttings, and direction." Elkin's caveat
contradicts his own mature artistic credo: "A picture, motion or candid or oil,
depends ultimately on content; that the content of art is *idea;* that any technique
without *idea* (and the validity of idea is based upon the pragmatic constant of
human nature) is only craftsmanship and skill." Along the way he bashes two
Aleksandr Dovzhenko films as "artsy," one Griffiths film, as well as most of
DeMille's because "they use human beings as though they were props."[3]

While writing for *Coffee* he was also developing and submitting original
stories. Shortly after Phil's death an unspecified story received a harsh rejection from *Antioch Review*, whose editor snarled, "I have also been wondering
why anyone but a specialist or a short story technician would want to read
it." A month later, Jarvis Thurston, with whom Elkin would have substantial

professional and personal contact, politely rejected an unspecified submission for *Perspective:* "Too much of the series of alternatives, parentheticals and appositives seems not adequately functional, a kind of authorial self-indulgence that is interesting but not *sufficiently* exploratory of mood or idea." A couple of months later, Ralph Freedman accepted "The Sun Light's Morning Game" for *Contact,* but the editors at *Western Review* refused to honor that commitment when they assimilated the magazine. The Elkin archive contains no typescript or other reference to a story with that title; it's probably an early version of "Criers and Kibitzers, Kibitzers and Criers." "Cousin Poor Lesley and the Lousy People" experienced a mixed fate with the widest-circulation venue Elkin had yet attempted. In July Peter Davidson of Atlantic–Little, Brown inquired about a possible novel based on characters and events from that story, which the editors of *Atlantic Monthly* had passed along to him. But three days later the journal rejected the story as "too loose-jointed for our purposes, but we read it with real interest." In September, *Epoch* rejected an unspecified story, and to complete the year, the *Berkeley Review* rejected "The Hero in the Alley" in October. It's likely that "In the Alley" is a revision, rewrite, or renaming of this story. If so, all the stories were accepted during the next few years.[4]

Despite the fact that so many editors defended their rejections of his stories based on length, or maybe because of that, Elkin was undertaking novels at this point as well. As teenagers he and Barry Spacks had argued about the relative literary gravitas of poems versus novels, and Spacks recalls that one thing they could agree upon was that novels were "serious" in ways stories weren't, and that "major" writers wrote novels.[5] A substantial planning sheet for what may have been his first novel attempt, likely composed about the time he left the army, focuses on "Magnitude" as a virtue: he mentions John Dos Passos's techniques, though he doesn't plan to emulate them, to achieve breadth: "Because scope is two-thirds of what we call greatness, massiveness of attempt." The few surviving pages of this fragment suggest that the story is based on the main theme of Elkin's juvenilia, his father's vocation. The hero, Jewish watch salesman Freddy Eckerstein, while driving through the Nebraska dusk on his way back to Chicago, has second thoughts about having changed his name to Frederick Ecker to counter the anti-Semitism he's encountered in business, in a wonderful imitation of Hemingway's style: "[N]ot ashamed of being a Jew. Not one bit ashamed. Didn't change my religion, after all. Just my name." As he answers nature's call in a cornfield, worried about what might happen if the farmer or a barking dog finds him there, he sees what he believes is a flying saucer. The fragment ends here, and it's tempting to speculate that the notion of extraterrestrials, while a popular motif of the era, simply didn't fuel Elkin's imagination. Or perhaps he was intimidated by the sententiousness of the Faulknerian theme he announced in his planning sheet: "Something I said on a Virginia porch [while in the army]:

Life [. . .] is not progress or stasis or retrogression. It's not anything at all to do with time. Time is merely the arena in which it all goes on. Actually, it's simple, so simple I figured it out. It—Life is—affiliation, a shift of allegiance, a transfer of loyalties; a concert only of epiphanies, the main themes; a constant accretion of civilization for the guy involved."[6]

A similar theme permeates a more developed undertaking, *The Glass Continent*. This novel was certainly in some draft stage before Phil's death in 1958, and I'm persuaded that it, not "The Sound of Distant Thunder," is the text on which Phil took his son to task for naïvely representing the quantity of a wholesale order. Someone, not Elkin, penciled on the archived draft, "[1952]—first novel, incomplete" but the bombast of juvenilia like "A Cup for God" suggests that this is a later work. It's set in 1951 with a flashback to 1932. Five sequential chapters survive, the last quite impressive in capturing Stephen Feldman's sense of tedium and simultaneous hope of moving on to the next sale, against his mortality and his awareness of the ways his deeds will be eclipsed when he dies. These are contrasted against his memory of Harvey Saturday, who mentored him early in his career and served as his role model—sort of a Dave Singleman to this Willy Loman. Many similarities exist between this fragment and Arthur Miller's great play, first produced in 1949 and filmed in 1951. But Elkin's Feldman is "less deceived," to borrow a phrase from Hamlet (and Philip Larkin), and part of his epiphany is the realization that selling is neither a vocation nor a way to gain immortality. Of greatest interest to the story of Elkin's artistic life—and the principal interest of this text is what it tells us about the process by which the young writer attempted to convert life to art—is that *The Glass Continent* is far more critical of the salesman's craft than mature novels like *The Franchiser*, chronicling Feldman's disillusionment as a result of his heart attack and recovery. A final chapter, not intended to follow the existing five directly (a typed note stipulates that this section "will come later in the development of the book"), takes up a visit by his son David, with whom Stephen has had a cool and distant relationship, to the family home in Brooklyn, and through the impetuous decision to take a nighttime cab ride to Oakland, New Jersey, where the family vacationed when he was a child. The fragment doesn't end—it simply stops after page twenty-two, complementing the ninety-one pages of chapters 1–5. Perhaps the autobiographical content of the second section, as well as the poignancy of the prolonged effort to convert Phil's life to art, discouraged Elkin from completing it. The loss for the biographical narrative because of his abandoning this story is great, but that for literature isn't, although chapter 5 gives us a hint of the promise that would manifest itself during the next decade.[7]

He was remarkably prolific during these years, in light of his duties as a new father, a teaching assistant, and an editorial staff member. Although several of his stories were rejected and abandoned, he was able to place two pieces. In December

1957 he got the dreaded note from *Tamarack Review* for "The Last of the Go-To-Hell-God-Damn-its." The editor explained, "We were a little troubled by this story, and I have difficulty explaining why, except to say that its intention and its characters both seemed to us a little cloudy." Although no final typescript for this item exists in the archive, the working drafts suggest that it's a Cisco Kid–Pancho buddy story about an unnamed narrator who becomes the title character's pal. Ed Hensall was probably based on Jack Mulligan, Elkin's bohemian friend from college. The story anticipates "A Poetics for Bullies" in exploring, from the perspective of the bully's victim, the process and effects of coercion. Ed, who writes lectures for his English professor, dates gorgeous women, breaks all the rules, and stars in plays he subverts, anticipates both protagonists of "Poetics," Push the Bully and John Williams, the "perfect" adolescent. Although clearly smarter than his fellows and the unchallenged leader of his subgroup, Ed "was a bully. His wit was often directed at people who could do nothing but cower before it, who were defenseless and who had, ultimately, to laugh with the others who were laughing at them or go under." The thirty-nine-page typescript in Elkin's papers cries out for tightening, as it struggles to show that the bullying is a veneer for an ordinary man. The narrator's epiphany, after their final meeting, anticipates central themes of *The Dick Gibson Show* and *The Franchiser*. He discovers that there are no great moments, that the ultimate truth lies in what Gibson later called a "strange displacement of the ordinary" (229): "[W]e were stuck and there was no such thing as a free spirit. Or if there was, you could bet it was a troubled spirit, a guilty spirit, tortured by what it was trying to do, knowing even in the first rush of air puffing up the out-stretched wings that it could never get away with it." The transformation is less than satisfactorily motivated; but any regret we might have that Elkin abandoned it is more than offset by the fact that he subsequently transformed the ideas to create "Poetics."[8]

He hit pay dirt when *Views* published "The Party" in 1958. His father had expressed reservations about the editor's motives, and the long delay in publishing annoyed Elkin, but he was in print while he was in graduate school. It's a dark character sketch, inquiring into the evasive personality, one who can't deal with the surrounding world but rather takes refuge in his reconstruction of alternative realities, in Stephen Feldman's case his own past. His evasions are motivated by a pervasive cynicism: "[H]e was convinced of the validity, the unremitting righteousness of his one unshakeable concept—the premise born hunch that things were terrible, and certainly, if God had been on our side, ought not to be"[9] (40). He commits nocturnal adultery not by having an affair, but by denying his wife connubial rights and living in a romanticized version of his own past, from visits to his grandmother's home in Brooklyn to legends of his grandfather's heroic death at the hands of Russian Cossacks. His wife plans a party to engage him with the neighborhood, but Stephen, preferring his work and his past, has avoided meeting the neighbors, to whom he feels superior: "If he had nothing (this was true) he would not at any rate settle for second best, not his wife's second best. It was too remedial, her party was to be a kind of patch hastily sewn on a tattered life. She could keep it" (44). Elkin later correctly dismissed "The Party" as amateurish, though in some ways it anticipates his problematic novella "The Condominium" as a study in the evasive personality, but it lacks a solid motivation for Feldman's rejection of his wife and their neighbors. His childhood memories, which seem to be less than fully assimilated, are most likely reconstructions of fragments of Elkin's own relocation as a child to Chicago. Stephen's mother is named Zelda and he recalls the sense of abandonment and awe that attended his last days in Brooklyn, as well as subsequent visits in which he discovers a preference for New York over Chicago. Elkin also wrote a fragment, which he never developed for publication, about yet another Stephen Feldman suffering a heart attack at his moment of climax with his mistress and their subsequent debate over whether and how to seek medical attention. The fragment reminds one of Philip Roth's contemporaneous "Epstein," but Elkin abandoned the project despite a planning note requiring Feldman's death: "Man has heart attack 1st time he cheats on his wife. Girl is married. Husband returns. Fellow dying in husband's bed."[10] A final fragment rounds out the family theme in Elkin's graduate school fictions. This untitled, heavily edited draft contains dense autobiographical elements, principally "Richard's" intense conflicts with a stern authoritarian father, his forced relocation to Nebraska (two states west of Illinois), and his attending a large midwestern university, where he becomes involved with multicultural friends and joins a radical movement—perhaps as close as Elkin would ever come to a radical protagonist.

Fortune wasn't finished smiling on the Elkins. In March 1959 *Perspective* accepted "Cousin Poor Lesley and the Lousy People," the earliest story Elkin chose to keep when he assembled his only collection, *Criers and Kibitzers, Kibitzers and Criers*. The next year he would become editor Thurston's colleague and they remained close friends for more than three decades. "Cousin Poor Lesley" had been rejected a year before by *Atlantic Monthly*, and Elkin apparently submitted another story, in multiple drafts, which Thurston rejected in October as "Still too ornate." In its final form, "Cousin Poor Lesley" is as close as Elkin ever came to an Our Gang comedy, minus the comedy. It does, however, have a gag line that anticipates the mature Elkin wit. When his schmuck-cousin Lesley joins the service, the narrator quips that his family "is not what you could call a United States Marine family. Ours is more a Certified Public Accountant family"[11] (220; *Criers and Kibbitzers*). Cousin Lesley from Chicago, who was the butt of all the jokes of the narrator's New York gang, the "Lousy people"—they had "*personality, outsized, grotesque, collective*" (221; emphasis in original)—is denied even the glory of a heroic end on the battlefield. He dies in an accident during maneuvers.

The story also chronicles entropic transformations among the gang while the narrator is in college. One is sent to jail, another wrestles in carnivals (anticipating Elkin's first published novel, *Boswell*), one sells suspicious insurance, and the others can't be accounted for. The gang leader, "our taste-maker" who "encouraged aberration for its own sake" (224), recovered from an auto accident caused by his reckless driving only to be committed to a mental institution. Despite its somber tones, in which no character with the possible exception of the narrator turns out well, Elkin ends "Cousin Poor Lesley" on an ambiguous note—one his craft isn't sufficiently developed to explore fully. After a tortured meeting with the narrator, presumably his only visitor since he arrived at the hospital, Danny, the leader, suddenly clams up. The narrator, after sitting in silence, departs: "Still he said nothing, but I did not miss the broad wink in the wild and knowing eye" (238). This wink implies that Danny is simultaneously mad and aware. But just how that counters the story's prevailing entropy isn't worked out.

Elkin also volunteered to work on the Illinois journal *Accent*, edited by Kerker Quinn. On the staff were his creative writing teachers George Scouffas and Charles Shattuck, as well as fellow Ph.D. student James Ballowe. His duties included screening stories for publication, sending rejection notices, and participating in editorial decision-making conferences. One of the new writers about whom Elkin was particularly excited was a young philosopher from Purdue University, William H. Gass. As Ballowe recalls, Gass's unusual stories were circulated among the staff, who didn't know exactly what to make of them, but they agreed that this was genius and Elkin vigorously advocated publishing them. After their publication, Gass was invited to join the faculty at Illinois, teaching classes in English, philosophy, and creative writing and serving on the *Accent* staff. When he arrived in Champaign, he heard Elkin read from his own work-in-progress and realized that this writer was truly special. As he got to know Elkin he concluded that this wasn't "just another guy trying to write—he was really good." They shared an office one semester, and Elkin later recalled watching Gass's art in progress: "[A]nd what he was doing was practicing his sentences, doing these endless, silent scales. He had a kaleidoscope on his desk, and he would turn it to the window to catch the light, and then try to write down what that kaleidoscope saw. You know, taking from the one medium and translating it to the other. That's a marvelous thing. It's much more important than the writer doing the social scientist's job."[12]

When Gass joined the faculty, a lasting and close friendship of men and writers who are very unlike each other began. Writing about those times twenty-five years later, Gass recalls his year at Illinois as less than ideal: "I would rather relive that year than rejoin the navy, but that's about it. Stanley Elkin was a welcome light in a dark time," recalling Robert Kipniss's comment that Elkin's humor made it possible for him to survive the army. When Gass gave a housewarming party, it rained so hard no one but the Elkins came, soaked to the bone from crossing the flooded street. Afraid the electricity would go out, Gass went to check the fuse box and suddenly became conscious of Stanley's presence in the knee-deep water in the flooded basement: "I thought if you were going to electrocute yourself down here [. . .] you ought to have some company." Gass recalled symbolically, "We set a new watermark that night." His friend was possessed by "his anecdotal history" of himself, "how Stanley, himself—always the subject—became objectified: became a character we all first heard, then felt we saw, emerge from our narrator's memory. Stanley also groused a lot. He wanted what he felt were his just deserts, his due, and to that end he kept accounts. Receipts, it seemed, regularly fell short. In addition he constantly complained about his health, which was precarious; and those complaints were hard to believe, he seemed so robust." In 2002 Gass again remembered Elkin as "something of a hypochondriac" back then, who complained about small ailments and injuries—of course, everything about him was woven into a larger story. One time he had a busted thumb, but Gass can't recall whether he punched someone or hit a wall in anger or frustration. Looking back, he believes an early manifestation of Elkin's lifelong nemesis happened in 1959 or 1960, a siege of temporary blindness, which no one recognized as a presymptom of multiple sclerosis. Ben Flesh, the hero of *The Franchiser*, suffers an identical first symptom, also in his late twenties.

Gass and Ballowe remember Elkin as an astute editor, a diligent and often original reader of submissions, and a generally congenial staff member. But according to Ballowe he could be "a little testy" when his opinion was challenged. Most of the time, however, he was "very astute, a real kibitzer" who knew exactly what he was doing in every editorial situation. Gass remembers a slightly more contentious relationship; he believes neither he nor anyone else anticipated the extent of Stanley's literary promise from his work as an editor, that he was often the "odd man out" in editorial decisions. His opinions were "quirky," sometimes "simply strange and cantankerous," but sometimes he'd catch something very important that other staffers had missed.[13] Certainly his time at *Accent* constituted what his character Dick Gibson calls an "apprenticeship," during which he learned how to reward good fiction and reject what wasn't so good—and it led to his meeting his first true literary celebrity, another adopted Chicagoan.

On the verso of an April 1960 rejection from *Mademoiselle*, Elkin handwrote, in red ink, to Saul Bellow: "We met briefly when you came to Champaign to give a talk. I am one of the people with *Accent*. I had some luck this past year with some of my stories. *Perspective*, *Accent* and *Chicago Review* each printed one. Perhaps *Noble Savage* can use this one." Bellow's reply was gracious, but no Elkin story appeared in *Noble Savage*: "I approve very highly of your story and am sending it on to the other editors with the hope that they will share my admiration for it." His postscript, however, sounds a warning note: "I particularly liked the grocery on 53rd Street and the employees and shoppers, but I was not sure that the last passages really bore the accumulated weight. It is too easy to float a conclusion with the support of certain Jewish symbols. I am a little suspicious of the use you make of them." From this comment we may confidently infer that the story was a version of "Criers and Kibitzers, Kibitzers and Criers." The visit to which Elkin refers happened while he was at *Accent,* and he mentioned this in response to a question about Bellow's influence:

> When I was at the University of Illinois, working on *Accent* magazine, Bellow came to Champaign to give a talk and *Accent* gave a lunch for him. I was a graduate student and one of the readers for the magazine, not a writer. I mean, I wrote, but I didn't consider myself a writer then. *Henderson the Rain King* [1959] had just come out. We were having lunch at the Urbana Lincoln Hotel, and for some reason every remark Bellow made—he kept staring at me, everything he said seemed to be addressed to me. And this lunch went on forever. Eventually I had to leave. When I got up, Bellow said, "Where are you going?" I said, "To the bathroom," and he said, "But you're coming back?" Later he invited me to have breakfast with him. What this means, I don't know. It probably means nothing, but you just mentioned *Henderson the Rain King* and I had the impression when I read the novel that he might have thought of me as a kind of Henderson.[14]

Although Bellow couldn't help Elkin get his story into print, they remained lifelong mutual admirers. Elkin consistently listed Bellow prominently among the writers who influenced his style, along with William Faulkner, Henry James, and Gass. Although he professed awe for Bellow's philosophical richness and his management of complex plots, he surprised more than a few interviewers by insisting on the elegance of Bellow's style. And the admiration was mutual. Shortly before *Ravelstein* (2000) came out, Bellow and I chatted briefly after an award ceremony in Baltimore. He was weary after his acceptance speech, but he brightened when I mentioned one of his loudest admirers. He smiled, then became very still, and said in almost a whisper: "I loved that man. I miss him so much."[15] And I thought of Charles Citrine, the protagonist of *Humboldt's Gift,* who sought even more than most Bellow protagonists to communicate with the departed, and his mentor, based on Bellow's own friendship with Delmore Schwartz.

Not all of his adventures at Illinois involved serving on an editorial board and meeting literary celebrities, however. There was the tedious matter of making a living, and graduate teaching assistants work notoriously long hours at low pay. He and Ballowe used adjoining carrels in the library as they prepared for dissertation work. Jim and his wife were close to the Elkins during those years, often visiting one another's residences, and from time to time going out together or babysitting Philip so Stanley and Joan could enjoy an evening out. Stanley "smoked like a fiend" in those days, so he often had to step outside and Jim sometimes accompanied him. They talked about their thesis work, their career plans, and their families. By this time Stanley was committed to a writing life, and saw university teaching as a way of supporting that choice. His later reputation as a fierce professor and a stern taskmaster wouldn't have been predicted by Ballowe's shared teaching experience with him.

Teaching assistants have to be on the lookout for ways to earn extra money, and in 1958 or 1959 Stan and Jim were invited to participate in a program teaching composition to servicemen making the transition to civilian life at Chanute Air Force Base, about fifteen miles north of town. They drove out together in a university vehicle and taught in adjoining classrooms in a barracks-like building. During those drives they shared anecdotes about their students, mostly sergeants and corporals who wanted to become public school coaches and principals. Ballowe, eventually a university dean, would bring a sheaf of corrected essays, the course book, and mimeographed assignments for the students. Stan brought a handful of model essays by professional writers—no book, no graded papers—and a package of cigarettes. In the adjoining room his class would echo with "raucous laughter" while Jim attempted to conduct a traditional, orderly lesson. Rather than a tutorial or a lesson, Elkin simply "held forth," especially after class, because students were willing to stay and he still had his audience. Looking back, Ballowe assessed Stanley's work in this program, as opposed to his own more traditional academic efforts: "His students had a good time. Stanley wasn't about to knock himself out teaching commas and participles to future basketball coaches and principals. He had an audience, who could tell him their lives." And he shared an experience with that audience, the military. He'd hated the army, and these students were eager to get out of the air force. One other element from that experience sheds light on the teacher Elkin would become: the English Department at Illinois had a strict protocol for grading student compositions: the department posted a list of ten prohibited grammar faults, such as dangling modifiers, comma splices, and so on. If the student had one of these on a paper, its highest possible grade was C; if two, D; three or more, F. The teaching assistants groused among themselves about the rubric's rigidity and many tried to find ways to change or circumvent it. Elkin simply ignored it. He didn't challenge the rules; he just paid no attention to them because they were irrelevant to what he valued.[16]

The home stretch at Urbana involved choosing a topic and researching a doctoral thesis. Ballowe was surprised that Elkin chose to write about religious images in Faulkner, a novelist whose characters exhibit morbidly fundamentalist Christian pathologies, for his thesis, because Elkin was an atheist from a Jewish background, but he had his Faulkner "down cold." He knew the work intimately and had a handle on its nuances. But his love for Faulkner was grounded in the rhetoric, the language, and the flourish, not the themes or abstractions. Elkin was most profoundly influenced by Faulkner's purple patches, his digressions, and his nearly absolute refusal to sacrifice the incident for the larger pattern.[17] In those days it would have been tough to get a dissertation on rhetoric approved, so Elkin turned, as he would say in the précis of the final product, to a class with his adviser: "This thesis developed from my impression in Professor John T. Flanagan's Faulkner-Hemingway seminar that William Faulkner repeatedly seems to incorporate the Christ figure into his novels. I had not anticipated at the time that the Hebraic-Christian influence was any more pervasive than that, but as I commenced to re-read Faulkner I gradually became aware that other elements of the religious tradition were equally important in his work."[18] As was frequent in those days, Ph.D. candidates went to their first employment "ABD," or with prelims passed but with the dissertation proposed but unwritten. He defended it in 1961, but it seems appropriate to discuss it here because it's the culmination of Elkin's graduate education.

Although he made a few efforts to publish "Religious Themes and Symbols in the Novels of William Faulkner" during his early years at Washington University, Elkin acknowledged in the 1970s that "[i]t wasn't a good thesis. What I then took for religious symbolism, I now see as a kind of religious *awe*."[19] Flanagan, his adviser, wrote in 1960 with generally positive reactions to the chapter drafts, even suggesting in August that Elkin revise chapter 6, "The Christ Figure in Faulkner's Novels," for journal submission. There's no evidence that Elkin did this, except for the global revision for submission as a book. But a month before Flanagan had been less enthusiastic about chapter 5, because he was unpersuaded by Elkin's claim that Mink Snopes, the tall convict from the "Old Man" section of *The Wild Palms,* and Lena Grove are Job figures. In the dissertation form of that chapter, Elkin offers an overview of what he thinks Faulkner achieves by adapting the Book of Job in a way that resonates in Elkin's own fiction and that of many of his contemporaries:

> Job's ordeal is a gratuitous test of his faith. This is perhaps its *central signifi-cance,* more important even than Job's ultimate faith or disillusionment. This is because the conditions of Job's ordeal reveal to the modern mind something of the nature of God. [. . .] God's motives in such an experiment might very well be questioned by reasonable or merciful men. The fact that Job comes out all right and that he ends up even richer than he was to begin with is, of course, irrelevant; the sop of reward he is thrown for his endurance does not in the least detract from the barbarity of the contest.
>
> In the story, God is, it seems to me, guilty of the sins of pride and arrogance. He is, for an omnipotent God, entirely too willing to test his strength at the expense of one of his servants. [Elkin cites epithets for God in several novels: "The Player" (*Light in August*), "The Cosmic Joker" (*The Wild Palms*), and the "dark diceman" (*The Sound and the Fury*)]. His final submission to his fate is a tribute to God's greater wisdom, but from the point of view of William Faulkner the modern Job comes off second best to the man who will fight

back, who will, as it were, curse God and live. [. . .] The implication is clear. Because Job is weak and God is strong, Job has no right to ask God for reasons, no right to demand that God explain the moral order of his universe.[20]

We may agree finally with Professor Flanagan's query on the persuasiveness of these Faulkner characters as Job figures, but the quotation offers substantial insight into the clarity of Elkin's perception, at age thirty, of the modernist interpretation of the Job story, focused not on his obedience, but on the capriciousness of the God who would kill his family and torture him to win a bet. Many years later Elkin created his own Job figure, Ellerbee, who is denied salvation in heaven. When he gets a chance to ask God about this irrational, even sadistic, banishment to eternal torture when his ethics warrant eternal bliss, Ellerbee snaps, "So no Job job, no nature in tooth and claw, please. An explanation!"[21]

William Butler Yeats, following in the tradition of William Blake whom he so admired, spoke about "creative misreadings." By that he meant that artists have a different agenda than critics or scholars in approaching a literary text. They may be less concerned with Truth (capital T), the verifiable analysis of data to produce a coherent and compelling theory of its meaning, than with the ways it can teach them their craft and art. "Religious Themes" is probably best approached in this way. Is it a contribution to Faulkner criticism and scholarship? Probably not. In many ways, it's at odds with itself, striving to explicate grand themes while secretly rejoicing in the intricacies of Faulkner's rhetoric. And when Elkin permits himself to focus on rhetoric, he produces gems like this: "Faulkner's basic rhetorical staple is the hyperbole. He uses hyperbolic characters, superlative characters, in the sense that their qualities represent the most extreme limits it is possible or those qualities to attain without spilling over into parody." This approval of a rhetoric of excess describes the degree to which Elkin, as he matured as a stylist, would be indebted to his mentor, so that his larger-than-life characters, be they a mad bailbondsman, a paranoid radio show host, a bad man, or even God, nurtured on the baroque rhetoric of Elkin, would amaze, repel, and delight us with their excesses. If he doesn't emulate what he termed Faulkner's taking the mythic road—"qualities which exist to the degree *that they become legendary*" (emphasis Elkin's)—he transforms through the rhetoric of excess a Chaplinesque British do-gooder (*The Magic Kingdom*) or an historically cursed "blue collar, horseshit man" (*George Mills*) or an entrepreneur bent on franchising America (*The Franchiser*) into figures of the imagination, larger than life in their hungers and their madcap energy. And a large part of Dick Gibson's problem is his desire to live a "mythic life."

While developing the thesis, Elkin undertook some field research to establish, not quite successfully, a biographical basis for the religious content he attributes to Faulkner's work. His introduction acknowledges that the Mississippi background is permeated by the revivalistic and evangelical strains of Methodism and Presbyterianism, and that only one Jewish family lived in Oxford, Mississippi, in 1960; in Faulkner's work, by Elkin's count, there are only four Jewish characters, so he sets a more ecumenical goal for his thesis, to show that Faulkner "falls back upon large segments of the Jewish-Christian myth to give ballast and meaning to his novels" and to deal "with the problem of being a good man, or, indeed, of being a man at all, in a world shaped by forces and wills which one can only guess at." He settled for this theological and ethical perspective only after his field research yielded evidence against Faulkner's being a member of any religious community. In 1960 he wrote Professor Harry Campbell of the University of Mississippi, who replied that he was unaware of any connection between Faulkner and the Presbyterian Church; in fact, he believed Faulkner attended Episcopal services intermittently. Elkin then contacted the rector of St. Peter's Episcopal Church, who responded that he believed Faulkner to have been born a Methodist but to have attended St. Peter's occasionally and concluded that any affiliation he might have had was Episcopalian. An apocryphal story has it that Elkin actually visited Faulkner while researching the thesis. Like most anecdotes from this era, there are many versions, all based on Elkin's first-person accounts. Here's the one he shared with Charles Gold, then a fellow teacher at Washington University. He and Joan, while driving home from Florida after visiting Tootsie, went out of their way to see Oxford, to soak up the atmosphere. Stanley impetuously asked for directions and drove out to the house. The person who answered the door

Washington University in St. Louis, main entrance. Photo by the author.

(in some versions of the story it was Mrs. Faulkner) said Bill was at the barn, but she would go get him; "Stanley said he panicked at his own boldness and said he [. . .] had to be on his way." Other versions have Stanley refusing, or accepting, an invitation to dinner with the Faulkners.[22]

Before he completed his thesis, however, there was the matter of earning a living. So Elkin went looking for a job in 1960, hoping to land a spot as an instructor and buying time to complete his thesis. He told an interviewer, "One Sunday I went to buy a newspaper. Now, I usually bought the *Chicago Tribune.* But that day, I picked up the *Post-Dispatch* and I saw a picture out here, outside Brookings Hall. It looked like a nice place, so I applied for a job here. If I hadn't bought that particular paper on that particular day, I wouldn't be here." Ballowe and many of his colleagues from graduate school were a trifle envious; they assured him that this was one of the Midwest's finest universities. Although Elkin understood this, he was uncertain whether he should take the offer because the money was less than what he might have earned elsewhere. Besides, some of their friends had offers of $100 to $200 more than Washington University's. That bothered him, but he took the job anyway. A year or two later Ballowe went to work at his alma mater (Millikin) for a few hundred dollars more than Elkin was earning at the time: "Stan was pissed." A few years later Jim moved to Bradley, where he got about $1,500 more and his old friend was "beside himself." To some degree, salary was a means of keeping score—of compelling the university to acknowledge his value. And he was notorious for asking direct questions about how much everyone earned. The autobiographical character Leon Mingus in *The Coffee Room* both bitterly resents, and poignantly whines about, his salary, which he discloses to everyone. And in 1989 Elkin shared this anecdote about his initial appointment: he agreed to a salary of $5,700 but when he got his first check, he discovered that it was based on $5,200. He asked his department chair to do something about the discrepancy. The chair said, "Resign" and Elkin backed down. It was the first of many conflicts over money between Elkin and his longtime employer.[23]

But that was to come. This was the summer of 1960, and the order of business for the Elkin household was to pack up their belongings and relocate 300 miles to the southwest, to University City, where a new job, new acquaintances, and their future lay before them.

🎕 5 🎕 "Become a Strong Man"
St. Louis, Europe, First Base, Full Houses, and the Big Time, 1960–65

"What shall I do to live?" "Oh, that," he said.
"Become a strong man."

—Dr. Herlitz, a character in *Boswell* (1964).

In the late summer of 1960, Stanley, Joan, and Philip moved to St. Louis. They rented an apartment on Leland Avenue in University City, a hefty walk from Washington University, where Elkin was about to launch his teaching career. St. Louis was a new community to learn about, a mid-sized, middle-American city, whereas Stanley identified himself as a New Yorker and a Chicagoan. He had a new job with new colleagues; very soon he'd encounter challenges in managing the time he needed to teach and write. An unfinished dissertation weighed against an expectation that an earned doctorate would be a condition of continued employment. Elkin arrived with a reputation as a professional writer, based on three stories in national magazines, an unfinished dissertation, a family to provide for, and inexhaustible self-confidence. By mid-decade he'd have a shelf of literary prizes, a substantial first novel, a widely praised collection of stories, and the first of a long series of appointments at writer's conferences, where he would reign as one of the most influential fiction writers in North America for thirty years. He would also be a visiting professor at a northeastern university and would be entertaining job offers from several others.

Jarvis Thurston, who had accepted "Cousin Poor Lesley and the Lousy People" for *Perspective,* feels responsible for bringing Elkin to the university, saying he had to do some fast talking to get him to sign on the dotted line. Leon Gottfried, a fellow Illinois alum, lobbied for him, based largely on fellow teaching assistant Jerome Beaty's telling him about this undergraduate who was the smartest student he'd yet encountered. Soon they found that having a true original on the teaching staff was a mixed blessing. As chair Thurston presided over frequent Executive Committee meetings trying to convince Stan not to do some of the things he liked to do in the classroom, one of which was reading from his own works-in-progress as the principal presentation. Looking back, Thurston feels that in his teaching, Elkin was as much an original genius as he was as a writer—brilliant, unpredictable, unconventional, and at times mercurial. Dave Demarest, who also joined the faculty in 1960, shared an office with the other new guy. Demarest had read a couple of Elkin's stories and was a little awed by the prospect of being the officemate of a published writer—a very good one at that. Because both young men were honing their craft as teachers while finishing their dissertations, their conversations often centered on teaching; their vocation was the source of what was evolving into a close friendship. Stan was dramatic, often hyperbolic, about both his writing and his teaching. Almost as much as he loved reading from his works-in-progress to students and colleagues, he enjoyed dramatizing his life in the classroom. Once, while he was giving a lecture in a theater-style classroom, a young woman in the top row kept asking questions that interrupted the flow of his talk. First he seriously attempted to answer her question and resumed his lecture. She asked the same question again, in slightly altered form, and this time he ignored it. Once more she inquired, again with slight modification, and Elkin snarled, "Miss ———, if you ask me that question once more I'm going to take off my glasses"—he dramatically removed his eyewear—"and fly up there and bite your neck."[1] Twenty-four years later, however, Bryanne Applegate thanked Elkin for his 1962 American literature class: although she took it as a "garbage course" to complete a curriculum requirement, "you actually made me think": "I don't believe I ever would have developed along the lines where I can now feel and see and understand images communicated on a paper if you hadn't opened my mind in the first place so pieces of the world would get in." Stan Tamarkin, also from that era, congratulated his former mentor on a major literary award, calling him "the best undergraduate teacher" he'd encountered and mixed high praise with low mirth:

> You were good, and you were demanding. The best course that I've ever taken [. . .] was a course called Hemingway and Faulkner. I shall never forget your probing, prompting style (although I should mention, and hopefully not be called a sexist, that not a few women were woefully intimidated by your questioning). One last memory and one last comment. I once followed you into the "john" after class to argue about a grade. You unzipped your pants in front of the urinal & said, "Tamarkin! Are you crazy? Get the hell out of here!" This anecdote must say something about my "chutzpah" and your patience. A lesser man would have thrown me out bodily. Another memory: I shall never forget how you half-sat in front of the class on the front of the desk and were deeply inhaling those extra-strong brown cigarettes. [. . .] I loved your story about (drunkenly?) calling Faulkner one night and talking to his wife.[2]

Both instructors had dissertations to complete, and Demarest's image of those days features the two of them sitting at desks facing opposite walls, pounding on bulky office typewriters during the summer of 1961. It was hot, it was humid, and there was no air conditioning. When they broke to talk or smoke, it often seemed as if their doctoral pursuits weren't delivering on the promise to escape the blue-collar world: "[W]e felt as if we were *really* working, like somebody in a factory." Although much of each hot afternoon featured quiet work, punctuated by the tapping of typewriter keys and occasional groans or curses when a typo required that a page be retyped, they found time to talk about their projects. "Stan idolized Faulkner as a writer," especially his skills as a storyteller and local colorist. Demarest wasn't at all surprised to learn that Elkin's work alludes to Faulkner more often than any writer except Shakespeare, or that he listed Faulkner and Bellow among his major influences. He remembers that at Washington University, Bellow was the writer young professionals were talking about in the early 1960s, and of course Stan loved to tell Bellow stories from the days at *Accent*. *The Adventures of Augie March* and *Henderson the Rain King* had opened up new possibilities in the picaresque tradition and humor, as well as Jewish American writing, but Demarest believes the personal acquaintance and the Chicago connection were paramount in Elkin's enthusiasm. "Stan was always proud and emphatic about his connections with New York and Chicago." He loved to talk about the Catskills and the Jewish resorts there, and often talked nostalgically about the family's camp in Oakland. Demarest too grew up in north Jersey and he suspects that Stanley's stories about Oakland may have been gilded somewhat, because from time to time he dropped hints that the camp wasn't all that grand. But usually he talked about it as a signifier of Jewish prosperity. He was "pretty promotional about his own myths" and deliberately presented himself as a "New Yorker who was on loan to Chicago for twenty years." He'd "wax enthusiastic about Chicago, but he usually qualified that by saying 'living in NYC is worth twenty points on your I.Q.'"[3]

But Elkin was in St. Louis to hone his craft as a writer, and neither the dissertation nor the classroom was as dear to him as his creative endeavors. Soon he got a carrel in the Olin Library and Demarest recalls his spending hours in it working over a single paragraph. He'd be satisfied if he could produce three or four good sentences in an afternoon, and he'd excitedly bring his new invention to the coffee room, where anyone who happened to be nearby would be corralled into listening to his recent efforts. He was extremely proud of newly minted metaphors or images or elegant turns in style. After a while, however, Elkin's afternoon performances wore thin, and Demarest and others sometimes found excuses to be out the office on late afternoons when Elkin headed back from his carrel. The prevailing impression in Duncker Hall at the time was that Elkin was more a poet than a fiction writer. "He would really labor over his writing, sentence by sentence, phrase by phrase, word by word, with a poet's attention to nuance and sound. Many of us felt that he was really more suited to be a poet than a storyteller."[4]

Elkin in his Washington University office, about 1963. By permission of Joan Elkin.

The young family expanded its social circle, beginning with, naturally, the university. Because they had so much in common, the Demarests and Elkins became quite close, until David moved on to Carnegie Mellon University. Joan and Marlene became good friends, and because both families had small children, they saw a lot of each other. They babysat for one another occasionally so the parents could enjoy an evening out. Demarest recalls that Philip seemed at times a little awed and intimidated by Stanley and suspects that he may have from time to time felt a need to emulate his own forceful father. Very soon, the Elkins formed one of their most lasting friendships with department colleague Naomi Lebowitz and her lawyer husband Al, a fellow writer, their tax adviser, and Stanley's closest friend. Soon he recommended Al to his literary agent, who helped him publish his first novel. Classics Department newcomer George Pepe became involved with the English Department because of their softball games, and he and Stanley remained close friends and eventually neighbors for the next four decades. Several times Pepe accompanied Stanley on visits to universities and other reading engagements. He was also frequently the instrument of Elkin's research. When he needed to check a fact for a story he was writing, often he'd call George and say, "Pepe, find out about this for me, will you?" Before he arrived in St. Louis, a mutual acquaintance had told George that she thought he'd find Elkin somewhat of a loner. She told him Elkin was a man of great talent, but he had the distinct feeling that there was something about Elkin she didn't like. Pepe was relieved to find that he didn't share these reservations. When Dan Shea joined the faculty a year later, Elkin was in Italy writing *Boswell*, so Dan knew him by reputation before meeting him. He was already legendary as a ferocious, unforgiving, uninhibited teacher. Dan heard stories about this from his colleagues, including the anecdote that he once asked students if they thought Moby Dick was a phallic symbol. When no one volunteered, Elkin drew a huge whale on the blackboard, stood amusedly aside, and asked, "Well, what the hell does *that* make you think of?" Shea recalls Stanley as a "big guy." He was a fairly large man, listed at six feet and 208 pounds on his army discharge papers, and a very loud one, who needed to be at the center of attention wherever he was. In a rumpled business suit, towering, with that powerful baritone voice, he literally took charge in the university coffee room or at a social event. Shea also recalls going to Cardinals games with the Elkin family and watching the 1968 All-Star game from St. Louis in Elkin's new home. During the decade, the Elkins also became friends with Eli and Lee Robins, both social scientists. Like Elkin, Eli developed multiple sclerosis, and "Why I Live Where I Live" provides a startlingly self-aware glimpse into the famous Elkin competitiveness, tinged with self-deprecating wit: "Eli's spread [. . .] is smaller, I think, than the palace at Versailles, but much grander than Madame Récamier's. And because, like me, he is a multiple sclerotic, much of the house is tricked out in the customized hardware of the handicapped, all the expensive gimcrackery of safety: stands of parallel bars like private roads, handles that bloom from the doorways like a steel ivy, cunning chair lifts like an indoor Aspen. Eli's electric cart, his motor pool." Eli, himself in the medical field and more advanced in symptoms, had every technology and device science could offer. Elkin was intrigued by and sometimes jealous of the technologies Eli acquired to deal with his symptoms and usually tried to get them for himself.[5] By the middle of the decade, however, his MS was as yet undiagnosed and the nucleus was formed for "Third Tuesdays," an informal salon-style meeting of intellectuals and friends that enriched and stimulated Elkin's intellectual and creative life and gave him an audience, so for a few hours once a month there was a forum for shouting down the silence.

Despite the pressures of the dissertation and teaching, St. Louis proved a much more welcoming environment than the Elkins had anticipated. Like Chicago, it offered professional sports; he took Philip to Blues hockey games during Philip's youth. His paternal affection is manifested by the fact that Stanley found hockey boring, but Philip loved it, and still does; his father, he recalls fondly, disliked the sport but loved taking his son to games. Toward the end of the decade, Philip played Little League baseball, and his father was a frequent, enthusiastic, and loud spectator. He rode his motorcycle to many games, creating quite a stir for himself—and an audience. He recalls his father as a good table tennis player, but sometimes he inexplicably couldn't consistently hit the ball back. When they came back to St. Louis after a Florida vacation in the late 1960s, Philip recalls that Stanley was neither serving with his usual ferocity nor rallying well. Now a paramedic, Philip thinks these may have been manifestations of as-yet undiagnosed MS symptoms.[6]

In addition to professional sports and excellent restaurants in the West End, exceptional bookstores at which he would later be a frequent reader and book signer, and a vital cultural life, St. Louis offered nearby Forest Park, with its magnificent vista across the street from the university, as well as summer concert venues, a fine zoo, and a major art museum, of special interest to Joan as a painter. The university was a lively center for performing arts, lectures, and recitals. Moreover, it had a medical school, which was a consolation because of Stanley's preoccupation with his health. "The Block" on Delmar Avenue, near Leland, provided outdoor cafes, theaters, and specialty shopping. All in all, St. Louis was working out. As he said in "Why I Live Where I Live": "Because, to me, it has always looked like what cities are supposed to look like" (260; *Pieces of Soap*).

On a university athletic field on Saturday mornings, men from the English Department congregated to play softball. Pepe recalls that Stanley could really belt the ball; he was a strong man with above average athletic ability. But he had a short attention span when it came to sports and played first base because he was left-handed, but primarily because there was often a base runner to talk to: "[W]hen he wasn't writing, he liked company, noise. We liked him playing because he was entertaining, but when the rest of us got caught up in the game, Stanley just couldn't understand that. He was serious about writing, and he was serious about his family, and I guess he was serious about literature. But there were a lot of things he wasn't serious about." Shea too thought Stan was a "pretty good first baseman who really loved to hit." When the ballplayers, by then in their forties and early fifties, had their aches and pains, Stanley gave it up, "but he didn't go willingly" despite mounting illnesses. Sports were about camaraderie, the sense of being with the fellows, hanging out. Whereas Wayne Fields, Pepe, Shea, and others competed, Elkin played. And he had an audience. This ritual sustained him until, and even beyond, a heart attack late in the decade.[7]

Poker was another competitive recreational outlet. A January 2004 blog posted this story, most likely a visit to Chicago after Elkin had achieved fame. It took place at a game in Bud Siegel's home. In one hand everyone folded except Stanley and Harry Richman, his lifelong friend. They raised one another again and again, until Stanley faced a poker crisis: "He was out of money; he didn't know what to do. [. . .] Stanley looked around again, desperate. Then he stuck his hand in his mouth. He yanked out his bridge and threw it on the table. 'I'll see you, and raise you $350, which is what I paid for this sonuvabitch.'"[8] When he got to St. Louis he was delighted to learn some of his friends played poker. They were pleased to have him in the game because he was funny and such good company. But not for long. The same lack of interest in the fine points of the game that exasperated his friends on the softball field proved disruptive at the prototypical American men's night out. According to Gottfried he was "always on"; he wasn't a bad player, but he was more interested in companionship than in poker. Pepe came to dread Stanley's card playing: "We hated to have Stanley play in those games, because for him it was just play, nothing else." He was loud, aggressive, and often competitive to a fault. In fact, once when he was losing but had a strong hand he bet even more than his bridge: "[H]e bet Joan, he bet his wife." Everyone knew it was a joke, but everyone was shocked and uncomfortable. During games he was disputative—about poker or any other subject, and about the money he won or lost: "Sure, he was fun to have there because he was Stanley, but at the same time he could be a pain in the ass." Al Lebowitz tells a similar story. Stanley wanted to be part of Al's game because "guys play poker" and it meant being part of the gang. He tried repeatedly to get into Al's group, but they wouldn't invite him: "I hear that the poker game is at Arthur's [Murati's] house. You're a neighbor. Can you get me in?" Al told him, "They're afraid of you. They're really afraid of what you might do to their game. They don't want to let you in because they're serious about poker." Stanley promised, "I'll be on my best behavior." Al talked to Murati, who replied, "I love Stanley, really, Al. But we have a good poker game here." Eventually they invited him, and soon Stanley was losing heavily. When dealer's choice came to him, he announced that the game was "Everything Wild Except Deuces"; immediately the game broke up as Murati slammed his fist on the table, shouting, "Goddamnit, I knew this was going to happen!" Later, Al confronted him, "They *knew* this was going to happen. But you promised me. And I vouched for you! Why did you do this?" to which Stanley replied, "I know, but I couldn't help it. It was too perfect." His brother-in-law recalls visiting St. Louis later in the decade and being invited to a poker game. Stanley was winning for a change, and he had a sterling hand. Suddenly he rose and looked at himself in the dining room mirror, and every player at the table folded immediately. Stanley guffawed, "Damnit, I only wanted to see if I had a poker face."[9]

While he was taking his chances and often losing at poker, he was betting full houses and hitting home runs on the professional front. The decade began with a flurry of publications, each more satisfying than the last, and by the mid-sixties, his dream was coming true. He was established as a novelist, he'd been included in *Best American Short Stories,* and the prizes were pouring in. In 1961 he began a correspondence with Robert Coover about "On a Field, Rampant." Jim Ballowe, his friend from graduate school, was the keystone in Stanley's campaign to get an introduction to Coover. Elkin's effort foreshadows the protagonist of his first novel, *Boswell.* He told Jim that he wanted to meet Coover, then an associate fiction editor for *Playboy:* "I'm thirty-one years old and it's time I'm famous."[10] By March, Coover congratulated Elkin on winning the Longview Foundation Award (for "In the Alley") and promised to take a new story "in the back door" to pressure other editors to look at it seriously. By mid-April he was encouraging Elkin: "I can understand your skepticism about *Playboy* acceptance. It isn't because it is empty of Jewishness and/or sex, but because it is not quite superficial enough for this magazine. Still, it might fool them. It's quite possible they'll 'dig the story line' as they say in the trade. Also it's long, of course. [. . .] Your handling of the difficult space/time problem in this contemporary legend was pure mastery." Days later he was convinced his editor "considers your story a masterpiece and will fight for it." They expected to pay $3,000. But Dan Gold, to whom Coover sent it with a strong recommendation, lost his enthusiasm and Coover prepared Elkin for bad news. Gold's note to Coover said that "this isn't right for PLAY-BOY" because all the four-letter words would need to go; "despite its grimness, it is a family story, with the bridge-game setting. We rarely buy family-oriented stuff." Finally, "[i]t is, in some ways, a trifle too 'literary' for us, particularly in the reader demands made by the s-o-c [stream of consciousness] passages." The other shoe hit the floor when a new editor took over and dismissed the story as "not lively enough for" the magazine; he was unmoved by Coover's argument that it would be good for *Playboy* to publish new writers of quality: "It is a most impressive piece, but not, at first blush, suitable for PLAYBOY. What it lacks in the vigorous, emphatic quality of most PLAYBOY fiction is made up by its sheer literary excellence." This disappointment may have been somewhat offset by an inquiry the day before soliciting material for the new *Longview Journal.* Needless to say, however, it wasn't paying even a fraction of $3,000. The story appeared in *Perspective* and was anthologized in *The Human Commitment: An Anthology of Contemporary Short Fiction,* edited by Dan Gold, the editor who had been unable to commit to publishing it in *Playboy,* in 1967. Again, neither came up with thousands of dollars.[11]

"On a Field, Rampant" is among the least typical among Elkin's stories, but it anticipates themes that emerge sporadically during his career, specifically a preoccupation with royalty, and it's the first manifestation of his novelistic technique, the picaresque. It follows the career of a nameless protagonist from his childhood, during which he's persuaded that he's royal, through many travels, to his simultaneous disillusionment and discovery that his selfish claims are reflected in the frustrations of the poor and the helpless. Although sketchily developed, the hero's preoccupation with celebrity and "greatness" anticipates the central concern of Elkin's first novel, *Boswell: A Modern Comedy,* and the character's grace, felicity in languages, and encyclopedic knowledge resemble, without the thematic ambiguity, John Williams, the co-antagonist of "A Poetics for Bullies." This interest in historical manifestations of hierarchy appears, in various forms, in Brewster Ashenden, the stylish inheritor of "The Making of Ashenden," and the hilarious relationship between the forty-third George Mills and King George IV of England, as well as the condescending, hierarchical attitude of the lord Guillalume toward "greatest Grandfather" in *George Mills.* Finally, Elkin would revisit this theme with comic abandon in "*Town Crier* Exclusive, Confessions of a Princess Manqué: 'How Royals Found Me "Unsuitable" to Marry Their Larry'" (1993). The progression is revealing. "On a Field" is generally dead serious, and possibilities for irony in the handling of the protagonist's illusions about his destiny are seldom worked through. Although the emulation of eighteenth-century styles, which Elkin would perfect in part 4 of *George Mills,* is clever, the story fails to exploit its latent ambiguities. And the final moment, in which the poor petition the hero to take up his greatness on their behalf, introduces a theme of the responsibility of power the reader isn't prepared for by the events of the story.

Endings were often a problem in Elkin's early stories, and the one that launched him as a major professional writer suffers from an overdramatic, even offensive, denouement. Shortly after the Elkins moved to Leland Avenue, a man claiming to be a friend of the family showed up at their doorstep. Ed Wolfe seemed lonely. He asked to spend a day or two with the Elkins and repeated, "I look out for Ed Wolfe." Sometime later, Elkin wondered what he might be worth if his assets were liquidated: "Without my thinking about it, the title which I had had for a month and a half before meshed with the idea of what I would be worth."[12] He began a story about an orphan who compensated for his lack of identity by being overly zealous as a bad-debt collector for a loan shark. His boss says while firing him, "A lot of people can't do it. You take a guy who's already down and bury him deeper. It's heart-wringing work. But you, you were amazing. An artist. You had a real thing for the deadbeat soul, I thought. [. . .] But Ed, you're a gangster" (43; *Criers and Kibitzers*). With his job, and therefore his identity, gone (a theme that resonates in Elkin's mature fiction, although he preferred the word *vocation* with its ecclesiastical and cultural connotations), Ed embarks on an absurd odyssey to discover his literal net worth, "the going rate for orphans in a wicked world" (55). The story is rich in tropes; Elkin ingeniously associates many objects Ed sells with the portion of the body each serves. Thus when he sells his clothes, he feels as if he's selling his skin; his phonograph and records, his ears, and so forth, until Wolfe has converted all his assets to cash. Despite the unfortunate ending, in which Wolfe forces himself into the company of some African Americans and eventually enacts a distasteful parody of a slave auction in a night club, "Ed Wolfe" was published in *Esquire*, Elkin's first successful foray into high-end national publications, and he received $700 for it, his first substantial payment. It was reprinted in *Best American Short Stories* (1963), then in *The World of Psychoanalysis* (1965) and *Writer's Choice* (1974). Until the 1990s, when racial sensitivity became a major editorial criterion for selection, "Ed Wolfe" frequently appeared in college literature anthologies as well. As he told Gass, "I sold a story to *Esquire* and I became an overnight sensation. Before it was even published I started getting letters from publishers, Atheneum, Atlantic–Little, Brown, Random House, Dial. Was I writing a novel? Would I show it to them if I was?" Very soon, his editor at *Esquire* asked to see portions of Elkin's novel-in-progress for publication, though he couldn't persuade his staff to accept them. On the advice of another *Esquire* editor, Fleet Publishing asked Elkin to send them a novel to consider, as did Houghton Mifflin a few days later. And the story led to another possible path in Elkin's career. In 1962 Jeffrey Hayden of Screen Gems inquired about developing "Ed Wolfe" for a television anthology show. The same day, his agents received a telegram from Screen Gems requesting a meeting to discuss Elkin's interest in writing for the popular series *Route 66* or *The Naked City*.[13] There's no indication that this meeting ever took place, but it was the first of many brushes Elkin would have with Hollywood and popular culture.

Largely on the basis of the Wolfe story, he launched yet another enterprise that would bear its greatest fruits in the 1980s, the familiar essay. Bob Brown, an editor at *Esquire,* humorously suggested some St. Louis topics for Elkin to pursue:

1) find some old lady who taught TS Eliot and interview her.
2) sneak into the Veiled Prophet Ball disguised as a socialite and report the scandalous doings.
3) someone says there's a revival of Greek architecture in some wood church in StL; Find out what this means, if it's true. Where it is, and if anybody cares.

Esquire commissioned the first of Elkin's essays, about actress Elizabeth Taylor, for which they paid $750. Brown's note suggests that was above the magazine's norm: "Since it is most important that Springer does not know about this [the sum]—or anybody else—I'd promised that I'd write to warn you that if word leaks out, we'll kill you." Soon after this essay came out he received a commission to write a 3,000-word piece on the Beatles, but *Esquire* turned that one down, paying a $200 kill fee because it seemed "[t]oo much a piece on you rather than the subject." Unfortunately, no copy remains. It was sent to *Dude* under the title "Idols of the Kinder," but the magazine apparently lost the typescript and claimed they'd returned it to agent Martha Winston. She couldn't locate a copy, so she asked Elkin for a carbon to submit to *Massachusetts Review,* whose editor seemed predisposed to accept it because of his fondness for Elkin's work. When Elkin couldn't find a copy either, she lamented that the "one and only manuscript of the Beatles piece has been lost. I just can't believe that you would not have made a carbon! Please, don't ever let any manuscript out of your hands without having a copy."[14]

Along with "Ed Wolfe" and "Criers and Kibitzers," "A Poetics for Bullies" is the most frequently anthologized of his stories and the one that defines the Elkin genius for many readers. He wrote it under contract with *The Saturday Evening Post,* but in December 1964 the magazine paid a kill fee, explaining that everyone liked it but agreed that it wasn't suitable for a *Post* audience. Within days *Esquire* grabbed it. Its genesis traces to a bow and arrow Joan made for Philip. A neighbor's kid said he could magically give him two arrows in exchange for one. The bully then broke the arrow and handed it back to a crying Philip. That was the inspiration for Push the Bully, Elkin's most original creation to date; he plays this trick on neighborhood kids in the story.[15] The allegorically named Push, the culmination of early stories like "The Last of the Go-To-Hell-God-Damn-its," is the first of Elkin's great antiheroes, a character possessing few endearing qualities but one we're forced to admire because of his rhetorical force and his peculiar brand of integrity in a compromised world. At first glance, Push is the perennial outsider, a boy who lives to rub his victims' noses in their weaknesses. As he says, "I love nobody loved" (197). But he's a unique bully, one who abjures violence, and Elkin's joke labels bullies who use force as mere "athletes." As he defiantly sees himself, "I have lived my life in the pursuit of the vulnerable: Push the chink seeker, wheeler dealer in the flawed cement of personality, a collapse maker" (198). At first blush, then, the conflict between Push and John Williams is the classic battle of good and evil. Williams is smart, sophisticated, handsome, athletic, and charismatic. He provides kindnesses and services to the poor and deprived. He attempts to help Push's victims overcome their shortcomings, whereas Push compels them to acknowledge them. But as the story works out, the do-gooder is a bully too. Subtly and with good will, he imposes his worldview on his subjects, who gradually lose their identities in his image of them. Thus, Push's refusal to be reconciled to Williams is a test of his integrity, even his identity. His gamble to recover his power by forcing Williams to beat him up backfires. All he has left is his defiance, his refusal to be reconciled, and this sole value alienates him even further from the playground community. But Push feels surprisingly vindicated by his "bully's sour solace. It's enough, I'll make do" (217). In this story, as in *A Bad Man,* Elkin compels his readers to consider the integrity of the bully's self-conception in the face of the challenges presented by model citizens like Williams who embody fairly ubiquitous bourgeois virtues.

The success with stories was intoxicating for Elkin, and he was receiving inquires about adapting them for the stage or television. Because of *Esquire*'s interest in his fiction and journalism, because literary prizes were coming in regularly, and because *Best American Short Stories* had included two of his stories ("Criers and Kibitzers," 1962, and "Ed Wolfe," 1963), Elkin was living his dream—except for one thing. He'd long fancied himself a novelist, not a short story writer. And after two years in St. Louis, he found himself with an inspiration for a novel, a growing national audience eager for his work, and an able literary agent, Martha Winston of Curtis Brown. But juggling the demands of teaching, parenthood, offers to write journalism as well as fiction, opportunities to read on college campuses, and efforts to publish his doctoral thesis, he simply couldn't find time to write his novel. This led to one of the strangest benefactions in literary history, the "Zelda Elkin grant." The novel originated when colleague Phil London told him about James Boswell's campaign to meet Voltaire. Although he'd taken undergraduate classes in "Dr. Johnson and His Circle" (English 349) and Alexander Pope (English 347), receiving an A in the first and a B in the second,[16] and although he deliberately modeled "On a Field, Rampant" on aristocratic assumptions of Restoration and eighteenth-century literature, he was unaware of the degree to which Boswell actually campaigned to meet the great and the near-great of his century, but on its surface the story "struck me as being so funny that I thought a modern Boswell, on the make for all the great men of his time, might be the source of an amusing novel." So he read Frederick Pottle's edition of *Boswell's London Journals,* which had come out during the 1950s, and learned that Boswell was a deliberate, practiced sycophant. Now he had his idea, and his research was complete. What he needed was the time to write.

When he complained that his teaching obligations stifled the inspiration to write, and in general that he "just hated my life," Joan encouraged him to visit Zelda. When he griped to his mother about the difficulties he faced, she challenged him to take up his destiny. Tootsie was economically comfortable because of Phil's great success, and she startled Stanley by making an offer he couldn't refuse: "Supposing I pay your salary [about $6,000] for the next year. Why don't you take off? I'll pay your transportation and you can go wherever you want to in the world." When the university approved a year's leave of absence, Joan, Stanley, and Philip headed for Rome. The empty space their absence left in University City is suggested by two letters from the Lebowitzes: "We have talked it over and we agree that the absence of the Elkin family has left a huge, unfillable hole in our hearts. The Demarests are even more desolate, if that's possible. Just try to imagine while yodeling in the Coliseum, genuflecting to the big, dull Pope, intercoursing on marble floors, the enormity of the crime you've committed against those who were committed to you." A month later Al described Demarest, Shea, and himself watching a baseball game in a bar, where Naomi "saw agonized pools of Elkin-longing." When they arrived in Rome, Elkin received a telegram containing the best possible news: "The first day we had settled in the place we had rented some guy came along tinkling a bicycle bell—the Italian equivalent of Western Union—'Elkeen, Elkeen, Elkeen!' The telegram was from the agent saying that Random House had taken the novel on the basis of the first two chapters. From then on I had an obligation—I was going to get paid—to actually finish the novel and no fooling around. I would rather have been eating pasta in Roman restaurants than working on this thing. But I worked very, very hard and had a novel." On September 28, 1962, he signed a contract for 100,000 words, with standard royalty agreements, and an advance of $2,000. Now he was really on his way to becoming a serious professional writer: "In effect, my mother changed my life by sending me."[17]

The family spent seven months in Italy and four in London. Philip recalls visiting Mount Vesuvius and fearing that dead people were still buried there after his dad told him about the great eruption. He also recalls seeing the Leaning Tower of Pisa,[18] so not all the time in Rome was work, work, work. And Stanley worried about his family's adjustment because "Joan still coughs" and "Philip's nose leaks clear plastic." "I figure I will be untroubled when we find an apartment and Philip can enter into a stable way of life. In the mean time, it is all too much for him. The other day, in Luxembourg, he looked out the window and said, 'Mommy, what city is this?' He hasn't slept in the same bed four nights running since July 12th."[19]

To pick up extra money Stanley got a job dubbing English in one of the decade's Italian cinematic extravaganzas. In 1963 he told Martha Winston that "in Rome I dubbed three minutes in a movie about Cleopatra, *the* Cleopatra, but not THE Cleopatra." During the months in Rome he'd developed a friendship with novelist/jazz musician Walter Clemons, a "kind of professional ex-patriot" who would be "a fine fellow if he liked me more." Clemons was romantically involved with Italian movie actress Carolyn de Fonseca. Stanley mentioned to de Fonseca that he'd like to earn some money dubbing English for U.S. releases of Italian pictures and she "allowed me to use her name and gave me private numbers of directors who hire dubbers." In his screen test Elkin stood before a screen showing clips from a movie about pirates and said, "Thank her majesty, and inform her that I mean to serve and shall steal only in her name." The director liked Elkin's voice and told him he'd call soon. "So now I may be a movie star. I hope so. I have always wanted to be a movie star."[20]

Perhaps because of the dubbing experience or the de Fonseca connection, Elkin was also hired for a small part in *A Bride for Caesar,* another Italian flick emulating the American fiasco starring Richard Burton and Elizabeth Taylor and directed by Joseph Mankiewicz, that was filmed to great scandal because of the stars' off-camera antics. *A Bride for Caesar* was scheduled to be released before *Cleopatra* in order to piggyback on the publicity it was generating. He played Sixtus, the son of star Akim Tamiroff, and had about eight lines. Overall the experience wasn't good. As he told the Lebowitzes, "I was lousy. The guy never called me back." He blamed his lines, banalities like "It is quarter past the hour of the second watch" and "I said it grimly, as grimly as he had put the question." The director wanted a more casual delivery, but Elkin didn't agree and inadvertently repeated the grim tone: "So when I saw the guy was getting sore I deliberately tried to sound bland. My blandness had reached something approaching Henry Aldrich in orgasm when the director finally bought it. But I heard the recording and it was stupid. The rest of my lines were all that sort of thing. [. . .] I sounded on the recording as if I were twelve years old."[21] Thus ingloriously ended Stanley's first experience with the film industry.

In addition to traveling throughout much of Italy, dubbing and acting in movies, and drinking deeply of Italian culture, from the magnificent museums to the splendid trattorias, Elkin, with a little prodding from editor Joe Fox and agent Winston, completed most of his novel in Rome. Because the apartment was small and hot, he developed a work habit that would serve him well throughout his life. Writing into mid-afternoon, he did most of the composing in an outdoor café. A typical day would feature Elkin, armed with two or three pens, a copybook, and a package of cigarettes, riding the bus to a favorite café, ordering coffee and pastry, and working uninterruptedly, except to refill or light up, for five or six hours—except for his natural gregariousness, which probably resulted in occasional interruptions and conversations. It's tempting to speculate that he emulated the habits of a favorite writer from his undergraduate days, Ernest Hemingway, whose style he imitated in a few unpublished stories, but as he gravitated toward Faulkner and James as models, he occasionally parodied Hemingway's work, as in the memorable episode from *The Franchiser* when Ben Flesh is hospitalized with Lieutenant Tanner of the Royal Air Force in South Dakota. In the mid-1970s he wrote an original film script, *The Art of War,* in which Papa figures prominently as a character. He certainly emulated Hemingway's work ethic. His flippant account of the stay in Rome also mimics Jake Barnes's self-effacing comments on his work in *The Sun Also Rises:*

> Once a week, I'd get an Italian copybook and go to Rosati's, a little café on the Piazza del Popolo. I had it all worked out. From 10 to 12, I'd drink tea, from 12 to 3, anisette, and from 3 to 5, Italian beer. All the time I'd be filling out this little copybook like mad. Some of the funniest scenes in "Boswell" were written in toto in those mornings and afternoons.
>
> Afterward I'd catch a bus home, and by the time I'd get to the house I'd be soaring. I could never make out what I'd written, and so the next day would be shot trying to figure out what was in the copybook.[22]

Early in the work, moreover, he encountered an artistic crossroads, which he solved by reverting to an eighteenth-century fictional technique—a logical association, given that his inspiration was Johnson's biographer. The first three chapters describe, in picaresque form, the prediction to orphan Boswell by his first celebrity, Dr. Leo Herlitz, that he cannot himself be great but will be a hanger-on to greatness: "Boswell, *voyeur*, Eye, Ear, you will pull your chair beside the roaring fire. Boswell, Boswell, Go-between, Welcome Guest, Reliable Source, Persona Grata. I weep for you" (18). Boswell as a result mounts a campaign to meet influential people, including Marty Penner, a buddy from the gym who has rubbed shoulders with ambassadors and royalty, and professional wrestler "The Great Sandusky." The chapter on meeting Sandusky sold to *Paris Review* and won that magazine's 1963 prize for humor. But early in the novel Elkin invites the metafictionist label he was later to repudiate by reminding readers that the "autobiography" we're reading is actually a calculated narrative by his protago-nist. No Huck Finn spontaneity here. For example, Boswell says out of the blue in chapter 2, "I've been going over some of my notes" (36), thus dispelling the illusion of a spontaneous narrator and calling attention to the strategic construc-tion of the narrative. In chapter 3 Boswell dips into his journals (like the historic biographer), and readers get portions of the story directly from the journals. The most memorable episode, Boswell's mythicized confrontation with aged wrestler John Sallow who styles himself "The Grim Reaper," begins as "an excerpt from my journal." Elkin's strongman-hero-schmuck builds Sallow via his imagination into the literal manifestation of his *nom de grappeleur*, and absurdly inflates a match, one-tenth sport and nine-tenths showbiz—he's supposed to lose, the outcome already decided—into an epic event: "In St. Louis I would whip Death's old ass" (99). As soon as the reaper hands him his young backside in the ring, a defeat Boswell inflates to ritualized death, the novel shifts once more into direct representation of his journals, the ostensible sourcebook for the narrative. Part 2, from his recovery after the beating Sallow gave him, through his campaign to meet financier William Lome and many others, including a Caribbean revolution-ary, are narrated from Boswell's American journals. This decision was calculated, as demonstrated by his planning sheets:

> BOSWELL Second part
> Introduce perhaps half a dozen new great men: (1) the great salesman and money man who gets Boswell his steady income; a famous (5) dictator; one of the survivors of one of the world's great families. A Medici; a (2) famous scientist; (3) a religious leader. Covers time through 1960.
> Close 2nd part with two scenes; 1st, Boswell's great statement about what he wants; 2nd scene in hospital room where in 1949 he rejects his own kid. *All from the journal.*[23]

In addition to the homage to Boswell and the English novel's origin in the epistolary mode of Samuel Richardson and Henry Fielding, the heavy reliance on journal entries also traces to a more proximate source. Bellow, whom Elkin knew and admired, had composed his first novel, *Dangling Man,* as a series of letters and journals concerning the time the Canadian hero, living in Chicago, spends awaiting his call to join the U.S. Army while he is bereft of friends, job, and family.

He finished *Boswell* in ten months, by which time the British rights had been sold to Hamish Hamilton. Portions had been sold to *Paris Review* and *Esquire,* though editor Rust Hills irritated Elkin and his agent by delaying publication until just weeks before the novel came out. Shortly after the Elkins arrived in London, the draft was complete. The final scene was suggested when they saw the Queen Mother, Princess Margaret, and Lord Snowden coming from a royal performance, "and that gave me a great idea for the last scene, the last paragraph has been written since last September." In that letter, however, Elkin was having second thoughts: "I have *very* serious doubts about *Boswell.* Doubts I can take. Sometimes, however, they are convictions and that scares the shit out of me. I have visions of Joe Fox tearing up the contract in my face."[24] And the *Boswell* saga was just beginning.

Fox wasn't tearing up any contract, but he was having aesthetic, legal, and practical problems with his emerging star. Like many editors after him, Fox tried to reign in Elkin's predilection toward excess. Although his responses were polite and at times gracious (not always true for Fox or his successors with later books), Elkin was usually adamant, insisting that his original text should stand. One amusing exchange will represent many: Fox objected to a scene in the Penner episode for reasons of taste, not merely aesthetics, but once again Elkin held fast: "There is, incidentally, only one place where I am dead set against one of your suggestions. On p. 44, Boswell, alone in Penner's room, declares, 'I stooped down and picked out his underwear and looked inside.' You suggested that the sentence be omitted and I presume your reasons are, well, reasons of taste. However, this is one of Boswell's most revealing gestures, an archetypal act for him. What he wants from other men, after all, is only to know that they are as bad off as he, as mortal as he, as linked to earth and death as he." Realizing that he wasn't going to change Elkin's mind, Fox replied, "One thing I will not change my mind about is the conviction that you have written a brilliant book. [. . .] I still disagree about the underwear business—this is not for reasons of taste, but merely because I started getting a little restless here,"[25] presumably with the homosexual implications of an act by a character who was at the time a weightlifter and gym rat.

Another concern was the title. Elkin planned to call the book simply *Boswell,* but Fox's market research suggested that this title would lead readers to expect a scholarly biography, whereas the target audience, novel readers, would probably ignore the book because its title didn't suggest a novel. In red ink Elkin scratched several suggestions, the first of which caught Fox's attention: "Boswell: A Modern Comedy; Boswell: A Modern Sequel; Boswell, Son of Boswell; Boswell, A Fiction;

Boswell: A Modern Boswell; Boswell: A Novel about the Self; Boswell: A Sequel; Boswell: An Extension." So Fox won this point, a better average than most of Elkin's editors compiled. Another he pressed because of advice from Random House's lawyers. The typescript called for Boswell to encounter actual celebrities of his time as well as fictional ones. Boswell attends speeches by both Adlai Stevenson and Dwight Eisenhower during the 1952 presidential election, carrying campaign banners for the opposing candidate to each rally. He seeks to meet atomic scientist Robert Oppenheimer, actor Orson Welles, and composer Igor Stravinsky as well as movie stars Kathryn Grayson and Esther Williams, whom Elkin claimed he encountered from a distance in Rome. The lawyer corroborated Fox's suspicion that the novelist could probably get away with references to politicians and public figures, but that movie stars would present a problem because they wouldn't be likely to give permission for their names to be used as objects of Boswell's celebrity hunts. Elkin was adamant, but relented after Fox took it back to counsel, telling him "to use imaginary stars, or dead ones. A great pity, but there it is." So Elkin tried a transparent dodge, introducing Kathryn Williams and Esther Grayson, but the lawyer squashed that as well.[26] Elkin conceded this point, but Boswell has brief conversations with Welles and actress Doris Day and mentions seeing Oppenheimer and Cary Grant. A similar legal problem would come up in his fourth novel, *The Franchiser*, when Ben Flesh meets Colonel Sanders.

Fox's greatest problem was getting the right jacket blurbs for the novel, and some of the results were devastating to Elkin. Naturally Random House sent inquiries to the major Jewish American novelists—Bellow, Bernard Malamud, Norman Mailer, Joseph Heller—as well as Lillian Hellman, Ralph Ellison, and Thomas Pynchon. In what must have been a stinging blow, Bellow didn't respond. Hellman, Ellison, and Malamud (who gave a reading at Washington University while Elkin was in Rome and must have heard about the novel-in-progress) politely refused to read it, pleading "busyness." Mailer too didn't respond, but Fox attributed that to "the fact that he and I bicker every time we meet." More damningly, Heller "tried hard but couldn't like it enough to give it a quote." Dwight Macdonald, approached after those novelists were unresponsive, dealt a crushing blow to Elkin's bruised ego:

> I'm afraid I don't like this quite enough to do a blurb. The first few pages seem to me pretentious, and while it gets better and funnier and sharper later [...] there are still too many false notes (as 109-a: "I have seen her breasts. Enough, you will go mad." You really can't write that way, even in fun) and also too much symbolism, or anyway some higher meaning than the literal one, or so one guesses, . . . He may do something very good later, though—I suppose his faults [...] are all the faults of a young writer, faults of excess and of a lack of self-criticism; but he does have a certain verve and richness of invention—and he's funny often (though not as often as he thinks he is).

Macdonald's sentiments were echoed by Jules Pfeiffer, who found the novel too long, with too much soliloquizing, and declined to offer a jacket note. Bruce Jay Friedman agreed: "I admire Mr. Elkin's intelligence, which is hair-raising; his writing skill is considerable, and yet he works on a frequency I don't seem to be able to pick up and I could not for the life of me work up any concern for his man, Boswell." Terry Southern, author of the recent *Candy* and *The Magic Christian*, offered a lukewarm comment, too late for the book jacket, although he disliked the final section: "How about : 'There are moments in *Boswell*—like the gym-scenes and the fantastic wrestling match between the Playboy and the Reaper—which indelibly mark Elkin as a great creative talent.'" When the book appeared, the only blurb was from relative unknown Alan Harrington, who gushed, "I congratulate you on having such a novelist on your list, and I congratulate Elkin on his courage. [. . .] *Boswell* is a hilarious and brilliant book." Just in time for the publicity campaign, the Southern comments were excerpted, and Alexander King chimed in, saying that it was the "finest novel of the decade."[27] Great praise indeed, but not from Bellow or Heller.

In addition to the challenge of soothing Elkin's rising frustration as writer after writer declined to praise or openly disliked his novel, Fox had to deal with Roger Machell of Hamish Hamilton, the British publisher. He and his staff were distressed by the thrice-repeated "mother-fucker" which "throws people here very considerably. None of them has ever come across it before" in serious fiction, and Machell requested permission to delete it in British editions. In fact, Machell typed the letter himself to spare his secretary the discomfort of typing the offending word. Of course Elkin demurred, and Fox did some fast talking to persuade him to agree to "mother lover" in the British version. But by the time Elkin agreed to the substitution, it was too late to make the change without incurring serious typesetting costs, so Elkin's original text appeared in the United Kingdom as well as in the United States.[28]

And on the personal front, yet one more frustration remained. Stanley and Joan decided to visit Barry Spacks before leaving London. They arrived in Cambridge on Elkin's thirty-third birthday (Faulknerian symbolism here!). The only thing on which the surviving adults agree is Joan's assessment: "the worst weekend of my life." Elkin insisted, against her objections, on taking the typescript with him. What happened from that moment forward depends on whom we hear it from. First, the Spacks version. Barry's cousin was "obviously proud" of his new novel, and wanted nothing so much as to read passages to him and Patricia, both of whom felt that it was "overwrought" and "we couldn't give Stanley the praise he so clearly needed." To defuse the crisis, Barry took him out to tour Pembroke College in the rain. Not surprisingly, Joan and Stanley recalled it differently. According to Joan, Barry asked what he was working on. When Stanley showed him the typescript, Barry retired to a couch and read it, making loud derisive noises, while everyone else was trying to have a conversation. Throughout that weekend, Barry conspicuously read his young daughter pieces from a story he was improvising with her, and it made Joan uncomfortable that Stanley didn't do these things with Philip. Stanley's own version suggests the amount of pain this episode caused him—the cousin with whom he'd competed from adolescence condescending to his firstborn artistically. Note the management of case, carefully transcribed to capture the ego proportions this confrontation took on for him—nearly approximating Boswell's mythicizing John Sallow:

> It was the most depressing weekend of my life. [. . .] I was afraid it would be lost in a fire. Joan told me—that Joan—she *told* me, stanley (she calls me with a lower case "s"), don't take the novel, it will only be read and bad things will happen." . . . Did you bring the novel, stanley (Barry too), Barry asked. Lie, stanley, Joan said. lie and don't tell him you brought The Novel. Yes, i did, BARRY, I said. what's it called *BARRY* said. Boswell, i said. OH, *BARRY* said, boswell, is it? So he made me bring it out and while Philip and his Daughter, JUDITH, were playing under his nose and singing camp songs, and his WIFE, PATSY, WHO JUST HAD ANOTHER BOOK PUBLISHED BY HARVARD UNIVERSITY PRESS, WHO HAD HAD ONE PUBLISHED BEFORE BY THE UNIVERSITY OF CALIFORNIA ON THOMPSON AND WHO WAS NOW PUBLISHING ONE ON THE SUPERNATURAL IN EIGHTEENTH CENTURY POETRY AND NEXT YEAR WILL BRING ONE OUT ON SOMEBODY ELSE I FORGET who AND IS WRITING A FOURTH IN CAMBRIDGE WHILE HER HUSBAND */BARRY/* *** WRITES HIS NOVEL, CALLED, ***—*** THE CHAMELION !—***—**** was showing us that not only can she write she is also the best cook in the world was drawing and quartering an ex for the evening meal and was having an argument with joan, right as i say under BARRY'S NOSE, *HE* READ IT. Hmph, He said when HE was through and asked me questions i couldn't answer. And so it went, a pitched battle to the death of EGO vs. ego, and I slunk on home, i slunk on home, and joanie carried me upstairs and it was my birthday and I got the mail.[29]

There must have been some small consolation for his wounded self-esteem when the mail announced that Martha Foley had selected "Ed Wolfe" for the *Best American Short Stories* anthology, and *Esquire* had offered $750 for the second chapter of *Boswell.*

And the disappointments didn't abate when the reviews came in. As the Spacks stories make clear, Elkin was at this time in great need of support because of his growing doubts about his new work. His friends, the Lebowitzes and Bill Gass, assured him that he had created something of great originality and importance, but Heller, Macdonald, the Spacks family, and even Bellow weren't supporting that assessment. So when the reviews came out in 1964, Elkin was hungry for praise and was therefore predisposed to exaggerate the negative press and minimize the positive. A decade later he recalled *Boswell* as his only novel that ever received negative reviews, bitterly remembering that Martin Levin, who blasted it in the *Sunday Times*, "made up a list of the worst books of that year and included *Boswell*. That hurt me." A decade after that he told a former student, "I believed every bad thing he said about me was true. I accepted it and went off like a stricken cur. Not even a *dog*, nothing so noble as a *dog*. Just this wounded, sniveling cur. I wanted to get naked in bed and suck my thumb. After a reasonable period of mourning, say three years, I felt much better."[30] In spite of his bitterness that lasted for decades because the book was poorly reviewed, most were in fact positive. Quite a few reviewers found it funny, satiric, and erudite, though several found it too long, with unresolved digressions—criticisms that aren't unfounded. Many felt that it promised a writer of true originality, one who would soon occupy an important place in American literature. A Dallas reviewer called it "one of the most gracefully inventive books since 'Catch-22,' and it is probably even better" while another Texan said *Boswell* was "as impressive and powerful a piece of writing as the decade has yet produced," propelling Elkin into "the first rank of American Letters." An anonymous reviewer in the *London Times Literary Supplement* called Elkin's invention "prodigious" and compared his combinations of the sensuous and the morbid with the legacy of John Donne. Finally, Joseph Haas in the *Chicago Daily News* labeled it a "major work, in conception and execution." The book received generally favorable responses, though it was less enthusiastically reviewed than any of his subsequent books. But the stings associated with *Boswell* had left him vulnerable, and the negative notices, which occurred in major outlets, left him on the verge of depression.

One review should have brought him great satisfaction, and it links with an important step in Elkin's career. John Ciardi in *Saturday Review* echoed the comparison with Heller's great war novel: "In point of style and of intellectual grace, the author of *Boswell* is to the author of *Catch-22* as a jeweler to a primitive potter."[31] This was a premier national magazine, and its books editor, Ciardi, was a prominent poet bringing out a brilliant translation of Dante's *Commedia*. He was also the leader of the Bread Loaf Writer's Conference, an annual congregation of writers in Middlebury, Vermont. Agent Winston nominated Elkin as a fellow in March 1964, sending along published excerpts from *Boswell*. She was hopeful that Elkin would receive tuition and living expenses. But Ciardi, upon seeing Elkin's dossier, wasn't having any part of Elkin as a fellow—he wanted him as a mentor. So the Elkins traveled northeast in August, and soon Winston joyfully reported, "[Y]ou made a hit at Bread Loaf." Conference historian David Bain labels 1964 a banner year because of new faces on the conference faculty: "Also hired—to teach fiction alongside Shirley Jackson, making quite a pair—was the wisecracking, thirty-four-year-old Stanley Elkin." At that conference he taught an emerging writer and later a close friend. Jerome Charyn recalls a "Talmudic sense of recognition between us" and the games of Ping-Pong he lost to "that big bear." There was also wrestling on the lawn: "I couldn't beat the bear. He whirled me around and around like a battered top. [. . .] He was the funniest man alive. He told stories with wonderful twisted jokes. He was always the essential victim of these jokes, the endless fall guy. Self-mockery was a kind of motor for Stanley: he lurched into long tales that always took advantage of himself." [32]

Elkin's public lecture, "The Endings of Novels," is a practical, witty account of three major paradigm shifts in the production of stories, one that hints at the worldview he was developing. Although it isn't terribly sophisticated in theory, its application of these paradigms is fresh and witty. First, he considers the classical, or tragic, vision, in which the narrative features God's striking down those who aspire too high: "*Talk about your jealous God!* It's interesting that humility is a nice word for mediocrity but even more interesting that it is the ultimate virtue in all religions—the saving gracelessness. [. . .] What is there left to assume but that God needs sheep and hates a hero? ("The Lord is my Shepherd? I shall not *want*"). The logic is easy. A hero, a does-it-himselfer, is a threat to God precisely because he does not need God. [. . .] Literature, then, in the bad old days, seems to have been about a single theme—the embarrassment of greatness. High art brought great men low." Later, with the advent of the novel, the paradigm shifted to a more secular mode of representation, with emphasis on society rather than the divine, and consequently the conflict centered on achieving material or ethical goals: marriage, success, rightness. "Men still get their lumps, but the lumps origi-nate within a rational matrix, and are probably deserved." And this rationality, Elkin contends, accounts for the comic orientation of the great age of the novel, from Fielding through Trollope. He cites a variety of nineteenth-century endings to support his claim that novels "conclude with major religious sacraments, which may actually symbolize beginnings rather than endings: engagements; weddings; births; deaths; vows; pledges. Or with major secular sacraments: kisses; fornica-tion; dawn. [. . .] The good are in their beds, or soon will be. The bad are in their graves, or soon will be." This orientation, he claims, mirrors the secular moral optimism of the enlightenment and the Victorian era. But something excit-ing and challenging confronts the novelist of the mid-twentieth century, during which the novel "has, I think, at least partially liberated itself from its creaky, rigid, moral lock-step. The absurd hero—I mean *any* hero, he doesn't have to be absurd; he has only to be sophisticated—doesn't have anything to fear but oblivion, has nothing hanging over his head but nothing. Consciousness rather than conscience has been dignified into a new value, and this in itself moves the novel to the border of a new metaphysics, a new metaphysics *every time* if you will, because it opens the novel up to the individual vision, to the eccentric vision." [33] This belief resonated with the young fiction writers in his audience, and it would inform the creation of Elkin's next three major protagonists, Leo Feldman, Alexander Main, and Dick Gibson. And, if the lecture drew applause among the conferees, it was Elkin's booming baritone voice holding forth in the sessions, on the porch of his cabin, that established him eventually as one of the great figures in the history of Bread Loaf.

Before the Elkins left for Vermont they had received encouraging news about the possibility of filming *Boswell*. "Artists Agency," a Curtis Brown affiliate, was convinced this was "the most important first novel" in years. In March they sent a prepublication copy to Stanley Kubrick, arguably the era's greatest director, on the assumption that only he could bring this fiction to the screen as he had Vladimir Nabokov's *Lolita*. There's no indication that Kubrick took an interest in the novel, but in June Lawrence Turman, who would shortly produce one of the decade's major films, *The Graduate*, offered high praise: "I cannot remember when I have read a book with as much enjoyment as I did *Boswell*," but it is "frustrating me because I have no idea whatsoever how I could make it into a film. And yet I want to, because I love it so much and I respond to your writing so strongly. [. . .] Meanwhile, if you can give me a clue how to make BOSWELL into a film, please call me collect" at either his private number or at the studio. It's unlikely that Elkin didn't reply, but the film was never made.[34]

After the Elkins left Bread Loaf, they journeyed to Northampton, Massachusetts, where he'd accepted a visiting lecturership at Smith College, at a salary of $8,800 plus moving expenses. Very soon he was involved in several negotiations that would affect his appointment as a university professor. By October, Washington University English chair Robert Schmitz asked for a clarification of his future plans: "As I go over [the correspondence] I find that you are looking forward to leaving the university every year or two, but I have no real sense of just where it is you look for refreshment, here in teaching or abroad in doing whatever you do away from here." Elkin clarified that he was asking the university for an understanding "that they would give me every third year off [without salary] in order that I might write a novel." Although Elkin preferred to stay in St. Louis, he advised Schmitz that the administration at Smith was sending out feelers about his interest in staying on. By the end of November, his former mentor Jerome Beaty, now at Emory, inquired about Elkin's interest in a creative writing appointment in Atlanta, teaching two courses per semester at about $9,000 a year. Elkin told Schmitz about the Emory offer, with the hope that "I would like very much to turn it down."[35] Schmitz offered a pay raise, but was unable support him for promotion before the annual Modern Language Association (MLA) conference, and by that time Elkin had two new stories, "A Poetics for Bullies" and "Perlmutter at the East Pole," based on a minor character from *Boswell*, in the publishing pipeline. Emory interviewed him in New York, and subsequently made an offer. As 1964 came to a close, Elkin, teaching in Massachusetts, with university affiliation in St. Louis, was on the verge of moving to Atlanta. One thing holding him back was the fact that the Rockefeller Foundation grant for which he'd applied depended on his being at Washington University the next year.

While he was at Smith, Elkin met a colleague who remained among his closest friends for the rest of his life. Helen Vendler recalls their first, inauspicious, meeting. While walking down the hall toward the department office during her first semester at Smith, she heard an increasingly loud male voice haranguing the departmental secretary. The voice was thundering by the time she entered the office. She saw a large man with horn-rimmed glasses looming threateningly over the secretary: "What do you mean you have no typewriter lying around? I never heard of an English Department that didn't have an extra typewriter somewhere." When the secretary, standing up valiantly to Elkin's irritation, continued to tell him she had no spare typewriters, Elkin wailed, "But what am I going to do? I need a typewriter. I'm supposed to be here as a writer. How the hell can I write without a typewriter? Why didn't you people tell me you couldn't afford a typewriter? I'd have brought my own from St. Louis." Vendler, who taught morning classes, interrupted, "Pardon me, but there's a typewriter in my office and I'm never there in the mornings. If you can be out of the office by noon, you're welcome to use my typewriter as much as you wish." Elkin was genuinely thankful. During the year at Smith he wrote in college exam books, then typed out second drafts, of *A Bad Man* and notes toward two novellas that would appear in *Searches and Seizures*—but only in the morning. He'd written during the mornings and into early afternoons in Rome, and it's likely that at Smith he confirmed his work habit. On that fall morning in 1964, a lifelong friendship began.

Although his was a visiting appointment, Elkin quickly developed a reputation as a smart, quixotic, intimidating instructor, very like the one he had at Washington. One local legend involved a blackboard eraser as a projectile. While teaching D. H. Lawrence's *The Plumed Serpent,* he was inspired to have his students chant the incantation to Quetzalcoatl toward the end of the book. He paced the room, chanting and encouraging the women to get into the spirit of his light mockery of Lawrence's theme: "We are not wasted. We are not left out. / *Quetzalcoatl has come!* / There is nothing more to ask for. / *Quetzalcoatl has come!*"[36] But the Smith women, unused to such teaching methods, demurred; they looked frantically into their notebooks or at one another, silent before this unconventional involvement. Without breaking rhythm in his chant, Elkin grabbed an eraser and fired it into the middle of the classroom. No one was hit, but no one joined the Quetzalcoatl chant either.

Because she felt more comfortable with poetry than the novel form, and because she was astonished at the brilliance and unconventionality of her new friend, Vendler audited one of his classes in the spring of 1965. After she got to know him, and to "listen while these jewels dropped from his lips, I thought, 'If anybody can teach me to "get" novels, it's Stanley, who "got" them intimately.'" This was one of the early incarnations of the Elkin "theory of the novel" class, which required that students read and discuss popular novel forms in comparison with serious literature. Students would read a nurse novel, a detective novel, and the like, then move on to Dickens or Faulkner (later, Elkin). The goal was that they would learn to recognize the tricks of formulaic fiction designed for mass-market consumption, and would subsequently appreciate the artistry of serious writing. Vendler was fascinated by the way he taught. "He was one of the best critical minds I've ever encountered." He conducted his class by asking the students a "hectoring set of questions" designed to point to the formulas and assumptions of popular fiction. "He would always teach by these questions; he never lectured." He demanded that they put these novels to the "real-life test"; that is, whether the plot twist could work in real life. "He was demanding that the students apply some meaningful aesthetic criterion, and he would conclude by asking the students why these novels, so transparent in their construction, were popular with the public." After the students read a genre novel, they would turn to a serious work and soon many students were beginning to comprehend the original architecture of serious fiction. "He was terribly funny, when he would recite the plot sequence of the nurse novels. I used to long to go into the class every day. It was better than a tonic."[37]

While he was at Smith, Random House and Martha Winston were negotiating another critical juncture in Elkin's becoming a strong man of American letters, his first collection of stories. They agreed that the new collection should appear within a year after *Boswell,* and shortly they had an agreement on eleven stories, including "The Guest," which had been hard to place with American magazines. The advance would be $1,500 against a standard royalties agreement. They would reach back to graduate school for stories like "Among the Witnesses" and would include new ones like "A Poetics for Bullies" and "Perlmutter at the East Pole," which brought $1,750 from *The Saturday Evening Post* in April. During the year, negotiations about the order of the stories, the title for the collection, and rights for "The Guest," which was held by the *Paris Review,* would occupy Fox and Winston, readying Elkin for the big time. While all this was happening, the author was starting his breakthrough novel, publishing "Everything Must Go!," a version of chapter 5 of *A Bad Man,* in the *Saturday Evening Post* in May 1965. Dr. Abraham Duker took issue with Elkin's portrayal of Feldman's manic father: "Must the *Post* supply a substitute psychiatrist's couch for Jews who feel the need of spewing out their own hostility toward their people, as a Mr. Elkin did in 'Everything Must Go' (July 31)? Let Mr. Elkin resolve his own conflicts with his 'Diaspora' in private. Why nauseate readers with his sickening and crude anti-Semitic outpourings? If this had been published in Germany, it would have been classified as neo-Nazi stuff." At editor Barbara Rosen's request, Elkin responded, and apparently his reply mitigated Duker's outrage. In August he responded, "I indeed appreciate your letter. I will re-read the story. Perhaps we will get together, if you are interested, for a conversation on it. I did not see your character as you had portrayed him. This is a matter of taste, but there is much more than that to it in the post-Hitler age." During the year at Smith, he arranged to visit Walpole Correctional Facility to learn about the physical facts of incarceration, though he consistently maintained that the visit yielded little of value in composing *A Bad Man*. His friends were contributing to his emergence as a major writer, too. Jim Ballowe, now at Bradley, invited him as a featured speaker at the Spring Arts Festival. Coover, living in Tarragona, Spain, asked for his help in pruning a new novel, *The Origin of the Brunists*, and for a prepublication comment. Demarest admitted that he read the *Post* in which "Perlmutter" appeared in a dentist's office and didn't buy it—"(I'm sorry, Stan)"—and perceptively noted a resonance Elkin would embrace for the rest of his artistic life: "By the way, I'm teaching [Henry James's] *Beast in the Jungle* now: could your story be the Beast re-romanticized?" The University of Oregon made an unexpected job offer as an associate professor two days after he formally turned Emory down, and Washington University, with strong support from Thurston, Vendler, Gass, Ciardi, and others, decided to promote and tenure rather than lose their emerging literary lion. Martha Foley selected "The Transient" for *Best American Short Stories 1965* and anthologies were seeking rights on many of the stories to be collected in *Criers and Kibitzers, Kibitzers and Criers*. Things were looking good on the Guggenheim and Rockefeller Foundation applications.[38] In the literary world, Elkin had become a strong man. He was ready for his breakthrough, which would happen very soon.

꩜ 6 ꩜ "Convicted of His Character"
Kibitzers, *A Bad Man*, Additions, and Catastrophe, 1965–68

"What the hell? I was new to dying."

—"Literature and the Heart Attack" (1968)

"We're in the homestretch of a race: your energy against my entropy. The universe is running down, Mr. Developer. [. . .] The smart money is in vaults."

—*A Bad Man* (1967)

The Elkins returned from Massachusetts in triumph. Stanley looked forward to a tenured appointment and an end to the anxiety of negotiating teaching contracts compatible with his writing commitment, but there would be friction sustaining these agreements for several years. He was in the final stages of preparing his collection of stories, which would culminate the work of the late 1950s and early 1960s, and would become his best-selling title, appearing in several editions, throughout his career. When *Criers and Kibitzers, Kibitzers and Criers* came out to rave reviews and excellent sales in 1966, Elkin found himself among the literary elite. Except for "Cousin Poor Lesley and the Lousy People,"[1] every story in the collection was anthologized at least once and four—"Ed Wolfe," the title story, "The Guest," and "A Poetics for Bullies"—many times. While awaiting those reviews he completed the novel he'd begun at Smith College, and the appearance of *A Bad Man* established beyond doubt that he was among the writers who would shape the serious fiction of the remainder of the century. While his career was flourishing on all fronts—in addition to the writing successes, he was courted by many universities to lead workshops and give readings, and quite a few invited him to join the creative writing faculty—Stanley and Joan expanded the family and bought a house. After several casual inquiries about *Boswell* and his stories, he received a serious option to film *A Bad Man*. By 1968, then, Elkin was realizing his dream as a writer and as a family man. Then the unthinkable happened.

If *Boswell* got Elkin noticed, *Criers and Kibitzers, Kibitzers and Criers* established his reputation. Although editor Joe Fox originally planned to include eleven stories, he and Elkin eventually agreed to eliminate two from the 1950s because Elkin habitually exceeded publishers' length recommendations. The reduction resulted in a handsome 272-page edition; an author biography approved by Elkin reminded readers that three had appeared in *Best American Short Stories,* an excerpt from *Boswell* had received a *Paris Review* humor prize, and two had won Longview Foundation Awards. The stories aren't printed in chronological order, though the final one, "Perlmutter at the East Pole," was written after *Boswell,* with the main character a minor figure from the novel. "A Poetics for Bullies" (seventh in the collection) was also recent. By contrast, "Cousin Poor Lesley and the Lousy People" (eighth) and "Among the Witnesses" (third) were written during the 1950s. The most popular story, "I Look Out for Ed Wolfe," is placed second, and the title story, probably a revision of the very early "Where There's a Minion," with other holograph titles including "Greenspahn and Son" and "A Man in Mourning,"[2] leads off. Because of Elkin's fondness for Faulkner and his seldom acknowledged influence by James Joyce, it's tempting to speculate that he intended some organic connection among the narratives rather like *The Unvanquished* or *Dubliners,* but if he had one, he didn't explain it and none of his critics has discerned it.

Along with "Ed Wolfe," the title story powerfully represents the sorrow dominating these texts, and its prominence, as the eponymous tale, as well as its intrinsic excellence, resulted in Elkin's being hailed as a "Jewish American" writer, a label he came to resist despite the fact that it linked him historically with Saul Bellow. Protagonist-merchant Jake Greenspahn suffers like a character out of a Bernard Malamud or an Edward Lewis Wallant novel of the American diaspora, rather than the vigorous, engaging hustlers of *A Bad Man* or *The Franchiser,* who are clearly descendants of Push the Bully. Jake's day—Joyceanly, the scope of his story—compels him to acknowledge and deal with many sorrows. Weary of the grind of selling, he views his very inventory as a burden, much as Ed Wolfe sees his life as assets to be liquidated. In a changing neighborhood, he wishes he could sell the business or dispose of his entire inventory. These business reversals are compounded by personal sorrows, for he recently buried his only son. His life stretches before him as an unending sequence of sad days like the one he undergoes in the story, bearing and hardly repressing his grief and anger.

Unlike the prototypical suffering Jewish American merchant, Malamud's Morris Bober in *The Assistant,* however, Jake is no saint and no patient sufferer. He carries his resentment of his life and his dashed expectations with him as surely as he suffers the constipation that crudely symbolizes his repressed sorrows. Even his friends and associates he resents, categorizing them as either "criers," who merely complain about their lives, or "kibitzers," who live vicariously off others' experiences. A 1930 film called *The Kibitzer,* based on a Broadway play by Edward G. Robinson, represented a Jewish money-grubber and busybody, very much the negative stereotype.[3] There's no evidence that Elkin saw the film, but his voracious appetite for movies and his having grown up in a tight-knit Jewish neighborhood support the conjecture that this manifestation of the kibitzer figure may have affected his construction of the class of observing busybodies that populate these stories and *Boswell*. The story's compounding irony is that, although Jake uses these labels to disparage the people with whom he associates, he is himself both a crier, missing few opportunities to complain, and a kibitzer, someone who holds no real cards of his own but lives through others, whether this takes the form of his dashed expectations for his son or his voyeuristic suspicions that his butcher and cashier are having an affair in his store. And he compensates for his grief by mistreating others. He fires the produce man for a trivial cause, though Frank has been instrumental in keeping the store from going under. Moreover, he alienates a wealthy customer who, he believes, tried to cheat him by demanding a discount on a loaf of bread, the wrapper of which she deliberately tore. Despite the fact that she's a doctor's wife (therefore well-to-do), a long-term customer (with, however, a history of stunts like the one with the bread wrapper), and a shopper bringing an abundantly loaded cart to the wretchedly unbusy checkout, Jake chases her out of his store as a *podler* (thief)— thereby doing injury to himself simply to assert identity and proprietorship. Jake also feels victimized by the chain store that opened nearby and especially by the customers who buy most of their groceries there, then take advantage of the loss leaders he advertises to entice shoppers away from the supermarket.

Thus alienated from his business, his associates, his fellow merchants, and his personal life, Jake faces with dread the *shneim asar chodesh* he'll observe for a year in his son's memory. His grief expands exponentially: Harold died childless, without having the chance to experience a full life—another "kibitzer" in Jake's classification. But life has yet one more brutal truth for him to face. When he fires Frank, the produce man blurts out that Harold was looting the cash register. And evidence accumulates indicating that, no matter how much Jake may repress or deny it, his son was indeed responsible for the thefts Jake blamed on others. Gradually he comes to accept this truth, and that evening in *shul* he grieves for his son, "twenty-three years old, wifeless, jobless, sacrificing nothing even in the act of death, leaving the world with his life not started"—and a thief. There's no end to Greenspahn's sorrow, only accumulation. Although it would be an exaggeration to call him a "loser" because of his ineffectual response to his sorrow, he has none of the dynamism, confrontational energy, or defiance of the heroes of Elkin's novels, who can be depended on to fight back against circumstance, even though they're fated to lose. But as a portrait in repressed rage and debilitating sorrow, Elkin's story is among the finest of that great decade, the 1960s.

When the collection came out, the reviewers adored it. Words like *brilliant, superb, beautiful,* and *genius* appear in comment after comment, many hailing the writer as an emerging major talent. Of particular interest is the fact that several reviewers applauded the power of Elkin's characterization, a criticism leveled at his novels before and after. *Publishers Weekly* called this an "excellent collection": "[W]hat Elkin has to say is universal and so competently does he engage the reader that the book is at once a totally personal experience and a philosophical one." *National Observer* hailed a "master storyteller" and a new writer of "formidable imagination; swift, evocative prose; and occasional stunning insight." The reviewer advised readers to "Buy these stories. They'll make you laugh, they may even make you cry, certainly they'll make you wonder. You won't soon forget them." Only a few demurred, but a couple of negative reviews appeared in large-impact venues: *Saturday Review,* a journal that consistently reviewed Elkin's novels favorably, lamented his bleak vision and "overworked literary themes." The *New York Review of Books* praised the linguistic skill, but derided the bleakness as well, concluding that the plot resolutions with their emphasis on suffering and defeat are characteristic of the "University Wits" currently taking over American fiction. Finally, the *New York Times* praised this "remarkable talent, composed of many important virtues: originality, wit, insight, an unusually sharp eye for irony, verbal exuberance, precision, detachment," but overall found the stories disappointing because they "are committed to failure from the beginning" and because Elkin offers his characters no choices that might amount to meaningful differences in their lives: "Elkin does not pull the rug out from under; he provides none to begin with." But the minority who objected to the stories did so on the basis of their vision, not their technique. Overall, the reviews were overwhelmingly and enthusiastically positive. Many agreed with *Southern Review's* estimate: "One of the most important collections of short stories published in years." When the collection was reissued under the Plume imprint in 1973, *New Republic* announced that the stories remained, after eight years, "as close to running, colloquial irresistible poetry as anything I've ever read"; there remain "some giants in the earth, and I now count Elkin among them."[4]

And the sales were very good. By January 25, the original printing sold out; a third was doing well in March. Fox stroked him, "Your collection is the equivalent of a best seller." He had, however, weeks before rubbed Elkin the wrong way by mentioning the success of another Random House writer whose story collections appealed to the critics but had limited mass market appeal, before he wrote a best seller: "Do you want to be slightly ill? The Capote *[In Cold Blood]* sold 17,000 copies on Monday alone, and by next week we will have 240,000 in print." By April, 5,500 copies had been sold, but Fox now fretted that Random House had "overspent on advertising" and therefore wasn't as far in the black as he'd hoped to be. And Bill Gass sent both a personal and a professional endorsement that must have meant more than any critic's praise. After enthusiastically praising the stories, he concluded, "You are much bespoke, beblessed, and beloved in this house."[5]

This long-term popularity and enthusiastic acceptance raises engaging questions. *Criers and Kibitzers* came closer to the combination of popular and critical success Elkin sought than any novel he wrote, or any collection of novellas except *The Living End*. In his 1990 introduction to the Thunder's Mouth edition, he complained that "for reasons not in the least clear to me" the book remained his "most enduring work," acknowledging the many reprints, film and stage inquiries, and steady income throughout the years, a "kind of widow's mite, a small annuity." Yet he virtually abandoned the story form at that point. He wrote only a few thereafter for magazines or journals. The obvious question is, why didn't Elkin continue writing stories? He continued to publish in popular and literary magazines, but these were either essays—some of which, like "Three Meetings," were short stories in disguise—or excerpts from novels in progress, or "Corporate Life," a story for *Chicago* (1985), and his final story, "Golf-Ball-Sized Hail" (1994), but he never again made a serious effort at publishing and collecting short stories. Thus, he chose not to follow up on the genre in which he had experienced his first great outpouring of critical praise, countless invitations to read and lecture, and material success. One explanation may be that in the late 1960s he discovered a fondness for the novella form and would publish three collections of these. The novella was in many ways the ideal genre for Elkin's talents, with its flexibility in plot development and room for stylistic improvisation. Nonetheless, the mystery is that he avoided the genre in which he received his strongest validation, both commercially and critically. Was this because he was, as he often maintained, convinced that the novel is a more substantial art form than the story? Barry Spacks confirms that in their youth they felt that the novel was a more "serious" venture, that major writers were judged by the novels they wrote.[6] Was he also persuaded by Fox's explanation that collections of stories don't sell as well as novels? Or did reviewers' insistence on categorizing his stories as Jewish American fiction, satires, and black humor lead him to associate what he considered a misreading with the genre in which he worked?

We can never know for certain why he stopped writing stories, though the simplest explanation is that he found the novella more amenable to his talents. Almost every magazine editor who accepted a story from the collection had advised substantial cuts, and there's no question that Elkin's are longer than stories by other top-tier 1960s writers of the genre, such as John Updike or Philip Roth—though "Eli, the Fanatic" is comparable in length to most Elkin stories, and very similar in theme and tone (raising again the "Jewish American" question). A slightly more complex rationale derives from the fact that many reviewers, eager to praise *Criers and Kibitzers, Kibitzers and Criers* in a context, allied it with three emerging literary movements: Jewish American writing; absurdist fiction, specifically black humor; and the more traditional subgenre, satire. Although all these labels apply to individual stories—"Poetics" is a triumph of black humor, the title story is among the best portrayals of a frustrated Jewish American in modern fiction, and "The Guest" plays brilliantly as satire—Elkin bristled at these affiliations. Throughout the next two decades, he explained to several interviewers how demeaning he felt these labels to be. A final explanation risks a venture into amateur psycho-analysis, but several close friends agree that it may explain something central to Elkin's artistic persona. Boswell, his first novel's protagonist, was based on an eighteenth-century biographer, but in one way he resembles his creator—or, more properly, his creator may have come to resemble Boswell. On the verge of realizing his lifelong dream, the foundation of a club for the great and near-great, Boswell unexpectedly subverts his triumph—on the eve of the grand opening he joins protesters outside, leading them in a chant, "*Down with the Club!*" He cannot cope with the realization of his dream, and consistently undermines that goal, first unconsciously, then deliberately. Is it possible that Elkin unconsciously subverted his own goal, the fame and respect of a successful story writer, because of a concern about being pigeonholed or anxiety about sustaining this triumph? There's no conclusive evidence for this theory, but something very like it would happen again while Elkin composed his magnum opus, *George Mills*.

Whatever his reasons may have been, America lost a gifted practitioner when he decided to stop writing short stories. Moreover, this resulted inevitably in his diminished presence in anthologies, which in turn acted against his desire to sell books. Most contemporary readers encounter a writer for the first time in an anthology and base future reading selections on writers whose work they remember from it. But as tastes changed in anthology-building over the years, Elkin wasn't producing new stories to compete with the emerging writers whose new works were filling the anthologies, several of whom Elkin had at one time or anther taught or counseled.

During the production of *Criers and Kibitzers,* Elkin was entertaining in-quires about film or television rights for certain stories, and interest in a couple of adaptations persisted into the 1980s. Security Pictures took an option in 1967, and to sweeten the deal, they tendered an offer on *Boswell* as well, guarantee-ing $15,000 if the options were picked up. The goal, however, was to lock in an exclusive on "Ed Wolfe." This company, operated by Philip Yordan, who would figure in Elkin's life for several years, sought an exclusive option on all the stories, with no cash up front, and a quantity discount: $5,000 if they filmed one story, $4,000 each if two, $2,500 each for three or more. But Security's lawyer advised Elkin and his agent in August that Yordan was having second thoughts about many of the stories and wanted to renegotiate the agreement—he'd pay $1,000 for an exclusive agreement on "The Bad Man" and a first look at Elkin's next two novels, with an option to purchase them at $15,000 each. Elkin complained in a draft response about "Yordan's periodic re-examinations of our piece-meal, Darwinian, evolving agreement"; he found the new proposal a "chipping away at my rights and future" and felt that his "bird-in-hand vision, a hit-and-run anxiety about the future" was being taken advantage of. He preferred to revert to the original agreement, selling exclusive rights on "Wolfe" and a one-year free option on the other stories. His irritation is evident in this comment to Yordan's lawyer: "My argument, then is that Mr. Yordan is not exactly discovering me, and that granting him all this time for nothing would be to suppress whatever movie chances may still exist for me." The lawyer salvaged the agreement by offering $5,000 for "Ed Wolfe" plus a one-year free option on *Boswell,* worth $10,000 if exercised, and a right of first refusal for a "reasonable period" (Elkin's penned in "10 days" was agreed to) for subsequent novels. By mid-1968, however, Yordan's interest in "Wolfe" had waned, and Bob Ornstein of Case Western Reserve sought permission to make an amateur film, using 16 mm silent film for the street scenes and television tape for the dialogue and interior scenes, then transferring everything to 16 mm tape and dubbing the dialogue. Ornstein promised Elkin "complete control of it, and if you want it erased, so be it."[7] The project wasn't intended for distribution and there's no evidence that it was made.

Other stories from *Criers and Kibitzers, Kibitzers and Criers* were from time to time optioned for film or stage. Elkin's 1990 Thunder's Mouth introduction notes that the title story was adapted as a radio play by the Canadian Broadcasting System in 1966, and it was also adapted for the stage, as was "The Guest," for which a television offer was made in January 1971, with a one-year option. In 1969 Richard Nolan Roth asked if Elkin had more material on Bertie that might be added to make a feature film based on "The Guest." He also asked whether Elkin had written any screenplays. In a separate venture, "The Guest" was adapted for the Chamber Theatre Ensemble in Evanston, Illinois, in August 1972. In 1983, Mark Crowell of Armory Free Theatre, an experimental laboratory at the University of Illinois, addressed the problem of genre, Elkin's use of an omniscient narrator who tells the story of Bertie's trashing his friend's apartment, by resorting, as film and stage adaptations often do, to a narrator, but at times Crowell's twenty-eight-page script reads like a parody of a Greek drama, a dialogue between Bertie and the narrator. Frank Galati produced a more compact and artistically successful adaptation at Northwestern University during the late 1970s, part of a series of collaborations that would result in film scripts for two of Elkin's novels. Recordings were produced of "Poetics," read by radio actor Jason Beck, the "voice of Bluto in the Popeye cartoons," and "The Guest," recorded by Elkin. Continuing interest in individual stories as adaptable for film or stage persisted into the 1980s. Hungarian émigré director Dezsö Magyar, who had filmed Hawthorne's "Rappaccini's Daughter," contracted for exclusive rights to produce "Perlmutter at the East Pole" in 1986, offering $3,000 on signing and another $15,000 when filming began. In late 1987, Elkin's agent told him Magyar was "as committed as ever" and had completed a script, but the project never went into production and there's no record of a script. In 1988 the Chicago Jewish Theater produced Arnold April's adaptation of "Criers and Kibitzers, Kibitzers and Criers," along with Isaac Bashevis Singer's "Fate" and Malamud's "The Magic Barrel." The Elkin production received good local reviews, but most of the ink was understandably devoted to the adaptation of recent Nobel laureate Singer's work. That same year, graduate student Peter Esmonde asked for nonexclusive rights to "Wolfe" and "In the Alley" for a two-year film project.[8]

There were yet two other reasons for Elkin's reservations about Yordan's attempt to claim first refusal on all future works. The first was that Yordan seemed eager to spend money on options for books he hadn't read carefully, then to express doubts about their viability as film projects. Although he remained interested in "Ed Wolfe" for some time, eventually he determined after signing the contract that he didn't want to film any of the remaining stories. This happened again with *A Bad Man*. The corollary to this roller-coaster ride was the gushing praise Yordan lavished on Elkin's prose, often followed by anxiety about his lack of name recognition and the suitability of his plots for film treatments. But something else was happening that discouraged Elkin from agreeing to a monopoly on his work, the strangest chapter in his artistic life to date, and another bizarre glimpse of the world that so fascinated him, Hollywood. It culminated in his first effort at original screenwriting and the unraveling of a real-life plot concerning money that would resemble one of his novels about commerce or his beloved Faulkner's Snopes books.

Enter Harry Joe "Coco" Brown Jr. (1934–2005), real estate developer, chairman of the Padua Playwrights Festival in Los Angeles, and the son of actor-director Harry Joe Brown (1890–1972). In 1966 Brown Jr. initiated a deal for Elkin to write an original script, with $3,000 to be paid for the outline, then, if accepted, an additional $6,000 for a first draft and a guarantee of $10,000 plus living expenses and a weekly stipend when production began. The problem was, Elkin had no clue what his topic might be. As he recollected in an introduction to *The Six-Year-Old Man* (1987), he misread the jacket note on Donald Barthelme's *The Cabinet of Dr. Caligari* (actually, *Come Back, Dr. Caligari*), concerning a sexual attraction by a teacher toward her thirty-five-year-old sixth grader. Elkin decided that a videoplay about a child who appears to be an adult would be interesting, so he wrote a treatment, which Brown enthusiastically accepted, and completed the draft screenplay, then revised it while teaching in California during the summer of 1967. At the time he was taking prescription amphetamines for weight control, so he had abundant energy to teach his classes and work on the project.[9] His plot invention, which never quite works in the final script, is that Paul suffers from progeria, the disease that afflicts Charles Mudd-Gaddis in *The Magic Kingdom*. By the time Elkin wrote his masterpiece, he'd learned about its symptoms and pathology, but while writing the screenplay he somewhat naïvely assumed that progeria was simply a linear acceleration of the aging process and developed a formula to calculate Paul's appearance at age six as approximating that of a healthy thirty-five-year-old adult. As his stage directions indicate, Paul is a "[s]trapping, six foot tall adultly formed male" who is "extraordinarily handsome." He speaks grammatically, reads sophisticated texts, and is generally precocious. The comic tension is that he has the emotional maturity of a six-year-old in this adult body; the humor comes from other people's assuming that he's what he appears to be. As Elkin would learn before *The Magic Kingdom*, progeria is a disease in which typical symptoms are shortness of stature, shrunken or birdlike faces, limited range of motion, dry scaly skin, dental abnormalities, and often a head somewhat too large for the body.[10] Thus the film script begins with a premise that's inconsistent with medical science, not itself inevitably damning but a mimetic problem of which Elkin didn't seem to be aware.

Fox, his editor, discouraged his undertaking the project, pleading that he should focus his energies on what he did best, writing fiction. He warned that this project would surely "take up more than three months of your precious time." By this point, *A Bad Man* was in production and Elkin was planning *The Dick Gibson Show*. He was bogged down in protracted and sometimes acrimonious negotiations with his university, and was being wooed by several others, including the University of California–Santa Barbara, where he received a preliminary offer for a tenure-tracking appointment in November 1966 and taught summer school in 1967. Joan's distaste for California persuaded Elkin that he was right not to have taken the permanent job: "We sub-let a furnished apartment for the summer. No grass, no sidewalks, the grocery stores were miles away, you had to drive miles to get anywhere. I hated it. I told Stanley, 'the only place I was willing to leave St. Louis to live was Brown University.'" But as often happened when Fox, a good friend and a shrewd editor, offered wise counsel, Elkin found ways to ignore it. He also was in need of ready cash, having signed a note with his agents, Curtis Brown, assigning any income he would receive from writing to them until a loan of $2,250 was repaid.[11]

His family responsibilities had increased as well; a second son, Bernard, named for Joan's brother, joined the family in 1966, and soon Molly was on the way. The Leland Avenue apartment was becoming crowded, and the Elkins began to think about moving—this in the context of job offers from Atlanta and Santa Barbara and inquiries from other distant places. A certain dissonance follows from simultaneously entertaining job offers that require moving and purchasing a home large enough to nurture a growing family. Fortunately, real estate prices dropped suddenly in the fashionable Parkview section of University City, less than half a mile from the campus, in the late 1960s because of anxiety about integrating neighborhoods; racial anxiety was pervasive enough that these homes briefly sold for considerably below their market value, so many faculty members could

Stanley, Philip, and
Bernard at the Leland
Avenue apartment, mid-
1960s. By permission of
Diane Brandwein.

afford houses that would have been out of reach a few years before.[12] During
1967 the Elkins moved into the tall gray house that would serve Joan as a studio,
the children as a wonderful home, and Stanley as a writing office, soon a center
for literary and social gatherings for members of and visitors to the St. Louis
literary community, and eventually a classroom for his graduate seminars.

For whatever reasons, then—a need for money, excitement about a new venture, frustration that book sales lagged behind critical acceptance, a lifelong love
of the movies, or a temptation to leave academic life and make his living as a
writer—Elkin completed the first typescript of *The Six-Year-Old Man* by March
1967, and Brown's fluctuating response was a prologue to problems to come.
He praised the "beautiful piece of writing" but said it would require extensive
changes to become commercially viable. Although he appreciated Elkin's giving
him "a more complete work" than the outline stipulated by the original agreement, Brown wanted substantial plot adjustments. He felt that the second half,
as the situations turn more bizarrely tragic, was weak in comparison with the

first. Additionally, he felt that the comic effects tended "to be too thoughtful at times," by which he apparently meant "dark" or "bleak," or to use a term Elkin disliked, "black humor." He insisted that the parents shouldn't be killed in the auto accident that coincidentally involves young men who allowed Paul to play in their souped-up car minutes before, that the effect would be "funnier and less terrifying and more acceptable" if they survived. As an indication of the growing tension, Elkin scribbled in the margin, in red ink, "kill *one* parent," though the final script has both surviving but severely injured, wrapped in bandages like mummies. Finally, Brown wanted to emphasize the chase scene, with the central theme "moving unconsciously and invulnerably through a world he has stirred into chaos, past an army of police or mafia or whatever, to his bicycle and back home." He sent three pages of commentary on specific points, generally seeking more realistic settings and motivations and pleading, "[O]nce we accept the absurd premise of Paul, the more realistic the outside events, the funnier and more valid the film will seem." Very soon Curtis Brown's Blossom Kahn, having undergone a "difficult negotiation" to pry the fee loose from Brown, posted $2,000 minus commissions to the Elkin ledger. And an undated note from Brown complains that, although there "are things in the script I found undisciplined or diffuse,"[13] he tried unsuccessfully to persuade Twentieth-Century Fox to produce it. He also gave copies to distinguished directors Arthur Penn and Mike Nichols. Although Twentieth-Century Fox coughed up another $6,000 in October 1967 to secure world film rights, and Hillard Elkins of Elkins Productions International asked to read it and the newly published *A Bad Man*, by the end of December the studio decided against moving forward, feeling that the amended script was "over long, undisciplined, and comically diffuse." Brown couldn't resist an I-told-you-so: "I must agree with them" and advised pruning to make an hour-and-forty-five-minute movie. The show business press widely reported that Brown had launched a bold new venture to produce new films based on works by exciting new fiction writers, and that he had signed Frank Conroy and Elkin for the project.[14]

In light of the increasingly personal antagonism developing between Elkin and Brown, it's tempting to dismiss Brown's criticism as philistine—the comments of a real estate developer dabbling with an avant-garde script. Brown had, however, produced stage versions of two daring new plays, Edward Albee's *The Zoo Story* and Samuel Beckett's *Krapp's Last Tape*, and as a Marshall Scholar had earned his M.A. in English at Oxford. Moreover, every studio executive he approached echoed his concerns about the script. For example, the plot turns on the babysitter's running away because she's surprised that Paul appears to be an adult, not a six-year-old (a scene that could conceivably be played with a sick sexual tension). The sitter's desertion is moreover a flimsy scaffold for the plot. Although she seems none too mature for a seventh grader, and although there were several things she'd prefer to do on a Saturday evening—her mother committed her to the job when Paul's father insisted that he'd pay far more than the going rate—simply abandoning Paul, without calling either her mother or Paul's parents, who gave her the number of the restaurant, seems irresponsible even for a middle schooler who'd rather be at choir practice or a teen party.

By now thoroughly frustrated, Elkin asked Fox and Martha Winston about the possibility of book publication. Fox recommended cutting most of the film directions, thereby reducing the script by about 25 percent, and combining it with at least four new stories. Elkin, already annoyed with Random House because of what he perceived as halfhearted effort to market *A Bad Man,* was further ir-ritated when Fox insisted that the new book shouldn't be published until after a novel that was still in the planning stages, *The Dick Gibson Show.* Elkin resisted his suggestion about the stage directions until Fox groused, "[A] writer you are, a director you ain't," mentioning his own apprenticeship in the television industry, often tasked with crossing out scriptwriters' instructions for directors. So when Winston came up with an offer to publish a truncated version in *Esquire,* Elkin accepted despite reservations about minimizing his text. Imagine his surprise when Brown insisted that the script was his property and demanded that he turn over most of the royalties. In August 1967 Brown complained that he only accidentally heard about the deal, and felt entitled to between $250 and $800 of that money. About these contract snarls, Elkin's publisher snapped, "Please, Stanley, next time let us do it. You create, we'll negotiate."[15]

The wrangling over money and rights to this script was far from over. Some time later, an undated message from the department secretary reads, in bright red ink, "Stanley: WOW" and includes a Las Vegas hotel number for Stella Stevens. This actress had played Appassionata von Climax in *Li'l Abner* and had costarred with Elvis Presley, Glenn Ford, Bing Crosby, and Jerry Lewis in a variety of mov-ies.[16] When she decided to try her hand at producing, Stevens took an interest in Elkin's script, and in 1970 she negotiated an option, for either $60,000 (Joan's recollection) or $75,000 (Stanley's). The problem was, the money, however much it was, never got to Elkin. Brown once again claimed ownership of the property, and he got whatever proceeds changed hands, though he later insisted that he barely broke even on the deal after legal costs. Brown claimed that Elkin had received $15,000 from him and Fox Films, and by this point things were so bitter between the two men that neither one's account is reliable. At any rate, Stevens told film critic Roger Ebert in 1970 that this would be her next project, and that Milos Forman was interested in directing it.[17] The final flap about *The Six-Year-Old Man* didn't happen until 1987, when independent publisher Bill Bamberger brought out a version with the *Esquire* cuts restored. Brown confronted Elkin's agent, who "confessed that we had made a deal with Bamberger." Brown wanted the entire advance, but said Elkin should keep all earnings beyond that. Georges Borchardt agreed, or perhaps wanted to avoid a nuisance, and asked Stanley to sign over his check to Brown. Elkin probably thought the sum ($225) was good riddance, but Brown blew a gasket when he saw Elkin's introduction. A long jeremiad arrived in February 1988. Brown began his compliant by professing his love for the work and his happiness that Elkin had reprinted it, but the tone quickly turned bitter: "When I picked it up and read your introduction I was shocked and dismayed. It was a particularly mean and paranoid piece of writing from someone whose wide gifts of humor and imagination I had once admired. Also in the simpler sense it was slanderous." A sample paragraph from Brown's diatribe completes this chapter in Elkin's Hollywood encounters:

> I don't understand your complaint. You were admittedly excited and turned on as never before when somebody came along and believed in you enough to commission you to write an original script. You were paid fully and correctly the price that we bargained for and whatever would have happened to the script afterward it would not have been your property and you would have had no legitimate gripe even if the movie had been made and I had made a million dollars. As it was you were the only person to make any money from it and also it further served to enhance and further your reputation and you received praise for the work. I don't want to debate with you the theories of private property and ownership on which our society runs but the only person who can successfully sell something and still keep it is a whore. [. . .] However, the tone of your attack on me was unfortunately not funny, it was simply bitter and mean.[18]

Two years later, Hollywood produced a film based on a premise similar to that of "The Six-Year-Old Man," and Elkin believed, as does his son Philip, that *Big* (1988), directed by Penny Marshall and written by Gary Ross and Anne Spielberg (both nominated for an Academy Award, as was actor Tom Hanks), was a knockoff. It's possible that Ross and Spielberg encountered Elkin's script, but the film seems no closer to plagiarism than your average television drama using a competitor's recycled plot. The joke is similar, with adults' expectations that Josh will behave like the adult he appears to be forming the nucleus, and the sexual tension in one scene mirrors the potential in that between Paul and his babysitter, or those in act 2 with Eleanor Glazer. But the film avoids the black humor and morbidity of Elkin's text—hence its commercial success—and its premise is sufficiently different to distance it as well. Josh wishes at a carnival for "bigness" and gets what he hopes for, as opposed to Paul's disease, perhaps misunderstood by his creator at the time.[19]

Although not as dramatic and public as these events, a minor episode from the period led Elkin in yet another direction, perhaps ridiculous enough to prove once more that the absurd twists we occasionally find in his plots may mirror some of the strange doings in his life. In January 1966, Gordon Lish, later an influential editor, teacher, and mentor, but then of Behavioral Research Laboratories in California, commissioned Elkin to write a piece for a government-sponsored study of the creative process. Very soon he had "A Prayer for Losers," and asked for a recorded copy, which delighted everyone at the office: "Lord, Playboy [many of Lish's salutations are epithets from *Boswell*], you're, like, you know, GOOD! [. . .] Listen, when the writing muscle wearies, I can always get you something in soaps." The boss piped Elkin's baritone throughout the office many mornings, so that it "has already become a classic." Lish apparently had big plans for a Job Corps project, based on the success of the creativity packet, but in June news came that he'd been fired from Behavioral Research Laboratories. "A Prayer for Losers" appeared in 1966, with a head shot of Elkin (about which Lish teased, "Tell me, do you always look so Jewish? [. . .] Imitate. It's all a matter of posture. That is, you *stand* Jewish, do you know what I mean? Learn to stand Gentile"), accompanied by seventeen multiple-choice questions designed, apparently by Lish, to assess the student's reading comprehension. "A Prayer" is hilariously tongue in cheek, though its value as a study of creativity remains dubious: "Make me gung-ho, for God's sake. Give me stick-to-it-ivity. Or whatever else it takes. Let me be reconciled at once. And lend me the power to forgive those who probably do not deserve it. For nothing counts now but getting on and I am not getting anywhere. Teach me, oh Lord, to play ball. *Make me square, please!*"[20] The loser's prayer closely resembles those of Leo Feldman and the inmates in *A Bad Man*, which Elkin was writing at the time, as well as Warden Fisher's obsession with middle-class values, and the concerns of a hitchhiker Ben Flesh picks up in *The Franchiser*, who advises him to "get a reality." A minor character from *The Six-Year-Old Man* makes a similar plea. Elkin and Lish had great fun parodying the core values of the very government that sponsored the project.

The great professional event of the decade was the publication of *A Bad Man* in 1967. It was inspired when Al Lebowitz told him about a lawyer who was sentenced to a prison term. Elkin became intrigued by the adjustment in worldview such a sentence would require of a white-collar criminal, and then added the crucial detail that Leo Feldman is technically innocent of the crime for which he's incarcerated—as Elkin was fond of saying, he's "convicted of his character." Elkin deliberately "upped the ante philosophically" by having Feldman "sentenced for his character." He told Tom LeClair that the "mixture of the classes is a very attractive theme," and Feldman is fascinated by the habits and interests of other inmates. While writing the novel and teaching at Smith College, he did some field research, Elkin style; as he told Gass and Jeffrey Duncan, "I decided that I had best get me to a prisonry." But he claimed that his visit to the Walpole Correctional Facility wasn't productive. "At the end of the day, I was absolutely delighted [. . .] because my prison of the imagination was much better than their real prison."[21] His created world, in which his first full-length, larger-than-life antihero would dominate, was a prison of the imagination, a structure lacking distinct shape or boundaries. In the first chapter, the deputy taking Feldman to the slammer makes ominous suggestions about the facility's mass—one can never know just when one is inside or outside. This prison contains the body, ensnares the mind, and ultimately absorbs the soul. In such a prison, mad bad men cultivate manic obsessions. Spatially, it's as strange and exotic as its inhabitants are, in some ways an extension of the warden's personality, but its surreal landscape recalls Salvador Dali, Franz Kafka, Lewis Carroll, and Monty Python—all at once. Whereas actual prisons are usually rectangular, functional structures, this one resembles a labyrinth. Corridors seem to go nowhere, but all passages ultimately lead to the center of the prison, the Warden's Quarters, directly over the execution chamber. And in this mad world, a funny, insane, and deadly serious conflict plays out between the stubborn individualist Feldman— though Elkin had used his mother's maiden name in an unpublished novel and many stories, this time he deliberately punned on the "felled man"—and an equally mad and bad apostle of order and decency, Warden Fisher, who may be the prototype for movie wardens in films as diverse as *Cool Hand Luke* (1967), *The Longest Yard* (1974 and 2005), and *The Shawshank Redemption* (1994). But one important difference demonstrates Elkin's originality. Whereas the Captain in *Luke* or Norton in *Shawshank* are pathological control freaks and sadists, as corrupt as the institutions over which they preside, Elkin's Fisher is so fixated on virtue and enforcing his own moral control over others that he paradoxically becomes more evil than the criminals he seeks to reform. Twice he puns on his name as a "fisher of bad men," suggesting ironically the passivity of the Fisher King in grail romance, who awaits the healing touch of the quest hero, as well as the New Testament promise that Christ's disciples would become "fishers of men" (Matthew 4:19). This evangelical mission evolves into fanaticism with the Warden's campaign to root out and segregate all the bad men in his prison. One of several paradoxes in the character of this, Elkin's first great antagonist, is that the Warden is an extraordinary evangelist for the ordinary, a man who passionately believes in the suppression of passions. A grand rhetorical moment occurs at Warden's Assembly, a mandatory convocation for cons, when the Warden's obsession with bad men—not all prisoners are "bad men," and the Warden gets to decide who is and who isn't—launches him into a religious zeal reminiscent of a fundamentalist Christian revival. Against him Elkin poses an entrepreneur who recalls the protagonist of "A Poetics for Bullies" as surely as Fisher recalls his antagonist John Williams. Feldman is, there's no getting around this, a very bad man, even if the final sentences read, "Why, I *am* innocent, he thought, even as they beat him. And indeed, he felt so." In the rhetorical and moral maze of this novel, reflected in the physical labyrinth of the prison, Feldman is persecuted by a zealous warden because he insists on his individuality, not because of what he's done—and there's plenty of which he's anything but innocent, including spousal abuse, child abuse, friend abuse, employee abuse, physician abuse, family denial, and about a thousand commercial code and local ordinance violations in the basement of his store. Lebowitz and Fox cleverly described Feldman in jacket copy for the first edition: *"What if all the barbarians had not been destroyed? Suppose, just suppose, one survived, one made it, one flourished?"* [22]

Even while he edited the text, however, Fox became nervous about its commercial potential, as did Winston, who cautioned Elkin against giving up his day job. Elkin, seriously considering becoming a full-time writer and getting out of the academic life, was sternly admonished, "I always get nervous when my clients talk about giving up a job. I'm the old-fashioned type who likes to know there's a pay check to take care of the rent"; she warned that although she considered Elkin one of the finest writers she'd ever represented, "there is always a question about how much dough you're going to make." She steered him toward focusing on the Guggenheim grant that Gass, Vendler, and others had recommended him for, and was relieved when he won the award in March. It provided a stipend of $6,000, mostly nontaxable, to free him to write. He soon learned that his application for a Rockefeller Foundation grant in the amount of $13,000 had been approved for the fiscal year beginning July 1, 1968. Fox advised restraint, pleading that Elkin cut as much as fifty pages: "Also, there are occasional passages where your rhetoric is simply overwhelming, where you tell three jokes where one would do, where your play with words exhausts the reader." He warned that it's a wonderful book, but "I have no idea how it's going to sell." [23]

So Random House undertook an ambitious and creative publicity campaign. Fox's associate sent letters to the editors of several university newspapers, asking for the name of a faculty member to whom Random House might offer a softcover copy for review in a local newspaper. Nearly twenty campuses responded, some with critics already famous and some soon to be. To each, Fox sent an advance copy with this note: "A BAD MAN is a provocative, funny, and distinguished novel and Stanley Elkin is an important American writer. However, in an era when vast numbers of books compete for attention, we would like to make certain that A BAD MAN reaches those opinion makers upon whom a writer's reputation so often depends. Therefore, we have published this Special Advance Edition of A BAD MAN, consisting of 500 paperbound copies designed for distribution to a selected group of readers and media who know, enjoy, and help to establish writers. We hope you'll be as excited about A BAD MAN as we are." [24] During this marketing campaign, Winston placed two excerpts in the large-circulation *Saturday Evening Post* at $2,250 each, the visit to Billy's classroom ("Feldman and Son") and Feldman's taking over the prison canteen ("The Merchant of New Desires"). She later placed "Everything Must Go," the story of Feldman and his crazed father Isidore enacting the "Diaspora in Southern Illinois," with the *Post* as well, but had less success with *Paris Review,* though George Plimpton liked the novel very much, and with *The Reporter*, where the staff found it "fascinating" but found no "excerpt that would be right for us." And the campaign for jacket blurbs was more successful than the one for *Boswell*, but not without its pitfalls. Heller, who had disliked *Boswell*, mellowed enough to plead that he'd love to read *Bad Man* but had pressing commitments. Kurt Vonnegut Jr. returned the review copy without comment, and of course nobody heard from Pynchon. Roth called to say he was "crazy about the book" and eager to review it or write a blurb, but within a week he entered the hospital and was unable to complete the task. And the comment Gass sent must have warmed his heart, though it didn't appear on the first edition: "Stanley Elkin is among a handful of American writers who, by employing all the resources of our life and language, are continuing to give the novel the qualities which in the past have made it so flexible, so rich, so great a kind. *A Bad Man* is large and beautiful in every way: in wit, thought, form, feeling, observation, sense, and style."[25] Lish wrote with characteristic flair, "You expect me to believe that bullshit about your not having first-hand knowledge of life in the joint? Listen, Elkin, you're an ex-con if I ever saw one. The cupped cigaret, the furtive glances, the dragging foot. And the eyes! Yes, it's mostly the eyes—a certain vacancy. The result of your having looked too much on greasy steel." The most unexpected response to the novel was an invitation to address the *Saturday Evening Post* staff retreat in Greenbrier, West Virginia, in April. Because three excerpts appeared in the *Post*, the editors asked him to talk about the book and a subsequent letter congratulated him on a well-received presentation: "Send me the bill. And send me stories, or chunks of the new book. The pleasure of publishing Elkin is a hard one to kick."[26] The first edition went into print with the Lebowitz-Fox comment on barbarians and a wonderful back cover photograph.

As Fox and Winston feared, reviews were spectacular but sales weren't. Writers in large and small markets praised the humor, rhetoric, surrealism, and antiestablishment themes of the new book, many agreeing with R. Z. Sheppard in *Book World* that it places Elkin among the "smartest, most imaginative, and most verbally gifted novelists writing in America today." A front-page item in the *New York Times Book Review* agreed: "[N]o serious and funny writer in America can match Elkin 'page for page'": he is "one of the flashiest and most exciting comic talents currently in view." *Life* announced that Elkin "now lays claim to his inner territory" and the *New York Times* praised the irony, absurdity, and wit that place its author "in the class of the best writers of the Jewish Renaissance." In fact, the reviews, although favorable and often raves, may have fueled Elkin's growing resistance to the categories in which their praise placed him. Quite a few agreed with the *Cincinnati Enquirer* that this is the "definitive black humor novel." Several noted the brilliant satiric effects. Even the few reviewers who had reservations complained because it so effectively exemplified the movement in

Book jacket photo for *A Bad Man*. Photograph by
John J. Oidtman, reproduced by permission.

American fiction toward black humor and the absurd; *New York Review* praised
Elkin's style but regretted his adopting the "apocalyptic formula" of the black
humorists. *Saturday Review* agreed, lamenting the "aura of the university even
though it unfolds almost entirely in jail." Most reviews, however, found the new
novel exciting, brilliant, and a promise of great things to come.[27]

Even if he was put off by labels like satirist, absurdist, black humorist, and
Jewish American writer—all of which apply to this novel—Elkin was gratified
by the unexpectedly warm critical reception. But as Fox and Winston feared, he
was far from the mark when he wrote Gass in March, seeking support for his
Guggenheim application, "Look to the people, Bill. Look to your mass markets
and your mass media. That is where the action is."[28] Twice Elkin had looked to

mass markets and twice he'd been disappointed. He earned advances on *The Six-Year-Old Man*, but it never developed into the commercial property he'd been led to expect. And sales of *A Bad Man* lagged in spite of the reviews. Winston and Fox tried to console Elkin, but he was looking for someone to blame. Random House was a convenient target. Weeks after publication, Fox reported that only 5,220 copes had been sold. Random planned to send 1,000 more to booksellers in anticipation of the front-page item in the *Times Book Review*. Elkin's handwritten response on the verso of Fox's letter poignantly summarizes his disappointment, one that would recur throughout his career: "I am very discouraged. This is the case for my discouragement. I had not frankly expected to get rich, with a best-seller, I am a 6000–7000 sales man. I will never write a best seller. The woods are full of us guys—R. V. Cassill, Jacob Lind, Bill Gass. However, I would have thought that my reviews—which I knew would be good, though not perhaps as good as they've turned out to be—would break that barrier, to reach, with luck, sales of ten thousand maybe." Elkin even called St. Louis bookstores and bitterly reported that one had no copies on hand, one had two, two had three, and two had four—for a writer who had captivated the St. Louis press as a local hero making the big time. And Fox's reply fueled the fire. He agreed that Elkin shouldn't be a 6,000–7,000 copy writer, "but at the moment I'd be delighted to sell that many" and reminded Elkin that Random House had printed a first run of 12,500. During the next few months Elkin pondered leaving Random House, despite Winston's and Fox's insistence that the house had overspent a generous budget for advertising and shouldn't be held responsible for poor sales. Fox also reminded his author that there was an unsold balance on *Boswell*, and that publishers carry these forward against future earnings. Elkin was frustrated and needed someone to blame for the book's commercial failure. He was even further annoyed when Fox told him that three or four of his salesmen reported that the rave reviews had actually worked against the book's sales by conveying the impression that it was "difficult," "too profound," or a "message book" and thereby actually discouraging buyers.[29]

He was concerned in part because he was eager to leave academic life and to commit to professional writing as his income source as well as his life's work, against Winston's advice. Poor sales for his best novel to date, along with the implosion of the effort to produce *The Six-Year-Old Man*, frustrated that goal. But one hope remained. Although Yordan had wavered back and forth in his plan to film "I Look Out for Ed Wolfe" and complained to his lawyer in August 1967 that he was developing doubts about the suitability of *A Bad Man*, on which he held an option, he suddenly decided to discuss it face to face. During the Christmas season he flew the family, first class, to Madrid. First class? According to Joan, *everything* was first class—an apartment, a limousine, servants who spoke as little English as the Elkins spoke Spanish, all the best restaurants.

From time to time Stanley actually spoke with Yordan, who could never find time to discuss the film. Soon Stanley became irritated about the stalling, and it eventually turned out that Yordan wanted a script in which Feldman was a good man, someone audiences could identify with.[30] On New Year's Day he paid $15,000 for an exclusive option for 1968 and renewed it the next year. He inquired about Broadway director Alan Schneider's interest in making this as his first movie and planned to produce it in 1969. Actor Robert Shaw expressed interest in the title role, and for more than a year Yordan insisted that the film would be made. Then in 1971 Elkin learned from Curtis Brown that Shaw's agent cabled with instructions to stop negotiations for a stage version, presumably replacing jettisoned plans to film it, "offering no reason at all for his desire to terminate them." So *A Bad Man* the movie never happened. Wayne Fields, who joined the Washington University faculty that year, found Elkin's anecdotes about the Spain trip irresistible. Stanley was full of funny stories about travel and movie people. He loved to tell about fancy hotels and restaurants he visited in Spain; he had a way of describing them with awe and with a certain amount of self-mockery about the fact that such luxury and ostentation could generate awe. He told Fields about a Madrid restaurant where waiters brought bars of silver to your table and pounded out spoons, but Fields, fully aware of Stanley's hyperbole, took that alchemy with a grain of salt.[31]

A Bad Man remained for many years an anchor in securing Elkin's literary reputation. Over the years he received other inquiries about filming the novel, but none came to fruition. His former agency advised him in 1976 that independent producer Donald Bradley was interested in adapting it and in 1994 Blackstock Pictures of Toronto wanted to "take a crack at" the story. It was translated into several languages, with the French version, *Un sale type,* creating considerable excitement in its 1976 rerelease, which inspired *L'Express* to rave, "A la fois documentaire, satire sociale, et fable métaphysique, ce voyage révèle en Elkin l'un des meilleurs romanciers américains."[32] Without a doubt, however, the greatest challenge was converting Elkin's prose into Japanese. He was lucky to have a skilled and diligent translator, who began a 1970 correspondence seeking clarification of linguistic and thematic elements. Yasuhiko Terakado inquired about thirty-nine words and phrases with which his English dictionaries couldn't help, including "the Fink," "the deuce and a half," "federal rap," "snug as a bug," "*Malleus Maleficarum,*"[33] "prick, fartass, scumbag," and "Quaker Oats box." He also asked subtle thematic questions, two of which might put to shame the pretensions of many formalist or poststructuralist critics: "1. The idea of a 'bad man' is hard to understand for me. Does it refer to simply any convict, or an intellectual or bourgeois convict who has a complex awareness? 2. Did you intend to write a modern version of John Bunyan's Bad Man? 'A bad man in the age of absurdity?'" As he made his way deeper into the translation, Terakado opened another of the book's more subtle thematic issues. Looking at the confrontation between Feldman and the developer, he asked for a clarification of Feldman's wonderful phrase, "your energy against my entropy": "a battle of the individualist against the energetic mass society shaper-developer. The developer is reshaping everything in the world into the ultimate state of homogeneity (entropy). And ultimately the last left heterogeneity (the developer) will also be thrown into homogeneity of his own making. Is my interpretation correct?" That's not quite what Elkin means—the interpretation requires that the developer, not Feldman, speak as entropy's advocate—but it places Elkin in a gestalt he shares with avant-garde writers like Pynchon, Coover, Don DeLillo, and others: Terakado observes that entropy remains a thermodynamic issue in Japan, but in the United States, the concept is "a key word for the nihilistic zeitgeist."[34]

In 1967, then, life was good in St. Louis. Sales weren't as bountiful as Elkin hoped, and he postponed the decision to exchange the academic life for the professional writer's because of disappointments with Hollywood and book sales. Moreover, some strains were evident in his ongoing negotiations with the university, focusing on three points: his desire to reserve time to write; frequent invitations by other universities to spend a term or a summer at their campus, often with an implicit suggestion that this could lead to a permanent appointment; and even the Guggenheim, one of many substantial grants Elkin would receive. Chair Jarvis Thurston, a strong supporter even before Elkin joined the faculty, was concerned because he felt that the university's contribution to the Guggenheim was contingent on Stanley's returning to the university, and Elkin was being aggressively courted by the University of California–Santa Barbara. Elkin's handwritten summary of their conversation summarizes these tensions:

> When he pointed out that as soon as I accepted money from W.U. I ceased to be a free agent, I invited him, *strongly*, to stop the checks; that I must consider myself free to enter the negotiations. I repeatedly urged him to do this; he, as repeatedly, declined, and I then said that I would accept no additional money from W.U., once California makes an offer which W.U. declines to approach in some counter offer, and I accept California—that, if this is unacceptable, the funds should stop at once.
>
> He was agreeable to leave it open, let it ride, until I commit the sin, & I told him that I did not consider such an arrangement a sin.[35]

The problem wasn't that his job was in jeopardy; market forces were in his favor, and he was invited to choose among a variety of appealing offers. His university, that year and the next, when he received a Ford Foundation grant, eventually found a way to accommodate him.

An anecdote Elkin told the Lebowitzes captures the social side of his persona during this, probably the happiest period of his life. He and Joan were at a nightclub where a promotion was "So You Want to Lead a Band." Of course Stanley wanted to lead the band. Al recalls, "It was Stanley's cup of tea. He had to get in there and win this contest." The ensemble was supposed to play exactly the way the leader directed them. Stanley felt that he did a magnificent job directing and was confident that he'd win. The other finalist was a gorgeous blonde with no musical instinct, but she did have a tight, low-cut dress, and the band played terribly trying to follow her lead. Stanley was so pleased with her bumbling that he could hardly keep a straight face. But the audience voted by applause and she won hands down.[36]

So he had it all in the spring of 1968: beautiful home, lovely family, excellent university job with offers to move on if he wanted to, invitations to lead workshops and give public readings, foundation grants, literary prizes, opportunities to break into the film industry, and a reputation as one of America's premier emerging literary talents. Then the unthinkable happened: he had a heart attack that spring. Although he would soon become the most identifiable literary celebrity suffering from multiple sclerosis, he often told interviewers that the defining moment of his life was the heart attack. He was almost thirty-eight years old.

Sure, he smoked too much, both tobacco and marijuana, but who didn't in the 1960s? Sure, he drank too much, whooped it up at parties at which he was the center of attention (or else!), and he was a little overweight, having resorted to prescription amphetamines to control his weight while writing *The Six-Year-Old Man*. His father had several heart attacks, and his mother had heart problems that limited her movement. Death was the central theme of his imaginative work; Feldman rants to his nemesis, the real estate developer, "[T]he smart money's in vaults." But Stanley was almost thirty-eight. He had a wonderful career going for him. He played softball on Saturdays and rode a motorcycle. Then, to borrow Heller's sardonic phrase, "his heart attacked him."[37] And his life, and his fiction, would never again be the same.

Outpourings of concern came in from agents, editors, readers, colleagues, and friends. Coover thanked him for his comments on *The Origin of the Brunists*, but ended, "Cool it. Make it into 1969. There'll be so many casualties this summer and fall it will be like a whole new world. They'll probably even forgive your heart attack, Stan." Yordan was shocked and admonished, "[N]ow that you have had the warning, for Christ's sake have some character and give up smoking." He also advised Elkin to give up his day job, move to Los Angeles or another warm climate, and live as a professional writer—apparently forgetting the documented, even in 1968, relation between stress and heart attack vulnerability. And Sol Yurick offered to "propitiate the gods" by slitting Bellow's or Malamud's throat on an altar "as a little instead-of-you sacrifice."[38]

During the spring and summer Stanley did two things that helped him recover from the physical and emotional malaise of the heart attack. He took a trip and he took up his pen. About midsummer, Herb Bogart called and Stanley told him about hearing from a former student in Germany who was having problems with a relationship. Herb spontaneously asked, "Do you want to go to Europe?" and without thinking, Stanley said yes. Herb sent the tickets, and off they went. Stanley was still recovering from his heart attack, and Joan, who had been through plenty with his illness compounding uncertainties about his future employment, was stuck for the summer with an infant (Molly) and a one-year-old (Bernie). Herb and Stanley flew to Germany; soon the student and his partner, now reconciled, took them on a trip to one of the concentration camps. While they were there, Bogart, a gentile, kept apologizing. Stanley suddenly asked, "Why? You didn't do anything." They continued to Norway and Sweden, where in a bookstore they saw one of Elkin's books in translation—a high point in his career. Overall, Joan thinks, her husband wanted Herb to "take care of him" in Europe, and that may have been an important step in the healing process.[39]

And during the year or so after being released from the hospital, another means of dealing with this was to fictionalize his recovery experience. He wrote two stories about the recuperation that lay ahead of him and the difficulty of resuming an important facet of his life, athletics. These stories, probably originally intended for publication but eventually abandoned, were written sometime after the attack and before 1970. The longer one, "Baseball Story," exists only in handwritten format, on university examination books. The absence of a typescript is evidence, though not conclusive, that Elkin discarded any intention of developing the story further; it had done its work as a therapeutic exercise, although its similarity to the first scene of the second story, "Colin Kelly's Kids" suggests that "Kelly" is a revision of it. Moreover, a portion of "Baseball Story" was revised for inclusion in his 1986 essay about owning a motorcycle. In both accounts, Elkin humorously balances his desire for a motorcycle, as a response to his need to appear "manly" after the heart attack, against his inept handling of the machine. The softball games that constitute the main plot matter of the two narratives have become part of the folklore of the university English Department, and most of the veterans of those Saturday morning contests remember Elkin as a power hitter who loved the camaraderie more than the competition. Toward the end "Baseball Story," while the principal character, named Elkin, has been daydreaming about the recuperation process, the cheating he's done on his doctor's advice, and the problems he can anticipate as he adjusts to living with an untrustworthy ticker, he's suddenly reminded that a ball game's going on, and that John Bernard, the one guy he was never on the same team with (because both were lefties and played first base) and a feared hitter, is batting; in a softball game, he's probably a pull hitter:

> Everyone gave him cigarettes—he took over a pack and a half a day from his friends. They gave him their cigarettes, their generosity keyed by deter-

mination—how, he supposed, that a man should be free, but because no one wanted to be parental, all ashamed of their tyrannies, determined to live if not to let live (and they were smokers themselves, each one, some of them now almost 37—his own age, when he had had the attack, nagged with each puff, bullied by the spots on TV, the Amer. Cancer Soc. ones. [. . .] Ill health was the new guilt, death a sin, more fearful than any religious proscription. It was better to be helpless.[40]

By contrast, "Colin Kelly's Kids" apparently was intended for publication, but it too was eventually abandoned. An evolution of "Baseball Story" minus the motorcycle story that would be recycled elsewhere, it's more developed and pruned, effectively capturing Elkin's reversion from a state of recovery to the conditions that exacerbated the heart attack. Like "Baseball Story," it's about the recovery process and Elkin's failure to follow the commonsense restrictions on his behavior as he recovers, but much more emphasis is placed on his surprise that he *is* in a process of recovery, that his strength and potency (closely allied in popular and sports culture, as well as stories and films about sports) are returning to pre–heart attack status. Ultimately this story is directed toward a more subtle, and atypical, Elkin theme—friendship and love among men. He reflects on the decency and kindness of his friends who do everything they can to help him through his crisis while doing all they can to disguise their generosity: "Their sportsmanship gave him confidence, allowed him to be himself, permitted his essential laziness as a fielder, and put him, out of respect, he supposed, for his memory, no further back than sixth or seventh on the line-up."[41] Gratitude, as well as the delight of being among his fellows and recognizing the generosity with which they encouraged him to resume his life, are atypical themes for Elkin. Although most of his fictional heroes are essentially loners, isolates who interact only at arm's length, this fictionalized "Elkin" is profoundly aware of the blessings of friendship.

A final act of recovery was a talk he gave at Purdue University in the fall. It's remarkable for its typical Elkin candor and the rough treatment he gives himself, much as he did his ego projections in the two stories. He charts a devastating curve in his responses, from entirely self-absorbed in his symptoms and prognosis, to a point of epiphany when "something human happened." After the initial shock of the heart attack, Stanley became intensely self-occupied, seeing his own health as the center of the universe. He admits to his physician, "Well, I'm a solipsist, Doctor" and remonstrates with himself:

> I had given him my poetic symptoms. (It is always what happens. I insist on proving my intelligence to professional men.) "It's as if," I explained, "a gauntleted fist were opening and closing in there, Doctor, the hingey, spikey knuckles of the clench dragging the meaty ruts like hauled lugs behind a truck. There's a quality of wetness; no, of wetness manqué; say rather of evaporation, as if the iron flanks of an automobile about the open wound with its gas tank

had been given sentient capacity and could feel the sharpish evaporative glaze of the last few drops of fuel fallen from the hose the attendant pulls from the hole. [. . .] That's where it hurts—the straw."

Instead of telling his physician his symptoms, he's telling him what he does for a living. And, as his hyperbole makes clear, Elkin realizes how self-indulgent his response to the illness really was. But in the hospital, "as much motel as hospital," and anticipating the great scene in *The Franchiser* when Ben attempts to connect with his wardmate, Stanley experiences a second episode that reminds him how absurd death can be. At 4 A.M., "I was feeling chest pain, the real stuff, just *like* the real stuff. And I thought, Shit. I thought, Jesus, and in my sleep, not running stairs, not moving furniture or shoveling snow. And, I thought, not fucking or over-eating or falling down drunk, not overextended, only sleeping, snuggy snug and tucky tucked, and I thought, not immoderate, merely asleep, and *still* this god damn son of a bitch pain can touch me, and I thought—well, I was very disappointed." Die he obviously didn't, but his roommate, a gnarled, unclean man, brought out the worst in him, partly because the guy was really sick, and partly because he was stupid enough to smoke with oxygen tanks in the room. Now on his moral high ground, Stanley demanded a transfer to a private room, when "[s]omething human happens and there's no discharge in the war." A fellow heart attack patient in a nearby room, far less advanced in recovery than he, received word by telephone of her brother's death. In her wail he heard the voice of sorrow that placed the egocentrism of his hospital stay in perspective: "I had not known the human voice was capable of such sound, as if what I heard were not grief so much as a sort of furious and oddly prescribed response to tragedy. [. . .] It was indecipherable and uninventable, and it must henceforth stand for me as the standard of grief and ruin, in a curious way as an ideal." In this ego chastening Elkin was on his way to an important kind of recovery, one that had the capacity to transcend the physical: "I had been an amateur to life. I guess that what I am saying is that my imagination took its beating too, you bet, and was finally humbled by the real, by its own awed sense of it, by the swarm of consequence."[42]

Now it was time for Stanley to get back to work. His heart had let him down, but it had bent, not broken. He'd play softball again, and he'd cheat on his smoking, diet, and drinking restrictions, just as he imagined he would in "Colin Kelly's Kids." And he'd never cease to be a smart guy and a satiric responder unwilling to suffer fools patiently. But that lament was in his heart, and before long it found its way into his fiction. As Stanley's health gave him more and more to complain about, he would realize and write that realization, that mortality puts us all in the same boat, and part of the writer's business is to show us how to stop some of the leaks, at least for a while.

ꙮ 7 ꙮ "Strange Displacements of the Ordinary"

Recovery and *The Dick Gibson Show,* 1968–70

> [T]here is no astrology, there's no black magic and no white, no ESP, no UFO's. Mars is uninhabited. The dead are dead and buried. [. . .] Your handwriting doesn't indicate your character and there is no God. All there is [. . .] are the strange displacements of the ordinary.
>
> —*The Dick Gibson Show*

Although he was laid up for only a few months after his heart attack, the world Elkin encountered during his recovery was transformed. Many cultural and political currents had been gathering force during the past four years, and the spring he spent in recovery saw two events that forever changed the United States. Civil rights leader Martin Luther King Jr. was assassinated in Memphis on April 4. Across the nation, protests, riots, and anxiety followed. Two months later, on June 5, presidential candidate Senator Robert F. Kennedy was murdered in Los Angeles, culminating a decade during which America reverted to a savage state, the politics of violence and assassination. Moreover, the impasse in Vietnam continued and compounded. About the time of Elkin's hospitalization, President Lyndon B. Johnson announced that he wouldn't seek reelection because of growing opposition to his conduct of the war. A bitter primary campaign between Senator Eugene McCarthy (D-Minn.) and Vice President Hubert Humphrey took shape as a referendum on the war. And the political landscape was itself changing as well. Resisting Democratic commitments to civil rights and opposition to the war, Alabama Governor George C. Wallace campaigned for the nomination, then, when frustrated in that bid, ran under the banner of the American Independent Party.

On the Republican side, former vice president (unsuccessful candidate for president in 1960 and California governor in 1962) Richard M. Nixon completed arguably the greatest political comeback in American history when he captured the nomination, asserting that his secret plan would resolve the impasse in Southeast Asia. Nixon's strategy transformed the Republican Party and laid the groundwork for the neoconservative takeover under Ronald Reagan, which in turn persisted for more than twenty-five years, reshaping America's political landscape once more. Recognizing the increasing rift between southern social conservatives and the national Democratic Party's commitment to civil rights, a war on poverty, and opposition to the war, Nixon wooed disaffected southerners to join the Republicans. The strategy worked brilliantly. Wallace siphoned off traditionally Democratic votes and several southern politicians followed Senator Strom Thurmond, who had switched parties in 1964. Nixon won the election, 301 electoral votes to Humphrey's 191 and Wallace's 46. Poet William Stafford wrote, "When they look back at our day and / ask their charts, they'll say / there never was such a time."[1]

The novel Elkin returned to after his health crisis, *The Dick Gibson Show*, ends with his most overt political allusion to date—Gibson's final caller on his "Night Letters" show is another Dick, "[t]he President of the United States. Dick, Bebe Rebozo [1912–98, Nixon's closest adviser] and I are terribly concerned about what's been going on in Vietnam...."[2] His novels and stories of the 1960s, however, hardly reflect the growing political and cultural turmoil that was swirling around him. Several early stories and the title work from *Criers and Kibitzers, Kibitzers and Criers* have as their settings the changing demographics of American cities, with the reshaping of commerce that involves. But reading *Boswell* and *A Bad Man*, one would hardly notice the political whirlwinds gathering throughout the decade. His closest friends recall Elkin as an observer rather than a participant in the political process. He did, however, receive a letter from editor Joe Fox in November 1968, apparently responding to Elkin's concern about the election: "Quite agree with you about the Nixon win." Near his life's end he and Norman Corwin commiserated on the "Contract with America," a 1994 movement that resulted in the neoconservative takeover of Congress: "Really, Norman, I haven't felt this bad since Nixon won his first term. I knew we were in for it. Now we're *really* in for it." For Stanley, however, politics was primarily a spectator sport. He wisecracked to Fox a year before Nixon's win, "I signed that War Tax Protest. When do they take me away? Will you still be my editor when I'm in jail? Do they have editors in jail? Do they have writers?"[3]

Marilyn and Steve Teitelbaum believe that if he actually voted (and both suspect that he occasionally did) he'd have been a liberal. Politically "he was probably interested in Nixon as fodder for his fiction, not as a political figure." Yet an event that shook many college campuses as the decade ended pulled Elkin as close to political action as anything ever did. In early May 1970, students at Kent State University in Ohio, and several campuses around the country, staged demonstrations against the recent U.S. invasion of Cambodia, an escalation of the Vietnam War. Many also protested the presence of the ROTC and the National Guard on campus. Tensions escalated until the morning of May 4, when Guardsmen opened fire on a crowd of students at Kent State, killing four and wounding nine. College campuses throughout the United States flared in protest, Washington University among them. Students occupied, and eventually burned, the ROTC building. Dick Hazelton of the English Department, who had led student radicals during the late 1960s, took part in the campus riot following Kent State; Dan Shea recalls Hazelton as "behind the anti-war demonstrators, but more political and angry." Stanley, Marilyn Teitelbaum and Joan believe, was intrigued by the behavior of Hazleton and student activist Howard Mechanic, jailed for throwing a cherry bomb at firefighters during the riot. George Pepe and he were present at demonstrations leading up to the conflagration; Stanley asked Pepe to "spectate." Both later testified on behalf of student activist Larry Kogis, subsequently convicted because of his part in the demonstration. Pepe believes, but can't confirm, that Elkin contributed to the Kogis defense fund.[4]

Stanley was fascinated by the drama of politics, and toward the end of his life he would write essays like "The First Amendment as Art Form" and "A Demo of Democrats" (unpublished, about the 1992 Democratic National convention). A confirmed atheist, he felt much the same way about religion. Like politics, religion could rile up the emotions of participants, and that passion produced a human drama that appealed to him as artist and social commentator. One spring morning between the time he got out of the hospital and the riots, he asked Pepe out for breakfast, as he often did. At the restaurant Stanley told George he wanted to visit the Shrine of Our Lady of the Snows, near Belleville, Illinois, a few miles east of St. Louis. When they arrived, Elkin was fascinated by the formal drive that takes visitors through the Stations of the Cross. A Roman Catholic, Pepe explained the symbolism and rituals to his friend, who was intrigued and far less sarcastic or mirthful than usual. When they arrived at the end of the drive, however, Stanley wanted to visit the bookstore to see if it stocked any of his books. Needless to say, it didn't.[5]

Bill Gass arrived at Washington University in 1969 and, with Howard Nemerov, provided Elkin two great literary friendships and role models, if from time to time competitors. A friend from the days at *Accent,* Gass apparently had some concerns about how his private life might be received in University City after a divorce. Stanley assured him, "What? Are you kidding? *Here?* In Fun City? Sin Town U.S.A.? No-oo. It's perfectly all right. Bring, bring. (Remember, though, I get to pin the 'A' on her breast, and I want dibs on your soul.)" He reassured Gass that "writers who preceded you have established precedents that you would be hard put to top," including a prominent homosexual poet "who once propositioned *me*" and one "who didn't" as well as a poet and novelist "who carried on!" Stanley looked forward to "laughter in the old house again" during the temporary appointment, which eventually led to a permanent one. And he insisted that Bill's turn to "get a Googy [Guggenheim]" had come: "After reading my letter of recommendation they might even give you to be held in perpetuity. They'll appoint you to the Fellowship the way men are appointed to the Supreme Court." During the coming decade, joint talks and readings by Gass and Elkin were among the most popular and eagerly anticipated events on the university calendar. The improvisation and interplay between the friends who were brilliant in far different ways sometimes threatened to outshine the readings, in which they from time to time read from each other's works.[6]

One adventure Gass recalls, however, sheds quite another light on his chum's attitudes toward readings. Shortly after Elkin's heart attack, Gass drove him to a reading at a private girls' school in St. Louis County. En route, Stanley groused about the small honorarium this event provided and grumbled that he didn't want to go. Bill reminded him that he'd made a commitment, and as they neared their destination Elkin chose his text from a typescript of his work-in-progress, *The Dick Gibson Show,* containing unusually ribald content, in which a respected druggist confesses to an unwholesome obsession with his female customers' secret parts. Gass was certain that he chose it deliberately to offend his hosts. If that was his motive, he succeeded memorably. The reception "was one of the worst hours I ever spent on the lecture circuit" with the hosts' response ranging between rage and embarrassment. Years later, Elkin had a similar adventure at a small Pennsylvania college. A surly student who met him at the airport told him he knew nothing about any reception and dropped him at the motel for the afternoon, where he had dinner alone. After he read to a sparse audience, his embarrassed faculty host confessed that he'd blown the budget on the honorarium, with nothing left for celebration. Back at his motel, Stanley charged food, beer, and liquor to the college, and invited fifteen or so people he met on the street to his impromptu celebration, much as Ben Flesh recruits guests for his Fred Astaire studio party in *The Franchiser.* On the way to the airport the next morning, he told the same surly student he was sorry the student missed a great party.[7]

By contrast, an event from these years shows a quite different side of Elkin's character, a warm, generous man behind the gruff exterior he liked to project to the world. After the 1968 Modern Language Association convention, Marvin Cohen inquired whether Elkin, whom he met at a conference party, might be able to suggest some reading venues in the St. Louis area. Cohen had told Elkin he'd love to teach creative writing but lacked the requisite degrees. He did, however, send a copy of his book. Instead of trying to find him a few readings, Elkin contacted the department chairs of five community colleges in the St. Louis area. On the verso of Cohen's January 1, 1969, letter, Elkin hand-drafted his response:

> I just spoke to Charles Dougherty [no relation to the author], the Chairman of the English dept. of the Univ. of Mo. at St. Louis (Normandy) about you.

The fact that you do not have a degree did not scare him off, and the fact that you have published a book at New Directions and that you will soon publish another led him on. He said that your chances to teach at the university as an instructor were "not impossible" but that you will probably have to wait until they lose an instructor [. . .] and that he will start looking around for a slot for you. Turnover, he tells me, is high. I would suggest that you get a vita together and perhaps a book to send him, and write him a letter reminding him of our conversation.

Nothing came of his effort and Cohen never interviewed for the job.[8] But the fact that Elkin made several calls and took an interest in Cohen's career suggests a generous professionalism quite at odds with the image Stanley usually presented to the world.

During 1969 Elkin accepted an appointment at the University of Wisconsin–Milwaukee as novelist-in-residence for the Summer Arts Festival. This in itself isn't unusual; he spent summers at a variety of institutions. And like Santa Barbara, Joan disliked Milwaukee; she took the children home to St. Louis before the engagement was complete. During that summer two important events took place, one of which became the basis for an important portion of the novel he was writing. After the family left, when he wasn't teaching or writing, he spent occasional evenings in Milwaukee bars, some of them biker joints. He recalls in an autobiographical essay nearly seventeen years later that "nursing a myocardial infarct already eighteen months old," it seemed to him as if all his colleagues drove motorcycles. "That summer I traveled in man's man circles on colleagues' long Leatherette bike backs, a sidekick sidesaddled as Roman wife." Upon returning to St. Louis he bought a Honda 175. In a story he was writing while he came to terms with his heart attack, about resuming his softball activities, he for the first time told his biker stories. Portions of that story were later included, with minor revisions and a shift to first person, in "The Mild One":

> (Though he rode it not very well. It was, indeed, the single thing he had ever *practiced*, having abandoned guitar lessons, given up typing, French, horseback riding, and the Australian crawl, grown impatient with every discipline save this.) Negotiating the simultaneous circuit between shifting and ground with his foot, accelerating and the release of the hand clutch. This he practiced, concentrated as a cryptographer, a scholar. [. . .] Thirty-nine years old and the only thing he had ever stuck with in his life. And still terrified, hugging the right hand margins of the streets and highways, his hands quite literally full. Why did he do it? The hard plastic helmet hid his bald spot and high-school girls waved at him in the park, but he never waved back, his hands too full with his bike's controls for that, feigning indifference, cool, suave, a girl in every port. [. . .] With them, he was cool, a different kind of rider.

As this recollection shows, he cut an amusing figure, an overweight academic tooling about the West End on a non-Harley. When he revised portions of "Baseball Story" as "The Mild One," he concluded humorously that his motorcycle was a classic symptom of male menopause, or compensation for the grim prospects of having rubbed noses with Death at age thirty-eight.[9] He kept the motorcycle until 1974; the odometer showed fewer than 1,300 miles when he sold it.

Another event from the summer of 1969 contributed a critical moment in *The Dick Gibson Show*. When he wasn't bumming rides on motorcycles, he listened to the radio, something he'd loved to do all his life, and he was at the time writing a novel about a radio personality. He'd long had a soft spot for call-in shows, and Gibson would eventually find "Night Letters" as his destined medium. In Milwaukee an irate caller telephoned to say his son had found an advertisement in a comic book, one that promised to instruct purchasers in methods of violence: "[H]ow to make bombs, how to become an assassin." Elkin became furious "that this kind of stuff could be available to kids in comic books."[10] As he brought *Gibson* toward its conclusion, he adapted this experience as Dick's last great paranoid gesture. A caller to "Night Letters" describes something very like what Elkin heard to Gibson, who, becoming once again disillusioned with his new format, finds in her story a chance to take an active, rather than a passive, role: "He made up his mind to kill the man responsible for the ad" (331). He launches an investigation to track down this source of evil, but as he's closing in, he realizes the quest is futile, that it "was too shabby—basement evil, the awry free enterprise of a madman. [. . .] How could he kill *him?* Nothing would change" (333) (these lines were, incidentally, added in Elkin's hand late in the editing process). Dick turns his information over to a frequent caller who's also a state's attorney.

For several years Martha Winston of Curtis Brown had represented Elkin to a variety of publishers, generally persuading them to meet his expectations for advances or payments greater than the publishers offered, and often, as in the case of *The Six-Year-Old Man* and the film contracts on *A Bad Man,* extricating him from situations he'd complicated by self-representation. She also nominated him for his first Bread Loaf position and advised against his leaving his university appointment and trying to make it as a writer, when others like director Philip Yordan were encouraging him to live by his pen, a fantasy that history conclusively shows would have been a disaster for Elkin. Had he remained the kind of writer he was, he and his family would have starved and he would have been forced eventually to compete for university jobs in a market that began to plummet shortly after he decided to stay at Washington University. On the other hand, savvy as he was, he could probably have made the necessary adjustments to sell more books, but that would, if successful, have dashed his hopes and expectations as a serious writer. Still, he was regularly disappointed by his sales, and in 1966 Winston contested his complaint that Random House didn't do enough to promote *Criers and Kibitzers, Kibitzers and Criers:* "I have no thought about your severing your connection with Random House." She argued that the publisher overspent the advertising budget, and that the results were good, as collections go. But as he approached his third novel, with a collection of novellas under contract, Elkin became convinced that he could continue to expect limited commercial success if he didn't do something dramatic. If he couldn't fire his publisher, he decided to fire his agent. Winston's reply of March 1969 suggests the personal as well as professional sorrow this caused: "Now that the personal hurt has simmered down to a dull ache, I must take a hard business-like look at the unhappy situation." She asked Elkin to study the contract for *A Bad Man* and clarify his position on the rights and responsibilities of Curtis Brown in ongoing negotiations, including the film contract. Elkin's penciled draft of a response on her letter suggests considerable animosity: "If you insisted on enforcing it you will be forcing my new agent to take action" and "be in touch with B"—Georges Borchardt, the New York agency that represented and advised him for the rest of his life. Winston's personal heartbreak was a harbinger of things to come, as Elkin frequently changed publishers and editors in search of an ideal combination of sales and aesthetic integrity, much as Gibson moves from radio station to station searching for his ideal format. A month later she wrote, "I still can't believe that this has happened. Stanley, the door is always open here if at any time you want to come home." But he never did. He frequently mentioned Winston fondly, but he never looked back.[11]

Before the heart attack he was making progress with a project that would take his literary reputation to an even higher level, one that skillfully combined communication theory with metafictional techniques. Elkin told an interviewer in 1975 that the inspiration for *The Dick Gibson Show* occurred while he was in the army, traveling from Fort Lee, Virginia, to New York in either 1956 or 1957. During a stop at a New Jersey Turnpike rest area, Elkin fiddled with the dial until he chanced upon a distinctive voice he was never able to identify. He was, however, intuitively certain that the announcer wasn't from a major market, but he was "very professional, very good, and there was something essentially so lonely" about his voice and his manner. At that point PFC Elkin began to muse upon the ways in which radio personalities were forming a new class of American celebrity and upon the connections among members of the audience listening to the program, as well as the needs these connections serve. This announcer sounded lonely, and "we were invisible and yet his voice was a link between all of us."[12] This experience simmered for nearly a decade before he began work on the novel.

He first mentioned this book in a 1967 response to a Rockefeller Foundation query concerning an eventually successful grant application: "I have only just begun the new novel. I call it *The Dick Gibson Show*, and it is, as I told you last year, about a radio announcer. The fellow had worked in all areas of radio, but at the time of the novel has his own program, a late night 'telephone' show on a powerful clear channel station in the midwest. The novel seems to me to be proceeding well." By August that year a City College of New York professor arranged for Elkin to read from "The Buck Gibson Show" as well as to present a lecture, "Art and Reality." On the next evening he was scheduled to read at the Hackensack YMHA and the professor expressed some reservations about the suitability of "Buck Gibson" for that audience.[13] We can infer that by August the project was well under way, for little in the first series of episodes, Dick's adventures at the Nebraska station KROP, would offend any but the most prudish auditors. On the other hand, the story of Marshall Maine's (the pseudonym Gibson used at the time) bus ride toward Pittsburgh after his Nebraska meltdown, and his erotic encounter, including repeated mutual masturbation, with Miriam Desebour might not play terribly well before an audience organized around traditional religion or ethics.

In November 1967 Gordon Lish congratulated his old friend because "your next protagonist shares in what I know to be the Only Truth: Radio announcing. For six years I was happy as such" while warning him that Ken Kesey was also planning a novel about a disk jockey. By then Elkin had two excerpts ready for *The Saturday Evening Post*. The magazine agreed to run "The Apprenticeship of Brothers" (the KROP episode) subject to Elkin's writing a brief introduction in February 1968, but the *Post* unexpectedly folded. Eventually "Apprenticeship" appeared in the pioneer edition of *Works in Progress* in January 1969, after being turned down by *Playboy, North American Review,* and *Harper's.* In late December he sent a typescript to his Random House editor, Joe Fox, and received the following telegram: "DICK GIBSON MAGNIFICENT STOP CONGRATU-LATIONS AND ADMIRATION," promising a less contentious editor-novelist relationship than what actually occurred. While the editing process went forward, portions of the controversial Hartford broadcast, "The Pharmacist's Tale" (Bernie Perk's narrative, the serial title acknowledging the influence of *The Canterbury Tales* on this entire section) and "The Memory Expert" (Pepper Streep's story) were offered to *Esquire,* where the fiction editor was Elkin's friend Rust Hills. *Esquire* ran "The Memory Expert," but Hills was outvoted on "The Pharmacist's Tale," presumably because it *is* risqué. *Playboy, New American Review, Harper's, Modern Occasions,* and *Locations* subsequently refused it.[14] In one of life's little ironies, the episode was eventually selected by Mordecai Richler for *The Best of Modern Humor* (1983). "The Dodo Bird" (a portion of the Mauritius episode) appeared in *Iowa Review* in 1970.

Fox, his copy editor, and Elkin wrangled throughout the editing process about the rhetorical opulence of the typescript, with the author resisting almost every effort to prune his prose. Fox mused, "[T]he sum effect of the novel is less than the whole of its parts; that is, individual scene after individual scene is absolutely brilliant, but when put together, no matter how skillfully, the overall effect is not as powerful as it could be." He was confident that this could be fixed through judicious cutting. Fox and the copy editor consistently urged restraint and substantial cuts, but Elkin usually insisted on retaining his original text. For example, both urged trimming, if not eliminating, Gibson's rhapsody on the relation of personality to place when he arrives in Mauritius: "Then something that has always been undeveloped in me—I mean my sense of place—suddenly surged up and overwhelmed me. Why, here I am, he thought, on Mauritius, one of three or four places on the globe which merely to have seen qualifies a man as a traveler, I mean a wanderer, one of those whose fate is to be troubled by laundry, mail months old, irregular bowel movements, a certain ignorance about time and a taste gone crotchety through nostalgia for things eaten long before. How did I get this way? I wondered." Maintaining that "less is more," Fox struck out the entire paragraph, much more than can be quoted here. No linguistic theory could be more alien to Elkin's practice and beliefs; he boasted of battling Fox about *Gibson:* "I had to fight him tooth and nail in the better restaurants to maintain excess because I don't believe that less is more. I believe that *more* is more. I believe that less is less, fat fat, thin thin, and enough is enough." Elkin testily penciled on the verso of the copyedited typescript, "you *can't* cut this. It's really as good as I get. It means that travel is no accident but the specific fate of a particular man, something I genuinely believe is true. Dick is encouraging himself here, too—this is the important thing—in the notion of his specialness, his view that he stands up (and out) in the landscape. (Hence deserts, seas, places where a man makes a mark). Please don't cut anything here. It's too good."[15] And Fox gave in. Despite his misgivings about the rhetorical abundance and the lack of verisimilitude in certain episodes, he usually deferred to Elkin's wishes and vigorously championed the novel as artistically profound and commercially viable, promising a solid return on the advance of $20,000 against royalties at 15 percent. Recalling Elkin's disappointment over *Bad Man* sales, and his blaming what he perceived as a lukewarm publicity campaign on the publisher's part, Fox wrote prophetically, "If we can't put you over the top on this one (and by over the top I suppose I mean a good hardcover sale, a good reprint sale, and superb reviews), then I would not blame you (and I'm speaking now both as friend and editor) for going elsewhere."[16]

In order to recover its substantial investment in *Gibson,* Random House designed an aggressive publicity campaign with a budget of $5,000, engineered to bring the novel to the head of the spring 1971 list. Fox asked Elkin to provide a list of all the campuses on which he'd read excerpts from *Gibson* in order to target those markets. He supplied the names of twenty-two colleges and universities, including Trinity College, Dublin University, and Leeds University in England. Throughout this process, Fox consistently assuaged Elkin's growing concern that it would prove to be yet another critical, but not popular, success. While it was in production, however, ominous signs appeared on the horizon. Random House offered options on the paperback edition to a dozen companies, five of which declined to bid, and others put off follow-up calls. Only Pocket Books made an offer, 80 percent of the $10,000 Fox hoped to get. Moreover, Random House sent copies for prepublication quotations to an impressive list of celebrities in the literary and entertainment world, including news and television personalities David Brinkley, Dick Cavett, David Frost, Chet Huntley, and Garry Moore; film directors Mike Nichols and Billy Wilder; and novelists John Barth, Kurt Vonnegut, and Philip Roth, who replied, "I'll try to get to Elkin's book soon; I do remember how generous he was about WSWG [*When She Was Good*] and I'll try to return that kindness." As late as December 1, 1970, however, Fox, having received "no word from anybody" except Gass, was both annoyed and worried: "None of the bastards has seen fit to say a word." Gass's blurb was a rave:

> Stanley Elkin established himself as a major American writer with *A Bad Man*. *The Dick Gibson Show* is, if anything, even more impressive. It is funny in the pure surreal way of the early silent comedies, yet it has enormous satirical and symbolic power as well. We are all on Dick Gibson's show—being interviewed, or phoning in—giving ourselves away. We are all "on the air." For anyone who loves language, this book is a feast. Composed with enormous skill and passion, its subject is creation and communication itself, and all the old and new excitements of "tuning in." The next novel to equal it will have to be written by Elkin himself.

For reasons lost to posterity, this comment didn't appear on the first edition jacket. It was featured, with excerpts from several reviews, in the full-column advertisements Random House bought. To compound the publicity problems further, *Time* magazine judged a teaser advertisement unacceptable because it mentioned the names of some of the nine radio personalities to whom the novel is dedicated without securing their permission (the "tenth" is "Joan Elkin: WIFE"). Finally, a company Random House hired to send bound review copies to out-of-town newspapers and magazines botched the assignment, then lied about it; therefore, the novel didn't arrive in the hands of the book page editors until within a week of the publication date, much too late for assigning, then receiving, reviews that might boost sales.[17]

With all these disappointments and foul-ups in the production, it was hardly a surprise, but nonetheless an annoyance, that the novel fell considerably short of sales projections. Although in December Fox persuaded Random House to increase the original printing from 8,500 to 12,500 copies, sales didn't follow.

As had been the case with *A Bad Man,* Elkin was once again a critical, but not a commercial, success, and *Gibson* was nominated for the 1972 National Book Award against formidable competition. Losing to a writer eight years dead rubbed salt in the wounded ego; Flannery O'Connor's *The Complete Stories* edged out a strong field, including E. L. Doctorow's *The Book of Daniel,* Walker Percy's *Love in the Ruins,* John Updike's *Rabbit Redux,* and Cynthia Ozick's *The Pagan Rabbi and Other Stories.*

As had been true of *A Bad Man,* reviews were predominately, but not universally, favorable; many were enthusiastic: Joseph McElroy announced that *Gibson* was Elkin's "best, a funny, melancholy, frightening, scabrous, absolutely American compendium that may turn out to be our classic about radio." R. Z. Sheppard predicted its place in "American folklore. As Dick Gibson, the paradox of his truest identity is that he is from Nowhere, U.S.A." By contrast, Christopher Lehman-Haupt complained that Elkin failed to integrate individual stories with the overall plot: a "stand-up, sit-down, and write-it-out comic." Lehman-Haupt wryly recalled that when he heard about the work-in-progress, he thought, "He can't miss this time. But I'm afraid he can." It took some clever excerpting to spin this as part of the ad campaign, but Random House managed to do so. And W. H. Pritchard groused in the *Hudson Review* with heavy-handed irony that one of "our leading sophisticates in this mode for years has been Stanley Elkin, who reaches something like mellow maturity in his latest effort. [. . .] The novel is frankly advertised as 'very dirty' but also as 'very funny,' which I can assure you it is not."[18] Elkin chafed yet once more about cementing his reputation as a critical success/popular failure. Perhaps the most meaningful comment came in the form of a 1971 letter from John Irving, who advised that Elkin become more "promotional," especially on late-night television, because *Gibson* "is a natural for talk shows on radio. I could have you all across the country. [It's] a pity, that lack of promo for such a good outrageous sharp book." Irving concludes in Chaucerian parody, "Stannystan, we are not so far apart I lern from your booke. Nobody understands the humor and illogical leaps of Chicago people, the whimsy, *lugubrious,* chivalry, rabid rationalizations, forced conscience, impatience, piteousness, pietic inventions, brutal *blaques,* boisterboosterisms, bathetic dips, the sexual Voice, as well as those chained to it."[19]

The *Gibson* saga, moreover, was far from over. Inquiries concerning film rights arrived quickly. James Lupton asked about writing a screenplay in April 1971; two years later Andrew Adleson of Jerry Shore Productions offered $1,000 for a one-year option, inquiring whether Elkin would be interested in doing the screenplay. Arthur Karp sought permission to produce an adaptation off-Broadway, but Borchardt advised against this deal because Karp's lawyer insisted on a very complex formula for subsidiary rights, and the off-Broadway earning potential was too miniscule to compromise possible future rights.[20] In 1978 Frank Galati, who specialized in adapting fiction to the stage, developed a student production of the Hartford episode as *The Dick Gibson Show* at Northwestern University. Upon learning that Elkin was reading in Chicago, and with considerable trepidation, Galati invited him to a rehearsal, and after that went well, to opening night. Despite the fact that, in the interest of brevity and possibly as a concession to public morality, Galati omitted the most outrageous monologue of the section, pharmacist Bernie Perk's confession, Elkin was delighted with the production. Soon Galati, actor John Mohrlein (Dr. Behr-Bleibtreau), lighting designer Geoffrey Bushor, and set designer Mary Griswold decided to take the show downtown, if off the Loop. They formed Novel Ventures, a production company whose debut, *The Dick Gibson Show*, opened October 15, 1979, to considerable local fanfare, including a radio interview with Studs Terkel. The Chicago-reared Elkin attended an early performance, and the production was a huge critical success in the Ruth Page Auditorium. It wasn't, however, profitable. Novel Ventures took it to St. Louis for performances at Washington University's Edison Theater in January 1980. There it played to packed houses for about half a dozen performances, and after the final one, a Super Bowl Sunday matinee, Elkin gave Mohrlein a huge salami (Behr-Bleibtreau in the adaptation grabbed one from Vendler's deli tray and brandished it to bully the other panel members) more than three feet long: "[W]e ate the whole damned thing after the show, watching the Super Bowl with Stanley and some of the Washington University crowd."[21]

During the late 1970s Galati and Elkin collaborated on another dramatic adaptation of the Hartford episode, this one suitable for larger theater or film production. Ray Wagner and Maurice Singer pitched it to several studios and although they got nibbles, the project didn't get beyond the talking stage. Again, in 1989, Evanston-based Charles A. Lippitz Productions very nearly resurrected the project as a film. His company paid $10,000 for an option, and by October 1991 they were moving toward an agreement with Novel Ventures on the script. Galati, having been nominated for an Academy Award for the screenplay for *The Accidental Tourist*, was very much in demand and couldn't commit to directing the film before 1994. With his blessing Lippitz sought another director, and he had indications of interest from actors Jeff Daniels and Joan Cusack. Mohrlein, who had played Behr-Bleibtreau in the Northwestern production, had committed to reprising that role and actively promoted the venture. By January 1993, Galati agreed to serve as executive producer and Peter Amster undertook a new film script. Elkin agreed to all these changes, and clippings circulated in the Chicago papers about the local filming of an all-Chicago production. Lippitz renewed his option in July 1994, paying $7,500, predicated on the understanding that this would have to be a small-budget film rather than a mass-market venture. Acknowledging that Elkin was by 1994 a niche-audience writer with a devoted following, Lippitz concluded after discussing the matter with several studio executives that it would do best at film festivals like Cannes and Sundance. He convinced Elkin that they would need to keep the production budget under $200,000, so that the Screen Actors Guild would permit actors to perform for lower fees. Although filming was scheduled to begin in July 1994, the production never got off the ground. Mohrlein believes the economic uncertainty of the early 1990s caused the production to go under: "[I]nvestors ran scared."[22]

While *Gibson* the novel was in preparation, Elkin, while not motorcycling, was working on two baseball stories related to his recovery process, and by the end of the decade he had refined the original to "Colin Kelly's Kids," a publishable story about softball as a form of recovery therapy and male bonding. It remained unpublished until 2006 because Elkin abandoned them to set off on a venture, arguably the one most suited to his peculiar talents, adapting the novella form that Henry James (whose ghost he invoked as a mentor more often than anyone except Gass, Bellow, and Faulkner) called "that blessèd form." He was also involved in an anthology project that was going to prove very controversial.

He was well enough established by the end of the decade to be offered a contract by Doubleday to edit *Stories from the Sixties.* Immediately Borchardt was concerned that Elkin, again negotiating on his own, had undersold himself. He labeled Doubleday's "a pretty poor offer" and vowed to improve it. Before long, however, the amount he'd be paid would be the least of Elkin's problems. He was originally hired to coedit the anthology with Herbert Gold, who pulled out. Lisa Johnson took over the project, and she was immediately troubled about the selections Elkin had made and the agreements into which he'd entered on Doubleday's behalf. Indirectly accusing him of cronyism, she complained about the writers he planned to include and even more about those he didn't, reminding him that the target market was college course adoptions. Doubleday wanted a collection "that would present a theory about the kind or kinds of fiction most representative of the '60s." Johnson feared that the writers Elkin had selected weren't really representative, except for Gass, Updike, Bellow, and Barth. She lamented the absence of African American writers, asking Elkin to reconsider works by LeRoi Jones, Ishmael Reed, and others. Moreover, she regretted the neglect of the black humorists and suggested that he include works by writers like Donald Barthelme, Kurt Vonnegut Jr., and J. P. Donleavy. Finally, she was mystified by the omission of Bernard Malamud; her perplexity seems justified, in that Malamud's *The Magic Barrel* won the 1959 National Book Award, and he published *Idiots First* in 1963; moreover, many of the stories in *Rembrandt's Hat* appeared in magazines before the close of the decade. Within weeks, Borchardt persuaded Doubleday that they had an obligation to abide by Elkin's choices and the publisher accepted both his selections and his preface. Later, there was minor trouble over "Love in the Winter" by Dan Curley, one of Elkin's mentors at Illinois and *Accent,* because of a permissions squabble. The implicit charge of cronyism is a serious matter, and the collection does contain stories by close Elkin friends like Al Lebowitz and Curley who were not widely read during the decade, as well as Bellow, Coover, and Gass, who were. Well-established writers whose works appear include Flannery O'Connor, Peter Taylor, and Tillie Olsen. All the deserving writers Johnson mentions, as well as Roth, Thomas Pynchon, and Eudora Welty, are omitted. In his preface Elkin scrupulously avoids explaining his principles of selection, with this exception: "Hopefully, the stories reprinted here are not stories of the sixties, though they were written back in those days."[23] He means simply that there's more to the representative stories of the decade than popularity or the reputation of the writer—a position anthologists almost universally proclaim. But the publisher's stated desire for representative stories casts some doubt on the degree to which Elkin conformed with the spirit, if not the letter, of his publisher's intention. He would, however, be asked to edit another decade anthology in 1980, and that one would be far less controversial.

That he was invited to edit the anthology, and that he was able to withstand the publisher's challenges about his selections, indicates the degree to which he had achieved his dream, becoming a recognized and respected writer. During the new decade's early months, he became involved in another strange project. Friends from *Tri-Quarterly* asked him to contribute to a Vladimir Nabokov special issue. But Elkin didn't know much about Nabokov, having never met the man; he could recall in 1989 having read only three of his novels, which he admired very much. When Charley Newman asked for a critical piece, Elkin told him, "I don't do that kind of writing." So, wanting to pay tribute to an important writer and to help out his friend, Elkin proposed a "comic memoir."[24] The resulting text, "Three Meetings," is a crossover between fiction and the familiar essay. It may well be the first manifestation of the imprimatur he was eventually to place on that long-dormant genre. He tips the reader to the fact that the "memoir" is pure fiction in several ways—most obviously that he describes two, not three meetings. Someone familiar with Elkin's life story will note the incongruity of the dates and places. The first meeting took place in 1941, when the narrator was "curator" of a highway zoo, and discovered when Nabokov visited it that they shared an interest in butterflies. Elkin was eleven in 1941, in a Chicago elementary school. And Elkin had never been in Venezuela (he toured that country in 1978), where "I" accompanied Nabokov on a hunt for a rare species, the Great Bull Butterfly—the name is a deadpan giveaway. On the Orinoco, the master utters one of Elkin's worst-ever puns: Nabokov's legendary interest in butterflies was due to their being a "metaphormorphosis." Finally, he parodies the tendency of Russian novels (from which country Nabokov emigrated to Germany, years before arriving in the United States) to use multiple names for the same character. Nabokov encourages the narrator to call him Dmitri and Vladi, both variations on the Russian's name, and "Boko," "Bozo," "Uncle Volodya," "Uncle," and "Steve."

Steve? Exactly what point all this serves is never clear, except for the fun. It tells us little about Nabokov or his work, except to remind us that he was an accomplished lepidopterist, which is hardly earthshaking news. The memoir includes some commentary on the changes that accompanied the interstate highway system during the 1960s and after, a theme that would become central to *The Franchiser,* but this is merely backstory here. Elkin's point is the fun of telling a story that foregrounds his own invention and rhetoric. This would happen soon again, with embarrassing consequences, when he visited London in 1971.

By the new decade's beginning, then, he had three novels and an important collection of stories to his credit; and he'd settled his dilemma of how to support himself and his family. While contentious negotiations with the university would flare up during the 1970s, he'd made his decision to remain in academia and deal with the adjustments this would involve. He'd won several awards, and *Gibson* got him very close to his first major competitive recognition. He'd taken his first fling at film scripts, and all his novels, as well as many of his stories, were under options for film production. And he'd initiated his avocation as a writer of familiar essays with one on Elizabeth Taylor and the failed (and, sadly, apparently forever lost) one on the Beatles, as well as the Nabokov spoof. On the more personal level he'd purchased the home in which he would remain for the rest of his life. His "Wall of Fame," a series of second-story bookcases devoted to his work, was rapidly being populated by translations of his work into French, German, and Japanese. He was constantly in demand as a speaker and lecturer, and his close friendships with Nemerov and Gass, both of whom lived nearby, would be crucial to his happiness as the 1970s began. And he'd survived his first great health crisis. Indeed, the 1970s looked like a very promising decade for Mr. Stanley Elkin.

8 "Blessèd Form"
Novellas, a Sabbatical Year Abroad,
and a Death Sentence, 1971–73

I don't like worrying, "Is anybody out there reading? Do they
know my name? Will they spell it right?" I'm tired of being
absorbed with myself.

—Elkin to interviewer Don Cricklaw, 1972

Despite Elkin's and many of his friends' concerns over the direction in which the country was heading under the Nixon presidency, his family was prospering in St. Louis, where a stimulating social life continued to evolve around his university affiliation and the broader literary community. Bernard recalls that when he was a child, his father enjoyed walking the quarter mile to school, then returning in mid-afternoon with Howard Nemerov, who often used the tall gray house as a watering hole on *his* way home. There was a lively mix of university politics, serious discussions, and gossip among several friends, especially Nemerov, during these pleasant afternoons. Stanley was always fascinated with the stories people were willing to tell, and sometimes even more with the ones they weren't. Nemerov also enjoyed a new pop culture phenomenon, *Monday Night Football*, which launched on ABC television in 1970. He insisted that George Pepe come to his house during the games because Stanley liked to be among the guys, but he wasn't all that interested in football. He held forth, often vociferously and loudly, on whatever subject occurred to him at the moment. But Nemerov hated distractions during the game, which he watched slumped forward and intensely taciturn. He told Pepe, "You've got to come to *Monday Night Football* to keep Stanley occupied." From time to time Stanley got caught up in the game, as he did occasionally with baseball during the World Series, but these, like the softball games of his pre–myocardial infarction days, were mainly opportunities to hang out and kibitz with his pals.[1]

While recovering from his heart attack, Elkin worked on two sketches, "Baseball Story" and "Colin Kelly's Kids." Perhaps because the material was overtly autobiographical, he felt that they were going nowhere. In New York he explained his writer's block to Joe Fox, who told him a story that changed Elkin's artistic life, and eventually added a legend to the Elkin saga:

He told me an anecdote about a friend of his who owns a gambling casino in London, and who had been mauled by a bear. [. . .] He had gone out to inspect the animals one evening, and put one of the animals, a bear, in a cage because she was in estrus and dangerous. [. . .] Well, he miscalculated, and got into the cage with the bear. The bear was still in estrus, and even though he had raised her since cubhood, the bear was about to kill him. It was only with the help of his wife and other people on the estate, who managed to distract the bear by poking poles at it, that he was able to escape with his life. It occurred to me as I was listening to this story, "My God, what I'm being told is not in itself a story, but *if* the man had to fuck the bear in order to save his life, *that* would be a story."[2]

He now had the story that would add a dimension to his career, because he discovered a new form to explore and develop: "I didn't think this was an idea for a novel, but it didn't seem like a short story, either. So I did it as a novella, and then after I wrote it, I thought, 'I want to write a book of novellas.' I like the length. It seems more important than a short story, and more manageable than a novel." This genre lent itself uniquely to Elkin's talents. He felt constrained by the "read-at-one-sitting" convention established for short stories by Edgar Allan Poe in "The Philosophy of Composition"; his early stories were often rejected on the basis of length, and he resisted editors' requests that he trim others to meet magazine guidelines. On the other hand, his predilection for flights of rhetoric, although the special appeal of his fiction for many fellow writers and other devotees, can be off-putting for novel readers who want the plot and characterization to move at a livelier pace, with less foregrounding of verbal pyrotechnics. Some readers may find that the demands of Elkin's intricate plots, often interconnected in less than obvious ways (but always interconnected), compounded by the rhetorical fireworks, render a novel intimidating. But a novella, with leisure for intricate plots, nuanced storytelling, and verbal display, seems perfectly suited to Elkin's gifts. Among the nine novellas he published, seven are masterworks of the genre. The only problem was, collections of novellas usually don't sell as well as novels do.

He set to work immediately after retuning from New York, developing "The Making of Ashenden" while wrapping up his teaching obligations and preparing to move the family to London, where they'd spend the 1971–72 academic year. When he began this project, he deliberately moved in two directions, an experiment in form and a totally original plot concept. "The Making of Ashenden" is a literary hybrid, part drawing room comedy laced with satire in the Henry James tradition, and part smoking car story and lurid beast fable. And it's James, a master of the novella, whose literary ghost oddly lingers in the shadows of "Ashenden." When Elkin introduces his hero, readers will recognize a cross-gendered version of the James heroine, say Daisy Miller, Maggie Verver, or Milly Theale—cultivated, smart, virtuous, philanthropic, naïve, and incredibly rich. Having been reared on a theme of noblesse oblige, Ashenden resolves that he has a duty to the family's future, so he embarks on a quest for a suitable lovemate with whom to spend his life, practice charity, and sire virtuous little Ashendens. Upon finding her, he intuits that she's mortally ill, which adds to the sentimental allure. By now the novel has morphed away from the James naïf encountering a vicious world and resembles nothing so much as the sentimental romances ("nurse novels") Elkin included in his "theory of the novel" classes. The sentimentality goes over the top when his beloved insists that he recover his virginity—apparently his virtue had some limits. Ashenden's preposterous quest leads him into scenes from famous paintings: "I am in art," he says more than once. The final setting is Edward Hicks's "The Peaceable Kingdom," a sentimentalization of colonial America as a new Eden. But Elkin's kingdom isn't exactly peaceable. In a brief but unforgettable climactic episode, a Kamchatka bear in estrus accosts Ashenden and he discovers that there's only one way out of this painting-forest. While he satisfies the bear, described in lurid, graphic imagery, Ashenden undergoes a transformation and alters his worldview. He ends the ordeal, and the story, a citizen of the wild.

Elkin never intended the abrupt shift to this extraordinarily salty story to surprise the reader. While revising, he told a student interviewer he feared that "I might have a great deal of difficulty in publishing it because of its length and because it is, as you say, filthy, although it's only filthy for the last 20 pages. [. . .]" The holograph title was "Fucking a Bear," so the final scene would hardly be a surprise; by the time he submitted the typescript, the title had changed to reflect the euphemism adolescents often use to describe having intimate relations with someone. But Elkin's pun added a dimension, for a new Ashenden is created, or made, from his encounter. Georges Borchardt replied that the story seemed "a little leisurely" and that, combined with the final scene, probably would scare off *Esquire,* where he hoped to send it. He also took the liberty to correct a few minor errors in Elkin's French, but the "English is excellent!"[3]

As author and agent feared, publishing "Ashenden" presented challenges. The culture was changing rapidly after the turbulent 1960s, and sexual explicitness was increasingly accepted in films and fiction. With nude casts and risqué themes, *Hair* premiered in New York in 1967 and *Oh! Calcutta* debuted off-Broadway two years later. The mild sexuality of *The Graduate* (1967) had already been eclipsed by European films like *Blow-Up* (1966); *A Clockwork Orange* (1971) mixed sexuality, sadism, and drug culture graphically. Anthony Burgess's novel on which that film was based had represented sadistic and brutal sex back in 1962 and Philip Roth's *Portnoy's Complaint* (1969) contained chapters entitled "Whacking Off" and "Cunt Crazy." The movie version came out in 1972. Although a lot was happening, America wasn't ready for bestiality. Gordon Lish at *Esquire,* aware of Elkin's distaste for editorial cuts, concluded, "I suppose it would be an outrage to suggest changes." But "barring changes, there is no way to proceed here." So Borchardt tried *New American Review*, which rejected it, then *Dutton Review*, where Jerome Charyn persuaded the staff to accept it. By mid-March, however, the staff had reconsidered and demanded extensive cutting; Borchardt and Charyn agreed that deep cuts wouldn't sit well with Elkin, so on it went to *Salamagundi*, then to *Tri-Quarterly*, which in July agreed to publish it as submitted.[4] It was collected as the second, although first composed, story in *Searches and Seizures* and would appear once more in the crossover anthology *Stanley Elkin's Greatest Hits*. The next year in London it contributed unforgettably to the Elkin legend.

By the end of August the family had moved to London for a year abroad that would change Stanley's life. He and Joan looked forward to returning to the city they'd visited a decade before during the final leg of the "Zelda Elkin grant." Supported in part by a sabbatical year at half-pay and an American Council of Learned Societies grant to complete the collection, they settled in a tiny flat in Putney, but were far from pleased with their accommodations. In November he complained to Nemerov, "Talk about squalid, talk about pastey, talk about grunge. My back's against the wall. [. . .] I keep waiting for someone to offer me a blindfold, I'd eat it. I'd smoke it. I'd fly it. I have learned from this here experience—I'm quick. I told Joan when we got off the ship that I was a goner anyway & that she should go on without me—that of all the emotions patriotism is the soundest. By God, sir, a man should venture no further than he can spit. They should hobble you at birth for your own good. Sources say that England is part of this galaxy. They lie." Nemerov taped a copy to the English Department mailbox and Naomi Lebowitz wrote that everyone was "in stitches over Stanley's letters." Shortly after his return Elkin reiterated his distaste for England, saying he never realized how much he liked St. Louis until he spent the year in London. He enjoyed the stimulating company of artists, writers, and intellectuals, and celebrated the social whirl this year afforded; his resentment was primarily directed at domestic accommodations and British snobbery. He groused about the tiny dwelling, "where one would ordinarily put a lawnmower or a rubber tire," and this, when he returned to his spacious Parkview home, which he had leased for one-third the rent of the tiny London flat, cast a pall on the London adventure.[5]

The most outrageous event of Elkin's professional life happened during this sabbatical. It involved, not surprisingly, "The Making of Ashenden" and for most of the decade versions of the story circulated widely among the literary community, earning near-legendary status. Elkin told one variation to interviewer Doris Bargen, and Jim Ballowe heard another from Robert Coover. Fox and Borchardt, among others, wrote about hearing the story told with approval while it was making the rounds. And Tim O'Grady from *Tri-Quarterly* offered to arrange for Charley Newman to wear "monk's robes" if Elkin would promise a reading like the one in Kent: "The bear visit this summer is being retold in bizarre places; the most recent occurrence being a lady from Atlantic Monthly Press." Coover published his recollection in 2006, the year we spoke, and because he was involved in the planning and was there, I will rely primarily on his accounts, noting minute discrepancies with other versions and quoting choice parcels from Elkin's own.

At a party in Putney early in 1972, Elkin mentioned that he'd welcome an opportunity to read his new novella in its entirety to test a live audience's response. A friend of Coover's arranged a public event in the Great Hall of Allington Castle, built for Anne Boleyn, one of King Henry VIII's unfortunate spouses, but could only come up with an honorarium of twenty-five pounds. Coover, aware of Elkin's competitiveness, advised him to say, "I gave a reading and you paid me £10. That worked." So the university rented the hall and the Carmelite monks—the castle had long since been a monastery—agreed to serve snacks and wine. A few days before the event, Coover prophetically quipped, "The whole of Kent is looking forward to your reading. Rumors of a vice squad raid on the monastery, etc." Coover's friend chartered a bus to drive his students from Canterbury. Some of their neighbors and friends made the trip, as did several of the Elkins' friends from London. A substantial, receptive audience was in place, and the reading went on for more than an hour. The Carmelites, pleased with the Henry James/sentimental novel portions of the story, had prepared wine, American pizza, and a hot potato for each guest, but the food was cooling and the reading wasn't over. So they began discreetly to serve the guests while Elkin approached the bear scene, and shortly before he reached the climax, a group on religious retreat at the monastery returned from their devotions and decided to observe the important literary event taking place in the Great Hall. The London and Kent crowds were "rolling about in our dropped potatoes," the Canterbury students were joining in the hilarity, and the folks on retreat were "frozen where they sat." The monks? Coover "glanced at the glass-windowed kitchen door and saw the pallid wide-eyed face of a horrified monk literally slide down behind the wooden paneling."[6]

The aftermath, according to Coover, "was somewhat cruel." The outraged monks indignantly refused to accept the agreed-upon payment for refreshments, saying it was the "tainted lucre of Satan." Elkin told Gordon Burnside, "I was a *Judas,* they said. We slunk away, having an overdone but free supper." A prior absurdly confronted Elkin, saying, "[I]f you're an example of what an American capitalist is like, it's a good thing we don't have them over here." And a teenager from the retreat asked him why he wrote that story. When he gave her a thematic explanation, she interrupted, "No, you wrote that story because you're the Anti-Christ." Some of her fellow retreat-goers chimed in, "That's right, that's right, he's the Anti-Christ." Nemerov later quipped, "I've been trying to imagine you as antichrist, but can't quite make it." Coover recalls a wild party immediately after—not, however, in the castle.[7]

Thus "Ashenden" found its way into literary folklore, but its story was far from complete. Shortly after *Searches and Seizures* came out in 1973, Elkin's agent received a call from Random House to the effect that *Gallery*, a pornographic magazine that "imitates *Playboy*," sought serial rights on "Ashenden," at $400 per installment. But the only part *Gallery* really wanted was, predictably, the bestiality scene and the deal fell through. Much more surprising is the fact that in 1990 Elkin received $1,500 for rights to a stage version written, produced, and directed by Larry Sloan (1959–95). The script was apparently faithful to the original; Sloan wrote in August, "Last part was the hardest, as you can imagine (no pun intended)." And *Ashenden* was actually performed as part of a Remains Theatre program called *Changing Nightly* that ran for twenty-one shows.[8] But it wasn't well received in the local press, and the tone of the comments suggests that these reviewers had done their homework. The *Sun-Times* reviewer commented, "[W]hat is, in print, a stunningly powerful metaphysical sexual act, turns into a crude burlesque when realized on the stage." Only the *Southtown Economist* was enthusiastic. That reviewer felt that it was by far the best of the three plays on the bill and praised "Sloan's smart transcription and direction of Elkin's hilarious, densely written fable." Elkin's friend Charles Gold saw the performance and told him the bear scene was the best thing about it, that the bear's orgasm was every bit as good as that of Meg Ryan's character in the memorable scene from *When Harry Met Sally* (1989).[9]

The Kent reading was a spectacular event, and the Elkins enjoyed a full social calendar during the London year. They hosted a variety of friends from America, England, and the continent, including the Lebowitzes, who recall a "fine party" in Putney that included John Gardner, Iris Murdoch, and Joyce Carol Oates with their spouses. It may have been that evening, certainly during this trip, that Stanley blurted, as Oates exited the flat, "I hope she cooks better than she writes," to which Oates angrily snapped, "I heard that, Stanley." That was Dan Shea's recollection of the story Stanley told him. It could have been a little more ribald than that, because after three draft beers and a bottle of decent wine I couldn't persuade Coover to tell me what he heard Stanley say to elicit that reply. Whatever he said to her that evening, Oates, who was suffering from depression at the time, remained morbidly fascinated with this writer whose temperament was so opposite her own for more than a decade. In a 1974 letter she told Stanley, "I know you don't like me—who would?—but such things can't be helped." And her *Journal*, published in 2007, contains several unfavorable recollections from that decade, of this other of two "Antithetical beings, no two people more unlike." She envied Elkin's morbid humor, his ability to charm and entertain audiences, and his eagerness to call attention to his "various illnesses, physical and mental, transposing them into jokes—and a very funny man is he!—Irresistibly funny." But she also saw him as a narcissist and pitied Joan's commitment to putting up with Stanley's antics: "[A]nd yet one can't help but remember the odd hysterical pathos of humor, famously 'gallows humor,' where mortality is ridiculed and jeered and made the subject of hilarity. . . . But to live with a man like that, how is it possible?????" (ellipses hers). In 1977 she praised John Updike's geniality "when a much lesser talent like Stanley Elkin is so unpleasantly egotistical." Three years later, at a meeting of the American Academy and Institute, she was delighted to learn that Howard Nemerov was "no longer shoving Stanley Elkin down our throats and [was] consequently pleasant." Whether it was what he said in London, or the impression of a genius of quite opposite character, Oates kept Elkin very much on her mind for many years. Lorin Cuoco and Bill Gass supply a bit of Elkinalia from university folklore that could be a variation on the same story: it concerns a female creative writing student whom Elkin told, "I hope you fuck better than you write." This version includes a riposte Elkin treasured: "That's something you'll never find out."[10]

Other visitors included Dave and Maureen Demarest, close friends from the early days at Washington University. Their special gift was child-sitting so Joan and Stanley could visit Germany. They stayed over in Amsterdam, then toured the countryside by automobile for about a week. The Demarests kept the children and lived in the flat. Unfortunately, Maureen washed Molly's (age five) favorite blanket, not knowing Molly was fond of certain odors at the corners, so she cried for three days until her parents returned. Bernard's strongest recollections of the trip include cramped family quarters and a nearby park in which his father played with the children. That year Stanley made up a series of "Marvelous Margery" stories as bedtime entertainment for the children. Because she was stuck all day in the tiny flat with two small children and a teenager, Joan insisted that Stanley put the kids to bed. He told them stories about a smart, adventurous Good Samaritan named Margery, about Molly's and Bernie's age. Each adventure involved her doing a good deed for someone, then suddenly the story would end, "and then she died." The children would cry and Joan would be angry with Stanley, but each night the children would ask for a story, with the caveat, "Don't let Marvelous Margery die, Daddy." He'd promise that she wouldn't, but then as the children were entranced with her adventure, something absurd would happen to kill her. Molly believes this was Stanley's way of teaching the children a "tragic vision of life" and eventually they became caught up in the theme and anticipated the end, often shouting out, "And then she died!" In kindergarten the children were assigned to tell the class a story, and Molly told a Marvelous Margery adventure. The teacher was shocked and insisted on a parental visit during which she demanded that Molly receive psychiatric treatments. It was bad enough, she thought, that the child told such a story, but it was inconceivable that she thought it was funny. Joan had a hard time convincing the teacher that there was nothing wrong with Molly, that her father had a rare sense of humor.[11]

The most important event of the London trip was, of course, the diagnosis of multiple sclerosis, a disease of which Demarest, Ballowe, and Gass recall observing symptoms nearly a decade earlier, but one that remained undiagnosed until London. In 1991 Elkin summarized, "In 1972, in England, I was diagnosed for multiple sclerosis. In '76 I started to use a cane, in '79 a foot brace." Gass recalls a period of visual impairment in graduate school that was suspiciously like a MS symptom, but it abated, and, because most of his friends thought of Stan as a hypochondriac, the incident was largely forgotten. Demarest, his officemate at Washington University, recalls occlusion of Elkin's vision and tingling in his left hand in the early 1960s as well, but the physicians didn't diagnose the cause as MS, and the symptoms again subsided. In Great Britain the tingling sensation reoccurred, and this time it didn't subside.[12]

Multiple sclerosis is a degenerative disease that affects the central nervous system by causing the myelin, or fatty tissue that helps nerves conduct electrical impulses, to be replaced by scar tissue called plaque, lesions, or sclerosis. This almost inevitably results in pain, often intense, on the nerve sites, as well as gradual deterioration, and eventual loss, of function in the extremities. Two of Elkin's most overtly autobiographical characters, Ben Flesh of *The Franchiser* (1976) and Jack Schiff of "Her Sense of Timing" and "Van Gogh's Room at Arles" (1993) suffer from MS. Flesh speaks one of the most poignant lines of the 1970s when he generalizes his and his creator's disease to the universal plaint, "Plague builds its nests in us." And it's a near-consensus in the commentary on Elkin's fiction that the work after *The Franchiser,* although maintaining its fierce satiric bite, takes a much more philosophical and sympathetic approach to human mortality and suffering. MS is incurable, with "remissions," or periods when the symptoms are less intense, but these are usually followed by more severe presentations of the disease. When he received his diagnosis, Elkin felt that he'd been handed a death sentence. Helen Vendler recalls his meeting her at Heathrow and when she asked, "How are you, Stanley?" he replied, "I'm dying, Helen." She thought he was joking, but he wasn't. He told the story about the diagnosis many times, and several variations circulated among his friends and colleagues, including these: Elkin told Demarest he learned about it by peeking at his medical records while the physician stepped out of the office. When the doctor returned, Stanley confronted him. The version he told Coover involved an irate Elkin, wearing a bathrobe over his hospital gown, storming across the street to a pharmacy to consult medical books, thus learning the terrible truth. Years later, he elaborated his feelings upon hearing the diagnosis:

> Actually, I had a kind of reactive depression, and I've never been a depressive personality. The thing started as a kind of tingling in my finger. When that didn't go away I went to the doctor. He said it was my posture. So he prescribed a course in physical therapy. I went to Roehampton Queens-Something Hos-

pital [Queen Mary's Hospital, Roehampton Lane], which was not far from where we were living at the time. I went every day, for an hour a day, until I was in the greatest shape I've ever been in. I worked with this old man in the hospital gymnasium, and he had me literally climbing up walls like a fly. It was incredible, the shape I was in. But the tingling was still there, in this hand, and spreading. The doctor put me in the same hospital where I'd had the physical therapy, in a tropical medicine ward, something that comes up in *The Franchiser*. Ok. So they gave me a lumbar puncture, which is what they use to diagnose M.S. I finished *Searches and Seizures* on May 14, and went back to the hospital on May 15 to find out the results. They told me I had multiple sclerosis. I thought that was a death sentence, that I'd be strapped to a wheel chair in about a week and a half. What I did was, I went to bed and read the drapes. These were the ugliest drapes in the world—thick, misshapen "u's" and "n's." And I stayed in bed for about three weeks until Joan said, "Come on, get up. We'll go home." Eventually I did, and that's when I started to feel better psychologically.[13]

The beginning of a long and inspiring story. The temptation to despair and self-pity is inherent in such a diagnosis, but as she would for the next twenty-three years, Joan told Stanley to stop feeling sorry for himself and get to work. Write and interact and deal with what had to happen. And that's what he did.

During the early symptoms and physical training he was working on the second, although last in the collection, of a series of four planned novellas; Fox loved his holograph title, "The Real Reason Why Martin and Lewis, Liz and Eddie, the Beatles, Gilbert and Sullivan, and Hitler and Hess Split Up: Four Short Novels by Stanley Elkin." His imagination returned to his youth in Chicago as the location for his least-successful novella, "The Condominium." Although an insightful portrait of a relatively new demographic, the gentrification of the North Side by a condominium enterprise designed to support a luxurious retirement for affluent senior citizens, the novella features a character who's marginally forceful to carry the burden of the narrative, and the theme is more depressing than anything he'd written since "The Guest." Both before and after writing this story, Elkin told creative writing students that writers should avoid the temptations to write disguised autobiography and to resolve a plot impasse by having a character commit suicide. Unfortunately, he did both in "Condominium," and the work was never popular with general readers, scholars, or Elkin himself. In July, Fox, with whom Elkin's relationship was growing increasingly testy, complained, "As you know I like the bear story very much, but I still think that *The Condominium* doesn't represent your best work, that it's too dense and obscure." As the collection moved toward completion, Fox remained unconvinced, but he realized that his ability to sway Elkin was gone: "I still feel that the first eight pages of *The Condominium* are pretty indigestible and will put readers off. I also remain convinced that the other points I wrote you about (like the lunch in Covington in *The Bailbondsman*) are as valid as when I made them, but I don't suppose I'm going to be able to convince you the second time around either."[14] Fox was wrong about "The Bailbondsman" but he was on target with "Condominium."

In setting and tone the story recalls Elkin's early, unpublished work and some stories in *Criers and Kibitzers, Kibitzers and Criers,* but it resembles nothing so much as "The Sound of Distant Thunder," a very early story that wasn't collected until *Early Elkin* in 1985, in its pessimistic look at the implications of demographic change. "The Condominium" begins with a mysterious brooding on the notion of "place"; Elkin had to explain to both Fox and Borchardt that it was part of a lecture being prepared by his protagonist, Marshall Preminger. In itself this should have been a warning—both were shrewd readers and arguably Elkin pushes the notion of in medias res beyond its logical limits.[15] And the milquetoast protagonist has an alarming assembly of Elkin characteristics. He's a "Ph.D. manqué" who grew up in Chicago, whose father was a dapper, successful salesman named Phil, who charmed the ladies at the condo and died of a heart attack, leaving Marshall a host of inheritance problems. Marshall, like Stanley having had a heart attack in his late thirties, is seeking a "place to live, to be!" and one element of the plot explores the distasteful subject of his disappointment that his father, whom he believed to be wealthy, left only the condo as an inheritance, with maintenance fees in arrears. He also suspects that a lady from a nearby apartment was having an affair with Phil, and a series of interminable letters eventually discloses that Phil's fatal heart attack occurred in flagrante delicto. Fond of eighteenth-century fiction, Elkin failed to resist the temptation toward epistolary narratives here and in sections of *George Mills.* Some of the names resonate autobiographically: Marshall is the name of Joan's brother, who told me that he was the model for an Elkin character, though there's no resemblance beyond the name here. A family that invites Marshall to dinner, he thinks to fix him up with their unmarried daughter, is named "Jacobsen," Joan's maiden name. What's surprising is that all these reminiscences of family history and previous stories yield a protagonist unlike either Elkin or his typical characters.

From sitting shivah with an erection to becoming a lifeguard at the pool in order to pay off obligations to the condo's developer, satirically labeled a "modern Aeneas" founding a new economic enterprise, Marshall is passive. While he prepares his lecture on the relation between place and being, he waits for the collective experience of the seniors' condo to give his thirty-seven-year-old life direction and meaning. When his father's lady friend sends signals, Marshall responds with the longest telegram in recorded literature—manifesting both improvidence and passivity. Her nonresponse to the faint signals in his telegram is one, but not the primary, cause of his suicide. He's also depressed by the increasing note of sadness in the shop talk (a favorite Elkin concept) around the pool; as he listens from his lifeguard's post, the talk shifts from the chatty to the sorrowful, and his parasitic grasp for meaning is again frustrated. Like Dick Gibson, who lived vicariously through the chatter of his Miami call-in show until the callers become morose and sorrowful, Marshall (a favorite Gibson alias was "Marshall Maine") has depended on this overheard conversation to make up for the emptiness at the core of his life, which has been exacerbated by his father's death. Whereas Gibson had his paranoia to direct him to new sources of illusory signification, Marshall hits on his dad's ex-mistress. Finally, his lecture thesis, "A Place to Live" doesn't stand up to the experimental test of the condo. That experience persuades him that a "life like his, even an altered one, could be lived in Montana or in Chicago. It made no difference" (221). His apathy gives way to despair in his public confession at poolside, his last substantial comment on the relation of place and being: "By moving here, I had thought to change my life, to alter its conditions by manipulating its geography, but now I see that this has little to do with it" (294). Elkin, living in London and learning that his adopted St. Louis is his "place to live, to be!" after transplantations from New York and Chicago, constructs a character so overwhelmed by disappointments that he can't face his life and plunges to his death, giving his final lecture on "place" as "Cage," "Net," "trap." Living abroad and suffering with mysterious symptoms that wouldn't go away and weren't yet diagnosed, he wrote his only story of a character too weak to challenge entropy with energy and will.

It can hardly have been a surprise that "The Condominium" was hard to place in a magazine. It was long, its theme was morbid, and it lacked the rhetorical zest editors looked for in an Elkin story. Although it contains many wonderful lines, like "What was curious about luxury was the low opinion it gave you of yourself because you had not anticipated your needs as cleverly as people who did not even know you" (222), it reads rather like Elkin grafted onto Bernard Malamud. Borchardt sent it to *Esquire,* where editor Pat Rotter liked it and "managed to carve an excerpt out of it." Borchardt didn't have to sell Elkin on those cuts, however, because Rotter's colleagues "just didn't think it was special enough." Lish, also at *Esquire,* aimed a dart at Elkin's ego, saying that except for sections of *The Dick Gibson Show,* there was no Elkin work he didn't admire, until now: "[E]xcept for a few moments, I don't like this one at all." *North American Review* returned it because of length; by June, it had also been refused by three more national journals, and Borchardt persuaded Elkin to accept an offer from *Works in Progress* for the first thirty-three pages at $750. Surprisingly, International Cinema offered a $500 option on the novella in 1975. Elkin accepted, despite the clause giving International unlimited rights to "change, alter, modify, add to and/or delete from" the text.[16] International didn't renew.

During the therapy leading up to the diagnosis, Elkin also began the second, though last in order of composition, in his book of novellas, "The Bailbondsman." This would result in the only Elkin story to hit the big screen, but it would be a major critical success as a novella and an equally major disappointment as a movie. He shared several variations on its inspiration, but the core story is that he was reading *Boss*, Mike Royko's biography of legendary Chicago mayor and politician extraordinaire Richard J. Daley, a portion of which describes a "saloon in Chicago with cops and bailbondsmen, and the word scared the hell out of me and at the same time intrigued me." He focused on the sheer power a bondsman has over those for whom he puts up bail, and, as was his practice, he began thinking about the implications of such a vocation. While plotting the novella, he experienced one of those serendipities on which he believed his best work depended: Nemerov sent him a clipping about an Indianapolis bonds- man, from the *Wall Street Journal,* which confirmed his suspicion that these are indeed menacing fellows: "I didn't know in the beginning I was writing about a man who had the power to loose and bind, but that's what 'The Bailbondsman' is about, a man who is himself a sort of government, who does to other people what governments do to the rest of us."[17] He was under way in developing the most engaging bad man in his fiction since Leo Feldman.

Much of "Ashenden" was set in England, but Elkin wrote most of the novella in St. Louis. By contrast, except for a dream sequence, "Bailbondsman" is situ- ated in and around Cincinnati, which he'd visited for readings, but Elkin wrote it in England and drew on London and Paris resources to establish his setting. He wanted to describe a hotel room minutely for one scene, so he rented one in Kensington and took notes. He also visited the Natural History Museum with his children, and found himself in a room with displays of human teeth. He returned the next day with pencils and paper, to draw and take notes on the teeth. He then wrote the section in which Alexander Main observes teeth in a Cincinnati museum. This section compounded an increasingly difficult relationship with his editor. Even in the final editing, Fox implored him to reduce the "teeth stuff" and the sarcophagus scene by as much as half, but he came up against the familiar Elkin resistance and capitulated in December: he was "not going to fight you" on edits, but "the tooth business and the sarcophagus opening seem to me dead spots—I'm not arguing about their symbolic value—and that is the *only* reason it seems to me they should be cut down. If the symbolism is more important than the fact that you're losing your reader's attention, so be it." He'd launched an angry broadside in September: "What about some paragraphing, for Chrissake!" Four years later Elkin was still annoyed by Fox's not approving the teeth episode, though he conceded that "I was overwhelmed by those goddamned teeth and I knew that I had to use them someplace, somehow, and though they really had nothing to do with the story I made them—serendipity!—the story." The final piece of research and serendipity involved a project on which Elkin was working simultaneously, a magazine essay on French actor Jean-Louis Trintignant that included an elaborate description of the Christmas preparations in Paris. The

editors cut the entire section, over Elkin's objection, but he felt that his description was the best thing in the essay, so he decided to "plagiarize from myself and
move it to Cincinnati."

Surprisingly, he once said, "I, myself, am closer to Main than any other character."[18] It was the 1970s, when we were all rebelling against "the Man," but Main
resembles Feldman more than Elkin, and this is Elkin's most explicit association of
himself with a created bad man. And Main is about as bad as any Elkin character,
even Feldman, gets. He's aggressive, brutal, at times sadistic, and defiantly racist.
He has contempt for the lowlifes whose bail he posts, for the lawyers he bribes,
and for the judges on his secret payroll. Alexander's driving force is his need for
the challenge and the chase. He seeks an adversary worthy of his skills, and in
more than thirty years he's never failed to bring back a client who attempted to
jump bail, except two, Oyp and Glyp, about whom he dreams and who have,
like Gibson's Dr. Edmond Behr-Bleibtreau, emerged in his private mythology as
larger than life and unusually powerful. Elkin told me that these names were the
result of his having noticed the license plates on two parked autos in London,
but artistically the silliness of their names corresponds with Main's elevation of
petty criminals who happened to get away to adversaries of heroic proportion.
The one way in which Main resembles his creator is his penchant for rhetoric
and the syntax of aggression. He verbally bullies his clients, the lawyers who send
them to him, his associate Crainpool, and, in a hilarious scene, the chancellor
of the University of Cincinnati, whom he tries to talk into a retainer for all the
students who may be detained during the campus riots of the late 1960s:

> *Mene, mene, tekel, upharsin.* If you don't read your student newspaper, try
> your Bible. It's Alexander Main, the Phoenician bailbond salesman. Listen to
> me, Doctor, [. . .] I got my ear to the ground. The University of Cincinnati
> is the biggest municipal university in the country. She's coming in like an oil
> well, it's going to blow. Already I smell smoke. State troopers are coming,
> the Guard. Fort Benning is keeping the engines warmed. Are you ready for
> this, Doctor? Where you gonna be when the lights go out? I'm telling you,
> you heard it here first, I think they've got their eye on upwards of twenty-five
> hundred kids. What'll your forty-five-grand-a-year job be worth when you
> got twenty-five hundred students in jail who can't make bond?

Main's reference to campus unrest was undoubtedly motivated in part by Elkin's
witnessing the riots at Washington University in the aftermath of the Kent State
shootings a few years before, but in this character's mouth a catastrophe of grave
public proportions morphs into a rhetorical hard sell to bully the administrator
into giving him business.[19]

Another Elkin dream came true when Raymond Wagner, who would be a
large part of Elkin's Hollywood life, contacted Lawrence B. Marcus (1917–2001),

a Hollywood writer who had written and produced television dramas and films, about writing a script for "The Bailbondsman." When they reached Elkin, he replied, "Terrific, get in touch with my agent, pay me money, do it." In September 1975 he signed the contract with Warner Brothers, with Dick Shepherd as the producer. The purchase price was $25,000 up front, with a percentage of all profits. The contract also called for credits: if the film were called "The Bailbondsman," immediately beneath the title would appear "Based on the Novella by Stanley Elkin." If not, "Based on the Novella 'The Bailbondsman' by Stanley Elkin" would appear below the new title. In any case, Elkin would have a nice check to cash, a cut of the profits, and the kind of recognition only Hollywood could provide. Everyone who was anyone in the literary community knew about Elkin—now it was the world's turn.

Or so it seemed. Almost immediately it became apparent that Marcus wanted to do more than a little tweaking to adapt this story, released as *Alex and the Gypsy,* to Hollywood. Early in the process he told Elkin, "We *mustn't dilute this for a minute.* We have to stick *word for word"* (emphasis his). But shortly after he began the screenplay, he telephoned Elkin, teaching at Iowa, to say, "Stanley, the thing I can't lick is the love interest."[20] Love interest? Anyone who has read the novella knows there's no gypsy in "The Bailbondsman," and the only love of which Main is capable is self-love. He was briefly married but is callously insensitive about his wife's death; now he satisfies his biological needs by taking favors from whore clients, and his most erotic experience is a wet dream about bailing out sarcophagus raiders, the new incarnations of Oyp and Glyp. By this time the studio had addressed box office appeal by contracting the able and extremely popular Jack Lemmon to play Alex—softening the character simply by giving him a nickname Elkin's character uses only in jest—and they were negotiating with Marsha Mason and Geneviève Bujold to play "the gypsy" Marcus invented to provide love interest. He told Elkin somewhat shamefacedly in June 1975, "Now when you see this I hope you're not going to get mad at me, because I've written a love story." When Elkin asked whether Marcus had kept any of Main's colorful speeches in the film, he responded, "Well, to tell you the truth, very little."[21]

Thus, a story of a forceful and energetic narcissist was transformed by Hollywood to a trite screenplay that suffocates the considerable talents of Lemmon, Bujold, and James Woods, who played Crainpool. The new plot is that the gypsy, arrested for stabbing her husband, needs bond until she must appear for sentencing, and Alex grudgingly posts her bail, then becomes erotically reinvolved with her, while several flashbacks establish their prior relationship and her dumping him. As Elkin lamented in an interview with the Boston University publication *Spectrum,* "'You know damned well that ultimately he will let her go because it's Genevieve Bujold.'" Or as he groused just after the film came out, Marcus "gave me assurances that he would be loyal to the character of Alexander Main.

But they were unwilling to make Lemmon a bad guy. [. . .] But I'm grateful they paid me. I hope the film does well. I have a small percentage, some points to be collected after everybody else has been paid off. I saw the movie at a screening and I turned to my agent and said, 'Well, Georges, there go the new points.'"[22]

As the press releases for *Alex and the Gypsy* put it, "To [Alex] there is a certain nobility in his profession, not merely a means of earning a living. His self image is that of a fighter for freedom, a protector of the persecuted, a defender of civil rights [. . .]"—about as far from Elkin's character as one could get. And Elkin's principal disappointment wasn't simply that director John Korty, making his first studio film, and Marcus, dumbing down the story for Hollywood, changed his text. He complained to *Spectrum* that he was disappointed "because it didn't seem better than your average made-for-television movie." Contemporaneous with the film's release, Pocket Books released a paperback *Alex and the Gypsy* featuring a cover photo of Bujold hugging a cigar-chewing Lemmon, but it didn't do much better on the shelves than the movie did at the box office. It had earned $3,867 short of the $5,500 advance when Pocket closed its books on *Alex* in 1978.[23]

And while the receipts trickled in, film critics gave it the cold shoulder. Despite the star power of Lemmon and Bujold, most simply ignored it. One of the few to note it in detail, Joel Thingvall, praised Lemmon's willingness to build on his breakthrough roles in *Days of Wine and Roses* and *Save the Tiger,* transforming himself from a comic actor to a force in serious drama. But he'd read Elkin's no-vella before seeing Korty's film and found the comparison inevitable: "Elkin's book has been completely transformed—from a study of a brilliant man's relations with the law of self and the law of courtrooms to a predictable kind of love story. And the losses of density and wiseass virtuosity are cruel." Thingvall felt that Korty's direction was "jagged, often sloppy" and Marcus's script was "confused."[24]

An afternoon at the Library of Congress, the only place I could find a copy of the film, confirms that Elkin and the critics were right. It's unrealistic to ex-pect that this or any Elkin fiction could be transformed without change to the screen, and several of Marcus's instincts to trim repetitive scenes and to eliminate Main's toxic racism were apt. But the hodgepodge he came up with in adapting the novella produces neither a good interpretation of the story nor a coherent or interesting film. The addition of a love interest reminds us that there are few love stories in all Elkin, though there are quite a few lust stories. The problem, however, is that Marcus adds a clichéd love story, one in which Alex's softer, more decent side is exposed by his association with and memories of Maritza (the gypsy). In one flashback she encourages him to remember his family, and this bad man turns out to be a frustrated idealist: his grandfather was a judge, and his father "was a saint, my old man" whose miracles usually fell through because he "trusted people. Nobody ever expected his ideas to work, except him [pause, softly] and me." Now we have a Psych 101 explanation for Alex's cynicism, and we can sympathize with his rage because we understand the pain behind it—a Hollywood cliché, not even remotely Elkin's character, and far from original or interesting. Twice Alex uses his muscle to intercede on Maritza's behalf, once trying to influence an ambitious public defender and later to persuade the judge that as a gypsy she'll never survive incarceration. Ultimately he helps her escape, feigning sleep after lovemaking (a joke that runs successfully through the middle reels) and taking a loss on the $30,000 bond, because he loves her and secretly hopes she'll take him with her.

The studio paid handsomely for the right to change the story, but the result is cliché-ridden. The film's other problem comes from hybridization, for Marcus at times imports Elkin's dialogue whole cloth into some scenes, which are energetic and call into relief the uneven pace and sloppy writing of the main plot. An early scene in which he convinces a young felon, charged with setting someone on fire because he winked at his girlfriend, that his family has resources and he's therefore bondable crackles with the morbid wit of Elkin's original. The scene between a Mafia representative and Main captures the verve of Elkin's repartee, and a related one between Main and the judge creates wonderful shtick on the screen. Elkin's jokes about Main's insistence that Crainpool comport himself as a character out of a Dickens novel play well too. But the end of the novella, in which Main forces Crainpool to resume his status as a fugitive, while the dialogue is straight out of Elkin, rings oddly in the context of the softened Alex, who fires shots over Crainpool's head, then forgets all about him as he tries unsuccessfully to renew his relationship with Maritza.

It's tempting to say that the film's failure is due to the difficulty of the bad-man-as-hero convention central to many Elkin tales, most notably *A Bad Man*, which was nearly filmed. This explanation, however, flies in the face of many facts. Antihero movies, in which the audience is expected to empathize with a bad man, were becoming increasingly popular during the decade leading up to the filming of *Alex*. A television actor emerging as one of the important figures in modern film, Clint Eastwood appeared in several Sergio Leone westerns about a murderous antihero with practically no redeeming qualities, but who was the emotional focus of the audience. This character is a bounty hunter, a vocation eerily similar to that of a bailbondsman, in the first two movies, *A Fistful of Dollars* (1964) and *For a Few Dollars More* (1965). Like the third and most popular of the series, *The Good, the Bad, and the Ugly* (1966), these films were produced and shot in Italy and Spain, but they were huge box-office successes in the United States. The fourth and by far most problematic in the series, *High Plains Drifter* (1973), was made in America and directed by Eastwood shortly before Marcus adapted *Alex*. In it the stranger terrorizes a town and rapes a citizen before joining forces with the townspeople against a band of outlaws, then coerces another citizen's wife to have unwanted sex. Moreover, by the time *Alex* was released, Eastwood had starred in three of the five "Dirty Harry" films about a ruthless, violent San Francisco policeman whose tagline became a pop culture slogan: "Go ahead, make my day," welcoming aggression so he could kill his enemy. Both the "man with no name" and "Dirty Harry" transformed the traditional western or cop film into something much darker and more ambiguous. So the explanation that the "bad man" needed to be softened to a more palatable Hollywood character to account for the failure of *Alex and the Gypsy* to be viable as a commercial film simply doesn't hold up. A much more cogent explanation is that the filmmakers dumbed down the character and the film halfway—they didn't abandon all of Main's bad man elements, but they softened his character enough to make him a hybrid that simply didn't work. But disappointed as he was both aesthetically and in terms of his aspirations for Hollywood recognition and rewards, Elkin would have more close encounters of the Tinseltown kind during the 1970s.

All along, the plan had been to issue a collection of four novellas. By mid-1972, however, Fox was moving toward a set of three, based primarily on the length of the two he'd seen. When Elkin sent "Bailbondsman," the deal was done. Except for a couple of scenes, Fox loved it and wrote in September to say, "I didn't take detailed notes [. . .] mainly because I got so absorbed that I would forget to do so, and then I didn't want to take the time to go back and find my quibble. [. . .]" Fox did, however, suggest some "judicious cutting" at a point or two, but by this time he didn't really expect Elkin to agree. He was unhappy with the collection title that Elkin had suggested, *Eligible Men,* and felt that the title of any one novella might be preferable. Elkin, however, insisted on a discrete title, and as publication neared, he doodled on Fox's November demand that they arrive at a decision: "Eligible Men"; "The Bailbondsman: Three Novellas"; and "Searches and Seizures: Three Novellas by Stanley Elkin." Fox liked the new title: "Al [Lebowitz] has come through again. I very much like *Searches and Seizures,*" but he suggested that the blurb should substitute "Short Novels" for "Novellas," to appeal to a broader audience. Lebowitz, a lawyer, had suggested a key phase from the fourth amendment of the U.S. Constitution, guaranteeing citizens protection against unlawful searches and seizures of property by the government, and Elkin was delighted by the puns that both terms added to his title. Throughout the galley stages, Fox and Elkin continued to wrangle about cuts to "Condominium" and "Bailbondsman," as well as Fox's suggestion that the point of view switches in the latter be eliminated, or presented as discrete chapters. In March 1973 he invoked "the strongest copy editor we have" to support the changes he recommended, but ended by stroking his author, "A strong book, and you should be proud of yourself. Well done." The postscript, however, showed that the tensions between the two were unresolved: "Of course, if you accept the changes we suggest, it will be even stronger."[25] As expected, Elkin nixed almost every change.

When Borchardt negotiated the British rights with Gollancz, with an advance of 400 pounds and a first refusal on his next book, a new problem emerged. The new title meant nothing to British audiences, and a crash course on the American Bill of Rights might not be good for sales in the United Kingdom. So the original title that annoyed Fox was reinstated and the book sold modestly as *Eligible Men*. Sales in the United States were somewhat better. Fox, sensitive to Elkin's concerns about sales, tried the audacious expedient of publishing simultaneous hardback and paperback editions. In the first month after publication, 3,176 hardbound and 4,446 paperbound books were sold, but Fox knew his writer wouldn't be happy: "I know you feel that we've botched our publication, but at least we've sold approximately 2,000 more copies of a new Elkin book than ever before."[26]

West of the Atlantic, reviews for *Searches and Seizures* were as enthusiastic as anything Elkin had ever experienced. It was nominated for the 1974 National Book Award, but had the misfortune of being up against John Gardner's *Nickel Mountain*, Isaac Bashevis Singer's *A Crown of Feathers and Other Stories*, and Thomas Pynchon's *Gravity's Rainbow*, the last two sharing the prize. Critics echoed Mark Cogan's *Book Week* observation that the collection is "irreverent and lewd, [. . .] Gargantuan & Aristophanic, and magnificently funny" as well as Christopher Lehman-Haupt's *New York Times* pronouncement that it signaled a "breakthrough" in which Elkin "has grown into his imagination." Only one North American critic, Philip Corwin in the *National Observer*, was harshly negative, and even he liked "The Condominium." Across the waters, however, it was nearly a reverse image. Martin Seymour-Smith in the *Financial Times* sounded a typical note: "If such an extraordinary exuberance could be disciplined Elkin might write a really substantial novel"; he concluded that "Ashenden" is "actually impossible." The *London Daily Telegraph*'s Nina Bawden was more blunt: "Ashenden" "made me ill." Wendy Monk in the *Birmingham Post* attributed her dislike to cultural differences: "Some of Mr. Elkin's shafts miss this side of the Atlantic. Pity."[27]

While he was working on "The Bailbondsman," an amusing development in Elkin's journalistic career took place as well. In August 1971, *Esquire* assigned him a story on French actor Jean-Louis Trintignant, who had become an international star in Claude Lelouch's 1966 *A Man and a Woman*. It was a good deal: $1,200 plus $300 travel expenses and a kill fee. In an initial mix-up, Trintignant's representatives nearly called it off: they wanted precise advance questions for this "interview" and Elkin testily replied, "It was my understanding when my agent proposed this topic in August, that everything had already been arranged. I am very surprised that you seem only now to be asking for information. [. . .] *Esquire* does not publish interviews. [. . .] From time to time the magazine commissions established writers to do rather serious studies of important figures either in literature or the arts, people who may or may not be celebrities." He flew to Paris during the Christmas season and delivered the piece in January, but

Borchardt found "Our Mensch in Paris" merely "amusing"; he had reservations about its being what *Esquire* had in mind. He was pleasantly surprised when the magazine asked permission to cut the beginning and heavily edit the rest, but almost immediately the magazine retracted its offer to amend and publish; in late February John Lombardi explained that he'd cut the essay "in hopes of making it work for us," but "there simply wasn't enough Trintignant in the story." Elkin complained about the magazine's imposing its profile on established writers, and this time Lombardi got testy: "Mr. Elkin's concerns with the limitations of the magazine's profile form, his questioning of the form's presumption, are, in my opinion self-indulgent and several years too late; other *Esquire* writers have questioned both, in our pages, and, from our point of view, there seems little point in doing this again." So *Esquire* paid the kill fee and Borchardt shopped the piece with other magazines. *Audience* returned it in May, sounding what became a familiar theme: "We like a lot of this, but it does seem to us that Stanley Elkin's way of doing the interview puts a somewhat heavy emphasis on him, and in spots at least, gets in the way of Trintignant." After several other magazines turned down "Our Mensch," the pornographic magazine *Oui* accepted it with the stipulation that the editors might make cuts. Elkin grumbled a few years later that *Oui* removed what he considered the best part of "Inside Jean-Louis Trintignant," the descriptions of Paris as the Christmas season approached: "I took a lot of notes and made up a lot of metaphors about the way Paris looked and smelled."[28] Undeterred, Elkin transported these descriptions to "Bailbondsman," relocating the Paris scene to Cincinnati.

During that year, several other journalistic opportunities came Elkin's way. Despite the dustup over Trintignant, *Esquire* paid his expenses for two more expeditions. The first was a summer jaunt to Detroit to write about the Johnson Smith company, a mail-order business specializing in gag gifts, but when he sent the typescript to his agent, even Elkin was dubious: "I don't know if they're going to want it. I do know that I worked very hard on the god damned thing and if he doesn't want it I hope he makes his mind up pretty quickly and that he'll send along my expenses and kill fee." Editor Ben Pesta loved it and "A la Recherche du Whoopee Cushion" came out in June 1974. It's unique among Elkin's essays in that it's actually *about* something, not about Elkin perceiving something. He liked Paul Smith, a physicist and mathematician who reads Proust and Wittgenstein in his spare time and once worked in the administration of the University of Chicago's atomic bomb project, but now manages the family business. Elkin sees mail order as "the democracy of matter" and reflects thoughtfully on the evolution of political correctness in the advertising of products like these. Much of what he learned about this manner of selling informed the novel he was writing, *The Franchiser,* which is also about the democratization of goods and services. *Sports Illustrated* also inquired about Elkin's interest in writing an article, but his agent stipulated that he'd be interested only in writing a piece on somebody breaking a record, and hoped editor Pat Ryan would suggest a topic. There's no indication that Ryan responded and *Sports Illustrated* missed out on Elkin's take on the world of sports. In 1974 Pesta assigned him to research the daily life of a "second-rate comedian." Elkin was at the Chicago Marriott in August, and sent the draft in October, but Pesta found it too long and threatened to withhold payment until revisions were satisfactory. Eventually he paid the kill fee and it was never printed.[29]

The Elkins' second London journey was a year of mixed responses. Obviously, the MS diagnosis clouded a future that was growing professionally brighter by the year. Once again face to face with his mortality, Elkin learned that this wasn't like a heart attack, from which one can recover and stand a reasonable chance of leading a healthy life by diet amendment, smoking cessation, exercise, and preventive measures—at none of which, however, Stanley was successful. Short of a medical miracle, MS offers no hope of a cure. Although 1970s therapies could temporarily relieve some of the symptoms, the progress of the disease is inevitable and the long-term prognosis is grim. One can, and must, endure. As Joan admonished him, one must get back to work.

Professionally, the year abroad was, except for the Trintignant fiasco, amazingly productive. He found a form that would showcase his unique talents for the rest of his career, one he'd return to every ten or so years. *Searches and Seizures* was moderately successful in North America, if not in Europe. And the ground was laid for one of his long-term dreams to be realized, the chance to have one of his works adapted to commercial film. The new decade would bring exciting opportunities in Hollywood and a second major breakthrough as a fiction writer. But before that, he would have to undergo more wrangling with his employer over the tensions between the demands of a writer as opposed to those of a teacher, and would once more test the depressed job market of 1970s English professors.

9 "Making America Look Like America"

Hollywood Beckons, a Breakthrough Novel, and a Cane, 1974–77

[H]e needed to costume his country, to give it its visible props,
[. . .] familiar neon signatures and logos, all its *things*, all its
crap, the true American graffiti, that perfect queer calligraphy
of American signature. [. . .]

—*The Franchiser*

So, hopefully, I have a form which will serve intentions
I've had all my life. Not just a form—a concept particularly
serviceable to me, the beauty that sleeps in the vulgar.

—Elkin to Scott Sanders, 1975

The journey back to St. Louis led to reunions with friends and university colleagues as well as a return to the daily grind of class work. Returning to his Parkview home was a special joy because the family had felt cramped in their Putney flat. Because Stanley was experiencing few symptoms of his newly diagnosed illness, he had some time to adjust to his changed prospects. He didn't need a cane, he wasn't using a walker, he hadn't moved into a wheelchair, though he knew these were coming. He realized an inevitable process of deterioration awaited him, but for the moment his symptoms were under control. As he morbidly quipped at the time, his British and American physicians assured him that multiple sclerosis was a manageable disease "if you don't mind going around with an earache in your right hand and a headache in your right toes every six months or so. My broken body was sending out good vibes, they said."[1] He was starting an exciting novel based on the emerging practice of franchising products and services, and he was negotiating for a semester as writer-in-residence at Yale and one the next year at Boston University, when one of his lifetime ambitions became a possibility.

Since childhood Elkin had been fascinated with film. High school friends recall his recording them on a voice recorder and his sister remembers his receiving a cutting-edge film camera during the 1950s. She visited Stan and Joan in Urbana while he was making an improvised home movie with it; he immediately assigned Diane and her cousin parts.[2] He wrote some excellent film reviews in graduate school. During his stay in Italy while writing *Boswell,* he dubbed English for one Italian movie and appeared as an extra in another. In the late 1960s, Philip Yordan bought rights to *A Bad Man* and *Boswell,* assuring him that commercial success was just around the corner when *A Bad Man* would be filmed. Other producers bought options on several of Elkin's stories as well as *Dick Gibson.* Stella Stevens inquired about filming his play *The Six-Year-Old Man.* While in England he received inquiries about writing a film script for *The Dice Man,* Luke Rinehart's satirical novel, for director John Schlesinger (1926–2003), but nothing came of this either—perhaps because Elkin priced himself out the market, asking $30,000 for a preliminary draft; Schlesinger decided he wanted someone with more screenwriting experience. And one of the novellas he wrote in England, "The Bailbondsman," would soon be filmed. That project was in development when his new opportunity emerged, so Elkin was unaware of the disappointments that would result from adapting his text for commercial cinema. While completing *The Franchiser,* in which one of Ben's business ventures is a cineplex in Oklahoma, he told an interviewer, with typical hyperbole, about the great moment of his life: the "happiest Joan and I have ever been in our married life" was seeing *The April Fools* (Stuart Rosenberg, 1969) in a "brand new theater in a marvy new shopping mall" in suburban Youngstown, Ohio. He told Joan, "What, what, what in this history of civilization, could be better than what we, you and me, baby, are doing right now, with enough money to buy the candy and the time to watch this stuff?'" So his response when producer Michael Ritchie contacted him about writing an original film script comes as no surprise: "Oh boy, would I! When does the boat leave, Mr. Ritchie?"[3]

Ritchie (1938–2001) was establishing himself as a filmmaker during the 1970s, and the fact that his letterhead for several of their early communications boldly advertised his upcoming film, "Robert Redford as the Candidate," probably made as strong an impression on Elkin as the note from Stevens about filming *The Six-Year-Old Man* a few years before or the casting of Geneviève Bujold, whom he met with starstruck awe, in *Alex and the Gypsy* soon after. Ritchie had done some television during the 1960s, then directed Redford in *Downhill Racer* (1969); he would build a reputation as a satiric-comic filmmaker with *Smile* (1975), *The Bad News Bears* (1976), and *Semi-Tough* (1977), in which Elkin told his son Philip he made a cameo appearance; an extra who looks very much like Stanley appears in a party scene and he visited Ritchie on the Florida set in March 1977. Ritchie initially contacted him about acquiring an option on *The Six-Year-Old Man,* but prophetically added, "[A]s a fan of your books my only complaint is that none of them seems adaptable for motion pictures." He inquired whether Elkin had written for the screen, or would be interested in adapting others' fiction. Elkin mentioned his idea for a screenplay, *The World Book of Records,* which would be about a boardinghouse owned by the character "Guinness": "all the boarders are involved in a sort of splendid and absurd over-achieving."[4] Echoes of the *Canterbury Tales* prototype in the Hartford episode of *The Dick Gibson Show* seem inherent in this concept but Ritchie was diplomatic: it "sounds wonderful" but seems more suited to the stage than the screen. Moreover, by this time Columbia Pictures had asked Ritchie to produce and direct a film about Robert Capa, the photographer who became internationally famous during the Spanish Civil War, the Sino-Japanese War, World War II, and the French-Indochina War, especially for his photos and covers in *Life* magazine. This Hungarian Jew, born Andrei Friedmann (1913–54), created a persona as the American photographer "Capa" so he could move freely in increasingly anti-Semitic post–World War I Europe and so publishers would print his stark photos of men at war. He later survived the McCarthy-era witch hunts, and by then his photos of World War II and the second Sino-Japanese conflict were hailed as masterworks. True to the violent world he covered, Capa died when he stepped on a land mine while photographing the French-Indochina War. Ritchie advised Elkin to examine Capa's autobiography, *Slightly Out of Focus* (1947) and the collection *Images of War* (1956); Elkin's script often connects scenes to specific photos from this collection. He also photocopied and annotated several other books: an *Encyclopedia Britannica* entry about China, with underlining in sections on the Japanese attacks of 1937, which Capa covered; Cecil Eby's *Between the Bullet and the Lie: American Volunteers in the Spanish Civil War* (1969); Lucien Bodard's *The Quicksand War: Prelude to Vietnam* (1963); and Vincent Sheean's *Not Peace but a Sword* (1939), which describes a few days that Ernest Hemingway and Capa spent with Sheean. In May 1973, Columbia Pictures formalized an agreement calling for Elkin to receive $12,500 for the first draft plus $2,500 for revisions, then $12,500 for a second draft. He sent Ritchie the university exam books on which he composed the handwritten draft, received feedback, and submitted a typescript. After Ritchie made extensive suggestions, changes, and deletions, Elkin completed the revisions. In August Ritchie wrote that "*Capa*" is a "great script" and many people "in Hollywood share that opinion."[5]

For an effort by an inexperienced screenwriter, *The Art of War,* Elkin's title, is surprisingly adept. The film would have been episodic, covering Friedmann/Capa's career from his achieving fame during the Spanish Civil War through his death. One archival text runs to 146 pages, with handwritten notes presumably by Ritchie and responses in Elkin's hand. Elkin's cinematic cuts are often sophisticated, moving spatially and temporally with great dexterity. Because he was a novelist, he overloaded the script with set descriptions and background details, something a director might want latitude to develop. But his composition by scene was natural for a novelist who typically created his narratives in self-contained stories, which later combined to form a whole. He once described this method to Borchardt as "exotic episodic." The scenes are linked chronologically, like the picaresque technique Elkin used in his novels, and through Capa's interactions with Gerda Taro, his mistress, and Hemingway, as well as his increasing anxieties about his life's work as a war photographer. The script is dominated by a larger-than-life Hemingway, to whose books the film script is rich in allusions and echoes (appropriately, *For Whom the Bell Tolls,* the great Spanish Civil War novel, figures prominently in this network of allusions), and whose clipped, terse style Elkin at times parodies skillfully. Although Ritchie's plan called for a biopic about Capa, the syntax of Elkin's subtitle is instructive: "A screenplay about Ernest Hemingway and Robert Capa." He later told Jeffrey Duncan and Bill Gass that what he found wrong with the scripts Columbia Pictures had commissioned before Elkin's was the absence of an emphasis on Hemingway.[6]

It's not unusual in fiction or film for a minor character to dominate the stage, and the Hemingway Elkin presents is a fascinating combination of macho bluster and private angst. He's at one moment the mythic tough guy–adventurer-stylist who casts a broad shadow over world literature. In one Paul Bunyanesque moment, probably based on a scene in *Not Peace but a Sword,* a flatboat gets stuck on the muddy bottom of the Ebro River and all the Lincoln Brigadiers can't budge it: Hem "takes the pole from the brigadier's hand and almost effortlessly moves the boat." Of course there's the sexual obsession that accompanies the Papa persona; he tells the Hispanic crew on his yacht watching for German U-boats during World War II, "None of you guys knows shit about screwing. A good lay takes four hours." Hemingway needs to "conquer" Gerda, opening a lasting wound between him and Capa, then to mock her: "That was a six year old screw, Friedmann, and besides that was in another country" (a phrase from Christopher Marlowe's *The Jew of Malta* alluded to in Hemingway's *The Sun Also Rises*). But Elkin's Papa, like Papa's heroes Robert Jordan or Jake Barnes, hides his vulnerability under a stubborn stoicism. When Capa visits Hemingway in a London hospital, confessing that he felt fear during the Normandy invasion, he parodies Hem's mantra: "Clumsiness under pressure." Papa shares his anxiety: "I sleep with a light on. Good at hunting, fishing, dialogue, and dropping articles from sentences. Fair country boxer—with hard belly and glass jaw. Refined, cultivated palate with gift for wines and trained eye for a well-turned cape. And that's as macho as I get, kid, and I sleep with a light on and all my life I've had black ass that hangs on like a summer cold. And my famous cajones [cojones] are just your ordinary balls. If you dip them in ice water, will they not shrivel? And that's no scepter between my legs but only a prick, self-serviced as the next man's. You got me? (very earnestly) *You got me?*" With the next breath Hem reverts to his public persona: "You tell anybody about this conversation and you won't have to worry about the Krauts killing you."

Elkin's point, however, isn't to debunk the Hemingway legend but to explore the damage a charismatic personality can inflict on a naïve protégé. When Elkin was writing this script, stories about Hemingway's bullying F. Scott Fitzgerald and John Dos Passos were circulating widely. A key theme of *The Art of War* is that Capa is mesmerized by his mentor's need for battle, challenge, and adventure. Therefore he pushes himself to take greater risks to get the perfect photo, to prove himself as an adventurer, an artist, and a man. He recognizes his fundamental problem, Papa-emulation: "I'm obsessed with him. I want to match him stunt for stunt. He bets character. I raise with my life. What's he thinking now, Gerda? Is he thinking, 'What's Capa doing?'"

Capa can't benefit from this realization, however; after photographing brutal images of man's inhumanity to man in attacks on an Israeli kibbutz, he decides he's finished with war photos and settles down to advertising and fashion work, only to be reprimanded by Hemingway: "Where's the composition? Take the blood out and you're lost. Pull risk and you're worthless; less good than the four-for-a-quarter machine behind the green curtains in the subway." As a result, Capa reconsiders his decision not to accept a dangerous Hanoi assignment, but once there his disillusionment returns. When he calls Hemingway from Indochina, his final question summarizes both the political and protégé themes of *The Art of War:* "Then tell me. Which side *are* we on?" The next day he meets the inevitable end of his life of chasing danger, but Elkin positions Capa's death as a suicide. He studies a land mine from all angles to photograph it, then "kicks the mine as one would punt a football."

The script ends with a spectacular montage, one that could work wonderfully on the big screen. Recalling the many scenes in which Capa's work took him to the front and the cry "medic!" summoned help for a wounded or dying soldier, a wounded medieval crusader, a shot Union soldier, and a bayoneted World War I British infantryman cry "medic!" in the voices of various characters from the story; and Hemingway, who committed suicide in Idaho, places a rifle in his mouth and calls out "medic!" in Capa's voice. This montage brilliantly links images of macho conduct, violence, disillusionment, pain, and "the art of war" over centuries.

For more than two years, Ritchie reassured Elkin that he'd make this film. He hoped to interest Gene Hackman in the Hemingway role and in 1973 Elkin told a St. Louis magazine that if the filming went through, he expected to spend the summer on location in Yugoslavia, Hong Kong, and England. By 1974, however, his tone had shifted toward bitterness. He told another interviewer that Ritchie was trying to line up Al Pacino and Jane Fonda, "but I don't have any confidence it will ever be made. I did it to order like a tailor. Like cutting a suit to order. The idea wasn't mine. [...] It wasn't a very pleasant experience. The money was pleasant." Ritchie shopped the script intermittently throughout the decade, but Elkin brushed off Ritchie's inquiry about sending a copy so he could once more approach a studio: "One of these days we are going to get that goddam film made. Sam Cohn & I feel it in our bones." Elkin scribbled in the margin: "Did not respond."[7]

While trying to produce *The Art of War,* Ritchie proposed a second screenplay, based on his idea about a circus movie. It never got as far as *The Art of War,* and the only surviving typescript is heavily edited in Elkin's increasingly undecipherable hand. The contract for a film script called "Circus Clown Story a.k.a. Mudshow" was formalized January 18, 1977. The cover page tells an ominous story: "Screenplay by Stanley Elkin. Story by Michael Ritchie." Throughout his professional life, Elkin did things Stanley's way; as he became exasperated that *The Art of War* was "written to order," he began to deviate from Ritchie's treatment to tell his own story. As the title suggests, Ritchie wanted a movie about a clown. That theme bored Elkin, so he included a clown as a minor character and focused on the owner-operator of a small-time traveling circus, a "mud show" struggling to survive as the large circuits grab up what's left of a diminishing market. His hero, Walter Kingman, recalls Leo Feldman of *A Bad Man* in his energy, his vigor, and especially his eagerness to impose his will on his environment. These qualities Kingman also shares with the great fictional creation Elkin was developing at the time, entrepreneur Ben Flesh of *The Franchiser.* Kingman persuades his trapeze act to work without a net. Originally motivated by the need to intensify risk, therefore to increase business, Walter quickly becomes energized by the need to win the point: "You're defiers of gravity. You want to know something? In the state of New York flyers are prevented by *law* from working without a net. You folks came to this country to get away from Mickey Mouse laws like that. It makes *real* flyers laugh. You know what they call trapezers at Madison Square Garden? They call them THE FLYING FAGGOTS OF THE STATE OF NEW YORK!"[8] Whether chatting up a performer, customer, or agent, Walter thrives on imposing his will through rhetoric or intimidation. And like Flesh and Feldman, he sometimes frustrates his own best interests to score a rhetorical point.

When he shopped the script with producer Michael Eisner, Ritchie was confident that the project would move forward if key objections were addressed: "It will be an acceptable shooting script if my [Eisner's] objections can be overcome." But those objections went to the heart of the script's cinematic and artistic flaw and they obviously weren't resolved to Eisner's satisfaction. He told Ritchie the script was "fantastic" up to the point at which Walter loses the circus, but that the final third contained a shift in tone that put him off.[9] His objection points out competing strategies within the script. The gruff, antiheroic, verbally aggressive Walter of the first two-thirds is a typical Elkin protagonist whom we like despite ourselves. He's funny, energetic, unpredictable, and strategic, a Push the Bully with a circus rather than a neighborhood to dominate. But after an aerialist falls to her death and a judge awards a substantial settlement against him,

Walter loses his circus and his vitality. Although there's a clever hospital scene that resembles the brilliant South Dakota episode in *The Franchiser,* the Walter of the final third of the script is an unresolved combination of defeated schmuck and sentimental romantic hero. He becomes paternally, but not romantically, infatuated with Elsie, his successor's daughter. Upon receiving some unexpected good luck, Walter tracks the circus down to rescue Elsie from it and her father: "C'mon, kid, we'll run away and join the real world." The ending implies that she's following him toward a middle-class life in Guthrie, Minnesota. Imagine Feldman in Hicksville.

The typescript of *Mudshow* is heavily revised in Elkin's and someone else's hands, with substantial deletions and jarring changes among scene sequences. This suggests that Elkin felt the need for major adjustments, but his revisions never attacked the core issue, the shift in Walter's character from typical Elkin hero to sappy good guy. It's possible that Elkin transformed him, as he refused to change his fictional heroes, out of a desire to provide the happy ending characteristic of commercially successful movies, but there's no hard evidence to sustain that, except that he was quite serious at the time about becoming a professional screenwriter. In any case, Eisner opted not to take up the project, and Ritchie couldn't interest anyone else for the rest of the decade; Warner Brothers inquired about its availability in 1979, but nothing came of that either.[10]

Between *Art of War* and *Mudshow,* Elkin had a different taste of Hollywood; it too was profitable but unpleasant. In 1976 MGM was shooting *The Demon Seed,* a science fiction thriller based on Dean Koontz's novel—the film has become a sci-fi cult classic. Its plot concerns a computer scientist whose creation rapes his wife, intending to propagate its identity and create a higher species. Producer Herb Jaffe and director Donald Cammell were dissatisfied with the dialogue for the computer character, "Proteus IV." They hired Elkin to rewrite this character's dialogue, working in California from December 14, 1976, until complete at a salary of $2,000 per week plus expenses. The problem clause was, "Your credit on the screen, if any, shall be determined by the Writers Guild of America." The producers were pleased with his work, as evidenced by this stage direction in an advanced shooting script: "Proteus should speak to Susan both while she is conscious, and while she is in the trance-like state of the Cosmic Voyage sequence. His voice can be heard *under* the music. Some sections of Stanley Elkin's Protean incantation should be adapted for this purpose (approximately one and a half minutes?)" But the producers felt that Elkin's contribution, as a work for hire, didn't merit screen credit. This omission ignited his competitive fires and he maintained that he deserved equal credit with Robert Jaffe and Roger Hirson. In January 1977 an MGM executive sent a registered letter pointing out that the shooting script "has been rewritten twice" since his revisions and asking whether Elkin insisted on seeking arbitration by the Writers Guild. Although he conscientiously marked the lines for which he claimed credit in the Proteus sections of the shooting script, he reluctantly gave up on getting his name on the screen after the executive advised him that the "Proteus Incantation" wouldn't be used.[11]

The Elkins' return to America involved much more than movie business, of course. There were reunions with friends and colleagues as well as preparations for semesters in residence and workshops, and more wrangling with university officials. One achievement was building a swimming pool in the yard of the Parkview home. Physicians would later prescribe water therapy for his multiple sclerosis symptoms, but at the time the primary motivation, according to Joan, was "pool envy." Bill Gass and Steve Zwicker, whose family had lived in the Elkins' home during the year abroad and then bought a house nearby, were combating St. Louis summers this way. Stanley quickly adapted, moving much of his reading and some of his writing activities to poolside when the weather was pleasant. This pool became the scene of an adventure that illustrates the challenge of chronicling Elkin's life. Introducing John Irving at Washington University in 1981, Elkin said Irving's son Brendan "almost drowned in my pool and would have if John hadn't had eyes in the back of his head." Years later, Irving told it differently: Elkin's daughter, about ten at the time, saw Brendan at the bottom of the pool and "Molly saved him." Molly, however, believes Irving deserves the credit: "I remember screaming that Brendan was drowning, but [. . .] Irving was the hero who did the actual rescuing."[12]

The family resumed their friendships with the Teitelbaums, the Lebowitzes, the Gasses, the Robins, and the Pepes—the "Third Tuesday" contingent that meant so much to their social life. Stanley's booming baritone resumed its rightful place as the central focus of those monthly get-togethers and much silence was shouted down. But one evening shortly after the return from London illustrated a temperamental side of Stanley's social persona. Steve Teitelbaum had begun a consultation practice and needed a new suit, so Marilyn bought him a fashion-able powder blue Johnny Carson with cuffs, bright buttons, and wide lapels. To celebrate his new practice she threw a "beautiful suit party," at which the guys modeled their best wardrobe and the women judged them. When they came back from England, the Elkins had brought the Teitelbaums Buckingham Palace dolls, which they'd placed on the staircase, down which the men strutted their threads competitively. In the fashion show, Steve wore the Carson, Al Lebowitz modeled a new Brooks Brothers, and Stanley wore a suit tailored for him at Savile Row. There was great mirth in the women's judging the fashion show, but in the end Al (and Brooks Brothers) won. Stanley, who had long been among the least fashionable of dressers, felt that a London-tailored suit should bring some sartorial respectability. He was so annoyed that he kicked one of the dolls down the stairs, so the judges named him "Mr. Congeniality."[13]

On the professional front as well, Stanley remained competitive. Department chair Jarvis Thurston recalls that after the London trip, Gass offered a philosophy and literature class that had to be moved to Graham Chapel because it attracted more than two hundred registrations. As this story made its way among the English faculty, Stanley decided he wanted to do the same thing the following semester. Thurston was anything but enthusiastic, but Stanley could be persistent. The class was scheduled and attracted quite a few registrations, but the numbers didn't approach Gass's and Stanley was disappointed. Then students dropped out in alarming numbers, so that by mid-semester only about twenty remained and they were moved to an ordinary classroom. By contrast, in 1976 Nancy Pope took Elkin's seminar in Faulkner's novels. In the first lecture, he promised to "teach my dissertation" to a class that he'd prefer to call "The Rise and Fall of a Great Writer." The idea was to develop the logic of Elkin's thesis as well as the conventional wisdom, that Faulkner's art peaked in the 1940s and deteriorated thereafter. Just before mid-semester, Elkin announced that he'd finished rereading all the novels on the syllabus and that his dissertation and the class plan got it wrong: he'd failed to appreciate the later novels when he was a graduate student, and there "was no 'fall.' Faulkner rises and rises and rises." Pope was shocked to hear a "professor admit to having been wrong anywhere, especially in his dissertation" and for her this was a formative moment: "I don't think I really understood before [. . .] that one could appear other than perfect, omniscient, and unchanging in front of one's students. [. . .] Or how big a man Stanley Elkin was." David Myers in 1979 told Elkin he'd left Washington University out of fear that he'd "completely assimilated" Elkin's approach, but now felt ready to return as a doctoral student. And the response to former student Robert Earlywine's impertinent question, "Why do you bite your students?," sums up this point in Elkin's teaching career: "It seems to me that anybody taking a writing course does so because he wants to be a better writer. If he wants to be a better writer he'd better learn how to write. That's why I bite my students. Gass also said that I treat them that way because I take them seriously."[14]

And from time to time he continued to haggle with his employer. The department and university were understandably concerned about his commitment and anxious about sharing him via visiting professorships at competing universities. He was miffed when the research committee turned down his request for funding in 1975, but his annoyance was mildly assuaged when Provost Merle Kling designated $700 to help with his typing costs. Although he wasn't outraged, as he had been a few years before over salary issues, he wasn't content and applied for teaching jobs at Smith and Southern Illinois. He also interviewed with Arizona at the Modern Language Association conference in 1972. But the shrinking job market of the 1970s made it impossible for these chairs to find a place even for a writer of Elkin's stature. On the home front, he felt that he wasn't a real player in the department and resented it. He often felt that people knew things they weren't telling him, and when Wayne Fields sat on the executive committee, Elkin regularly sought him out to get the lowdown: "[H]e was always looking for the figure in the carpet." But the generous man who later said he couldn't recall casting a single vote against tenure for a colleague came through as a friend and mentor. Fields's own tenure review divided the department, and during that dark time Elkin "was supportive in meaningful ways. He made it clear that it was OK for me to be here."[15]

The saddest moment of these years was his mother's death on September 13, 1974. Tootsie, who had always supported Stanley and his family emotionally and economically, succumbed after a long bout with heart disease in Miami, where she'd lived for several years and where Stanley and the family had frequently visited her. Memorial services took place in Hackensack, New Jersey, two days later. He later said, "[G]rief tunneled my vision and left me the impression that the town was all graveyard."[16] Despite his profound sorrow, Elkin the professional writer would draw on this emotion for a scene in *The Franchiser*, which he was writing at the time; Ben assists a mourner in selecting a casket at his funeral franchise. A decade later he credited this sad time with inspiring *The Rabbi of Lud*.

His fiction during this period was gaining increasing recognition and he was in demand on the lecture circuit and as a workshop guest and mentor, as well as spending summers or semesters in residence at Iowa (1974), Yale (1975), and Boston University (1976). *Dick Gibson* had been nominated for the National Book Award in 1973, as was *Searches and Seizures* the next year; Elkin was mentioned three times in the *New York Times* story. Neither, however, won. He was asked in December to serve as a judge in the 1975 competition, won jointly by Robert Stone's *Dog Soldiers* and Thomas Williams's *The Hair of Harold Roux*. Later, Elkin expressed regret that he didn't vote for Joseph Heller's *Something Happened*: "Fifteen or so years later, however, I find that I've a better memory of Heller's book than I do of either of the others." Heller's refusals to write jacket blurbs for *Boswell* and *A Bad Man* may have soured his reading of this important, misunderstood novel—he'd certainly felt insulted by Heller's snubs. In 1974 Elkin also received an award from the American Academy of Arts and Letters and sent some of the pink examination books in which he composed his first drafts for an exhibit: "I am pleased, of course, by the Academy Institute's selecting me to receive an award, but not so much pleased as moved. Money, of course, always comes at just the right time, an eleventh hour thing. [. . .] Money's timing is perfect. But the other, the acknowledgment that one may be on the right track after all is much rarer and much sweeter."[17]

This acceptance was further manifested when national and international journals asked to interview him. He'd been the subject of local interviews for many years, in St. Louis as a regional writer attracting national attention, or at universities where he was a visiting professor or workshop leader. Suddenly, national scholarly journals wanted to print what Mr. Elkin had to say about literature, life, America, the upcoming bicentennial, and his experiences. In November 1973,

Contemporary Literature published Scott Sanders's interview. During the next year, Elkin and Gass jointly interviewed with Jeffrey Duncan for *Iowa Review* and Phyllis and Joseph Bernt interviewed him for *Prairie Schooner.* He hit the big time when he received a brash request from Tom LeClair of the University of Cincinnati, who had written an important article on his work to date and who expected to publish the interview with the essay. He was also arranging an Elkin reading in Cincinnati. LeClair promised "No money, little fame, but a chance to tell all the anxious professors the truth about your fiction—how it really was in prison, how to fuck a bear—or to make up stories outrageous enough to make Nabokov's herrings pale." Upon completing the interview, LeClair surprised everyone by offering it to *Paris Review.* George Plimpton, who had published an excerpt from *Boswell* in 1964, asked for only a few cuts. Elkin was now big time and international. Moreover, Allan Guttman, who had written on Elkin's short fiction, asked him to support Doris Bargen's research toward a doctoral thesis on Elkin's life and work. Another border crossed—they were writing dissertations about him! The academy was taking him seriously. In February 1975, Bargen interviewed Elkin when he read at Smith and while he was in residence at Yale. She recorded the conversations and appended the transcript to her dissertation and subsequent book. Finally, in 1977, Larry McCaffrey of San Diego State proposed a special session at the annual Modern Language Association conference on Elkin's and Gass's fiction.[18] The kid from Chicago had hit the academic big time. He'd schmoozed many an MLA convention, but now they were convening sessions about him.

His summers had been hectic with movie efforts, teaching and workshop assignments, and travel, so he hadn't had an opportunity to return to the Bread Loaf Writer's Conference since 1964. But in 1976, the year he began using a cane to manage some of the MS symptoms, he began what would prove to be a regular and sustaining part of his writing life, one most of his immediate family recalls as high points of many summers. He would return for three consecutive summers, then four more during the 1980s, establishing himself as part of Bread Loaf's folklore. Although he was less mobile than before, and wouldn't be able to wrestle Jerome Charyn as he did at the 1964 conference, his cane could lean against a wall while he plied his greatest strength, simply being Stanley and holding forth. Conference historian David Bain paints this memorable scene: "Over the years at Treman Cottage, he found himself embroiled in a delightfully contentious dialogue with John Gardner that somehow combined respect for each other's individualism with disdain for each other's work. To younger writers sitting literally at their feet, their conversations were Olympian as they hurled thunderbolts at each other's feet with sardonic grins on their faces." The colorful, controversial Gardner, whose *On Moral Fiction* (1977) lambasted the "immorality" of many contemporary writers, including Elkin, was himself a flashy wordsmith and many conferees looked forward to Vermont confrontations between these titans. They'd been close friends, but Elkin resented Gardner's dismissal of him and many others in *On Moral Fiction*. Their conflict came to a head when Gardner read a screed in which Elkin's name came up while Stanley was in the audience. A few years later Gardner's cancer was diagnosed, and a conferee, unaware of their rift, rushed up to Elkin, effusively lamenting this great writer's illness. She was shocked when he replied, "Too bad," but her surprise converted to melodramatic hyperbole, and she wailed, asking in the light of the Cosmic Injustice of Gardner's illness what possible reason there could be for continuing to live or write. Stanley interrupted to tell her and the growing group of auditors that he could think of a reason: "God reads."[19]

Other writers Elkin befriended during these years include Richard Ford, Anthony Hecht, Hilma Wolitzer, Linda Pastan, Geoffrey Wolff, Gail Godwin, and John Irving, all of whom he would develop warm relationships with during the next several years. Wolff wrote in 1980 that the only reason he planned to attend Bread Loaf was that he'd been assured that Stanley would be there. Bain also recalls the family narrative of those happy years, including the Elkin children— Philip played soccer, Bernie hung out and fished, and Molly stayed near the writers and the talks. And they added anecdotes to the Middlebury saga: "For several years Bernie Elkin cornered the market in five-cent aluminum cans, going so far as to pay younger children three cents for a can and pocketing the commission. His sister Molly volunteered to help the social staff during a barn dance; helpfully, she began setting up new drinks by retrieving almost-empty plastic cups from around the Barn and pouring the flat, forgotten beer into new cups—which the sweaty dancers downed without missing a beat."

Marlene Charyn, however, recalled Bread Loaf and a writer she adored differently. In 1977 she lamented "the very fashionable despair of the tortured souls in the sweet Vermont woods coming to good meals set before them by me and my fellow waitership winners and having nothing more taxing to do, day and night, than talk." Her bitterness extended to the personal; she felt that Stanley had resisted her charms back in 1964: "[A] warm and funny man, a compassionate man with the strength to resist a young and luscious morsel because he was not a cheat. I can't believe he was done in by multiple sclerosis." She felt both rejected and disappointed: "I saw something beautiful in you at Bread Loaf and I can't believe it's gone completely or that I was simply wrong." Jerome confirms that Marlene had been institutionalized both before Stanley introduced them and after their divorce, about the time she wrote this letter. He believes the letter means that Stanley didn't take advantage of her vulnerability, which may have been expressed as an advance to someone who represented success and achievement. George Pepe heard a similar story from Elkin himself about a younger colleague's wife who made repeated visits to his Washington University office about

Molly, Joan, Bernie, and Stanley at Bread Loaf, 1984. Photograph © Miriam
Berkeley, used with permission.

this time, usually fragrant with perfume, gin, and cigarettes. On her last visit she
propositioned him and Stanley told her politely to go away. Pepe doesn't know
if that was due to virtue, familial values, or a case of being unable or afraid to
complete the moment; the most logical explanation is Stanley's concerns about
Joan's feelings. Pepe isn't sure why Stanley told him this story, but he did so more
than once, and he doesn't know if Stanley ever told anyone else. Late in his life
he told Joan and the Milofskys a similar story, in his living room, about a young
woman who came on to him after a reading: "Jesus, I thought I was going to get
laid!" Milofsky didn't for a moment believe there was any sexual scandal there,
but simply Stanley habitually saying outrageous and suggestive things.[20]

All the while—visiting professorships, conferences, film adventures, adjusting
to his diagnosis, dealing with grief at Tootsie's passing, and managing a growing
family and a work situation he was accepting as inevitable—Elkin was developing
his most ambitious work to date and one of the most extraordinary bicentennial
American novels of them all. *The Franchiser* was ready for the spring 1976 list
of his new publisher, Farrar, Straus and Giroux, who promoted it as a novel of
America's two-hundredth birthday, like best sellers geared to the celebration,
E. L. Doctorow's *Ragtime* (1975) and Gore Vidal's *1876*. His inspiration was
a *Time* magazine cover story[21] on the successes of McDonald's franchiser Ray
Kroc. Technically, Elkin's protagonist is one who buys franchises, whereas a

"franchiser" sells them; in the novel, "Colonel Sanders" tells Ben, "If you bought franchises you'd see the contract calls you the 'franshisee.'" Elkin parodies this success story early in his novel by casting the narrative of Ben's life as one that will never make the magazines or even the *TWA Ambassador,* for which Elkin would soon write a commissioned piece. He contracted for the novel in January 1974; an excerpt, which he wanted to call "Benny in the Bucket," in which Ben opens his Brooklyn Kentucky Fried Chicken franchise, appeared in *Fiction* (1975) as "From *The Franchiser."* Another, from the Travel Inn section near the end, appeared in *Iowa Review* (1976). By April 1976, his agent received an inquiry from Michael Lobell Film Productions about adapting the novel, of which Lobell had seen an excerpt, for the screen. The filmmaker entertained a vision of Kroc, now the owner of a major league baseball team, "telling members of the Padres over the PA system how lousy they are."[22]

Like *Ragtime, The Franchiser* is a new kind of novel about America entering its third century. Whereas Doctorow elected to chronicle the first two decades of the twentieth century, as America came to terms with its international prominence, technology, attitudes toward cultural pluralism, and the second generation of robber barons monopolizing its capital and resources, Elkin focuses on mid-century, a culture of conspicuous consumption, show biz, entrepreneurship, diminishing resources with increasing competition for them, and the relatively new phenomenon of franchising business operations. The protagonist, whom critics described as a variation on the Benjamin Franklin figure, the self-made man who because of ingenuity and pluck constitutes a folkloric American hero, was originally "Harold Flesh," the name of a character from both *A Bad Man* and *Dick Gibson.* That name was based, Elkin confided, on a real estate sign he saw while visiting his mother in Florida. Elkin switched to "Ben" in part to echo Franklin while retaining the reminder of mortality the surname brings. Ben, an American naïf who makes good in business because of serendipity and despite his many miscalculations, discovers his life's work while going to the Wharton School of Business, where he expected to study typing and bookkeeping on the G.I. Bill—something else that shaped mid-century America: "He was excited because he knew that he had something going for him now. He would discover which men's names were for sale and he would buy them and have that going for him. He would have them at the rate banks gave their favored customers and he would have *that* going for him, too. He was very excited. He had never been so excited" (50). A key cultural and economic transformation happening during the decades leading up to the bicentennial was the increasing displacement of local businesses, with their tendency toward uniqueness, local flavor, idiosyncrasy, and individualism, with the heavily regulated and uniform franchise, in which an entrepreneur purchases the right to represent a regional or national logo providing a product or service. For the consumer, whom Elkin always took more seriously than most of his contemporary writers did, this meant the appearance of uniform product quality as well as brand recognition, especially for whose who were traveling, a double motif in this novel; Ben is on the road more than most American heroes, in effect living in his Cadillac while driving from town to town, much like Stephen Feldman of Elkin's unpublished *The Glass Continent*. And the Americans to whom Ben aims his franchised products and services are also on the move—his great achievement, the "capstone of my career" is a Travel Inn franchise, a locally owned motel that looks like Travel Inns everywhere else in North America, except that "[h]e owns it all. Yet in a certain sense, though it's his, it's his by charter" (316). Travelers from far and near can depend on the quality and supervision by the franchiser to assure them that franchisees like Mr. Flesh must purchase materials from them and meet standards promulgated by the home office (stoned on marijuana, Ben tells the gala at his Chicago dance studio, "I come from Fred Astaire" [63]). Yet Elkin was virtually alone in this apparent endorsement of the franchise business in 1976. Most artists and intellectuals lamented this dilution of American culture, and more than a quarter-century after Elkin's novel appeared, intellectuals continue to complain about standardization in food suppliers, hotels, shopping centers, media outlets, and newspapers. By contrast, Elkin declared that he intended Ben to be "the man who makes America look like America" and summarized, "Our salvation is the Franchise business": as Ben puts it, "it may be a franchiser, I think, who'll save us. [. . .] Yes. Speaking some Esperanto of simple need, answering appetite with convenience foods" (258). When pressed about his identification with Flesh's goals in 1983, Elkin backed off toward the intellectual mainstream: "For a long time that was the game I talked, but I'm a lot more comfortable in the Hotel Pierre than [. . .] the Holiday Inn." He adamantly maintained, however, "Ben manages, I think, to rise above the kind of thing he's doing."[23]

Because of its subject matter, *The Franchiser* is even richer in topical allusions than Elkin's other work. Probably no serious novelist except John Updike in the Angstrom novels has been equally adept in capturing the look and feel of America in its transition from the authentically regional to the corporately tacky. Leafing through its pages we discover a shrewd archaeological rendering of the emergence of cineplexes, KFC stores, Dairy Queens, dry cleaners, and even funeral parlors. Elkin boasted that the only research he did for this book was a library carrel full of catalogues from Sears, Roebuck and Neiman Marcus: "I work directly from the illustrations in the catalogues." He also checked into a Holiday Inn for two days and "took a lot of notes about the *appearance*" to give the final chapters verisimilitude.[24] Moreover, he included a funny encounter with someone Ben could idolize, Colonel Sanders, the Kentucky Fried Chicken icon. Because of his publisher's anxiety about brand name infringement, however, Elkin agreed to change this character to a "doppelganger," one Roger Foster who impersonates the Colonel. For another piece of the story, however, he didn't have to do much research.

The defining element of *The Franchiser* is Ben's multiple sclerosis. Elkin stubbornly if not persuasively insisted to interviewers a decade apart that there was nothing autobiographical about this, that the disease occurred to him as a metaphor while the novel was in progress.[25] It proves to be a spectacularly successful trope, linking the progressive deterioration of Ben's physical being with another topical issue, the energy crisis of the early 1970s—the first such crisis in American history, and one that, in its consequent impact on related industries and services, bubbled over to create a decade of economic and cultural uncertainty. The novel describes brownouts, in which energy suppliers deliberately limited the amount of power to be transported over a grid, thus reducing energy for lights and producing a dimming effect. Like many Americans reacting to the energy crisis, Ben hoards absurdly. He carries cans of gasoline in the trunk of his Cadillac and thereby drives a gas-guzzling bomb. Like him, many Americans refused to accept (and still do) the inevitable logic of conservation as a means of reducing energy demand. And like Ben's MS, the energy crises of the 1970s and beyond have been punctuated by periods of remission. For brief periods, stable or even reduced energy cost lead consumers to hope the crisis has passed, only to learn that higher prices await. Ben's MS, like Stanley's, would move through plateaus, from relatively good health to periods of sensory deprivation and discomfort. Wonderful figure that it is, Elkin's insistence that the novel isn't autobiographical seems disingenuous. As Peter Bailey says, it's "exceedingly unlikely that Elkin would ever have thought of using multiple sclerosis as a cultural symbol had he not himself been afflicted with the disease, but the awareness of its autobiographical roots, rather than diminishing our sense of his achievement [. . .] tends instead to make our admiration for his ability to transform a physical reality into a complex symbol that much greater."[26]

There are other reasons to suspect that *The Franchiser* is Elkin's most overtly autobiographical published work to date. Ben's use of marijuana mirrors Stanley's, which evolved to therapeutic after the MS symptoms intensified. The moments of euphoria Ben feels, especially as he faces economic ruin, correspond to Stanley's own occasional bursts of ecstasy, especially after he accepted the diagnosis.[27] And one of the Finsberg twins and triplets who become Ben's responsibility when he accepted his legacy from his father's business partner is called "the Insight Lady." Ben has an affair with Patty in the Rockies during which they engage in a wonderful exchange of aphorisms during coitus: "We read shapes. The culture is preliterate!" and "It's tactile, a blind man's culture" (195) cogently describe the change from a culture of words and ideas to one of media packaging and sound bites that was taking place. Some of Ben's insights are solemn: "*I want my remission back!*" (196) suggests the tragic theme of the novel, that we cannot hope for a cure from our shared mortal condition. The best we can reasonably expect is respite, which in turn means another cycle toward entropy, suffering, and death—

something Ben and Stanley know too well: "Vouchsafed to die of his disease, it was as if here, in nature, where everything was a disease, all growth a sickness and the trees a sickness, too, with their symptomatic leaves and their pathological barks, the progress of his disease could leap exponentially, travel his bloodstream like the venom of poisonous snakes or the deathbites of killer spiders" (199). A colleague of Stanley's called "the Insight Lady" appears under that name in his radio play *The Coffee Room*. She's also credited with the epigraph in their mutual friend Howard Nemerov's "The Author to His Body on Their Fiftieth Birthday 29 ii 80": "There's never a dull moment in the human body." When I knocked at the door to interview Naomi and Al Lebowitz, she greeted me, "Hello. I'm the Insight Lady." This is not to say that Patty Finsberg is Naomi, but the name and properties of a close friend were appropriated for that character—a tactic that would bring Elkin considerable cause for regret in his next novel.

There's yet another reason for saying that Flesh is Elkin's most autobiographical character. As Bargen points out, the novel is organized around three trips Ben makes to inspect his franchises, with the largest portion treating a 1974 trip from Harrisburg, Pennsylvania, where Ben buys television sets for the motel he plans as his culminating achievement, through the Midwest, and ending with his Oklahoma City cineplex operation. Flashbacks take Ben to a 1971 journey from St. Cloud, Minnesota, to Colorado Springs. And the final, framing narrative is his effort at finding stability in his Travel Inn venture, in 1975. These are placed nonsequentially in the text and on the whole the itinerary constitutes one of the book's major motifs and symbols. Ben tells his god-cousins "I live along my itinerary" but in Oklahoma comes to his existential crisis: "[H]is itinerary. Which was what he had left in lieu of a life. [. . .] Only that. His itinerary. He could have wept" (245).[28] The notion of a journey instead of a life, which constitutes one of the novel's tragic themes, is based on his father's life. Essays Elkin wrote after *The Franchiser* made clear the reverence he had for his father and the degree to which that affection was grounded in Phil's professionalism. As a youth Stanley accompanied Phil on much of at least one itinerary, something he cherished as a key adventure of his life. In his early years he wrote several stories and novel drafts in which the hero, usually named Feldman after Tootsie's family, was a traveling salesman. And many, though not all, of the midwestern cities Ben visits in 1971 were on Phil's route. It's nearly inevitable that in this, the most important novel he'd written to date, Elkin contrasted anxiety about his own mortality against his father's grand American dream, the immigrant version of the dream Franklin personified, "the spirit of America's first champion of the commercial, the civic, and the secular" hero.[29]

In another important way *The Franchiser* is a breakthrough novel for Elkin. The hero ultimately commits to the well-being of others, not himself, and that commitment has tragic consequences. Flesh is the first Elkin hero to transcend the self-interest and indifference to others that characterized Main, Gibson, Boswell, and Feldman. When he accepts the prime rate as the legacy of Julius Finsberg, his father's partner who cheated him in a business deal, he accepts responsibility to fund the lives of his eighteen god-cousins, outwardly identical but each containing the unique genetic code that signals her or his mortality. In some ways the surrogate for Fritz-Allan Jay, the sole single (and still) Finsberg birth, Ben also inherits some of Julius's optimism. Facing his death and passing on the legacy of economic advantage to Ben so the surrogate can manage the fortunes of his god-cousins, Julius stubbornly maintains an optimism few Elkin characters, or those of any other serious writer of the times, can approach—a section of the novel Gass still reads brilliantly and joyfully in public performances: "So! Still! Against all the odds in the universe you made happy landings. What do you think? Ain't that delightful? Wait, there's more. You have not only your existence, but your edge, your advantage and privilege. You do, Ben, you do. No? Everybody does. They give congressmen the frank. Golden-agers go cheap to the movies. You work on the railroads they give you a pass. You clerk in a store it's the 20 per cent discount. You're a dentist your kid's home free with the orthodontics. Benny, Benny, we got so much edge we could cut diamonds!" (24–25). This euphoria in the face of imminent death constitutes a central theme of this novel and expresses a seldom-heard element of Elkin's fiction. As Ben faces his Travel Inn's certain failure, for the funding of which he has sold or mortgaged his successful franchises, he too feels a strange euphoria. The final paragraph has puzzled and fascinated reviewers, critics, and general readers; but it echoes Julius's dying optimism rhetorically and conceptually:

> He was broken, they would kill him. The Finsbergs were an endangered species and his Travel Inn was a disaster. They would kill him. Within weeks he would be strapped to a wheelchair. And ah, he thought, euphorically, ecstatically, this privileged man who could have been a vegetable or mineral instead of an animal and a lower animal instead of a higher, who could have been a pencil or a dot on a die, who could have been a stitch in a glove or change in someone's pocket, or a lost dollar nobody found, who could have been stillborn or less sentient than sand, or the chemical flash of someone else's fear, ahh. *Ahh!* (342).

Of course Ben was smoking weed while he spied on the sorrows, disappointments, and perversions of his few guests, but his euphoria is more than chemical and more than an illusion. It's a manifestation of a heretofore-submerged Elkin theme, that life is good in spite of certain defeat and that we should cherish it while it leads us to disappointment and death. He told an interviewer that euphoria is a manifestation of MS and throughout his post-diagnosed life he experienced inexplicable moments of elation.[30] Ben's grief has a deeper source

than his business failure, powerful as that motive must be. He has failed the
Finsbergs, whom he has grown to love. Although they're anything but loveable,
he transformed his responsibility for them to affection. Moreover, as he grew
to care about them, he became vulnerable to their indifference. Elkin's previous
heroes were self-contained men, able to absorb and ignore others' rebuffs. But
Ben can't, and his vulnerability elevates him to a higher moral and tragic stature
among Elkin heroes.

Aaron Asher, Elkin's new editor, was less aggressive than Fox had been in
demanding cuts, though he too unsuccessfully pressed for economies. He was,
however, enthusiastic about the novel and overwhelmingly gratified when the
prepublication blurbs flowed in. Nemerov concludes, "The only comparison I
come up with is Melville's *The Confidence Man*, about a century and a quarter
ago. But Stanley's reading fits us better; suggesting that in this world no villain
need be (though we have villains as well); with everyone cadillacking about trying
to make an honest nickel the result is still the weird and wonderful interlocking
fuck-up that keeps us going till we stop. What a fine vision! Love till die and
laugh till cry. And the whole marvelous mechano-organism goes on." And Coover
was equally enthusiastic: "This comic valentine to plastic blacktopped America
is a capital roadshow entertainment. It beats *Oklahoma* by a country mile, spins
circles around *Carousel*. [. . .] Five stars."[31] But the book came out to mixed reviews. Although most major reviewers recognized its originality and genius, a few
found it turgid and fanciful. *Publishers Weekly* declared it a "funny-sad tour de
force" that is "powerful, disturbing and occasionally hilarious." *Saturday Review*
called it Elkin's best novel organized around a "brilliant conceit." And the *New
York Times*, while guarded in its praise, concluded that it was "one of the more
original works of the season." Wolff in the *New York Times* and R. Z. Sheppard
in both the *New York Post* and *Time* praised the book's scope and virtuosity. The
Baltimore News-American declared it "a rare and unforgettable treat." But the
Book-of-the-Month Club, often a test of a book's market potential, damned it with
faint praise in the "also recommends" section, calling it "everything a good novel
should be, and more. It is brilliant, funny, serious, and combustible, possessing a
driving force that is rare in the American novel these days. It is also maddeningly
complex, overblown, discursive, unstructured, self-indulgent. [. . .] Stanley Elkin
writes in the tradition of other good-bad novelists—notably William Gaddis and
Thomas Pynchon—but he is funnier, more accessible and more humane."[32]

Not all the reviews were kind, as these titles demonstrate: "Rich in Character,
Thin in Story" (*Baltimore Sun*); "Elkin a Many-Talented Writer, but Glitter Seems
to Fade" (*Boston Sunday Globe*); "America under Microscope Is Funny, Boring"
(*Hartford Times*); "The American Zombie Portrayed" (*Greensboro Daily News*).
Although the raves considerably outweighed the negatives, and although even the
negatives generally conceded the originality of the conceit and Elkin's rhetorical

virtuosity, Elkin wasn't accustomed to negative reviews after *Gibson* and *Searches and Seizures*. Moreover, he felt any tiny reservation more keenly than the most grandiose praise. It was consoling to get letters from colleagues and friends praising the book while the stings from a few lukewarm reviews cooled off.

Helen Vendler captured the tragic themes with a reference to *King Lear:* "The real physical horrors—in the hospital, in the twins, in the MS—are extreme like Gloucester's blinding, with the grotesque, though it's there, not nullifying the extremity, something it seems almost impossible to get away with." Diane Wakoski read the book after Bread Loaf and wrote, "What a remarkable, wonderful, awful, brilliant book. My God, Stanley, your imagination gets wilder and more wonderful with every book. And how I identify with that terrible need to drive America, be all over the roads, the automobile giving place to the 20th century quest for the adventure which will replace the finding of the grail. [. . .] Oh Stanley, Stanley, what a book." And how gratifying it was to hear from the scholar who advised his doctoral thesis: "[B]ewildered and impressed by the allusions and references in your novel," John T. Flanagan marveled at his former pupil's knowledge of the day-to-day operations of so many businesses: "[Y]ou have captured enough of the idiom, the lingo to make your descriptions sound authentic." He concluded, "[P]erhaps Ben Flesh might become a cinema vehicle for Robert Redford," but prophetically acknowledged the problems of translating *The Franchiser* to film.[33]

Elkin had more disappointments to endure. Sales didn't meet his or Asher's expectations. The first month saw only 4,202 copies shipped, yielding an unearned balance of $11,409.42 against his modest advance. By March 1977 the unearned balance had dropped to $9,939.69, but returns quickly cut into that and by the year's end it increased to $10,188.82. Farrar, Straus and Giroux undertook to recoup some of its losses with an English-language agreement, once more advancing $15,000, and Casa Editrice in Milan paid 800,000 lira for translation rights. To make matters worse, in July Borchardt had received no paperback reprint offers—so the publisher couldn't recover any losses that way, and Elkin wouldn't have the opportunity for larger, if less profitable by individual book, sales. There was no paperback of *The Franchiser* until Boston publisher David R. Godine brought out a high-class trade edition of *Searches and Seizures* that sold out advances in 1979; buoyed by that success, he hoped to revive some out-of-print paperbacks. He wanted to bid on *The Living End,* but "I can't for a minute believe that it won't bring the big bucks. And, by God, it *should.*" Godine was interested in *A Bad Man,* but agreed that a quality paperback of *The Franchiser* would serve literary as well as commercial interests. The book came out with Gass's foreword, also published as a *New Republic* essay, which has since become one of the indispensable pieces of Elkin criticism. For a welcome change, this printing was commercially viable. Godine originally planned to print 3,500 copies, but he doubled that when the Quality Paperback Book Club selected it as an alternate. On the basis of that success, he printed another 3,500 copies of *Searches and Seizures*. Throughout the 1980s and 1990s, the Godine paperbacks played a major role in keeping Elkin on the literary radar; these two books were subsequently reissued with a handsome cover photo of Joan's painting of Stanley. Godine sent some welcome news in November: "More good news—you are about to be the recipient of some royalty monies. Don't go buy Joan a fur coat, but you're now well in the black and going strong."[34]

Only a year before, Elkin had switched from Random House to Farrar, Straus and Giroux because of his feeling that Random House's failure adequately to promote his books caused their poor sales. With a new publisher, and by his and many critics' assessments a more important novel, sales were even worse. Shortly after the publication of *The Franchiser*, yet another disruption in Elkin's publishing career emerged. Based on weak initial sales, Farrar advised Borchardt that they could offer no more than $6,000 advance against his next novel, soon to be titled *George Mills*. Borchardt negotiated a better deal with Henry Robbins at Dutton. To sweeten the deal, Dutton was willing to commit to reprinting several out-of-print paperback titles, and for many years the Dutton paperbound versions of all the books except *Searches and Seizures* and *The Franchiser* provided readers with an inexpensive introduction to Elkin. In September, the deal was complete. Asher wrote to say that he was sorry to lose Elkin after only one book "even though I completely agree with your position." At that point, total sales of *The Franchiser* were a puny 5,300,[35] and a brief relationship with a talented editor ended.

Movie inquiries came in for *The Franchiser* even before it came out in book form, but the most hopeful sign that this bicentennial novel might become a feature film occurred during the late 1970s, when former television stars Henry Gibson and Lily Tomlin, major contributors to *Rowan and Martin's Laugh-In* (NBC, 1968–73), expressed an interest in producing and starring in a film version. Both had recently acted in Robert Altman's *Nashville* (1975) and hoped they might interest Altman in directing. Borchardt discussed the project with Gibson in Los Angeles and they toured Altman's studio, but as was so often the case with Elkin's novels, the project died of its own weight. There was never a screenplay. In 1979 Godine mentioned that Warner "is interested, but they haven't yet made a move." In 1992, Lydia Pilcher, a producer who would make her mark with *The Talented Mr. Ripley* (1999) and *Vanity Fair* (2004), and Ed Lachman signed a "deal memo" to film *The Franchiser*, advancing $5,000 against a purchase price of $45,000 or 2½ percent of the profits. Because of Stanley's poor health, the agreement identified Joan, Philip, Bernard, and Molly as "Assignors." In 1994, however, Pilcher and Lachman notified the Borchardt Agency that they didn't intend to renew the agreement, and Ben Flesh never made it to the big screen.

Although the novel would present considerable challenges for the screenwriter, it could, with imaginative cutting and directing, form a major motion picture on the transformation of America as the country turned 200.[36]

By 1977, then, Hollywood had flirted, but she had rebuffed his eager response; yet Stanley wasn't done with the movies and he still harbored ambitions to write for the screen. His most comprehensive novel to date repeated the theme of his writing life with a vengeance: commercial failure, artistic success. And the grim prognosis of the MS diagnosis was proving true. He needed a cane to walk any distance, he was being hassled by his doctors to lose weight and stop smoking, and his handwriting was virtually illegible. Yet his fame among those who really mattered, his friends and colleagues in St. Louis and his wider family in the writing community, continued to increase and he was widely viewed as one of America's most important novelists. His spirit undimmed by disappointments, he looked forward to completing the trilogy of novellas he began for Bread Loaf and to completing a very long novel about a blue-collar man from St. Louis.

10 **Heaven and Hell, St. Louis
and Mexico, the First Crusade,
and South America**

Life's Greatest Hits and a Major
Disappointment, 1978–82

> You don't seem to understand. Stanley Elkin doesn't
> believe in spit. My characters do. And while I'm writing
> them, you know, maybe I think, hey, that's a pretty good
> line. They might even talk me into it. But I'm writing
> these characters. I'm making up those beliefs. They believe
> in spit, not me. . . . The most I can give them is not my
> sympathy, but the best lines I can think of to give them.
> But that's my business—to give people the best lines. I'm
> like a speech writer. For Reagan.
>
> —Elkin to Roger Hahn, 1983 (ellipses his)

The decade's final years were the most prosperous and controversial of Elkin's writing life. Despite his disappointments about the movie of
"The Bailbondsman" and the failure to film *The Art of War,* renewed interest in
filming his works flourished as his most influential work to date, *The Living End,*
amused, delighted, or shocked various audiences. Unlike its protagonist, God,
who "never found my audience," Elkin found himself in the unusual position of
having the literary community's attention in ways he'd dreamed about but had
never before experienced. With his multiple sclerosis under control, his novels
being optioned for films, magazines competing for his essays, and *The Living
End* generating enthusiastic praise and strident condemnation, Elkin took up his
long-cherished idea of a novel about a blue-collar man victimized by a thousand-
year curse. While completing what he considered his magnum opus, he brought
out *Stanley Elkin's Greatest Hits.* He and Joan also traveled to South America as
U.S. cultural representatives and he discovered the inspiration for his next novel,
The Magic Kingdom, during a London vacation. Family life changed dramatically too, with Philip joining the army and Bernie moving to a Massachusetts
boarding school. The decade ended with a sad note when Joan's father died in

June 1979. Although the MS continued to cast a long, grim shadow—one he mirrored by making his own morbid fashion statement, affecting suspenders bearing the images of skulls and crossbones—Stanley was at the top of his writing, film, teaching, and performing career.

His return to Bread Loaf in 1976 initiated a project that would increase his fame and fortune. Contemplating his reading for the 1976 conference, he enjoyed another of his life's serendipities. Awakening at night, he asked himself, "What if all this stuff about heaven and Hell were true? Literally. I was impressed with the idea, but too lazy to get a pencil and write it down. It was the first time in 22 years that something like that had come to me. So I woke Joan [. . .] and asked her to remember it. I don't know if she did. I didn't have to test her. I remembered. It was very easy to write, it all came fast."[1] This inspiration led to easy writing, perhaps because, despite its over-the-top subject matter, the triptych is Elkin's most linear narrative since another big hit, "The Making of Ashenden." Although written in successive summers among a variety of competing activities, the three stories are direct and easy to follow, in comparison with the intricate flashbacks in *The Franchiser* or *George Mills;* they combine to form a unified narrative of Minneapolis, hell, and heaven.

Ellerbee, the hero of "The Conventional Wisdom," takes his place among several uniquely modern adaptations of the biblical Job figure. For twentieth-century writers, this narrative of God's testing the righteous man has morphed from an encomium on obedience to a questioning of the grand design. Robert Frost's *A Masque of Reason* (1945) playfully contests the rationale by which God permits his most loyal subject to suffer only to demonstrate loyalty to him. *J.B.,* the 1959 Pulitzer Prize–winning play by poet Archibald MacLeish, uses the biblical text as a framework for his wealthy banker who refuses to renounce God despite his awareness that it was with God's consent that he lost family, friends, possessions, and hope. Perhaps taking his cue from MacLeish, Elkin makes his Job a businessman, a man of virtue and decency virtually absent from Elkin's fiction and most modern literature; Ashenden of the novella is also virtuous, but his decency seems less meaningful than Ellerbee's because it's grounded in a culture of wealth and privilege. Although operating a fiercely competitive enterprise, Elkin's liquor store owner behaves with exemplary virtue despite the tendency of his vocation toward cutting ethical corners. Murdered in the last of a series of holdups, Ellerbee meets St. Peter at the pearly gates with the reasonable expectation that his virtuous life has earned eternal bliss. The reader too is shocked when St. Peter says, literally, "Go to hell." The rest of the novella traces Ellerbee's timeless sojourn in hell, "the ultimate inner city" trying to come to terms with the injustice of his punishment. His chance comes when God answers Ellerbee's prayer to the "Old Terrorist," "God the Godfather," and pays a visit. No longer a loyal and obedient servant—he wants "no Job job, no nature in tooth and claw"

(38–39)—Ellerbee demands the explanation his biblical prototype didn't. God's answers are legalistic technicalities, such as disobeying the fifth commandment: Ellerbee cheerfully honored his adoptive parents, but the commandment requires him to honor his biological progenitors, despite the fact that he never knew who they were; or his breaking the seventh when he developed an erection while the wife of a murdered employee, whose salary Ellerbee continued to pay, came on to him. The "sins" go on and on, always the letter rather than the substance of the law,[2] and all that's left for Ellerbee is to endure eternity in hell with the meager consolation that he's really been screwed over.

Geoffrey Wolff recalled the excitement with which he heard Elkin read "The Conventional Wisdom" at Bread Loaf in 1976 and Hilma Wolitzer remembers raucous laughter followed by stunned silence, a reading she still thinks of as "the most stellar" experience of all her Bread Loaf years. Because of its controversial content, however, it was turned down by *The New Yorker* and *Esquire,* but eagerly accepted by *American Review.* Editor Ted Solotoff mentioned that like "some of the other readers here, I find that the descriptions of the torments go on a bit. Otherwise I don't see much to do with this story except publish it and rejoice." It proved to be one of Elkin's most frequently reprinted pieces, snapped up for *Best American Short Stories 1978* and included in *Stanley Elkin's Greatest Hits.* In 1983 it appeared in Tobias Wolff's *Matters of Life and Death: New American Stories.*

Early in the trilogy's composition, Elkin decided that each story's title would be a cliché, in part because there's a correlation between the function of clichés as packaged speech expressing a cultural truism and the inspiration for the novel, that everything about heaven and hell is true—hence pearly gates, streets paved with gold, heavenly choirs. A small inconvenience attended the publication of the collection when Henry Robbins, his new editor, received a complaint from John Bart Gerald, whose book *Conventional Wisdom* had been published by Farrar, Straus and Giroux in 1972. Gerald felt that Elkin's new book, then projected as *The Conventional Wisdom,* infringed on his title. Robbins was convinced that the law was on Elkin's side, and Gerald didn't proceed against Elkin or E. P. Dutton. Soon, however, Robbins began using the title of the second novella, *The Bottom Line.* A University of Nebraska student newspaper described Elkin's November 1978 reading of that story: It "had the audience in hysterics at times, especially during the dialogue between the saintly ones. [...] Even those who were offended by the sacrilegious account had to be impressed by Elkin's command of language and imagination."[3]

"The Bottom Line" was reported as far away as Kent, where Robert Coover heard from Wolff about Elkin's "great reading of your god's-little-chillun" and predicted that these Bread Loaf events might someday rival the Ashenden episode in the monastery, now "a permanent part of Kentish folklore here." Coover also sounded a note of personal concern: "Geoffrey said you looked fit, but scared everybody with pillpopping routines."[4] This second installment of the hell story, subsequently published in *Antaeus,* was a hit wherever he read it. And its content gets Elkin into even more controversial theology than "Conventional Wisdom." It concerns the reconciliation of Ellerbee and Ladelhaus, an accessory in the fatal robbery, but the tone shifts when God pays a second visit to hell and mistakes a smart remark by one of the damned as emanating from Ladelhaus. In His rage He banishes Ladelhaus *from* hell. This has two direct consequences. First, Ladelhaus hears "God's under-the-breath 'Oops'" and concludes that not everything we heard about omnipotence is true: "He means me, He makes mistakes" (50–51). This introduction of a less-than-goof-proof God set the stage for the final story, but it also enraged fundamentalists of all creeds who ever heard of Elkin or *The Living End.* Elkin's explanation is an explicit challenge to the conventional wisdom of God's infallibility: "He makes a tiny mistake every now and then. So what? He's God, he's entitled. That was the idea, don't you see? Creating somebody so powerful, so immensely powerful, that he can do anything he wants to. God's not subject to the kinds of laws we're subject to."[5] It also generated big sales.

The second consequence of God's mistake is, where does one go when one is banished *from* hell? Heaven's out, and there's no purgatory in this theology. So Ladelhaus becomes "the only dead man" decomposing but retaining consciousness in the only grave in a deconsecrated plot that's now part of a high school athletic field. His encounter with an obnoxious hypertensive groundskeeper leads to wildly funny and petty efforts to get revenge on the dead man who won't leave Quiz alone, including a fictional war between Minneapolis and St. Paul. As the episode ends, God visits an amateur concert and exhibits another absolutist attribute. Hearing a child play "Sheep May Safely Graze," He takes Flanoy to heaven immediately because his music "made me all smarmy." Unable to dissuade God from ending the child's life, Ladelhaus exploits "His mistakes" to get a small revenge, telling Him to take Quiz: "God, who knew nothing [not omniscient?] of their quarrel but owed Ladelhaus a favor, struck Quiz dead" (84).

Unlike "Conventional Wisdom," this story isn't self-contained; it can only be understood in the context of the previous one. By this time Robbins had embraced Elkin's description of the larger narrative frame: "I've come more and more to like the word 'triptych' as a description of the book's form; it really does have certain resemblances to those early Renaissance triptychs with their three panels depicting different aspects of the central theme." He also regretted Elkin's deleting a reference to Dante in copy for Dutton's catalogue.[6] When the book came out, "triptych" appeared prominently on the cover, recalling the connection between Trinitarian doctrine and the religious references that center the text. But "The Bottom Line" is a pop culture crossover, a cliffhanger for Installment 1979.

Ladelhaus's banishment from hell isn't resolved, the injustice of Flanoy's death is in the balance, and what will God do with Quiz? And what about Ellerbee? Tune in next year at Bread Loaf.

The conference regulars, and by now much of the literary community, were on tenterhooks with excitement about how Elkin would top "The Bottom Line," and he didn't disappoint. Although he resisted comparisons with Dante in advertising brochures, the triptych aligns cleverly with the *Commedia* in this respect: the first "panel" is about earth; the second, about hell; and "The State of the Art" is about heaven. But in spite of choirs of angels, pearly gates, and reunions of the blessed, heaven isn't happy. Flanoy misses his family and Minneapolis until he and the Blessed Virgin establish an emotional symbiosis. Jesus, "the magic cripple" whose portrayal offended Christians of all but the most liberal type, displays His wounded hands and feet to remind God of His suffering, insisting that He, like Flanoy, preferred earth: "I loved it there" (96). When God asks Jesus' forgiveness for smiting Quiz in Minneapolis, the response is puckish, but not conventionally divine. Jesus rescues Quiz from hell, where he's been the loudest of the gripers. Jesus' bringing a self-centered egotist to heaven, while a virtuous man like Ellerbee continues to suffer damnation, reminds us that Divine Justice may be capricious. The portrayal of the Holy Family delighted iconoclasts everywhere and enraged true believers. Joseph is a whiner, a stage Jew seething with resentment of his cuckoldry and stubbornly refusing to believe Jesus is the Messiah. And Mary is morbidly frigid, bitterly resenting the sexual connotations of virginity and birth, as well as the exploitation of her sexuality in missionary practices. If Ezra Pound once described *The Cantos* as a "commedia agnostica," "The State of the Art" is a "commedia atheistica."

The final pages, God's "gala," attracted cheers from the irreverent and playful and fury from the reverent. God, the pitchman-showman Creator, clarifies everything, from how to buy good used cars to who assassinated President Kennedy, then explains the ultimate mystery, the presence of suffering and death in this best of all possible worlds: "What do you make of Me Who could have gotten it all right the first time, saved everyone trouble and left hell unstocked? Do you love Me? Do you forgive and forget as easily as I do?" (126). This may seem like amateur theology, but the gravity of the question behind the question remains: if God is capable of creating a world without suffering and sorrow, why do we suffer and why do people go to hell? God's explanation resonates with anyone interested in literature: "It was all Art. *Because it makes a better story is why*" (129). Of course it's an artist's rather than a theologian's explanation. But our penchant for telling stories is one thing that makes us human. And stories have their basis in desire, the belief that things ought to be better than they are. Tragedies, comedies, romances, farces, and especially satires begin with the perception that life is imperfect and the imagination can diagnose, manifest, or theorize an alternative. Indeed, the notion of the Fall produced *Paradise Lost* and the New Testament and much of Melville and Faulkner.

Neither Stanley nor God was finished with the audiences giggling at Bread Loaf. God reminds the living and the dead, the blessed and the damned, that he's given humanity more second chances than we deserve: "All right, that's it! *Kairos!* Doomsday!" (129) and sets into motion the end of days. It's arguably the most apocalyptic ending since Stanley Kubrick's *Dr. Strangelove, or How I Learned to Stop Worrying and Love the Bomb* (1964), and in some ways Elkin's apocalypse is even more audacious than that other Stanley's. The end of time in *Strangelove* is the result of human incompetence, stupidity, and aggressiveness; in *The Living End*, nature ceases because God "never found My audience" (133), because creation, religion, and philosophy lacked the imagination to appreciate divine magnificence. Thus Elkin's God is the Artist Alone, the solitary creator who cannot be understood by creation and who therefore really has no one to talk to—rather like the artist Dylan Thomas describes in "In My Craft or Sullen Art," who writes "in the still night / When only the moon rages / And lovers lie abed." Like Thomas's autobiographical artist, who writes for lovers who couldn't care less about him or his creation, Elkin's God creates for a humanity that can't comprehend or appreciate His achievement. The apocalyptic tone of *The Living End* guaranteed that God's creator would at last find his audience, even if a portion of it would be loud, angry, and hostile.

When he presented the final installment at Bread Loaf, his new publisher was eager to rush his new, high-prestige author to its catalogue. But although the book was complete, the naming wasn't. At one time or another, Elkin tried each story's title as the collection's name. It was contracted as *The Conventional Wisdom*, but Robbins bought cover art for *The Bottom Line*. Elkin wasn't satisfied, and he discussed his predicament with the Third Tuesday crowd in St. Louis. He held a cliché contest, with people shouting out bromides to complement the ones he'd used for the individual sections. Kathleen Shea yelled "the living end" and Elkin stopped the contest: "That's it!" After he persuaded Robbins to have the cover art reprinted, he had the title for his most popular work. Her autographed copy reads, "For Kathleen, who gave me the title for the book."[7]

Even though Borchardt, Robbins, and John Irving assured him that this would be the book that would make him rich as well as famous, Elkin was edgy. He'd heard this before, if not as eloquently as Irving put it while congratulating Robbins on publishing the book: "He's always had critical respect—the highest kind—but I see this one as having the potential for winning him the broader audience he deserves. Stanley Elkin is a very serious man, but he is also the best entertainer now writing." Consoling as such praise from a fellow writer about to make the big time with *The World According to Garp* must have been, there were disappoint-

Artwork for the dust jacket of *The Bottom Line*, subsequently published as *The Living End*. Copy of dust jacket in Elkin Archive, by permission of Joan Elkin.

ments along the way, and Elkin tended to focus on these. John Barth and William Gaddis praised the book but refused to offer cover comments; Gaddis professed that "blurbs are so often a kind of self-advertisement on someone else's jacket" and Barth protested that his "vows to the muse prohibit the giving or soliciting of advertising testimonials, but I share your enthusiasm for Elkin in general and *The Living End* in particular." As usual, Coover came through with kind words: "[O]ne of the great visionary God stories of the past three to four thousand years. Hold your sides and look out for lightning bolts . . . !8 Then Elkin's hopes were dashed by his new publisher's catalogue foul-up, which produced one of the funniest and most poignant letters ever written about the writing life as art and business.

At literary conferences, Georges Borchardt often speaks on the challenges serious writers face getting published. He began to quote Elkin's January 1979 letter at Bread Loaf and Sewanee, often with Stanley laughing louder than anyone at the combination of petulance, injury, and the desire to "find his audience" the letter proclaims. Because Stanley drew so much pleasure from his letter's being introduced as articulating the inevitable tensions among artist, publisher, and agent, Borchardt sometimes deliberately placed it late in his remarks so he could watch Stanley squirm because he hadn't yet heard it:

It is I, Georges, the crybaby of the Western World. I want to tell on Henry [Robbins]. I want to report him, Georges.

I'm beginning to get the picture. I'm never going to be rich and famous like John Gardner, John Irving, all those other Johns. Henry is publishing THE LIVING END now, Georges; it used to be THE CONVENTIONAL WISDOM, then it was THE BOTTOM LINE there for a time; now it's THE LIVING END—but self-fulfilling-prophecy-wise the handwriting is on the wall, handwriting-on-the-wall-wise. Henry has sent along Xeroxes of a nine page ad that will proclaim Dutton's Spring list in PUBLISHERS WEEKLY. I thumbed through the full page stuff and past the two books to the page item and found myself where by this time I should have learned to look first, stuffed in with the Honorable Mentions and the books about veneers and the time-tables for the old New York Central. There it was— THE BOTTOM LINE (it wasn't THE LIVING END yet when it went to press), with its price, $7.95, a buck less than what it was when it was in the catalogue where it was still THE BOTTOM LINE but $8.95. Already discounted 6 months before publication. But that's all right. Prices are subject to change, the catalogue says so. But downward? Have I licked inflation single-handed? Will I get a thank-you note from Jimmy Carter? Well all this is sarcasm, Georges, it don't mean a thing, it's just my way of getting a cheap laugh. But then I understood! Exclamation points stuck like daggers in my consciousness, like banderillas! And that's sarcasm, Georges. But, Georges, the stuff about the title was inadvertent, it was an inadvertency, and the stuff about the price of the book may have been an error, but they left out the part about $30,000 ADVERTISING, they left out the part about $20,000 ADVERTISING. They left out the part about the AUTHOR TOUR, and the part about COOPERATIVE ADVERTISING AVAILABLE and even the part about COOPERATIVE ADVERTISING AVAILABLE IN NEW YORK CITY. I guess they <u>had</u> to leave out the BOOK-OF-THE-MONTH CLUB ALTERNATE part, and the BIG PAPERBACK REPRINT part, but couldn't they have said WORD OF MOUTH advertising available after all this talk of BIG BREAKTHROUGH in their catalogue copy and their ad copy? I can't stop being sarcastic, Georges, I don't want to shift tones. I want to be consistent. As I will be when THE LIVING END, or whatever may be its title by June, is published. Reviewers will tch tch about how I should be more widely known, and the paper people will agree but remind that business is business—they're going to sell 3,432 copies. I get those vibes, Georges. I'm going to get good reviews and nobody is going to make a penny, and Dutton will be able to say how it done good by literature. I'm good for publishing's image, a feather in the cap of free enterprise, a kind of artsy loss leader.[9]

Convinced that, despite enthusiastic responses at Bread Loaf and on the reading circuit, he'd once more be an "artsy loss leader," Elkin felt that he was again the victim of publisher incompetence, carelessness, or disinterest. Yet again, it seemed as if his work would never reach the larger public and he'd fail to sell out another advance. But this time he was wrong. The initial run of 12,500 hardcovers immediately sold out, and another run put Stanley in an unfamiliar position—he was in the black. A generous paperback contract, also with Dutton, promised even wider circulation and readership. Borchardt arranged an autograph party at Books and Company on Madison Avenue. By August 1979 Stanley was where he'd always wanted to be, on best-seller lists: number ten on the *New York Post* list and number eighteen on *Ingram Newsletter*. Foreign-language presses eagerly bid. Jonathan Cape, who had published Elkin before, grabbed up British rights; Rowholt Verlag bought German rights for *Himmel und Holles: auch eine Göttliche Komodie*. Gallimard in France found it "too immoral," but Laffont offered 25,000 francs against a generous percentage for *Au commencement était la fin;* and in February 1980, Borchardt entered an agreement with Zmora-Bittan-Moran for Hebrew rights. In 1987 Empuries translated it to Spanish and Editora Schwartz to Portuguese. The underground Polish house Wydanicto Przeds´wit, with the perestroika movement and the fall of Communism imminent, translated it among American books, especially the most risky of them.[10]

One can only imagine the challenge of translating *The Living End* with its theological irreverence and lexical playfulness. French translator Jean-Pierre Carasso, who had rendered *A Bad Man* as *Un sale type,* expressed the tribulations of many who undertook the task: "[I]t is an atrociously hard book to translate, harder still than the *Bad Man* in spite of the fact that it is shorter. [. . .] I'll do everything I can to make the French readers weep as you made me weep and laugh as you made me laugh (this seems rather impossible, in fact) and if you have any piece of advice [. . .] I would appreciate it very much if you'd let me know. How about the title, for instance? Would le professeur d'anglais let me know what the real writer had in mind, so I can devise a French equivalent that would not be too *indigent?* You're the hero of Heaven, I call upon you!"[11] And the reviews were, overall, generous with praise. It was lauded for wit, exuberance, playfulness, and especially irreverence by most of the critics in the major markets.

Not only did reviewers praise the book extravagantly, but readers wrote to express their delight as well. A friend from Michigan raved about it and Irving's review, but also fretted about Stanley's health, asking if he still swam regularly and ending with a doleful recollection: "You know when I think about you the most? Holding onto a rail and walking up and down steps." Chuck Gold gave a copy to a judge for the Pulitzers.[12] Letters from people Elkin didn't know poured in too. Laura Wilson of Corvalis, Oregon: "*The Living End* gave me nightmares, it was so good. I found myself, a bad Catholic, praying for everything I learned in Sunday School not to be true. If it wasn't for your delightful humor I could not loan that book to my less-than-stout-hearted friends." Michael Ledeen of *The Washington Quarterly:* "You got God and Joseph perfectly and Hell sounds the way I remember it. I gave a copy to [former Secretary of State Henry] Kissinger for his birthday . . . with inscription so that he will know how to behave when he gets there." Arthur A. Leff of Yale Law School called it "magnificent": "It is not CHURCH DOGMATICS or SYSTEMATIC THEOLOGY or even RELIGIO MEDICI, but as the only successful marriage of Brueghel and Bosch, it is a lot closer to a modern Thomas à Kempis than one would have thought possible." His former editor, Joe Fox, sent a touching card: "I'm still here and I miss you." The Library of the American Academy and Institute of Arts and Letters requested one of the university examination books on which Elkin wrote the first draft of "The Bottom Line" in connection with a citation, the inscription of which reads in part: "A trinity of tales in which a literal imagination works upon the persons and eschatology of our sacred books. [. . . T]hink of Laurence Sterne doing his version of the Inferno; or, to adapt a remark of Horace Walpole, 'the adventure of an orthodox rabbi in Bedlam.'" Public Broadcasting Service inquired about a radio production based on *The Franchiser* and *Dick Gibson,* culminating with a discussion of and reading from *The Living End.* A decade later David Gregory from Santa Fe praised the challenging theology of the novel and one of its successors: "*The Magic Kingdom* should be required reading in medical schools and *The Living End* in seminaries and vice versa."[13]

A friend who remains anonymous sent the funniest letter. "Pearl Lee Gates" of "1979 Eternity Road, Orlando, FL" asked, "How dare you write such a terrible book!! Why would anyone read such trash!!" and confessed that "she" was offended by the time she got to page forty-six: "It would be awful enough if there was only one dirty story, *but to write three such filthy stories in the same book cannot be forgiven!!* Again, have you no shame? Your language is as bad as my first and fourth husbands used!! The more I think about all this crap, the—the more anger I feel!!! Literature is supposed to cause reflection in people Mr. Elkin, it's used to change the way people think and act . . . this horrible book couldn't change the way anyone thinks . . . the very idea . . . *this book should be sent to burn in the vast meadows of Hell among its fiery hills!!!*" To encode the tongue-in-cheek tone, "Ms. Gates" undermined her objections to the dirty language: "People should not write books that make fun of God and Jesus and all-that-stuff!!!! The most terrible thing is your use of all that filthy language. Damn! Your book is nothing but a big bunch of shit!! So there!!!"[14]

Not all the correspondents were as witty as "Ms. Gates." Some took pen in hand to vent about its irreverence and blasphemy, none so vociferously as a lady from Rhode Island who wanted her money back. Her rabbi mentioned it during an adult education class, so she bought a copy: "It is such an affront; so crude, so gross, so disgusting, that I could not finish the book. Naturally it's beyond the 3 days allowed to return it without a receipt!! So I am sending it back to you to hopefully recoup my $7.95 plus 6% Rhode Island tax."[15]

With few but occasionally strident exceptions, reviewers in the major markets and national magazines in the United States and United Kingdom enthusiastically encouraged their readers to read *The Living End*. A few dailies in local markets demurred on the basis of irreverence, but most followed Irving's lead in the *New York Times Book Review:* "His talent and compassionate laughter have always been huge. Now he has a novel—a narrative and a vision—that can contain the tendency of his robust imagination and his ribald language run amok. 'The Living End' is a big book for Stanley Elkin, and a fine and daring novel for our literature." Tom LeClair in *Saturday Review* invoked Dante and Geoffrey Wolff compared it with Melville, concluding "The book is a man-made miracle." Terence du Pres informed *Washington Post Book World* readers that this is a big book "in every way but length" by the "magister ludi," concluding, "Hard and unyielding as his comic vision becomes, Elkin's laughter is remission and reprieve, a gesture of willingness to join the human mess, to side with the damned, to laugh in momentary grace at whatever makes life Hell." Paul Bailey of the *Times Literary Supplement* (U.K.) thought it "the most sustained and dazzling performance that vaudeville's answer to Sir Thomas Browne" has achieved. James Frakes urged *Cleveland Plain Dealer* subscribers to buy the book and cheerfully shared a reader's possibly tongue-in-cheek concern for *his* immortal soul: "My friend, I will pray for you. Do you realize that in your article you have blasphemed. [. . .] Please, James, ask GOD, Jesus, for forgiveness."[16]

Like the *Plain Dealer*'s correspondent, a few U.S. and U.K. reviewers complained about Elkin's lack of reverence. *Kirkus Reviews* damned it with faint praise, labeling it a "spotty, minor work, perhaps but with flashes [. . .] of brilliance." A reviewer for the *Spiritual Studies Center* charged that Elkin must have concluded that "saying 'fuck' no longer shocks so he has turned to blasphemy." The *Baltimore Sun* groused that the triptych shows that "Americans seldom blaspheme with style" while readers of the *London Times* were warned that Elkin "works hard—too hard?—at his verbal fireworks. A bit fancy, as they say in Yorkshire." Not to be outdone, the *Irish Times* snapped, "Hands off Bethlehem, smarty boots."[17] Although the negative reviews enjoyed the rhetorical advantage of righteous indignation, they were a loud minority whose outrage probably contributed to the novel's sales. Maugre their carping, this was Stanley Elkin's Greatest Hit. It had wowed 'em at Bread Loaf, on the lecture circuit, in serial form, in hardcover, and with the reviewers. And another exciting chapter awaited, one that nearly completed the dream of fame, fortune, and artistic integrity.

Michael Ritchie, the producer who was still shopping around two scripts Elkin had developed for him, found "The Conventional Wisdom" "delightful but resolutely non-commercial. How the hell do I do Heaven and Hell?" Raymond Wagner, who had brought the idea of filming "The Bailbondsman" to Warner Brothers, wasn't so cautious. Fellow producer Maurice Singer owned film rights for *The Living End* and approached Wagner about a joint venture to produce it. Upon reading the triptych and some reviews, Wagner realized that this was truly special, a story with enormous social implications, but a film they'd need to approach with great care because of its controversial content. After having weighed the risks against the potential aesthetic and commercial rewards, Wagner called St. Louis to inquire about Elkin's interest in writing the screenplay. Although they hit it off immediately, Elkin was unwilling or unable to undertake the project. He'd recently returned from South America and was behind schedule with *George Mills*. Elkin suggested Frank Galati, who had adapted *The Dick Gibson Show* for the stage. The first problem was that Galati was on a Caribbean cruise. When Wagner finally reached him, Galati was excited about the opportunity to adapt another Elkin work, but he was after all on vacation and he was aware of some of the challenges *The Living End* posed. So he promised to give Wagner a decision in ten days. Within that time he'd completed most of a draft. He flew to Los Angeles where he, Wagner, Elkin, and Singer hammered out an agreement; then he and Elkin discussed the screenplay. They signed a formal agreement, with Elkin agreeing to "polish" Galati's drafts with compensation of $3,000 on completion and $25,000 more upon making the picture.

Galati returned to the Caribbean, where he revised the first draft. When it arrived in Los Angeles, Wagner proclaimed it "wonderful" and arranged for Galati, Singer, and himself to meet Elkin in St. Louis over the Fourth of July to work on revisions. As the consultation proceeded, however, one seemingly insurmountable difficulty persisted, a problem when reading the book that would be much greater when seeing the film. In "The Bottom Line," God decides to take a child. This is consistent with the theme of God's capriciousness, but to visualize the child's death—the film script has him struck by lightning—seems gratuitous. In a St. Louis restaurant, Wagner told Elkin and Galati that this scene would never fly, that it would turn audiences against the film. Galati was also uncomfortable with the episode, and Elkin agreed to think about it. After midnight, Galati's hotel room phone rang: "This is Stanley. I know why God killed Flanoy." "This is good news, Stanley. Why?" "Because he wouldn't practice." Click.

Despite their misgivings about this episode, Wagner and Singer went ahead with the project. They secured an understanding with Peter O'Toole (b. 1932) to play the role of God, and Ken Russell (b. 1927) agreed to direct. But the film, like the triptych, stands or falls on Ellerbee, the Job figure. On pure hope, Wagner sent the script to the agent of *Saturday Night Live* comic genius John

Belushi (1949–82) who had branched out to film with *Animal House* (1978), *The Blues Brothers* (1980), and others. Soon Wagner received a lunch invitation from Belushi, who came right to the point: "Ray, I don't laugh a lot. I just don't find that many things funny. It's just the way I am. But while I read this script I laughed so hard I almost fell off the couch. When I got near the end, I wouldn't finish it, and the script lay open on my table for two days. My wife said, 'John, you gonna finish this script or what?' and I told her 'This is too good, there's no way they're not gonna screw it up at the end.' But when I got the nerve to finish it, I knew I wanted to make this movie."

With the principal actors and the director lined up, Wagner turned to the problem of scheduling, when, weeks after the lunch, the disaster that torpedoed the film occurred. Belushi fatally overdosed and the project began to unravel. They considered other actors, but Russell began to emphasize the fantastic physical effects of heaven and hell, beyond even the lavish special effects Galati's script demanded, and eventually the project imploded. Looking back, Wagner regrets that the film wasn't made, but realizes that it was too daring for its time and much too daring for the first decade of the new millennium. Its content scared away many investors, who feared the public's reaction to a visual representation of Elkin's mercurial showman God and his unflattering portrayal of the Holy Family.

When Wagner flew Elkin to Los Angeles for a production conference, another manifestation of Elkin's starstruck alter ego manifested itself. They went to lunch at an upscale restaurant on Pico Boulevard. While they were ordering, Stanley repeatedly asked, "Are we gonna see any movie stars today? I want to see some movie stars, dammit." Wagner was replying "Who knows?" when a warm voice said over his shoulder, "Hello, Ray." When he turned to greet Jacqueline Bisset, he noticed that Stanley's mouth was gaping and his eyes were luminous. Ms. Bisset accepted Wagner's invitation to sit and chat for a few minutes, and Stanley was able to manage some small talk. But he remained starstruck for the rest of the lunch, and "his mouth was wide open all the time we were together that afternoon."[18]

Frank Galati, who identifies this as the second major step in his journey that would lead to his Academy Award nomination for the 1988 screenplay of *The Accidental Tourist*—the first step was his adaptation of *The Dick Gibson Show* for the stage—was cautious in developing the script. Kubrick might get away with cinematic apocalypse, but Galati and Wagner weren't eager to risk it. In the film script, Ellerbee becomes an agent of reconciliation when he gets into heaven via a circuitous route, finally bringing an end to the bickering between Jesus and God. Forgiving God for his time in hell, Ellerbee suggests that they "have a few beers." God introduces his new chum to Jesus and the final stage directions form a tableau quite opposite Elkin's apocalypse: "Jesus looks at his curled hand. He extends it slowly and gradually the fingers bend. He proffers it to Ellerbee now

clean and free of stigmata in an inviting handshake. God stops Jesus' right hand
with his own. God's right hand grasps Jesus' right hand. Jesus reaches across
their clasped hands and takes Ellerbee's left hand in his own left hand. God's left
hand grabs Ellerbee's right wrist and lifts it above their heads in triumph."[19]

Even though the triptych is Elkin's shortest work, Galati recognized the need
for compression, especially because his script calls for frame-consuming establishing shots and transitions, such as Ellerbee's ascent to heaven. To accomplish
this, he eliminated Ladelhaus, transferring to Ellerbee his role as the only dead
man and completing the circuit—living virtuously, viewing heaven, suffering
hell, lying dead, and entering heaven in triumph. He also eliminates the distasteful Quiz, thus tightening the relationship between the dead Ellerbee and the
children, especially Flanoy, and setting up the most important change Galati
made in order to give the story a Hollywood ending while remaining faithful to
Elkin's portrayal of a dysfunctional Holy Family. Galati's Jesus rescues Ellerbee
from death in response to Flanoy's longing, and in part to annoy His Father and
please His Mother. Ellerbee's ascent of course sets the scene for reconciliation in
heaven. Although he consulted on the script, Elkin soon became displeased with
these transformations. In 1983 he told Robert Earlywine that Singer and Wagner
continued to exercise their options, "but I don't think it will ever be made. Not
with the script they have."[20]

In addition to Bread Loaf, work on *The Living End,* and work on *George
Mills,* the Elkins embarked on a unique adventure in 1978. A curious letter from
Wolff expresses hope that Stanley will "knock them out of their socks in Brazil":
"If they spit on your limousine or poke you with anti-gringo placards, viejo, let
me know promptly and I'll have my Assistant Secretary of State drop bombs on
them." Except for a whimsical, fictional "reminiscence" in which he professes to
have met Vladimir Nabokov in Venezuela, there had been no indication of any
interest Latin America in any of Elkin's writings to this point, though he was
setting a small but critical section of *Mills* in Mexico. Coover and Gass had gotten consulting jobs with the United States Information Agency as, in the jargon
of government authorization, an "American Specialist." When he heard about
this combination of travel on the government's nickel and modest pay, Stanley
wondered, "Why can't I get a job with them too?" He suddenly insisted that
he'd always wanted to visit South America, though he didn't speak Spanish or
Portuguese and had only a dilettante's interest in that continent's literature and
culture. Joan summarized the trip in an undated note: "State dept sent Stanley
to Brazil and Venezuela. Paid for his airline ticket and paid him $832 + $50 per
day for 15 days." Because of his MS, he petitioned to claim Joan's airfare as a
necessary business expense.[21]

They landed in Rio de Janeiro and then flew to Brasilia on February 9, 1978.
In Rio an embassy staff member warned them not to discuss state secrets or

nuclear power plants; Elkin was there to give a lecture to South American high school English teachers. They were told that they'd speak with South American diplomats, and they had dinner with at least one ambassador during the trip. They loved Florianopolis, which struck them as stunningly beautiful and socially exhilarating. Like Brasilia, it featured well-planned social events with fascinating intellectuals and politicians. Caracas, Venezuela, was another story: "It scared the hell out of us" because of the oppressive poverty all around. The hotel at which they stayed felt like a fortress; everyone was well dressed, dinners were elegant and beautifully served, and there was a bar mitzvah in the hotel while they were there. But Joan was afraid to take a walk, even around the hotel, and wherever they went by cab or state department car, they encountered great poverty. They felt generally isolated for the few days they spent there. Stanley went out to give his talks and returned, but their social life was confined to the hotel. The trip's only unpleasant reading happened in Caracas; at an arranged meeting with a local book club, Stanley read excerpts from *The Franchiser*. Unlike the high school English teachers to whom he gave his prepared talk, this audience spoke practically no English, so he'd read a sentence, then a translator would render it in Spanish. After about an hour of this, still only a few pages into his text, Elkin said, "You know, I don't think we'll go on with this," and the audience applauded politely. His prepared remarks for the Venezuelan Writers Association and academics from various regional universities went very well, as suggested by this state department assessment: "Although his lack of Spanish presented some difficulties, partially overcome by a post-supplied interpreter, he was well received by all three levels. He was given an especially warm and understanding welcome by the academic audience at Central University. [. . .] They came out in large numbers, regardless of semester break, to listen to and exchange views with this prominent, witty, and controversial novelist." The Brasilia embassy made a similar assessment, though Joan remains annoyed by their caveat. His talk was a "[s]uperb, beautifully crafted presentation. Unanimous audience request for printing, distribution of manuscript" and the overall assessment was that in both the talk and the discussion sessions, "Elkin exceeded in all aspects." The caveat? He had trouble climbing stairs, so visits to seminars in third-floor classrooms had to be canceled. In fairness, the embassy is critical of poor planning by the United States Information Agency, not of Elkin, and the report closes with an urgent plea that the embassies be made aware of special needs, in this case elevators, for all impaired guests.[22]

The speech he adapted for the South American tour—he'd given versions of it to North American audiences, including the University of Denver—was a sophisticated look at the "Writer in Society." It began with his apology for "not being more famous," a best seller, or a Nobel laureate: "[M]ea culpa me for the disease of my obscurity. Forgive me the sin of anonymity and excuse my un-fame." While this could be construed as counterproductive and even self-pitying, as usual

Elkin knew exactly what he was doing. He points out that even popular writers aren't widely read and that serious writers like Saul Bellow, Barth, or Gass might walk "unrecognized through not only airports but through actual libraries." By contrast, Truman Capote, Norman Mailer, or Gore Vidal might be asked for autographs, but only because people recognized them from television talk shows, not because they've read their books: "Fiction simply isn't popular. Even *popular* fiction isn't popular." After slyly demonstrating that Peter Benchley's *Jaws* (1974) was the quintessential American novel for its time and that Harold Robbins (1916–97) was the model of the successful novelist, having sold 200,000,000 books by 1978, Elkin addressed his real theme, that a preoccupation with society's approval guarantees bad writing. Invoking Henry James, Leo Tolstoy, William Faulkner, and, with a nod to his Latino hearers, Gabriel García Márquez, Elkin returned to a theme that remained constant throughout his writing life: "A writer writing has no sense of his audience, let alone his society, less notion of them than a child praying has of God. The writer writing *is* his audience. He is talking to himself. [. . .] The point I'm trying to make is that the writer finds his audience by *being* his audience." This was pure Elkin, a thoroughly original riff on the theme of the artist's obligation to his society and the notion of verisimilitude. It also represented his preoccupation with the issues of representation while he worked on two of his most imaginative works, *The Living End* and the first section of *George Mills*.

Elkin as cultural ambassador? In December 1979 he repeated as a "professional associate" for the East-West Center, in a Honolulu conference about "The Global Situation." His "Address to the Hawaiians" is a variation on the South America talk, with a similar theme of the futility of associating the writer's work with his culture, but this version introduces the notion of cultural pluralism. Improvising on C. P. Snow's concerns about the growing abyss between the sciences and the humanities, Elkin hypothesizes that "Snow was wrong I think. He underestimated. Like some early astronomer he names a planet and thinks he's found the sky. Two cultures? *Two?* There are two thousand. Two million. Too many." And the competing frequencies of these diverse cultures on "my bi-cameral mind" render cultural representation distracting and impossible. To compound the problem, Elkin reminisces about the traditional role of the "writer in society," which, he insists, was once clear-cut: "They were shamans or bards. They brought the news, explained the battles, identified the laws, passed on what God had told them in visions. [. . .] It's only in our own century—the romantic tradition is an exception with its lung stained poets and garret nesting bohemians—that the writer is no longer an instrument of the priests and the rabbis." This isn't nostalgia for the days when writers occupied a central social position, but an embracing of cultural pluralism and its consequence, that writing must be individual and idiosyncratic rather than "social" if it is to matter.[23]

Although his experience with *Best American Short Stories 1969* had been marred by controversy and charges of cronyism, he agreed in 1979 to serve again. For months his mail was cluttered by letters from writers, some famous, some not, asking him to consider their stories for the annual. Don't worry, writers. I'm not naming names. With expert assistance from Shannon Ravenel, Elkin avoided controversy this time. The only pal whose story made the final cut was Gass, whose stature is beyond question. A solid cross section of established writers like Donald Barthelme, Grace Paley, Elizabeth Hardwicke, Peter Taylor, Mavis Gallant, John Updike, and Isaac Bashevis Singer is complemented by a handsome assembly of newer ones. The only controversial issue was the inclusion of two stories by Gallant, which Elkin explains glibly: "That also was a decision easily arrived at. What was tougher was the problem of whether to include a third, 'The Burgundy Weekend.'" The introduction is pure Elkin, a leisurely combination of reminiscence and political jeremiad, ending with a plea for the absolute subjectivity of taste. While other editors might lament the difficulty of choosing eleven out of 125 stories prescreened by Ravenel, Elkin defiantly announces, "[M]y decisions were a breeze, easy as rolling off a log. Because these are, quite simply, the very best short stories published in American magazines in 1979, and they declared themselves to whatever sense I have of the wonderful as succinctly as so many logos." The introduction argues that all taste, aesthetic or political, is subjective. He points out that Ronald Reagan, the "conservative Republican [presidential] front-runner," is a fiction of political tastes—"But what did Mr. Reagan actually *do* that was conservative?"—and concludes that "conservatism is only another opinion, only, that is, a kind of taste, as liberalism is, or fascism, too." And he announces that the taste that informs his work as an editor [as in his writing] is "rhetorical sacrament. We are dealing with *solace*, the *idea* of solace, art's and language's consolation prize." For fiction is about our recognition of eventual failure in the context of life's disappointments, and what matters is how we face those certainties: "But life's tallest order is to keep the feelings up, to make two dollars' worth of euphoria go the distance. And life can't do that. So fiction does. And there, right there, is the real—I want to say 'only'—morality of fiction."[24]

Another project on which he worked during this period was his first anthology of previously published writings. *Stanley Elkin's Greatest Hits* won the 1981 *Southern Review* prize, but was far less successful in the marketplace than he and his new publisher had hoped. The inspiration was a compilation stereo album, *Neil Diamond's Greatest Hits*. While listening to this album with his children, he asked about the title and learned that rereleases of previous materials are common in the recording industry. "I thought, 'that's nifty, to have a Greatest Hits,' and I thought wouldn't it be wonderful if we had Stanley Elkin's Greatest Hits, the world needs it. It was the only way I could think of to get my name above the title." Borchardt couldn't sell the idea to Warner Paperback, which had reissued several of Elkin's books, but Dutton agreed to try a hardcover in January 1980.[25] Although a compilation of stories, two novellas, and chapters from previously published works, it's nonchronological. The first work, "The Making of Ashenden," is followed by a chapter from A Bad Man, which was written almost a decade before; the next excerpt, from The Dick Gibson Show, was written between the preceding pieces; the next two items are short stories, written the earliest of all; but the final two entries are recent, a selection from The Franchiser and "The Conventional Wisdom." Musical artists often select cuts from several albums or disks to form an anthology, but ordinarily there's a chronological sequence. In an important foreword to Greatest Hits, Coover points out that the selections move from youth to age and the hereafter, "a kind of parodic 'seven ages of man.'" His introduction concentrates on Elkin's tragic vision, one of the first commentaries to address this theme that gathered force after the MS diagnosis, and compares Elkin with another great tragic-comic writer: "It is a joke Elkin shares with Samuel Beckett—you must go on, I can't go on, I'll go on—just as he shares with him a love for rhetorical flourish and comedy. The pursuit of whimsical strategies, a belief in the alliance of vision and the vulgar; though Beckett is more cerebral, more demanding, Elkin is more transparently in love with the world."[26] Although there were few reviews, those that came out were almost unanimously positive, sounding the familiar refrain about an important writer who deserves to be more widely read with a new urgency and telling readers that this collection is an ideal introduction; the Dallas Morning News: "For truly wild, outrageous, belly-laugh humor, no one surpasses Stanley Elkin. Yet, as Stanley Elkin's Greatest Hits demonstrates, it is humor used primarily to illuminate the human condition. [It] belongs on any Top 40 list."[27] But though the reviewers loved it, the collection didn't even approach selling out its modest advance. Although it won the 1980 Southern Review prize, it became a collector's item more quickly than anything else Elkin ever published.

While all this was happening, he was working on what he considered the final and defining novel he'd write. But yet one more opportunity too good to resist came up while he was working on Mills. National Public Radio launched an ambitious project in 1971 to broadcast radio adaptations of existing texts as well as original radio plays by established authors. By the late 1970s, Earplay focused on developing new scripts by established authors from other media such as fiction. Elkin, Donald Barthelme, and Gardner were asked to participate, and, despite his misgivings over the many projects taking time away from Mills, Elkin decided that the challenge and the guaranteed $2,000 were too good to miss. Casting about for a subject, he was sitting in the department coffee room, a now-reassigned-for-offices-and-workspace area adjacent to the chair's office where faculty congregated between classes to chat, gripe, gossip, and kibitz. Department veterans recall this as Stanley's room, where he held forth, made terse and witty comments, opined loudly, combated fiercely, judged ruthlessly, and shouted down much silence. Although nearly everyone recalls being the object of one or more of those moments of verbal aggression, no one resented it—it was just Stanley's way of being collegial. This morning one of those serendipities in which he so passionately believed occurred: "One of my colleagues popped in and said something familiar (familiar in the sense that he'd said something like it before). Then another did. Then another. And it occurred to me that it is impossible for anyone—I don't exclude myself—to say anything that is 'out of character,' and that, in a way, it's what we're likely to say to each other—the anecdotes we tell, the complaints we complain—that constitutes character in the first place—that we speak, are *compelled* to speak, a sort of *déjà vu* lingo, repetitive and crazed." With this insight, Elkin probably came closer to practicing realism than in any work since "The Condominium." Portraying real colleagues in thin disguises, his radio play captures a slice from a morning in the coffee room, during which people drop in, gripe about workloads and deadlines, defame administrators, gossip, talk about teaching, and complain about money. The chief agitator-raconteur is Leon Mingus, Stanley's alter ego, who toward the end breaks down complaining bitterly about his frustrations and his poor salary. Although NPR's announced goal was to encourage original drama, Elkin acknowledged that this "room-realism" concept was really the trope of modern American drama from Eugene O'Neill to Edward Albee (and he might have added that great force influencing American drama, Beckett): "[P]lacing people in a room and letting them talk to each other, the conversation shifting from smalltalk to accusation to confession. Secrets are surrendered and given up as if theater were burlesque, a sort of noble verbal striptease."[28]

The Coffee Room broadcast featured established comic actor Fred Gwynne (1926–93), who had starred on many television sitcoms, most notably as Herman on *The Munsters*, as Mingus, and Edward Hermann. After NPR dropped *Earplay* in 1981, Elkin approached Lorin Cuoco, who was interviewing him for local affiliate KWMU, about producing a new broadcast. She'd never produced a radio drama, but Stanley agreed to help with the production on the condition that he'd get to play Mingus. So Cuoco talked with her boss, an amateur actor, and wrote a grant to the Missouri Arts Council. Elkin adjusted the salaries for inflation and they went into the studio with thirteen local actors, but Stanley was ill during the taping sessions, "popping nitroglycerine the whole time." Still, he managed to keep the production cast in stitches throughout the taping, and Cuoco only later learned how sick he was: "In the studio, with the actors, I think he was in heaven." Within weeks he'd undergo heart bypass surgery. This version of *The Coffee Room* was broadcast on KWMU, but never nationally. It was also featured at Washington University library's 1996 Milestone Celebration of the acquisition of its three millionth volume, along with "The Stanley Elkin

Show: An Exhibition of Books and Manuscripts." In the program for that event, Naomi Lebowitz spoke for those whose characters and voices had been frozen in time: "We, the Coffee Room constituency, didn't mind being used to serve Stanley's artistry. Watching our funny wills on automatic pilot rocket past each other, warmed into life by the just and loving humor of the Master, we embraced the privilege of being painted by his brush. Stanley created the coffee room in our own image, divining that it was that social gathering place to which we all retreated *into* the world, agreeing to play our parts so comfortably that we did not prod the cliché into life."[29]

But the decade's big task was completing his self-proclaimed magnum opus. He told Helen Vendler in the mid-seventies that he wanted to write a novel about a common man, and for the next several years he worked on his longest and favorite book. The central premise for this novel led him far from the signature Elkin concerns. No matter how diverse his books had been in vocation, geography, rhetoric, and plot, they had uniformly been picaresque, arranged around the life of one forceful character readers are challenged to empathize with despite many misgivings about the hero's ethical or personal qualities. However unlike they are, what unites Boswell, Feldman, Gibson, and Flesh includes vitality, a zest for life, and the force of will to take charge of a situation, however difficult. The central conceit of *Mills* works against what Elkin did best—unlike the typical Elkin hero, the millennium of Mills men are second-raters, blue-collar men fated to be at the periphery of history, to be acted on rather than initiating. Thus his biggest novel was going to require that he rethink the very foundations of his fiction, the capacity of men of strong will to engage the world, often tragically. For against the "vocation" premise central to his novels to date was the fact that blue-collar men are seldom rhetorical dynamos. So Elkin's long-standing habit of giving everybody else the best lines, which really meant projecting his own voice onto his characters, would come up against the notion of verisimilitude, in that Mills men are by education and habit of mind passive, unlikely candidates for the Elkin flourish. Yet he had determined even as he began the book that it would end with the most rhetorical of acts, a sermon. The first section as well ends with a variation on a sermon, when "Greatest Grandfather Mills" dazzles the barbarians with his message of nonviolence—"I have come to tell you not to hit" (41) and "Ain't gonna study war no more!" (42)—even if it may be the horse's movement rather than the content of Mills's lecture that gets them safely out of eastern Europe, and the history of Europe doesn't exactly persuade us that the barbarians internalized his pacifist message. The contemporary Mills's sermon, to explain why an unbeliever feels saved, constitutes one of the unifying motifs of this long and complicated saga.

The first, and best, installment of the Mills story came to Elkin as another serendipity. He was one of the first American writers to acknowledge television

Stanley and Joan at home during the early 1980s. By permission of Joan Elkin.

as a potentially viable entertainment and information medium. Whereas most serious writers of his era embraced, often with little critical reflection, Newton Minow's 1961 characterization of American television as a "vast wasteland," Elkin, perhaps because of his disability but more likely because of his insatiable appetite for mass culture, watched selectively. He was probably the only American author in 1980 who could acknowledge that television inspired one of his best works: "I had the compulsion to write about ordinary men, but I couldn't get a handle on the subject. I've never worked in a factory myself or swilled beer with workmen. I hope this doesn't sound elitist because I don't mean it to be." What it suggests, of course, is the distance between Elkin's life and his proposed topic: "It wasn't until I watched a sequence in that wonderful [Jacob] Bronowski television series, 'The Ascent of Man,' [1973, thirteen segments, BBC] that I saw a way into the book. It was the sequence where Bronowski talked of a Polish salt mine a thousand years old and still being worked. If the mine still existed after a thousand years, so did the George Millses of the world who worked in such jobs. If Bronowski hadn't made that point about the salt mine, I don't think my book would have been written." His epic began with a story suggested by Bronowski's images of Wieliczka, a salt mine near Krakow, Poland, that has been in existence since the thirteenth century and that contains many religious images carved in the salt. Several years later he acknowledged, "The first sentence that came to me was, 'Because he knew nothing about horses.'"[30] He constructs an elaborate, fanciful narrative of literature's third great draft dodger (after Achilles and Odysseus), the youngest son of a British family low in the peerage pecking order, who takes an ignorant stable boy as his squire on a journey to join some crusaders bound for the Holy Land. Elkin's new editor John Macrae unsuccessfully lobbied him to substitute "Guillaume" (William) for the name Guillalume "which is unpronounceable in French or English."[31] But Macrae, who took over editing Elkin after Henry Robbins's sudden death in July 1979, didn't fare better than his predecessors had in changing Elkin's made-up mind. Elkin liked the compound foppishness the extra syllable suggests, and he may have wanted to echo Edgar Allan Poe's gothic masterpiece, "Ulalume." Guillalume has no desire to crusade and defers the pathfinding to Mills, who defers it to his horse, so they get lost in Eastern Europe, eventually becoming captive laborers.

The core narrative of "The First George Mills" is Guillalume's pronouncing the "Mills Curse" while both are in danger of becoming captives, when presumably elements of character like intelligence, determination, and pluck would trump social standing: "There are distinctions among men, humanity is dealt out like cards. There is a natural suzereignty like the face value on coins. Men have their place" (12). This may not apply universally, in that Guillalume is doing all he can to escape his destiny as a youngest son, suitable for Crusades and early death. But the problem isn't what Guillalume believes; it's Mills's acceptance of it: "You've doomed me. [. . .] You've cursed my race" (12). More problematic is that this is the stuff of oral history, and all the Mills sons hear and pass on the legend of the Millses' place at the periphery of events, as handymen, not originators. Of the three remaining Mills men in the novel, two have their own Guillalumes, bosses who assume "natural" superiority and the suitability of horseshit men like Mills to follow instructions, no matter how ridiculous or odious the tasks may be, and to expect no advancement or reward beyond what the superiors volunteer. The metaphysical conceit, fantastical as it is, that Elkin derives from this premise fuels the narrative's politics: for the next thousand years, each Mills will sire one, and only one, son, to whom he'll pass on the oral history, and that son will enact the role of blue-collar man in his generation, thus perpetuating the curse into another. The politics, which Elkin artfully avoided when commenting on the novel, is that consent to entrapment in history requires collaboration between the oppressor and the oppressed, with the ultimate responsibility attaching to those who consent to their victimization. Only once did he admit this possibility, and even then he insisted that the Mills history is "manufactured history, something I invent" and that it's not "particularly political." But the conflict is a "matter of *us . . . them*. I guess that's the essence of all political thought. *Them* oppresses us. *Them* oppresses Mills and his people."[32]

"The First George Mills" remains the funniest and most satisfying section, rich in invention, rhetoric, humor, and social relevance, and for many readers the remaining four sections, or 90 percent of the novel's volume, are anticlimactic. It was published in *Tri-Quarterly* after having been issued as a handsome, signed chapbook by Pressworks of Dallas, Texas, with illustrations by Jane E. Hughes. Hilma Wolitzer, a friend from Bread Loaf, singled the section out in her praise for the novel: "God, HORSELAND! What an insane little boy Stanley must have been."[33]

More than 60 percent of the novel treats the life of a 1982 George Mills who moves furniture for a St. Louis eviction specialist. This Mills ends the line, and the curse, because he has no son to whom to tell the story. The first scene portrays Mills resisting a seduction attempt by his still-winsome wife Louise, setting into motion the pattern of sexual reticence associated with his character and introducing the central conceit of the contemporary saga, "salvation." To explain his lack of response to Louise's enticements, Mills tells her he's saved, and this impromptu explanation quickly becomes the central truth of his yeoman-life: "He was saved, lifted from life. In a state of grace. Mills in weightlessness, desire, will and soul idling like a car at a stoplight. George Mills, yeomanized a thousand years, Blue Collar George like a priest at a timeclock, Odd Job George, Lunchpail Mills, the grassroots kid, was saved" (59).

Mills's salvation is in some ways the most troubling element of the novel. To an astonished Reverend Coulé, a former televangelist intrigued by Mills's serene assurance of secular salvation, he explains his racism and the absence of consequences as "salvation": "I parted them niggers like the Red Sea. They never touched me. You know how they do people in those projects? They never did *me*. They never will. Who *says* I ain't saved?" (69). By contrast, Mills's final sermon, in Coulé's church, amounts to recognition that his secular salvation was a way of legitimating his habit of subservience, the key fact of the Millses' life for 1,000 years. While honoring his promise to Coulé to preach on the subject of his grace, that "nothing could happen to him," he has a pulpit epiphany and reverses his premise: "Hell, I ain't saved. [. . .] Being tired isn't saved, sucking up isn't grace" (516, 518). Elkin often said that he, like Mills, felt saved in the sense that all the bad things that had happened to his body made him feel somehow immune: "Well, I feel the same way. Nothing is ever going to happen to me again. But that's simply as result of my multiple sclerosis."[34] Mills's epiphany also has an autobiographical element: he insists that the "meaning of life is to live long enough to find something out or to do something well" (518) and Elkin told me that this was his core philosophy. To illustrate his sympathy with Mills's profession that "I don't *know* anything" (515), Elkin mentioned universal product codes, a technology that revolutionized shopping and inventory in the late 1970s; he sat at the market while Joan checked out and wondered, "I don't understand this. I don't understand how the world works." In one way, he felt that his own "salvation" was the complete control of the possibilities of language as a compensation for being denied the benefits of health and full mobility, and he often insisted that *Mills* was the vindication of his craft as a writer. Often he used the phrase "I felt as if I owned the language" as he completed this novel, to which Benjamin Chambers quipped, "[Y]our impression was correct. You DO own the language (I'm wondering if I might apply for fair use)."[35]

Elkin was by 1980 painfully aware that even his supportive critics complained about his verbal overkill and his tendency toward digressions, something he defended as a shared quality with Faulkner and Charles Dickens, a writer he often included in his "Theory of the Novel" classes—with the good stuff (i.e., Faulkner and Elkin). Readers had, until *The Living End,* frequently voted with closed pocketbooks, and the consistent disparity between literary recognition and poor sales rankled Elkin. After his extraordinary critical and substantial popular success with the triptych, he reverted defiantly to the very qualities that stood between him and the popular audience he craved. For *Mills* is more expansive, more digressive, than even *The Franchiser* or *Gibson.* A large chapter of part 2, for example, treats George's early adolescence in the medium-spiritualist compound in Cassadaga, Florida.[36] The story of his formative years is essential to his breaking the curse, but this chapter is massive—in most editions it runs to 101 pages, two sections of which were excerpted as magazine publications in *Tri-Quarterly* and *Playboy.* Within the chapter, which is digressive in its handling of the bildungsroman motif and has little direct bearing on George's developing the resources to defeat the curse, is a huge "sub-digression," larger than a chapter in most novels. Spiritualist Dr. N. M. M. Kinsley receives a letter, twenty-eight pages in print, concerning a Vermont blacksmith with strange obsessions about family, work, and horses. While this offers a variation on the horse-lore of Greatest Grandfather's tale, it's a stretch to say this lurid beast-fable has much to do with the novel's plot or themes. Elkin defended *Mills* as a "story factory," and the Cassadaga section in particular as "the most inventive fun I ever had, and I love the book for those hundred pages or so alone." But this story taxes even the most patient reader, and it would be no great surprise if copies that turned up in secondhand bookstores showed signs of wear through the first 150 or so pages. The chapter ends, however, with an imitation of a key scene in Faulkner's *Absalom, Absalom!,* in which Reverend Wickland, the spiritualist who mentored him and apparently cuckolded his father, helps George imagine the series of events leading up to his sister's birth, something that, if true, breaks the family curse because Mills men sire only sons—but Wickland hints that he fathered the daughter when he explains why George's father's broke his promise not to tell his son the Mills narrative. Elkin acknowledged that he was thinking about the mutual reconstruction of Sutpen family history by Quentin Compson and Shreve MacLaughlin when he constructed this end to the chapter—a suspicion that initiates Mills's eventual search for his lost sister. Tom LeClair, friend, interviewer, and critic, had a unique take on the Cassadaga section. In a postcard from Athens, he wrote, "[Y]ou have spooked me" because LeClair himself lived there at about George's age: "It's a beautiful piece of artistic/astral projection. I await the rest, nervously. Don't want you messing around in the nights of my present life."[37]

The 1980s Mills narrative involves an unlikely cast of characters—members of a local university community, many based on people Elkin knew well. One of his planning sheets includes George and Patty Pepe, close friends in the Third Tuesday group; Patty figures prominently in his essay "Why I Live Where I Live." He also planned to include the Finebergs, next-door neighbors Joan recalls as an odd couple, she a political activist and he a scientist who "was very dull," as models for members of the wealthier class Mills comes to know. And his representation of one family nearly cost him a friendship. He specifically planned to represent Parkview (the gated community in which he lived) as "like a Jane Austen rendering," whereas Mills's world, South St. Louis, would be "dark comedy filled with real-world terror."[38] The links between these worlds are Mills, his new employer, and the acquaintance who introduces them. Except for the Mills family, all are characters from the Elkin circle. George loses his job and a Meals-on-Wheels provider present at his father-in-law's death introduces him to an acquaintance who is dying of cancer and seeking a driver-handyman to help her make a desperate journey to a Mexican Laetrile clinic. During the 1970s and 1980s, many prominent Americans, including actor Steve McQueen (1930–80) traveled against their doctors' advice to Mexico to receive this treatment, based on extracts from almond or apricot pits. Because friends with the best of intentions frequently sent Stanley letters or notices of MS therapies not sanctioned by the American Medical Association, it's no surprise that this narrative would figure prominently in *George Mills*, and that Judith Glaser, the wife of a wealthy university dean, would be this Mills's Guillalume.

In the planning document, Judith Glaser is called "Laura Mae," her husband "the Leon character." And that's how Stanley earned the ire of Leon Gottfried, who had been dean of the faculty at Washington University during the 1970s. Both were Illinois Ph.D.'s, and Gottfried was by all accounts an exemplary university citizen. No one recalls any animosity between the two; Joan remembers cordial meetings at parties and university events, though they didn't visit each other's homes often. Gottfried played poker with Stanley during the 1960s. His wife Laura Mae tragically developed terminal cancer in the 1970s, and, after her husband had accepted the chair of Purdue University's English Department, went to Mexico for the Laetrile cure. She eventually, according to Pepe, accepted her death and designed her own funeral—something Judith does morbidly in the novel. It would be cruel enough to see one's family's grief represented in such thin disguise in a work of fiction, and not a few friendships have soured this way over time. Of course Elkin's friends knew their foibles might eventually be grist for his comic mill(s). But despair and dying aren't foibles or amusing; moreover, both Judith and Dean Sam Glaser are represented as thoroughly unlikable people. She's the supreme test of Mills's humanity, to which he responds heroically in a "Marco Polo" episode in Mexico that brings tears to one's eyes even on a fifth reading. A medical practitioner sent Stanley a card for his fifty-ninth birthday saying that scene "tells about what I do as powerfully as I ever need to be told, and reading it, and sharing it has made me a whole lot better washer of feet, once the tears dried." But Gottfried saw a portrayal of his wife as a caustic, morbid, egocentric, rich bitch. Dan Shea empathized with him: "And others winced too. On the other hand one could say that the Masked Marvel, death, was always showing up in Elkin fictions, and sharp-edges and off-balance thrusts were Stanley's style of combat, no harm to real persons intended." Moreover, Gottfried had long been an Elkin advocate at Washington University, but friends in Indiana warned him that elements in *Mills* were alarmingly similar to his family situation a few years before. He found reading the novel "very hurtful" and drove to St. Louis to confront his old friend about the effect this cruel representation might have on his daughters. Elkin pleaded the "writer's line" that this was art, not life, and that he didn't intend to critique the family's lives, but eventually he apologized and they parted amicably. But Gottfried "never felt the same about our relationship after that. There was a lingering sense of betrayal."[39] Although they never formally reconciled, Gottfried attended the Elkin memorial at Washington University in 1995.

The principal link between Mills–South St. Louis and the Glasers-Parkview is Elkin's most autobiographical character, even more so than Ben Flesh, and it's not a pretty picture. Years ago I mentioned some similarities, but Elkin laughingly brushed the identification off: "Cornell Messenger, *c'est moi?* [. . .] I don't write autobiographical things." Before we revisit that claim, here's an inventory. Cornell Messenger, a writer, believes his books haven't sold as well as they deserve, one story of which was optioned for a movie that was never made; he teaches at a prestigious university; his father was a jewelry salesman; he has three children, including a learning-disabled son and a precocious daughter; he suffered a heart attack and became reconciled to his reputation as a bad driver; he smokes recreational marijuana and becomes sentimental over Jerry Lewis telethons. And Elkin's planning document confirms that these similarities aren't accidental. In the early planning, the Messenger character was called "Elkin." The device linking the worlds of Elkin-Messenger and the Glasers was in place early in the planning: "Elkin learns about Laura Mae's illness asks what he can do—she asks him to drive her turn at the Meals on Wheels—(this is how he meets Mills)." The point isn't that Elkin fibbed in distancing himself from Messenger—he may well have forgotten that Messenger was originally "Elkin"—but that he's as ruthlessly critical of this character with his pompously quoting Joseph Conrad ("the horror, the horror, hey Mills") to the unlettered Mills as he is of any other character. In some ways Messenger is the writer incarnate, the continual observer and prodder, one who interprets and re-creates what he observes. And unlike Elkin, he's a terrible parent.

As digressive as the Cassadaga section may seem, Elkin had one more surprise for critics who carped about indulgence. Section 4 (112 pages) introduces the adventures of a new Mills, George 43, who migrated the family to America. Like Cassadaga, this is marked by invention and wit, though some of Elkin's editors counseled compacting it substantially or eliminating it entirely. His *Playboy* editor had a critical and creative suggestion: "It seems like a dirty trick to the reader, designed to show off Stanley's talents. But we *know* he's talented: what we want is more of George. [. . .] There are other things he could do with the section. He could sell some of it to me, for instance—what is *Playboy* for if not to publish stuff about harems?"[40] But Alice Turner had already committed *Playboy* to two excerpts, and the book's publication date was imminent. Part 4 is a spectacular set piece, treating the meeting of Mills and King George IV in a delightful parody of Restoration comedy, with chortles, asides, and overt references to human sexuality. Mills makes another journey, this time to Persia, where he becomes a Turkish Janissary and eventually the only uncastrated male in a sultan's harem. Elkin learned about Janissaries while reading Michael Arlen's memoir *Passage to Ararat* (1975). He was so engaged by the chapter on these colorful, ruthless Turkish special forces—"they were fascinating to me, so when I saw this I had to include them in the novel"—that he chose to fabricate their decline in this narrative of a Mills once more at the periphery of history.[41] Whatever digressive defiance the Turkish story may impose on the Mills narrative—and Turner was right, it could stand alone as a novella or a serial—it's among the funniest, most· ribald delights in the Elkin portfolio.

By this time it had become almost inevitable that Stanley would complain about his publisher's failure to market the new book aggressively. He asked in 1981 to be released from his contract to publish *Mills,* with the expectation that he'd repay the $5,000 advance he'd accepted in 1976. This extraordinary request, with the novel nearly completed, was based on three elements: he felt that both his Dutton books had been poorly promoted, so that should *Mills* come out "with a good-enough-willed but minimum effort," the result would replicate past efforts, great reviews and tepid sales; second, he perceived a "less than enthusiastic" response from Macrae to his partial typescript; finally, he was convinced this would be his final novel: "I'm fifty-one years old, not in the best of health, worried to the bone, and that's just not good enough anymore." When he recovered from his shock upon receiving the request, Macrae soothed his star writer's ruffled ego by assuring him that he and the second reader were excited about *Mills* and that they intended "to make it a major title for next fall." He explained Dutton's marketing *Greatest Hits* as a project they inherited when they acquired Elkin's paperback rights, but never really wanted: "[I]t was Warner's idea" but despite reservations, Dutton made "an honest effort" to market the hardcover, in order to set up paperback sales that never materialized. He defended the *Living End* campaign, reminding Elkin that they sold 20,000 hardcovers. Macrae concluded with a plea and a promise: "Please finish *George Mills*. Once I have the manuscript, I'll respond with a specific publishing plan for the book. If you don't like the plan and if you don't believe we're enthusiastic then we can talk about a separation. But here you're talking divorce and we're not even married. We want you, Stanley. Tell me GEORGE MILLS can make the fall list." And it soothed Elkin enough to submit the remainder, to which Macrae replied, "Allow me to say that GEORGE MILLS is a magnificent book, demonstrating the full range of your talents and, for my money, a stylistic masterpiece." He kept his word about aggressive advertising; a half-page ad, featuring a wonderful David Levine sketch of Stanley typing in his bathtub, along with praise from Wolitzer and excerpts from six positive reviews, appeared at least twice in the *New York Times* during the run-up to publication. The amended contract called for Dutton to budget $35,000 toward promoting the book.[42]

As Elkin expected, even if he hoped against expectations, the reviews were positive and sales were dismal. It was his most-awaited and most widely reviewed work, benefiting from the buzz created by *The Living End*. Nearly all the weekly and monthly magazines covered the publication, as did several academic journals; all the major market newspapers did too, often with a brief biographical piece or an interview; a large number of secondary and tertiary market papers reviewed it too. Most were very positive; quite a few were raves. *USA Today* rejoiced in a "fabulous 500-page beast of a book" that should rescue Elkin from obscurity and *Publishers Weekly* called it his "most memorable to date," adding that no one since James Joyce is a "better serious, funny writer." The executive director of the Modern Language Association was very positive in *Washington Post Book World* and the *International Herald-Tribune*: "[A] master of comic effects, [. . .] a laureate of lamentation" and "one of our essential voices." LeClair in *New Republic* declared it Elkin's best book, but sounded a prophetic qualification that was echoed frequently, that the rhetoric might overwhelm an audience unfamiliar with "Elkin's excess." The *New York Times* voiced a similar reservation; individual episodes are excellent, "But what—one gets tired of asking—does it all add up to?" Of course, a few disliked it. The *Philadelphia Inquirer* judged that *Mills* confirmed Elkin's status as a cult writer and the *Boston Globe* pronounced it "wayward and plotless," "about nothing."[43] But these were minority voices; the number, tone, and quality of positive reviews could easily have turned the head of a lesser man. But Elkin had heard all this before. Great reviews were warm and fuzzy, but his files were full of great reviews. Too often, these didn't translate into sales.

The letters of congratulation poured in—but unlike the letters he got about *The Living End*, these were all from his friends. Nemerov compared the visions of *Mills* with *King Lear* and Rabelais, concluding that it's "a fine, rich, telling book, probably as good as you think it is." Gold, who reviewed it enthusiastically for the *Chicago Sun-Times*, wrote to say he'd given his review copy to his wife with "instructions not to cook, work, or screw until she read it." Richard Ford opted for minimalism: "Funny, you're funny. Smart you're too." And John Irving shared a Gilligan's Island of a story about his Mills experience. Reading a prepublication copy on his sloop half a mile offshore, he got to the point where Mills describes his state of grace; Irving felt "jarred into a consciousness of myself" and closed the book, reflecting on his own emotional and romantic entanglements. Just after he closed his eyes, a squall came up and the boat capsized, plunging Irving, Mills, and the sailor into frigid New England water. They held onto the boat for dear life, fearing hypothermia if rescue didn't come, but Irving refused to let go of Mills; back on shore he devoured the rest of the "whole bloated and page-loose thing" and volunteered a blurb: "Jesus, what a plot. It seems a very different book for you, while the voice, the voice is what gives it your usual conviction."[44] Of course, Stanley knew he was good, and he knew his friends knew he was good. But where were the readers he didn't know? What were they thinking? And when was the book going to sell?

All the good wishes from friends and enthusiastic reviews were appetizers to the feast. *Mills* won the National Book Critics Circle Award for the best fiction of 1983 against formidable opponents including Bobbie Ann Mason's *Shiloh and Other Stores*, Anne Tyler's *Dinner at the Homesick Restaurant*, and Cynthia Ozick's *Levitation*. No longer a runner-up on the big stage, Stanley was front row center. Bernard Malamud was the first of many to tell him, "You fully deserve it," and Chancellor William Danforth of Washington University held a banquet to honor Stanley, as well as Bill Gass's and Mona van Duyn's election to the American Academy and Institute of Arts and Letters. The university, and Stanley, were having a good year. Danforth also sent a gracious note: "I feel very fortunate always that you are associated with Washington University. You do a great deal for us. Indirectly we receive honor because of your accomplishments. Moreover, you give a lift to our spirits." To be honored by one's peers is always an occasion of joy. Macrae told the *Times* that sales picked up in February following the announcement, "not enormously, but measurably,"[45] but that was a blip on the dismal radar. Was the book ever going to sell?

Well, no. Just as Stanley had feared, sales were initially tepid, then they cooled down and the returns warmed up. The initial shipping of 9,637 copies in October

1982 was promising, but the return of 2,741 in mid-1983, with no new orders from booksellers, set off alarms; by 1984 the Dutton Obelisk paperback was selling "slowly but steadily" and the company decided to remainder 5,000 hardcovers. Then an inventory revealed that things were even worse; Dutton offered Elkin or Borchardt as many of the 8,488 hardcovers in stock as they wanted. Adding insult to injury, a French publisher acquired a translation subsidy from the Centre National du Livre, but Borchardt's French representative was mysteriously obliged to cancel the contract. By decade's end, Borchardt entertained offers from David Godine and Thunder's Mouth Press to publish specialty paperbacks. The 1990 Thunder's Mouth edition had sold 4,149 copies by the end of 1992.[46]

Despite the reading public's harsh judgments, Elkin stubbornly held to his conviction that *Mills* was his best work, and he had decided while writing it that he'd write no more novels. But it's historically important for one more reason: it's one of the first novels by a "serious" or "literary" writer to have been composed in large measure on a word processor—an early CPU designed solely for word processing, in this case a Lexitron. Most serious writers had reservations about this intersection between creativity and technology, and Stanley's decision wasn't entirely voluntary. His handwriting, marginally legible before his MS was diagnosed, deteriorated steadily during the decade. His fingertips became increasingly painful while he was writing *Mills* and *Living End,* and touching typewriter keys brought agony. Shea, his colleague, visited him during a hospital stay and pledged to persuade the dean to find funds for a word processor—they cost a lot back then. The first several chapters were written in the famous university exam books and typed by someone else. But the final sections were composed and revised on the word processor; eleven 5¼ inch diskettes contain pages 260–466 of the print-out. Years later, Elkin would hyperbolically assess the importance of his "bubble machine," as he called the Lexitron. When asked what was the most important event of his writing life, he replied "June 6, 1979, when my word processor was delivered. Not just any word processor, but a dedicated word processor. Not even just a dedicated word processor, finally, but a devoted one."[47]

Because of the popularity of *The Living End* and the excitement Dutton and the literary community were stirring over *Mills,* Elkin appeared on *The Dick Cavett Show* in March 1981. Cavett's program was widely considered a thoughtful alternative to late-night entertainment shows like *The Tonight Show.* He recruited much more controversial guests, and the conversation often went into far greater depth than the "my-newest-movie/album/book/play" promotions that still bring guests to late-night television. One of Cavett's major innovations was scheduling only one guest for an hour-long show, thus allowing for in-depth discussions. He was also well prepared, witty if at times glib, and occasionally sarcastic. Perhaps for these reasons there were problems with network support. ABC ran the show from 1969–75, then CBS picked it up for a season. PBS began broadcasting it in 1977. It was on PBS, toward the end of Cavett's run, that Elkin appeared. Although he found his audience with Cavett, it was a PBS audience, not the real big time, but pretty big nonetheless.

His appearance was legendary for his refusal to be intimidated by the host, quite in contrast with earlier encounters with celebrities. Coover was concerned about whether he'd be able to walk unassisted onto the set, because his cane sometimes now gave way to a walker. And Elkin was apprehensive. He told a *Newsday* interviewer about his anxiety about appearing on national television: "'It scares the ――― out of me [. . .] I'm not afraid of Cavett; I'm afraid of me. I respect that show. I've bought books off it." And, although the interview didn't make the "Dick Cavett's Greatest Hits" DVDs (there really are three of them), Elkin acquitted himself well, wearing his skull-and-crossbone suspenders under a rumpled suit and smoking during the live show. He took control of the conversation, discussing the role of the writer, *The Living End* and its theology, the book he was writing, and his word processor, which itself elicited many letters of congratulation. A couple of friends commented on how Stanley found his audience on live TV. Gail Godwin: "First of all, you were the only person (except, perhaps, JK Galbraith whose total style is not as lovable as yours) I have seen stay in control of the show, and not let Our Dick demean or diffuse or confuse or antagonize you by his asides to gossip, trivia, etc." Coover agreed: "[A]nd whaddya know, there he is, the Man himself bringing us the Holy Scripture and looking much like I imagined the Pope to look according to his medical bulletins." More than twenty years later, Coover delighted in his friend's gaining control of the interview; despite his apprehension, Elkin appeared very much at ease before the camera, and he had a wonderful time playing off the theme of the artist as God from *The Living End*. And because Stanley managed Cavett's well-prepared questions so well, Coover observed with some pride that his friend was considerably smarter than the television host, and that Cavett realized and respected this. But, Coover feels, Cavett didn't know exactly how to deal with a man of such quick wit and stubborn intelligence.[48] Several admirers wrote to tell him they wanted to read his books because of the Cavett appearance. Once more, Stanley seemed to have his audience, but it wasn't one of the big three networks, and it was a modest comfort as the *Mills* sales plummeted.

II Disney World and Alaskan Rabbis
A Masterpiece, a Flop, the Elkin Essay, and More Bad Medical News, 1983–88

> The doomed and the dying are Elkin's loved ones. [. . .]
> Stanley Elkin has always been amazing at taking the guy
> who's down and burying him deeper; he has a real thing for
> the deadbeat soul, indeed; and you better believe that it's
> heart-wringing work.
>
> —John Irving reviewing *The Living End*, 1979

Of course Elkin was disappointed with the poor reception *George Mills* received in the bookstores despite excellent reviews and a major national award. It was his most ambitious undertaking, and, he was positive, his best novel. Critics and judges got it. So why didn't the public get it? Why didn't people buy it? Why did the stores keep sending back returns? But that's not why he decided to end his career as a novelist. He'd made that decision while writing *Mills,* and it may account for the self-indulgences that fueled returns and consumer disinterest. Having decided that *Mills* was his final novel, he had even fewer compunctions than usual about writing this one for Stanley, including whatever interested him at the moment: Janissaries, spiritualists, unflattering descriptions of friends and their homes, Jerry Lewis telethons, universal product codes, and an anachronistic vision of the DNA molecule. Despite several disappointments in Hollywood during the past decade, he wanted to try film writing again. His reasons illustrate yet again the tension between the serious literary profession and popular success that drove his creative life. He told Bill Gass in an interview focused primarily on *Mills* that he was burned out; he'd had it with serious, "literary" fiction and he wanted to move into something less demanding: "I saw myself becoming a hack, wanting to be a hack, like a limousine turning into a taxi, because I thought writing *George Mills* would take it all out of me."[1] After all, he spent seven years writing that book. To the gregarious Elkin they seemed like lonely years, sitting over the exam booklets, and later in front of the word processor, composing for five to seven hours a day, then reading student compositions, books by friends, books by competitors, and material for the workshops and story contests he was regularly asked to judge. Friends, former students, publishers, and people he'd never heard of sent books for publicity comments and manuscripts for advice about revising or publishing. And he seldom ignored such requests, however meager the submission. But it seemed a lonely life and he fondly recalled interacting with Frank Galati, Maurice Singer, and Ray Wagner while adapting *The Living End,* and collaborating with Michael Ritchie on his screenplays. So he decided to stop writing serious novels and take up a more comfortable and remunerative business; he would undertake smaller units, like essays, or more collaborative efforts, like plays or film scripts, so he could hang out with directors, producers, fellow writers, and actors.

Perhaps pursuing that goal, he wrote "The Saturday Visit," a one-act reminiscent of Edward Albee's short plays, in 1982. *Esquire* was eager to publish it, having received very positive responses to his essay "Why I Live Where I Live" in 1980 and having commissioned "Alfred Kinsey: The Patron Saint of Sex" for 1983, but the magazine soon lost interest; there was also some discussion of its being performed at the Louisville Arts Festival, but that didn't happen either. It was eventually published in *Colorado Review.* Editor David Milofsky suspected that this was something Elkin had written years before, and he was delighted to receive and publish it: "Of course we had to pay Stanley more than we paid anyone else." The play is a "room drama" with only two characters, dapper fifty-eight-year-old Phil and his rumpled son in a Manhattan tearoom after visiting the Metropolitan Museum of Art. Like many works Elkin was writing at the time, the father-son conflict centers this text with obvious autobiographical overtones. Phil—Elkin's father's name—can't reconcile himself to Sean's/Stan's not following his advice to dress better, wear his hair more conservatively, or learn socially useful arts like Spanish (Elkin's recent trip to Brazil is recalled when Phil tells Sean "the smart money's on South America"). They bicker over small matters, like a Mets game, and large ones, like the tension between Phil and Sean's mother. As they depart—to see the Mets—the increasing light reveals that many other tables are occupied by fathers and sons or daughters on Saturday visits of their own, though the occupants of only one have tiny speaking parts.[2] At this time the theme of the broken home and the absent father was close to Elkin's imagination. He'd soon write a series of essays on his relationship with the real Phil, and the autobiographical character Cornell Messenger in *George Mills* struggles with his relationships with his three children who in many ways resemble Elkin's—in a draft copy of the excerpt "The Griefs," the children are Philip, Molly, and Barney (a nickname for Bernard); they become in the published versions "his son," Jeanne, and Harve,[3] and the point of view switches from Messenger's narrative to omniscient.

From the early 1960s onward, Elkin had from time to time contended with Washington University over issues of salary, scheduling, and release time. He'd entertained several job offers in the late 1960s, and actively sought appointments elsewhere during the early 1970s. A few inquiries came in about his directing writing programs, but administration wasn't one of his strengths. He needed time to write, not to sit in meetings. By the late 1970s, Elkin was still unhappy about his pay, but he was no longer the feisty employee of years past. His letter protesting his appointment for the academic year 1979 sounds a note of bitterness, petulance, and powerlessness:

> As you know, I am very unhappy about my salary—unhappy and hurt and humiliated. I'm not going to list my "credits" for you. This isn't an audition. I'm not going to parse the history of my sense that I'm undervalued at Washington University, or make invidious comparisons. This isn't a catalogue of grievances. I have only one grievance and I've already stated it. I am aware that we, as a department, are generally underpaid. I've always felt—hoped— that this would resolve itself over the years. It hasn't, and I think the time has come for me to speak out as an individual, because it's as an individual that I feel hurt.

His only threat, and he acknowledged it as a "paltry hole card," was to withdraw from the Writers' Program if his demand for a $1,900 per year increase wasn't met: "Should I get it I will still feel underpaid. Should I not get it, I will feel, well, punished." Chair Dick Ruland took him seriously, pleading in a three-page letter that his demand be met. Ruland based his case on the familiar argument that a writer of Elkin's stature brings honor to the university, then added a pragmatic twist: "If this relatively small public finds us worthy, by *their* intellectual lights, they will send us their good students—and, indeed, they will send us good faculty or want to come themselves." Ruland was able to influence the salary decision enough that Elkin remained in the Writers' Program. In 1982 the decades of contention ended when the university appointed him Merle Kling Professor of Modern Letters. This endowed chair brought prestige, a budget, a reduced teaching load, and a salary increase. Kling, for many years provost at Washington University, felt honored that Elkin occupied a chair bearing his name. Shortly after the appointment, Kling, then president of Mercy College in New Jersey, wrote, "I am vain about the link between my name and your stature as an author." After learning from the *Washington University Record* about Elkin's Assembly Series lecture, Kling waved the newspaper before administrators at Mercy and "insisted that they now exhibit proper deference toward me." Dan Shea felt that his friend's installation was "a kind of Camelot": "We're none of us going to be here forever, and this was a high point in the intellectual and creative life of the university."[4]

With the professional situation settled for the rest of his life, Elkin could enjoy his colleagues and the special role he enjoyed as the department's social center for witty, pithy, sarcastic observations. His family life continued to undergo radical transformations as well. After college and the army, Philip returned to St. Louis in 1982, only to move to Cleveland the next year "to get away" and make some changes in his life. There was no bitterness; he warmly appreciated Stanley's efforts to secure his admission to the University of Arizona, and he remains convinced that Stanley "would do anything for the family."[5] In Ohio Philip worked in a nursing home and later trained for his present vocation as a paramedic.

And his wasn't the only emptying of the Parkview nest during the 1980s. Bernard is dyslexic, and some behavioral problems accompanied his learning disability. From age ten until sixteen (1976–82), "my thing was making things," especially things that blew up. How ironic that Elkin had included an episode on the dissemination of information about making bombs in *The Dick Gibson Show,* when Bernie was five; later his son would search magazines for similar instructions, then see how well they worked. Once he and a friend combined nitrogen fertilizer and pharmaceutical chemicals. Sometimes he was injured, sometimes his experiments damaged property, and "there was debris in the pool all the time." Once Stanley refused to let Bernie build a tree house as punishment for one of these experiments. He was also interested in picking locks and ordered his first pick set from *Spy* magazine. From time to time he tested the picks without his father's knowledge. These experiences may have prepared him for the locksmith business he now operates, but they were an increasingly serious concern for the family. By the end of the decade it was clear that intervention was necessary, and Bernard attended the Churchill School summer program in St. Louis "for treatment of severe learning disabilities [. . .] caused by a neurological disorder." In 1983 the family reluctantly concluded that more intensive treatment would be necessary. Joan's and Stanley's research convinced them that the Landmark School in Beverly Farms, Massachusetts, provided the best prospect for success. It would be costly, because Landmark is a boarding school, classes were very small, and there were many tutorials. Although he hated to leave his family, Bernie enjoyed the school, but while he was there a family crisis took place. Later Elkin wrote Saul Bellow that he and Joan had decided against telling Bernie he is adopted because of the problems attending his dyslexia, but at age eighteen, at Beverly Farms, Bernie received a telephone call from his birth mother, "who lays it all out, tells him 'Guess Who and Guess What,' and knocks him for a loop that could have been avoided if we'd told him at three what he needed to know." By contrast, there was great joy when his dad received an award from Brandeis University (unanimously selected by Albee, Bernard Malamud, and Geoffrey Wolff) and took Bernie out of school to travel with him during his time in New England. Today he appreciates the love and sacrifice Joan and Stanley made for him during this time, but they felt keenly his absence during those years.[6]

Before the mid-1980s, then, the only child remaining at home was Molly, with whom Stanley had a special relationship. Although he dearly loved his sons, she was the apple of his eye, the most intellectual, verbal, and witty among the children. And their relationship was always marked by humor, love, and mutual respect. But it wasn't always easy. When she was eleven, Molly took figure skating lessons and soon moved on to competitive skating. Unlike Philip's baseball and soccer, Stanley wasn't interested in skating, once telling her it was "ridiculous." But as her skills improved she participated in competitions and exhibitions. While other parents shouted encouragement during warm-ups, Molly was mortified to hear her father yell, "My daughter! She's assimilated!" A few years later he was flying to New York for a function at the American Academy of Arts and Letters. He and Molly quarreled over who would use the shower first. Stanley had a plane to catch and Molly didn't want to be late for school. The argument intensified, and when he insisted that his urgency trumped hers, Molly went into a pout and decided she wasn't going to school at all. By the time Stanley came down for breakfast, Joan was beside herself. Advised of the situation, he asked, "Well, what do you plan to do?" Molly replied, "I want to go to New York with you today." To her, and her mother's, utter surprise, he replied, "OK. The plane leaves in two hours." Editor Bill Whitehead arranged last-minute tickets for *Cats*, that season's Broadway hit. She recalls the hotel as "lousy" and the restaurant at which they had dinner as "wretched," but "it was one of the best days of my life. It was wonderful to live with someone who might tell you in the early morning, 'Hurry up, we're going to' someplace like Hollywood, Disney World, New York, and to get a plane at Lambert and be on your way—on someone else's tab, because after he became famous, Stanley never paid plane fare. If someone wasn't willing to fly him to a place, he wasn't going." And there was a Stanley-wrinkle on the usual paternal anxiety about high school–age daughters at parties or on dates. When she arrived at home, perhaps after curfew, she'd hurry quietly to the third floor, but her dad would inevitably call out softly as she passed through the second, and would want to know everything anyone said, about whom, to whom—"an unappeasable taste for gossip." This persisted through high school, college, law school, and into her practice in Washington, D.C.; he always wanted to know with whom she rubbed elbows at parties or business functions.

Molly learned to drive while her parents were on a trip. As was often the case, they left Bernard, if at home, and Molly supervised by some of Stanley's graduate students, something both teens loved, and in 1982 one of those students taught Molly to drive. Four years later, she overheated the family car's engine—a total loss. But that wasn't why her parents were mad at her during the days before and after her high school graduation. It wasn't a very good car and Stanley had his eye on a Saab. After all, Howard Nemerov had recently bought a Mercedes. They were mad at Molly about a pool party. She had permission to have a "couple of friends" over while her parents were away, to celebrate her imminent gradua-tion. "It quickly turned into about 200 of my nearest and dearest friends." The crowd was loud; poolside was alive with noise, splashing, and drinking. Molly worried about the havoc and about annoying the neighbors. She asked people to go home but they wouldn't, so she called the cops: "Terrible things were done to this house": some of Joan's paintings were removed from the walls, but fortunately not harmed; debris and beer stains were everywhere; and some meat was removed from a basement freezer and left in plastic garbage bags. Molly didn't find that while cleaning up; by the time Joan discovered it, the meat was unsafe to eat. When her parents came home, Joan was shocked and angry: "I can't believe you did this to me. What have you done to my house?" By contrast, "My dad was pretty cool about it, as he was about most things like that." He subsequently wrote Molly a graduation letter challenging the very "tragic vision" he'd made it his business to teach the children: "He always had this problem with me being happy. He felt that I needed to be more serious about things, that I should have a tragic vision. When I graduated from high school, he wrote me this wonderful letter that says, in effect, 'I was wrong.' and concludes, 'The tragic vision is for blind people.'" But he hadn't forgotten the party: "[I]f I've been giving you a hard time in these last few days when skinhead goblins have been swinging on our chandeliers, dancing on our dining-room tables, walking their dogs on our oriental rugs, unfreezing our lambchops, thawing our turkeys, sitting on our meat and setting fire to our cars, hey, that shit happens. It really does. I should have remembered. I love you, Molly. I won't forget. Commence!"[7]

And where were Stanley and Joan during the pool party? They were scheduled to be in France, where Marc Chenetier was organizing a conference devoted to Elkin's work, or at a German symposium "which was supposed to have been about me"—two international events "about me" in one spring, no less. But he couldn't attend either because Molly wasn't the only Elkin about to "commence." He and three others received honorary doctorates from the University of Illinois on May 26, 1986. There would be other conferences in Europe, one in Nice organized by Chenetier and another in Stuttgart organized by Heide Zeigler. But there's only one honorary degree from one's university. It wasn't the first time Elkin had been considered for an honorary degree, but it was the first time the deal got done. Jeffrey Duncan, recalling several successful Elkin appearances at Iowa, inquired about his interest in receiving a degree in 1981, in conjunction with a reading from *Mills* and from his essay "Plot." Apparently Elkin expressed some reservations about appearing to seek this honor, because Duncan assured him, "*You* are not applying. *We* are. Because we believe in you and your work."[8] Moreover, he'd received the Brandies University Creative Arts Award earlier that spring.

In this climate of changing family life, expanding intellectual and professional recognition, exhilaration about the commercial and popular success of *The Living End*, and grim disappointment about the chilly response to what he considered his most important book, Elkin reluctantly took up his most daring project, a radical departure from anything he'd ever done. He'd been resisting the temptation to begin a book about the practice of offering a dream holiday to terminally ill children since a 1980 London trip, mainly because he'd decided not to write any more novels. As they prepared to see a play, he saw a BBC news item covering the departure of terminally ill children from Heathrow for Disney World. An early version:

> Joan was getting ready and I was watching the news on television, and I saw this three-minute filmclip of these kids being taken off to Disney World— British children—and there were seven of 'em. At the time, I said to Joan—first of all, tears were rolling down my face. This was the saddest thing I'd ever seen in my life. And I said "Joan"—this is what I do with the sad things in my life— "this would make an incredible novel. It would be wrong to do it, but it would make an incredible novel." [. . .] I meant that the temptations to be maudlin, opportunistic, sentimental, and manipulative would be immense. I mean, [. . .] the material is so fraught with that, with those things, that it would be wrong to try and write a novel and succumb to those temptations.[9]

With this inspiration, qualified by concerns over the tendency of such a narrative toward sentimentality, Elkin eventually embarked on his version of academic research. He called physician Steve Teitelbaum, "the unofficial consultant for diseases" in *Mills* and the new novel, as well as the reference desks at Washington University Medical Center and the Olin Library, to collect information on the pathology of various diseases. He kept photocopies of entries from *Dictionary of Medical Symptoms*, second edition, edited by Sergio Magalini (1981), and *Current Pediatric Diagnosis and Treatment*, sixth edition (1980), on each of the diseases afflicting the children in the novel. There's also a handwritten entry listing symptoms for these seven deadlies. One he'd written about before. Charles Mudd-Gaddis suffers from progeria, or premature aging, a disease Elkin had treated in the play *The Six-Year-Old Man* for Columbia Pictures in 1968.[10] His library research complete, he launched a campaign to mooch a free visit to Disney World.

It's axiomatic among his friends and family that Elkin hated to pay his own airfare. After all, if someone wanted to hear from an important writer, that institution should pick up transportation and hospitality checks. Compelling the organization to do so was a measure of his success and prestige. So he began angling for a trip to Disney World. He turned to his editor at *Playboy*, Alice K. Turner. The magazine had committed to publishing two sections from *George Mills* (November 1982) and Elkin had a long if checkered history with it.[11] In addition to his history with the magazine, he'd been fascinated with Disney World as a microcosm for transformations occurring in American consumer culture in *The Franchiser*, in which Ben Flesh's grand design is to take advantage of new travel habits associated with the Florida theme park. And in *The Living*

End Ellerbee aroused the Almighty's Eternal Wrath by comparing heaven with a theme park. Moreover, Elkin was developing quite a following as an essayist, writing irreverent, personal essays on diverse subjects.

So with these three things in alignment—a renewed relationship with *Playboy*, a lasting fascination with the social and cultural implications of Disney World, and a track record of developing personal essays about subjects of general interest—Elkin gathered brochures about the theme park and Make-a-Wish Foundation, and gauged Turner's interest in an impressionistic essay on Disney culture. Turner's reply suggests something about the strained relationship between *Playboy*, at that time considered outré and a "men's magazine" and the sanitized worldview promoted by Disney and satirized by Elkin in the novel:

> I have some interesting news for you on the Walt Disney front; not only can you not use us for credentials, you're dead if you mention our name. The reason is the attached piece ["A Real Mickey Mouse Operation" by D. Keith Mano], which ran in the December 1973 issue and permanently pissed off the Disney people. [. . . Y]ou are going to have a very hard time getting backstage at Disney World with any sort of credentials—they'd as soon have a family of tarantulas as a writer back there. The image of the whole park is predicated on magic, and they don't want the world to know what turns its wheels. They don't want you to know that inside the Mickey shell is a teenage girl hunchback, and they will go to great lengths to steer you clear of such knowledge.

With that option dead on arrival, Elkin took Bernard and Molly to Disney World in 1983. His agenda was to collect information and impressions, but as he told several interviewers, the monument to fantasy and conspicuous consumption struck him as underwhelming. Although the children were amused with the rides and displays, Elkin attributed his own boredom to the children. He summarized the visit tersely: "[T]he magic kingdom is just rides and bullshit." Six years later, he declared that Disney World is "no place to take a terminally ill kid because I don't think he would last out a week if he went on all that stuff. However it's a marvelous place to take them in a novel."[12]

On the trip he saw three things that would affect his construction of the book, but for the rest he felt that he could have stayed in St. Louis: he was intrigued by the sophisticated animation in the Hall of Presidents, and that technology forms the centerpiece for the subplot in which Colin Bible prostitutes himself with a park employee in order to acquire schematics to give his lover, a wax artist at Madame Tussaud's. Elkin also watched with fascination the nearly innumerable parades that take place in the Kingdom—his archive contains several snapshots of Disney parades—and these morphed in his imagination to arguably the most important scene in the novel, the "people parade" Bible takes the children to see, in which watching the watchers proves to be the most therapeutic event in their Florida visit. After helping the diseased children enumerate the deformities of the "healthy" observers, Colin leads Noah Cloth to an epiphany combining the universality of imperfection with the only antidote, compassion, spoken in American cockney: "Jesus weeps! [. . .] He weeps for all the potty, pig-ignorant prats off their chumps, for all the slow-cloth clots and dead-from-the-neck-up dimbos, and wonky, puddled clots and gits, goofs and goons, for all his chuckle-headed, loopy muggins and passengers past praying for" (227). Elkin also cited photographs by Diane Arbus, Nemerov's sister, as a source for these "passengers past praying for."

Elkin's children loved the lake and the speedboats, the scene of the most splendid rhetorical moment of the novel, probably in all of Elkin's prose. On the final day, Stanley was less than enthusiastic about the children's going out on the lagoon again because they were soon to depart. Against his wishes, they rented motorboats, but Molly's broke down. Bernie maneuvered his boat to rescue her. As they limped Bernie's boat toward the shore, they saw Elkin furiously beating the dock with his cane in impatience and concern; Molly was afraid he was going to have a heart attack. In an interview that aired on National Public Radio shortly after the novel's publication, Elkin credited Bernard with the inspiration for the second grand therapeutic moment in *The Magic Kingdom*.[13] In the Discovery Island sequence, Bible again takes charge of the expedition, and, with Mary Cottle's assistance, bullies and flirts with the young man who rents the boats, then leads the sickly seven to Discovery Island, where they sunbathe and enjoy a magical moment of privacy and, amazingly, an appreciation for their frail, broken bodies—something they've never experienced because of the public spotlight and prodding medical attention. The chapter (part 3, chapter 5) ends with the most astonishing, the most elegant, the most beautiful language in all of Elkin: "And it was wondrous in the negligible humidity how they gawked across the perfect air, how, stunned by the helices and all the parabolas of grace, they gasped, they sighed [. . .] how, glad to be alive, they stared at each other and caught their breath" (257). To several interviewers, Elkin maintained that the main thing he discovered at Disney World was the room Mary Cottle rents to secure privacy for the "bouts of furious masturbation" to which she resorts to soothe her nerves. It became for him the real magic kingdom, and the magic there is by no means limited to the visual distortion of the false Mickey and Pluto as seen through an inverted door lens or the snow that falls only on Disney World, not in Orlando.

With the room, the automaton displays, the parades and spectators, the mandatory silence among Disney's "cast," and the lagoon in place, Elkin embarked on an artistic journey that would lead him into murkier, more perilous waters than any he had encountered in his art, to a subject that seems to be philosophically and aesthetically a dead end. Nothing is sadder, or more frustrating, than terminal illness among children. The Make-a-Wish Foundation seems naïve and perhaps exhibitionistic in its good intentions, and the practice rubs the child's nose in the fact of her impending doom, even if she gets to meet a major leaguer, a rock star, or Mickey Mouse. Only one child, Lydia Conscience, actually wants to go to Disney World. Benny Maxine prefers Monaco to this "tarted-up Brighton." Yet one feels compelled to do *something*, even as one acknowledges that whatever one may do is futile. We empathize with Eddy Bale's and his ex's frantic, failed search for cures for their dying son Liam, dragging him from chemotherapies to operations to holy places to quack cures in a desperate effort to prolong his wretched life. As Bale tells the Queen of England in the novel's funniest scene, "We never rewarded him for his death. He should have lived like a crown prince, Queen" (17). One of the novel's most touching moments occurs when Eddy, midway though the journey, conjures Liam's presence to apologize for insisting on painful therapies, quack cures, and miracle hunting, all focused on the illusion of bringing about an impossible cure and in the meantime adding to Liam's suffering. So what's an adult to do? Try for the magical cure, or pack them off for a week in Disney World? The one unconscionable thing to do is nothing.

While the novel was in publication, ominous signs gathered on the horizon. *Southwest Review*, which had agreed sight unseen to publish an excerpt after Elkin read from the work in progress, asked to be let off the hook when Borchardt sent them chapter 2, in which Bale assembles his staff; although "brilliant in spots, it's not quite strong enough to stand on its own as written." *Vanity Fair* and *Antaeus* soon followed suit. No section of the novel was published separately in a commercial magazine. Editor Bill Whitehead loved the typescript, but found "several scenes" troubling and felt that several conversations "go on too long." Like many editors before him, Whitehead counseled restraint, and like them he was largely ignored. He asked Elkin to drop the second dream sequence and to rethink one character: "*Should* Nedra be as disagreeable as she seems here?" He also requested cuts in the account of Nedra Carp's family background, feeling that the pace is "too leisurely," to which Elkin responded, "incremental, info building." Whitehead's main concern, however, was fully motivating the conflict between Bible and Eddy, and on that issue he fared much better than his predecessors; Elkin's response was a checkmark, and he tightened that thread, thereby addressing another of Bill's reservations, Bible's motives. Whitehead even successfully suggested a cut! When he complained that the scene at Heathrow should be tightened or eliminated, Elkin placed another checkmark in the margin and went to work.

Whitehead's last suggestion, while the printing was in progress, produced mild titular confusion. The title page was originally set up with the author's name above the title, a mark of his having made it. But after the galleys were set up, Whitehead had a brainstorm; by adding an apostrophe and an *s*, the title became *Stanley Elkin's The Magic Kingdom*, recalling the anthology *Stanley*

Elkin's Greatest Hits. Elkin wasn't at all opposed and the first edition carried
that title. It was featured as a Literary Guild alternate selection. French press
Editions Albin Michel agreed on translation rights, with a 30,000 franc advance,
and Jean-Pierre Carasso, who had translated several Elkin novels, would oversee
a new translator's work on *Le Royaume Enchanté.* A Portuguese edition came
out from Publicacones Don Quixote in 1986 and a Japanese translation was
contracted with Shinchosha in 1989. British publisher Arena bought paperback
rights in 1985. Although sales on release were "not spectacular," according to
Whitehead, both the hardcover and the subsequent paperback held its own for
two years. By the end of November 1987, however, Dutton took the title out of
print, offering Elkin 5,381 hardcovers and 1,646 paperbacks at reduced rates. In
1990 Thunder's Mouth Press brought out a quality paperback of this and several
other titles.[14]

   The biggest surprise is that someone paid $5,000 for a film option. Darrell
Kreitz had been a production assistant for *Blood Simple* (1984) and an actor in
Trespasses (1986).[15] Elkin was happy to cash the check, but I can't for a moment
believe he ever thought this film could be made. He'd sold options on several
novels that could have been adapted as good films, but he had to know this one
was undoable. The subject matter, deformed and dying children, wouldn't play
well at any box office. Sex sells movies, but not the kind in this story—Cottle's
masturbation and Bible's homosexual liaison in a Disney washroom aren't the
stuff of commercial cinema, which leaves the Romeo and Juliet story of Rena and
Benny. That could play on the big screen, but the director would have to soften
the emphasis on early-adolescent sexuality and the visual pathology of Rena's
nasal discharges resulting from her cystic fibrosis. The final glorious copulation
between Bale and Cottle would work better in a stag film than a commercial
one. Moreover, the most important scenes in Elkin's text can't be filmed. The
Shipwreck Island moment would be a visual atrocity, because Elkin emphasizes
seven nude sunbathers' acceptance of their broken bodies, but what a moviegoer
would see is deformity; and the parade scene features the dying children mocking
the swellings, varicose veins, tumors, cellulite, rashes, and other imperfections of
the "healthy" observers. And not even Ingmar Bergman or Stanley Kubrick could
film the true center of this Kingdom, Elkin's language. The rhetoric of the novel,
while sometimes excessive, is at times poetry few novelists, or poets, approach.
The contract's provisions for a made-for-TV movie or a series were probably
"lawyer-speak." But they highlight the obvious question: what was Kreitz thinking? Elkin was too smart not to have asked this question, and far too smart not
to have cashed the check quickly.

   It's, after all, a spectacular, morbid, dark box of logic. The book's refrain,
simultaneously ironic and literal, is "Because everything has a perfectly reasonable
explanation." And if there isn't a humane explanation for disease and death hap-

pening to children, an unremitting logic of cause and effect defines our dilemma. If we act, there are risks. If we do nothing, the child will die and we'll never forgive ourselves. If we take the extreme cure route, the child will still die and we'll second-guess ourselves as Eddy does. And if we take the Dream Holiday, the child will die—despite physician Morehead's careful selection based on the patients' survivability, one dies on this journey and another died before it, while opening the envelope that announced his selection, and the remaining six will shortly after the novel ends. And we'll still be wondering what we might have done—because the unacceptable answer is the only true and logical one: There's nothing we *can* do. In his final interview Elkin acknowledged that he began the novel knowing one child would die, but he didn't know who: "It was love that killed the kid because cystic fibrosis is a lung disease, and she can't get past the orgasm. The punishment fits the crime."[16]

All of which introduces yet another sadly reasonable explanation: these children will be denied not only life but its most intense pleasure. Another poignant moment occurs when Benny asks Eddy about sex, a subject Eddy avoided with Liam. When the surrogate son asks the faux father if sex is "all it's cracked up to be," Eddy mournfully tells Benny what he wasn't man enough to tell Liam: "I'm afraid so" (183). So there we have it. That's why. These children can contemplate the happiness from which they'll be excluded, much as Noah Cloth can indulge his acquisitiveness in a massive shopping spree when he learns he can charge purchases to the rooms. But the risks are intensified if the children attempt to experience the more intimate pleasures from which they'll be excluded. When Rena and Benny attempt intimacy, they accelerate her death. Donne and the metaphysical poets got that right, substituting the metaphor "die" for sexual climax. Her dying—both ways—in Room 822, reaching out to Benny, whom she has come to love, is moving enough that Mickey Mouse, actually park employee Lamar Kenny, weeps inside his costume. But it's the opposite of the clichéd death of a young lover, the stuff of sentimental ballads about a love frozen in time and memory from the Top 40 charts. It's Romeo and Juliet without the catharsis and political reconciliation, a grim reminder that these children, like a modern Moses, may glimpse the magic kingdom of sexual maturity, but they're never going to get there.

If *The Magic Kingdom* is Elkin's darkest novel in its presentation of the pathologies of seven dying children accompanied by five zany chaperones, it's also his most experimental work. While experimentation was a hallmark of Elkin's technique, most of his novels are picaresques punctuated by flights of rhetoric— *Mills* takes picaresque to the third power, with narratives of three Millses—but this time he attempted a truly multiple point of view novel, once again proving that form follows function. Although Elkin insisted that Bale is his protagonist,[17] Eddy isn't sufficiently forceful to carry the burden of being the narrator or point of view character. Therefore ("everything has a perfectly reasonable explanation")

Elkin distributes the point of view among several characters: each caretaker is introduced with a life history in which he or she is the main character—sort of a mini-picaresque—as is each child. Mr. Morehead is the protagonist of his private Florida agenda, interviewing a holocaust survivor to corroborate his zany if profound theory that the predisposition to disease is the key to human pathology. Mary is the heroine of her story, leading from failed pregnancies to the refusal to have her tubes tied, through her noxious cigarettes and masturbation as efforts to control her nerves, to the renting of Room 822. A lengthy digression flouting realism, and recalling the Finsberg twins and triplets in *The Franchiser,* chronicles the sequential displacements of Nedra's family, leading to her compensatory identification with nannies and her carping preference for those children assigned to her care, against the interests of those assigned to Bible, Morehead, and especially Mary—she becomes in the book's funniest line, "a patriot of the propinquitous" (125). Ultimately, Bible displaces Eddy as the central character and becomes the most effective caregiver and the one who can manage bureaucrats and keep the expedition from falling apart after Rena's death. But just as readers become comfortable with Bible as the focal character, Elkin at his most metafictional restores the shaken Eddy as his protagonist, as he and the genetically flawed Mary Cottle have sex with the intention of creating a flawed child. As the perspective shifts for the next-to-last time, Mary recalls the magnificent Molly Bloom soliloquy that ends *Ulysses* as she deliberately conceives a monster, a "troll" or a "goblin." The outré sexuality of the final scene, with its affirmation of life in spite of suffering and death, outraged some reviewers. Others' moral indignation was fueled by Mary's masturbation, Bible's homosexual prostitution (and Elkin's naming a gay male "Bible"), Benny's sexual curiosity, and the disastrous results of Rena's maturation. So it came as no surprise that the reviews were more mixed than any novel since *The Franchiser,* another Elkin groundbreaker.

Kirkus Reviews decried Elkin's "weakest novel so far, with strain and self-consciousness on constant display," whereas *Newsday* included it among the best of 1985 as "darkly delightful." *Library Journal* complimented Elkin's "wonderful world where affirmation cavorts with pain and death." In the national press, Max Apple told *New York Times Book Review* audiences that Elkin's comic vision is "both hysterical and profound. Part sick joke, part lyrical meditation on the nature of disease, the journey to this magic kingdom earns its place among the dark voyages that fiction must endure." The *New York Times* praised "an idea for a novel only he would dare to attempt," and *Vogue* celebrated the "blackest comedy" of a "black humorist of Elizabethan exuberance." By contrast, Anne Tyler lamented that it's really two books, a "comedy about commercial crassness and sentimentality" and "a dark angry book about the children themselves. It can't be both at once." *USA Today* complained, "Elkin is an incorrigible showoff" who has "great gifts. [. . .] If he'd be less self-indulgent—stop masturbating with words, so to speak—he could also write consistently good [novels]." The most hostile review, from the *Washington Times*, complained about Elkin's treatment of sexuality and his didacticism. Most reviewers were excited about the new book, several were on the fence, and a louder and larger minority than for the previous two novels disliked it.[18] And sales were modest at best.

Between the time Elkin completed the novel and its publication, fate intervened with one more cruel irony. As 1985 dawned he had ambitious plans: get *Magic Kingdom* through publication; complete a mentor residency at The Loft in Minneapolis; develop a new novel; negotiate a screenwriting deal with director Bob Rafelson, who had produced and directed *Five Easy Pieces* (1970) and *The King of Marvin Gardens* (1972) and was interested in making a father-son film for Paramount; lead an advanced session in fiction writing at the Mark Twain Sesquicentennial Commission; and deliver a new paper at "A Day of American Literature" in the Paris Metropolitan Museum.[19] The only one he completed was the Minneapolis residency, where he dropped a memorable but prophetic line. When the workshop broke for lunch, organizers suggested healthy, natural food restaurants nearby, but Stanley growled, "Lunch! That means a hamburger!" And a paragraph in the speech he planned to deliver in Paris, which Marc Chenetier read in his absence, sounds another ominous note. Explaining that reading literature is "a young man's game," Elkin launched into a screed on the body's vulnerability, one that echoes several riffs on disease as the natural condition in *The Magic Kingdom*: "By admitting up front that something awful happens to us, that there's this hardening of arteries, some arteriosclerotic stiffening of enthusiasm, a piecemeal wearing away of the glamour glands, that shuts down the pores of excitement and clouds zeal, ardour, earnestness, interest—all poetic complicity's gratuitous good grace."[20] His point was that our aesthetic sensibilities tend to calcify with experience and age, but his vehicle was the familiar theme of the body's inevitable inheritance of disease and death.

And who would know more about that than Elkin? His MS was progressing, and each year well-intentioned people sent him clippings, announcements, and summaries of miracle cures for MS, much like his character Judith Glaser's Laetrile cure in *George Mills*. He applied for an Albert Einstein College of Medicine trial of Copolymer 1, an artificially produced substance that "supposedly imitates in certain respects one of the substances, myelin basic protein, which is found in the brain and the spinal cord," but was turned down because his disease wasn't progressing at the rate required by the protocol for the trial. He'd had a heart attack back in 1968 and his family history carried ominous portents for cardiac problems. But MS had trumped heart, and his focus had been on adapting to it. Like many of us in the 1970s, he didn't give up smoking tobacco because he didn't try hard enough. An Australian physician painted a clinical portrait of a mentor courting heart trouble: "I can't say I wasn't anxious when I saw you at

Bread Loaf, sitting on the porch, overweight, sweating, pale as death, frowning, smoking one cigarette after another, taking to chewing gum as if it would block the poison, the pain in your legs, pain in the chest, that I suspected would shake you eventually, and bring down the whole edifice, the famous writer, [. . .] metamorphosing characters and their actions, neglecting himself, forgetting that man is paper-mâché tied tenuously together with a few bits of string." Overweight? Stanley ordered a cavalry shirt from Sew It Seems in Arizona, giving his neck size as 17½ and sleeve length as 35, both within reason for a husky six-footer. But when asked about his chest and waist measurements, he scribbled in the margins, 47 and 46, respectively. And he was "popping nitroglycerine" while taping the St. Louis version of *The Coffee Room*.[21]

In the spring of 1985, Elkin underwent quadruple bypass surgery, a procedure that was much more dangerous than it is today, in St. Louis's Barnes Memorial Hospital. Whether he had a heart attack that spring remains in question, but the blood flow to his heart was sufficiently restricted to warrant risky surgery with a long recovery period for a healthy person, to say nothing of someone whose MS complicated his prognosis. Another old enemy raised its ugly head again, and that old dread that accompanied the first heart attack, sending him running off to Norway to choose life and escape over death and disease, was now bidding trumps. When the dread had first loomed, he was a relatively healthy, overweight man with two sedentary occupations who didn't take good care of himself. Now he endured constant pain, neurological damage, motion restriction, and the certainty his MS was getting worse. So what is there to do but go on? Even when one of his lungs collapsed in 1987 and he had to undergo painful surgery to reinflate it? With Joan's help, he went on.

Of course he had to cut back a little. He gave up judging for the Literary Awards Committee of the American Academy and Institute of Arts and Letters; William Gaddis served out his term. Elkin's misfortune sent shock waves through the literary community. Heather McHugh wrote sympathetically, "Stanley, did your bypass help? Are you uncomfortable all the time? What makes you want to live? (Is it love? People? Guts? Curmudgeonliness? Work?)," but Hilma Wolitzer told Dr. Eisenberg that by August 1985 he had "recovered sufficiently to shine at Bread Loaf, the old philosophical self sitting on the front porch discussing this and that."[22] By year's end he'd resumed his full schedule, with plans to judge for the 1986 PEN/Faulkner Award, to participate again in Minneapolis's Loft program, and to serve as "featured instructor" at the Duke Writers' Conference. He also changed publishers once more. When Bill Whitehead left Dutton for Macmillan, Elkin sought formal permission to accompany the editor with whom he had enjoyed such good rapport. Yet fate once again scowled at Stanley. Whitehead, among the first generation of AIDS victims, died in 1988. Elkin's eulogy touched Cynthia Ozick deeply: "[T]his gentle, kind, generous, childless man, who, when

I took it out of the closet, and handed back his beautiful tweed, raglan-sleeved overcoat, seemed, if no longer my boss, then, however tenuously, a sort of father still." Whitehead's brother Allen was also touched by Stanley's eulogy.[23] The loss of a friend and trusted editor would leave its mark on Elkin's next novel.

Before the heart episode Elkin embarked on one more solo journey that would also have a profound impact on his work-in-progress. Raymond Carver, having heard Elkin was going to "that shebang in Fairbanks," warned him about perpetual daylight and advised him to visit the Mad Dog Saloon. Jean Anderson, affiliated with Fireweed Press and the Midnight Sun organization that sponsored the literary celebration, had worked out the deal by August 1983: he'd be expected to judge 150–300 pages of short story submissions, then join the winner (he selected Nancy Lord) for readings, radio interviews, and meet-and-greets in Anchorage, Fairbanks, Juneau, and the winner's hometown, Homer. Elkin balked at the volume of submissions, so Anderson volunteered herself and two colleagues to winnow these to the best ten. He arrived in Anchorage on July 30, 1984, to a higher-than-usual interest in the celebration because of the publicity surrounding his presence. Some of his excitement about visiting Alaska is explained by Anderson's terse comment about a raid on an Alaska marijuana farm, "Looks as if your visit came just in time." Stanley was delighted to learn cannabis was legal in small personal quantities. When he heard there were pot farms near Fairbanks, he insisted on visiting one. In fact, his hosts felt that he wasn't going to leave Alaska until he did. Someone connected with the events knew about a farm operated by a group of ex-hippies, one of whom had a federal grant for growing hydroponic tomatoes in Alaska, but he was also experimenting with cultivating weed in an inhospitable climate. Elkin was enthralled with the farmer's ingenuity: "That's what genius looks like." He was fascinated with the high-tech practices they were developing, and after the visit he declared, "That's what it must have been like at the beginning of time, when they were inventing the wheel." The farmers were amused by this older gentleman with a cane and such enthusiasm for their craft. But there's no indication that he was offered any samples.[24]

When Elkin arrived in Anchorage, his MS was severe enough that he needed a wheelchair to navigate the air terminal. His hosts were relieved to discover that he could walk short distances, and therefore had few mobility problems during the several days, four cities, and miles of driving that made up the Alaska adventure. He was in excellent spirits throughout, though he from time to time exhibited symptoms of homesickness. He talked frequently about his family and how much they might enjoy the Alaskan scenery and culture. He read a different text at every event. Most were from his work-in-progress, *The Magic Kingdom*. But his hosts recall primarily his conversations at restaurants or during the trips between readings. After a successful interview by a Homer radio personality, Elkin confided to them that he now knew that his next novel would be the story of a journalist who relocates to Alaska and has to adapt to the culture and the market for local news. Of course, that vocation didn't pan out, but the trip clearly inspired the central section of *The Rabbi of Lud,* in which protagonist Jerry Goldkorn spends a season as "Chief Rabbi of the Alaska Pipe Line." And like Rabbi Goldkorn Stanley was overwhelmed, as are many visitors to Alaska, with the prices of consumer products and the bravado gestures of generosity and hospitality. During Goldkorn's flight, he observes competition in hospitality resulting in the hyperbolic gesture of "six-packing the plane." He also learns about the Native American custom of potlatch, an extravagant and sometimes competitive ceremony of giving that occasionally involves the destruction of valued property, something Elkin converted to the core metaphor of *Rabbi.*

But his habit of not suffering fools patiently didn't change. Although he was able to bite his tongue through a disastrous radio interview in Anchorage, in which the radio host was ill-informed about his work and Lord's, several received a touch of the acerbic Elkin wit. In an Anchorage restaurant, a younger writer's enthusiasm for the current Association of Writers and Writing Programs (AWP) trend of aiming for an unobtrusive style and writing in the present tense set Elkin into a tirade against the minimalists' "damned pretentiousness." For the rest of the evening he mocked the style, saying things like "Now I place my hand on this glass of water." At a reception in Homer, the talk turned, as it often does in Alaska literary circles, to infringement of native resources, with most of the speakers maintaining that non–Native Americans shouldn't write about indigenous cultures, until Elkin shouted, "Anyone should be free to write about anything he damned well wants to." He would write about twin Tinneh Indians and the potlatch in *Rabbi,* very tongue in cheek and perhaps recalling that conversation in Homer. And while in Alaska, Stanley told Anderson what he experienced as a "visionary insight" into what it would be like to be dead. He recalled being at a party and going to use an upstairs bathroom, then standing at the stop of the steps and looking down at everyone else enjoying the party. "I knew at that moment that this is what it's like to be dead. Everyone else is having fun and you're not."[25]

He was well into *The Rabbi of Lud* before his heart attack, and this text had drawn on two other life experiences, his mother's death and his youth in Chicago. The central idea of *Rabbi* originated with Tootsie Elkin's burial in New Jersey. Stanley and Diane arranged the burial, thus launching the novel's main conceit, that Lud's sole industry is the burial of Jews from New York and Connecticut. He wondered what it must be like to officiate at the funeral of someone one doesn't know.[26] Because vocation always appealed to Elkin, he started thinking about what kind of person would be able or willing to do this. He settled on a rabbi who isn't very good, who, like Stanley, was a terrible Hebrew student and therefore couldn't get into a respectable rabbinical school, so Jerry (like some contemporary physicians) studied offshore, in the Maldive Islands, and his low self-esteem consistently battles with his egocentrism: "God's little own welfare cheat" (11). Even the event that shaped this most unlikely candidate for rabbi has autobiographical overtones. Jerry's first sense of belonging happened on Chicago's South Side, when Rabbi Herschel Wolfblock organized his "all-boy minyan and original Little League davening society." Among the members were friends from Elkin's youth, Billy Guggenheim and Harry Richman, as well as Stanley Bloom (his New York relatives were named Bloom). As a rabbi Goldkorn makes a good living and has no lasting involvement with grieving families and their dead, never having known them. But the main reason he stays in Lud, despite his daughter's overpowering need to get away, is what happened to him in Alaska.

What chased Jerry back to Lud was his experience as Chief Rabbi of the Alaska Pipeline. In the great north, Jerry learns that the world is complex and dangerous, that people are eager to scam one another, and that he's subject to credulity and uncontrolled religious enthusiasms. And the section raises questions about authorial ownership that aren't unique to Elkin. He said Rick Moody was the only reviewer to understand the Alaska section. Jerry became involved in "the biggest scam ever to hit the Alaska pipeline" involving three phony Torahs, one self-referentially called "The Old Testament's greatest hits." Elkin did his kind of research, calling the Hillel Foundation to learn the price of a carefully prepared Torah ($10,000)[27] but those foisted off by Tinneh twin Phil go for half a million, suggesting that big money attracts cons and scams, taking advantage of even religious institutions. As Jerry becomes more a Protestant Fundamentalist than a Jew, running Arctic Circle religious revivals, he discovers his own vulnerability to hoax and his penchant for religious enthusiasm. He retreats to Lud, where the customers are dead and the mourners will go away in a day or two, where he can make a nice living by doing very little. In the process he harms those he loves most—his daughter, his wife, and his mistress.

The book contained the usual dedication to Joan, but also one to Whitehead, whose sickness may account in part for its remaining the least influential of Elkin's novels. Years later he said, "If *Rabbi of Lud* had had an editor, it would have been a good book." For the record, Whitehead loved the novel, considering it Elkin's best plotting to date and thinking the Alaska section "brilliant but perhaps over-explained [!]" and the Connie sections among Elkin's best writing to date: "[H]e's one of your very best characters. The book offers a lot of smart thinking on Judaism, death, law, families—(all the good stuff!)—and it's laugh-out-loud funny." Because of his illness, Whitehead, who had earned Elkin's respect as few other editors had, couldn't be closely involved in the process; his absence during the editing may have contributed to the arbitrariness of the plot connections in that book, for if Elkin would have listened to anyone's advice, it would have been Bill's. Moreover, it's his first sustained experiment with first-person central since *Boswell,* the other weak link in the Elkin chain. When asked about this choice to move away from the tested, signature omniscient with flexibility to move into first central for short stretches, Elkin said, "I liked Goldkorn's voice. [. . .] I began in the first person and just liked the sound of the man's voice."[28] But clever as it is, Goldkorn's voice may have been an aesthetic trap. He's smart, glib, and funny, but he's also an avoider of reality, both outside and in. When he moves to the closing epiphany, the reader is shocked to learn that this self-absorbed avoider is capable of serious self-analysis. But the bridge between glib and self-critical never quite convinces us.

If Jerry's voice isn't a sufficient vehicle for the sustained development of the narrative and explication of its ironies, it serves as a magnificent instrument for the epiphany. Jerry has to deliver a funeral service for someone he knows, all too well. One of Shelley's best friends, and Jerry's mistress, is killed in an absurd hunting accident; while delivering her eulogy, he comes to an understanding of his own strategies of avoidance. On the invitation to the bar mitzvah of Steve Zwicker's son, someone, not Stanley, wrote "For the sins which we have committed against thee in the wrong communities For the sin à by too much talking up death & grief not enuff,"[29] language that would, with considerable modification, evolve into Jerry's rare Kaddish. In his real feelings for and empathy with Joan and her absurd death, Jerry becomes an authentic human being who can see into his own cowardice and avoidances. The section also became the source for one of Elkin's oddest artistic crossovers.

In 1986 he contracted with the Mid-America Dance Company (MADCO) to compose a work suitable for interpretation by dancers. Choreographer Ross Winter explained, "I have choreographed to classical and contemporary music, to ethnic and traditional music, to sound collage and to silence—but I have never choreographed to the accompaniment of human voice." Elkin adapted the final section of *Rabbi* as "Notes toward a Eulogy for Joan Cohen," to be read while dancers interpreted the language by movement behind a transparent screen. Joan designed the dancers' costumes. By all accounts it was a spectacular performance, with Elkin hobbling out to a lighted reading table in front of the curtain, and dropping his cane loudly, then reading in that powerful, inflected baritone. His voice served as the music the dancers would interpret behind the transparent screen, their slim, lithe bodies in silhouette contrasting with the frail, drooping body of the seated reader. The contrast wasn't lost on Elkin, who recounted in "The Muses Are Heard" (1988), "We are practically colleagues, these toned, flexible, almost jointless young men and women in their twenties and the crippled-up fifty-eight-year-old man who has to negotiate the high step into the van by means of a high step onto a milk case, a breathtaking piece of choreography in its own right." The essay was reprinted in *The Best American Essays 1989*. "Notes toward a Eulogy for Joan Cohen" was part of MADCO's program for three St. Louis performances; one in Winfield, Kansas; and one in Springfield, Missouri, after which, Elkin recalls, "There are curtain calls. I get roses" from the 250 attendees. The performances were favorably reviewed in St. Louis, with Martha Baker in *Connoisseur* making an eloquent case for the contrast between Elkin's "voice, swaying in swags of Yiddish, pull[ing] the audience toward the story of a rabbi burying a woman with whom he has had a memorable sexual encounter" and the "force of Winter's dance, performed often behind a scrim as distancing as a mourning veil, pulling the audience back toward the dancers." His voice was recorded so "Cohen" could be performed on the road, but I've found no record of performances other than the summer of 1987.[30]

Like *Magic Kingdom*, *Rabbi* encountered serialization problems. *Chicago* magazine had committed to an excerpt from chapter 1, but the editors decided to phase out fiction; they would publish what Chris Newman had committed to, but would consider no more. The *New Yorker* liked the book as a whole, but found nothing to extract. Editor Daniel Menaker "had some hopes for the Alaska interlude in general, but it ended up being more diffuse and protracted than I had hoped it would." Scribner's tried its best to generate interest through strategic advertising, placing large ads in the major newspapers, including the *New York Times, Chicago Sun-Times,* and *Los Angeles Times,* as well as most St. Louis dailies. They also planned special promotions in the St. Louis area; an author's party at the American Book Association (ABA), which Stanley would attend; and to feature his new book in their ABA booth. The prepublication comments were raves. Ozick praised this "genius of language, laughter, and the irresistible American idiom" while Coover reminded readers that Elkin remains "one of America's great tragicomic geniuses." Wolff called him "an irreplaceable treasure" and Richard Ford quipped that "if we didn't have him to read, we'd need to invent him. But we wouldn't come close." And John Irving, quoting Goldkorn, called Elkin a "'coach of character'—not to mention, a divine exploiter of the idiocies and intricacies of our language. There is always in his work the understanding that however recklessly we behave, life is to be cherished."[31]

But the old story played itself out with a new twist. The reviews were for the most part enthusiastically positive, except for William Pritchard's nasty one in the *New York Times,* but there weren't many. More than 80 percent of the few that came out were positive, and more than half of those enthusiastically so, but Elkin knew by now that good reviews have little impact on sales, and a couple for *Rabbi* were the worst he'd encountered since *Boswell*. The only earnings entry in the archive shows an unearned balance of $24,804.29 against an advance of $35,757.00 in 1990, with only 5,271 hardbacks sold and the paperback long in press.

Rabbi was also the occasion of another interlude with the movies. Denise Shannon of Borchardt's pitched the novel to Disney, whose Magic Kingdom franchise Elkin had satirized in his previous novel. But Disney wasn't interested; Cynthia

Sherman loved "this delightful book" and thought Goldkorn's ditzy wife Shelley might be an ideal part for comic actress Bette Midler. But Sherman diplomatically passed on the project because "the essential part of the tale is what is internal to Goldkorn's development and change as a man. Externalizing his conflict too much might destroy the beautiful balance achieved in this book."[32] Elkin probably wasn't surprised, and the novel would indeed be hard to adapt to the screen, for the reasons Sherman suggests and several others: the core conflict between Goldkorn and his daughter, while adaptable to film, would require considerable imagination and tact to avoid the "drawing-room comedy" effect; moreover, Connie's revenge, promiscuous sex with underage boys, would offend many viewers, and her claim of visitations from the Blessed Virgin would upset many Christians; the Alaska Pipeline scam is so dense that most commentators didn't get it in a narrative text—how could it be explained cinematically? Finally, even "the divine Miss M" would be hard-pressed to make Shelley Goldkorn's stage-door Yiddish credible or funny. Some films shouldn't be made; this was one of them.

Elkin never expressed affection for *Rabbi* or even regret that the book didn't sell well. Perhaps he was getting used to books that didn't sell, but he seems to have accepted that this wasn't his best effort. He was, however, heavily engaged in another enterprise through which he'd be part of a minor literary revolution, the reassertion of the personal essay. Since his earliest pieces in the 1960s, he'd encountered problems with editors because the essays they commissioned came back more about Stanley than about the ostensible subject matter. Essayists of Elkin's generation and beyond were taught to eschew the personal, to conceal opinion, and to write so the subject matter, not the writer, was the primary focus. By contrast, Elkin's main interest was always personal, and his speeches and introductions to his own and others' work were consistently rich in personal anecdote, quirky and unique in style, and funny, with a defiantly personal slant.

During the late 1970s, *TWA Ambassador,* a company magazine provided for travelers to read while flying, had asked Elkin to contribute something. His 1981 essay "Withdrawal of Expectations," later published as "Turning Middle Aged" in *Washington University Magazine* and as "My Middle Age" in *Pieces of Soap,* initiated a series of autobiographical essays that suggest that Elkin was beginning to evaluate as well as to exhibit his life and the choices he made. He contrasts his own "middle-aged spirit, this balding pot-belly heart" with his father's dapper, rakish, fashion compliance and assumes that most readers of *TWA Ambassador* will identify with Stanley's acceptance of reduced expectations. He speaks with startling candor about visits to barbershops ("to me a haircut is a kind of affectation") and professional disappointments. He even speculates on his possible interest in a one-night stand with no obligations, but "[i]t hasn't come up and I no longer expect that it will." Yet while the essay is at times painfully autobiographical, the tone is neither self-pitying nor bitter. In the tradition of the great personal essayists of centuries gone by, Stanley is simply and eloquently offering up his own experience as a model for all those TWA fliers who are, or will be, going though the same lowering of expectations.

Like "My Middle Age," "My Father's Life" (1987) tells fond stories about the long shadow Phil cast over Stanley's life. Because this essay informed part of chapter 2, I only mention that its assessment of the father and his power is once more unremittingly candid, with no mitigation either of Phil's capacity to inspire awe or of his failings. Stanley recalls his dad's materialism, a theme that plays out in Stanley's professional life. His cousin Bert Bloom told him about one of Phil's visits to his sister's home while on a business trip, and Jean fretted that Phil was fatigued, in pain, perhaps ill; she admonished him to slow down and take care of his health, when Phil muttered softly, "Listen, [. . .] if I have to live on ten thousand like some ribbon clerk then I don't *want* to live."

He also undertook to revisit and understand his past in the army ("Summer: A True Confession" [1986] and "Where I Read What I Read" [1982]), his clothing choices ("My Tuxedo: A Meditation" [1985] and "My Shirt Tale" [1989]), and his motorcycle period ("The Mild One" [1986]). He wrote an introduction to a colleague's edition of plays by Austrian writer Arthur Schnitzler (1982), which is more about Elkin and playwriting than about Schnitzler, as well as introductions to three small press volumes of his own works (*Early Elkin* [1985], *The Six-Year-Old Man* [1987], and *The Coffee Room* [1987]). There were a few traditional essays, with the emphasis somewhat more on the subject than the writer, such as "Plot" (1980), "Performance and Reality" (1983), and "Alfred Kinsey, Patron Saint of Sex" (1983, widely reprinted and sometimes retitled "A Kinsey Report"), a clever account of Dr. Kinsey's pioneering studies not as good science but as opening up a national conversation on human sexuality—and it tells the story of Stanley's and two friends' visit to a whorehouse during the "dark ages of sex" in 1948. The sheer volume of these pieces, as well as their stylistic brilliance and sometimes painful candor, suggest that Elkin was indeed fulfilling part of his plan, to turn from writing novels toward producing essays that went against the "objective" grain of American prose. They were eagerly contracted, often at handsome fees and with few expectations of editorial censure, by mass-circulation magazines like *Esquire* and *Chicago* as well as more specialized venues such as *Antaeus* and *Art and Antiques*. The volume is astonishing, considering Elkin's ill health and his other commitments. And the candor and elegance suggest that he knew he was participating in one last revolution in style, the resuscitation of the long-dormant familiar essay.

One of the most important of these personal essays, with the first-person pronoun defiantly appearing twice in the title, is "Why I Live Where I Live," originally published in *Esquire* in 1980; it's a paean to contentment, to acceptance of the 1960 decision to place his roots in University City. He parses contentment with the Third Tuesday crowd, "who will listen to me speak Self like a challenge dance," and mentions familiar names like Lebowitz, Teitelbaum, Robins, Pepe, Gass, as well as a few others. The essay is a charming ode to friendship and comfort in an intellectual environment that stimulates without stressing—exactly, Stanley realized, what his art needed.

As this stage of his life completed itself, Elkin was a much sicker man than he was in the early 1980s. His MS was worse, his heart had attacked him again, and his lung had collapsed. His third straight novel had disappointed his hopes for a sales breakthrough. But he was curiously happy, having accepted his adopted home, having renounced his decision against writing more novels, and having taken up the familiar essay as a new art form. And if the public didn't buy his novels, he'd by God continue to write for Stanley and Bill Gass, Howard Nemerov, and Bob Coover, the only critics whose praise he needed.

And one more great moment awaited, one that would bring him the recognition he craved for one grand New York evening. He was one of twenty-six honored as a "Literary Lion" in November 1987, and they spelled his name right three times in the *New York Times* account.[33] He got to hang out with Raymond Carver, Harold Pinter, Wilfrid Sheed, Isaac Bashevis Singer, Judy Blume, Garrison Keillor, Carolyn Kizer, and William Meredith, as well as Bill Blass, Estelle Parsons, Oscar de la Renta, and Jacqueline Kennedy Onassis. The rich and famous, the style setters and trend makers, some brilliant writers—and Stanley, sitting where he'd always dreamed of sitting, among the celebrities.

12 "But I Am Getting Ahead of Myself"

Back to the Movies, Another Trilogy, More Awards, and the Last Years, 1989–94

But you do not know that I am ill. What you may know is
that I have multiple sclerosis and difficulty walking. Sitting
down I am still a relatively healthy man. Asleep, I'm the
Übermensch.

—Elkin to Paul Gediman, 1988

I just got back from seeing King Lear. And you think you
got problems, dad?!

—Molly Elkin from London, 1991

In a poignant moment from "Pieces of Soap," Elkin confesses
that his lifetime habit of collecting mini-soaps from hotels and conference centers,
a hobby that undoubtedly traces to his father's nomadic lifestyle and the souvenirs
Phil brought home from his travels, had recently undergone a radical change. For
many years friends, admirers, colleagues, and associates sent him hotel soaps from
exotic and ordinary places around the world. The essay joyfully acknowledges
that with these, like much of his life and art, excess was Stanley's rule. Various
baskets and hampers contained five or six thousand mini-bars. But by the early
1990s "I have begun to use the soaps, a different one every day. (What was I
saving them for, a rainy day?)" Elkin acknowledges his mortality—the silence
will absorb the last word, sooner than we'd like. His life horizons were growing
dimmer, his fiction was appealing to an ever smaller and more select audience,
and his new interest, the familiar essay, was emerging as his most influential work.
Even before he began using the soap he'd begun a process of self-archiving.

In September 1984, a small press owner had approached Elkin about collecting some early work that appeared only in journals, often with limited circulation. They agreed on one relatively new essay, "Where I Read What I Read"
(*Antaeus* 1982), three old stories ("A Sound of Distant Thunder,"[1] "The Party,"

and "Fifty Dollars") as well as "The Graduate Seminar," a 1972 fictionalization of Elkin's review of an Anthony Burgess novel, which was turned down by his publisher and subsequently transformed into a story about a professor who takes his class on a field trip to the Carnegie Museum. Bill Bamberger wanted these stories for the proposed collection, along with *The Six-Year-Old Man* film script, with $250 up front against 20 percent of gross retail sales. Upon assembling the collection, however, Bamberger found it too bulky and therefore set the play aside.[2] *Early Elkin*, with a new introduction confessing that his early stories are autobiographical—"I tell my students to avoid their lives and invent their texts, but how, I wonder, did I get so smart?"—appeared in 1985 to a good reception for a small press collection, and Bamberger decided to gamble on *The Six-Year-Old Man*. That limited edition of 1,000 copies came out in 1987, also with a new introduction by Elkin. What he probably didn't realize at the time was that he was beginning to self-archive. He hadn't up to this point been terribly concerned with his legacy as a writer, preferring to think in the immediate future: next book, next contract, next public reading, next award, next story. But now, with scholars taking him and his art seriously, holding international conferences devoted to his work, interviewing him wherever he went, writing essays and books about his work—Peter Bailey's *Reading Stanley Elkin*, on which Elkin had commented generously while it was evolving from a Ph.D. thesis, came out in 1985—he began to think about his legacy.

He had long experimented with the personal essay, making the form his own, as Leonard Kriegel recalled in a posthumous tribute: "[S]uperb as his fiction is, he is at his richest in the personal essay. He molded his pain to the form. Writing 'I' allowed him to dig into the unremitting destiny of disease."[3] He found in this form an ideal opportunity to let Elkin be Stanley, to cast his original, inquisitive, and mirthful eye on the foibles of American culture and Elkin autobiography, a love story that's simultaneously narcissistic and a mirror for the culture. He memorialized his friendships in St. Louis, his army days, his meeting T. S. Eliot ("My Shirt Tale," 1989), his father's life, and his advancing middle age. He also wrote personal essays on public issues, including "The First Amendment as Art Form" and "Some Overrated Masterpieces." For some time he'd been thinking about collecting his essays. Then came a dramatic incentive to archiving: the silence crept several steps closer in June 1989.

Over the years he'd become accustomed to Barnes Memorial Hospital, but nothing prepared him for spending the end of June until mid-August there. The recovery period got him released from teaching duties for the coming semester, so he made up the lost time developing his new novel. But it was a dreadful price to pay for a semester's relief; the clinical history reads like a soap opera. He told the story to several correspondents, including Bob Chibka, whose novel *A Slight Lapse* Elkin had favored with a jacket blurb in May and whose academic tenure

he'd promised to support. When Chibka apologized for seeking a recommendation in light of Stanley's terrible summer, Elkin generously indicated that a letter
was a small nuisance compared with this hospital stay:

> June 29th I went into the hospital to get a dose of Solumedrol with a Cytoxin
> chaser on behalf of my exacerbating m.s. Before this could happen, however,
> it was discovered that my throat needed cutting—an endoarterectomy—on
> behalf of bringing blood to my brain lest the transient ischemic episode I was
> experiencing (in which I tried to explain to my wife the existence of an awful
> headache I was having as "a terrible haircut" and, realizing the mistalk I'd
> made but unable anyway to find the word "headache" in my vocabulary, I
> went on to suggest that I could be coming down with a stroke and told her
> I might be having "an Australian crawl"), dry me up like a desert in that
> direction. The operation was entirely successful but the anesthesia gave me a
> heart attack. I was, after a time, permitted to go home, with the understanding
> that I return in two weeks for a heart catheterization to determine whether
> I should be "managed medically," given angioplasty, or, for the second time
> in just over four years, a heart bypass. *Well.* "No bypass," I told the doctors.
> "Never again!" I told them. Well! But those nude pix, Chibka, those naked,
> X-rated pix of my angio. It was bypass or pass on. So, on behalf of my life,
> and in the interest of letting them keep doing it till they get it right, I permitted
> them to crack my breast open for a second time.[4]

This litany of diseases provides a context for the health history of Robert
Druff, the protagonist of the novel Elkin was writing. Like Stanley, Druff exhibits
many maladies, including anxiety about "aphasia, or Alzheimer's, or the beginnings of senility, or anything importantly neurological" (11) to explain his sudden
inability to recall names and facts that seemed to be on the tip of his tongue.
Druff doesn't, however, have MS. Amid Elkin's improbable complications—MS
treatments and small strokes leading to yet another heart attack and another
bypass—it's not surprising that the notion of collecting his essays would be a
high priority during recovery. Shortly before the crisis he'd told Rick Moody,
who as editor at Farrar, Straus and Giroux had inquired about collecting the
essays, about conversations with Borchardt concerning sixteen of them. In the
meantime he wanted to complete two that would prove to be among his best.
In April 1988, Stanley and Joan visited Hollywood for a working vacation that
would yield "In Darkest Hollywood: At the Academy Awards."[5] Then in January
1989, he flew westward alone to research "An American in California."

While "An American in California" offers a humorous, quirky, quasi-socio-
logical view of the differences between the West Coast and mid-American culture,
"At the Academy Awards" takes us to the heart of Tinseltown darkness. A friend
was nominated for best screenplay based on previously published material. Frank
Galati, who credits Elkin with launching his career as an adaptor of fiction to

film, had transformed portions of *The Dick Gibson Show* for the stage and had written the screenplay for *The Living End*. In 1988 Galati and Lawrence Kasdan were nominated for scripting Anne Tyler's *The Accidental Tourist,* but Christopher Hampton won with *Dangerous Liaisons.* Elkin punctuates his essay with the clause, "*Maybe because Galati never returned my calls,*" something Galati regrets to this day. He was busy with a nominee's social whirl and intended no slight or disrespect to his friend and mentor, though Elkin didn't see it that way at the time.[6] The essay forms a core narrative of America's fascination with celebrity culture and the way we value ourselves in relation to the celebrities we know and court, much like the hero of Elkin's first novel, James Boswell. And Elkin doesn't assume Olympian distance from the infection of the starstruck. He includes anecdotes about his own encounters with the famous and powerful, including his first general, who was, "to use Faulkner's word—my first avatar." He also confesses "the worst thing I ever did." In 1975, while a visiting professor at Yale, he was invited to a reception for former senator, vice president, and presidential nominee Hubert H. Humphrey. They met briefly before the event, but when Elkin arrived at the cocktail party, Humphrey greeted him effusively, "*Saay,* I didn't know you were *that* Stanley Elkin." *That* Stanley's b.s. detector clicked on; "I was being patronized. I knew it and it annoyed me." To get even, Stanley, having fortified his chutzpah with a few drinks, waited until the senator was holding forth on public issues to a large group—and then loudly asked Humphrey to get him a Coca-Cola from a nearby cooler. Mildly irritated, Humphrey reached around and handed him a can of soda, but Elkin insinuated that Humphrey's manners were deficient because he didn't open it: "I might cut myself. I better not try opening that." The senator, however, won that round of chump the celebrity by breaking the aluminum opener and handing it back to Stanley, saying he couldn't do it either: "He'd won, the happy Warrior, and by now he probably had all too clear an idea about the kind of Stanley Elkin I really was." Later he told Molly about meeting newsman Walter Cronkite at a party in Kurt Vonnegut's New York apartment, but he was having a difficult evening and realized that this guy looked familiar, someone he saw nearly every day. When it started to connect, he also realized he was standing with his cane, bearing some of his more than 200 pounds, on Cronkite's foot. As he lifted it, he realized this familiar person was the face of CBS evening news.[7]

"In Darkest Hollywood" expands this notion of a starstruck Stanley, who delighted in his nine seconds of fame when his and Joan's image appeared on the giant screen while the camera panned the audience, to indict a culture that thrives on narcissism and celebrity, not only within the show biz community but also in the larger public interested enough to watch this drivel on television or to attend and even to write essays about it: "At the Academy Awards, it's a drawn-out, almost fastidious, customary kowtow" (154). This spectacular blend of confessional autobiography and acute social commentary was chosen for *Best American Essays 1990* with "The First Amendment as Art Form" among the most notable essays of 1989. It's tempting to speculate that the merciless satire that drives "In Darkest Hollywood" is Elkin's revenge for the many disappointments he experienced in writing original screenplays or having his novels optioned for movies that, with one dismal exception, never got made; but the target of his satire isn't mendacity or shabby artistic standards in Hollywood, but rather the systemic phoniness that is often commented upon, if seldom so keenly or so well.

The 1989 solo trip was organized around the "California salute" celebrating the return of President and Mrs. Reagan to California shortly before his second term ended, but side trips were arranged for a Lakers game and tapings of two game shows. The entourage journeyed north to San Francisco, where he visited the Center for Independent People, which specialized in meeting the needs of handicapped citizens, and collected a substantial amount of information on that facility, though little of this appears in the essay. "An American in California" appeared in two 1990 issues of *California,* accompanied by Lou Beach's wonderful illustrations. With the companion piece, "At the Academy Awards," Elkin justifies Carter Revard's praise: "Now that you have invented Essays, novels & plays & poems will just have to eat their hearts out. The earth was without prose, and void, until Stanley noticed. Let there be essays, and there were essays, that's the true Gen." Revard playfully worried, however, that Elkin might someday try his hand at poems: "[F]or God's sake stay away, I don't want to have to play in *that* league if you join it."[8] "An American" narrates Stanley's California idyll with typical, disarming candor, not omitting his being overwhelmed by the transformation of TV executive David Milch, whom he knew at Yale in the 1970s, teaching Stanley the art of the California tip and the shop talk of horse betting. He portrays himself as an uncouth midwesterner, "a theory-*shtupped* middle-American cripple," a "self-proclaimed geography guru, volunteering to explain California like some miracle rabbi [obliquely referring to the Alaska section of *The Rabbi of Lud*]" (107). But it's far more than self-deprecation or autobiographical candor that gives "An American" its charm. The unique California culture has long been part of the American mythology. All this comes to a head at the Reagan gala, a celebration of the mix of Hollywood, Washington, power, image, and politics that transformed America, for better or worse. We have journalists aplenty to interpret California and media for us, but Elkin brings rare imagination and wit to the task. Even his title suggests an alien quality of California culture, and only his imagination would portray the Reagan event as "a bar mitzvah with secret service, G-men in tuxes. [. . .] I've never been so forcefully made to feel the lack of due process before" (112). His sights are lethally focused on the empty gestures of intimacy and friendship, the preening and celebrity consciousness. He captures the event's political core while describing comedian Don Rickles's fawning insult-*schtick,* "predictable, yet remarkably fitting," and suddenly blossoms into revelation: "[W]e're all of us at, oh, court, say, in Shakespearean tragedy, and Reagan isn't just the president, he's the *king,* and Rickles isn't a comic, he's the court jester, and it's very scary, really, and I'm wondering if perhaps there shouldn't be a constitutional amendment somewhere about the separation of State and Show Biz" (115). His metaphors dazzle with variations on this leading-edge culture writ large. Californians' love for the automobile is explained not as transportation, but as a "sort of prosthesis." The tipping ethos makes it "the gratuity state." And it's the "quality-time capital of the world," the "New Wave State," the "Support Group State," "a choice one makes, a blow one strikes for hope" (126, 136, 135).

But the month the second installment of "An American" appeared, something else led Stanley to focus on his legacy. Longtime friend, colleague, and drinking buddy Howard Nemerov came down with a sore throat that proved to be esophageal cancer. The gruff, healthy Howard wasn't going to outlast his chronically ill friend. By the end of March an exploratory surgery confirmed the worst, which Elkin called "a let's-not-kid-ourselves prognosis. This shit grows, it spreads, it has its way with one." Howard struggled against the silence for more than a year but succumbed in July 1991. Helen Vendler tried to console Stanley: "I don't know what Howard would have done without your pool to come and sit at, your conversation to relish and reply to, your satiric streak to match his own, your language that came new-minted. He wasn't one to sit in everyone's back yard." Elkin delivered a moving tribute at Nemerov's memorial service and a year and a half later confided how much he missed him: "You're right about Howard. I find I give him more thought now he's dead than I did when he was alive. The *strangest* thing. About two weeks ago, for three or four nights running, I woke up in the night and couldn't for the life of me be certain that he'd died. Because I'm superstitious about such stuff I won't tell you his name, but both Howard and someone else at the University—this after I'd waked up—came into my head and I had to concentrate to distinguish which of the two had died. Creepy, but it goes to inform how even unconsciously he is still a presence to me."[9] Even the tough poet laureate couldn't conquer the silence. And Stanley, who loved and missed him, who now couldn't get around without Joan's help and a wheelchair, for whom the walker was becoming a nostalgic image of freedom, needed to think once more about his legacy.

While he worked on the final novel he'd see into print, he completed plans for a collection, then entitled *My Tuxedo and Other Essays.* The holograph title essay, published in *Chicago* in 1985 and later excerpted in *Harper's* as "In Praise of Tuxedos," tells the story of Stanley's one and only purchase of a tuxedo, occasioned by the fiftieth-anniversary celebration of *Esquire* magazine (a black-tie gala by a publication with which he had a long and checkered history) and the wedding of his cousin Burt Subin's child in Scarsdale. He told Wyatt Prunty a back story that appears only indirectly in the essay, involving the wedding of Burt's elder child. Stanley didn't go to that wedding because Subin specified that it was black tie, but he attended a younger child's nuptials in formal attire.[10] Stanley, who often said that he dressed like someone on *Bowling for Dollars*, found himself in the market for a tux. He was surprised by the transformation it made in his broken body—he looked good, and "maybe *that's* the meaning of the tuxedo. It corrects nature, it covers up flaw. It's designed, that is, to hide you. Like a kind of sartorial White Out." But enamored as he was with the tuxedo piece as his collection title, when Lorraine Glennon of *Art and Antiques* asked for a new essay on radio, he countered with his soap collection: "There might be an essay in something like that, an essay about the nature of souvenir actually, and I'd be just the fellow to do it, but I'd want top dollar, and I'd want more than 1,200 words." The title of the new collection was decided upon when he realized that this wasn't an appendage to the collection, but among the finest things he'd ever written. John Updike sent Glennon this accolade: "The Elkin piece on soap was amazing, like all he writes—his incorrigible excess. But fascinating, the way he ties it into his advancing disease—this mountain of stolen soap, this increasingly useless body."[11] So it was *My Tuxedo* on November 25, 1990, but *Pieces of Soap* by December 15. Simon and Schuster brought out an unusually handsome book adorned by a replica of one of Joan's paintings, a cocky, bearded, hatted, caned Stanley strolling in the snow-filled park across the street from their Parkview home. And a nice surprise came while the collection was in publication. Almost out of the blue, Vendler volunteered to write an introduction for it. They were longtime friends; Stanley would soon introduce her as a candidate for an honorary doctorate at Washington University and he was well aware of her reputation as a scholar. His tribute climaxed with "The lady is a gent, I think, and lives in this state of human grace. She has heart by the heart, I mean, and I've never known anyone as smart or kind." He apologized for having hinted that the collection might need an introduction, but with typical assertiveness he admonished her a year later about the "familiarity" of the introduction, asking her to "Elkinize me," to refer to him more formally, as a writer rather than as a friend. With Joan's painting, Vendler's introduction, and Stanley's essays—a few didn't make the cut, including his first mass market essay on Elizabeth Taylor, the Jean-Louis Trintignant essay that appeared in a porn mag, as well as book reviews and scholarly efforts from the early days—*Pieces of Soap* strode forth in 1992 to unanimous accolades, one of which touched Elkin deeply. Saul Bellow wrote, "I've been reading your pieces of soap, agreeing, mainly; here and there differing. Admiring. [. . .] Some pen pal you got yourself. I still hope to be a true pen-pal. Saul." Like Boswell, Elkin could be celebrity-struck, and Bellow had a Nobel Prize, Pulitzers, National Book Awards, and the homage of an international literary community. When Elkin listed writers who influenced him profoundly,

Bellow was inevitably among the final four. Maybe the ultimate vindication occurs when one's idol offers to be one's pen pal and says, "The U.S. has no expression like 'cher maître' and I can't think of any approximate equivalent." Elkin's response expressed the sincere thanks of a writer whose work was falling out of favor and simultaneously honored by someone he too considered a "cher maître": "Maybe one or two times a year tops I get a letter that makes a difference in my life. And, at the outside, once a generation I get one that makes soul clap hands and sing. Yours [. . .] did it all, and throw into the pot, too, a desire to kick up what I have left for heels and dance." Bellow, Updike, and Vendler were echoed by Frank Conroy, who quipped, "Meaner than Mencken, smarter than Bellow, more powerful than Webster's Third! Elkin is simultaneously out on the edge, high on the wire, and in your face. Irresistible, and a marvel."[12]

And the reviews were even better than those his novels received—near-unanimous high commendation for wit, style, and the quality of his insights. But there weren't many. Most of the major dailies, including the *New York Times,* the *Washington Post,* and the *Chicago Sun-Times,* chimed in with lavish praise. But the weekly magazines, except for *Newsday,* remained mum on the subject of soap. Only *Kirkus Reviews* and *Publishers Weekly* among the library journals had nice things, or any things, to say. So the old story was writ even larger: huge critical success, popular failure. Books of essays don't ordinarily sell terribly well, and although several judicious critics saw the originality and brilliance of *Pieces of Soap,* the book's sales were yet another disappointment.

Frustrated as he was with the sales of this new venture, Elkin had more essays to write, one of which would generate as much controversy as anything he ever sent to press. Read at the Sewanee Writers' Conference in July 1992 to raucous laughter and uncomfortable chuckles, then published in *Harper's* in January 1993, "Out of One's Tree: My Bout with Temporary Insanity" chronicles something that happened while *Pieces of Soap* was being prepared for publication, just after *The MacGuffin* came out. Because of his MS and the many breathing problems complicated by it, Elkin was taking increasing doses of prednisone, a corticosteroid commonly prescribed for inflammatory diseases including MS. But prednisone can have severe side effects, including disorientation, confusion, dementia, and depression. Early in this therapy he'd been delighted with the results, once writing Molly, "[I]t puts a tiger in your tank."[13] But in April 1991 Stanley found himself sitting naked in the shower with no idea how he got there or what he was supposed to do. When Joan informed him that he hadn't read or written for two weeks, that he'd sat on the bed flipping through the television channels, he disputed her account: "I'm crippled, not lazy. All I can do is work." He also worried that his "Wall of Respect"—large bookcases that prominently display all his books, stories, and essays, as well as translations of his work, and all the interviews he gave and the books and papers written about him—was a fraud, that he was a fake, that he'd written none of it. Joan sent him to Barnes Memorial on April 19, 1991, where the medical teams spent five days adjusting his prednisone and prescribing counter-medications for his dementia.

An important theme in "Out of One's Tree" is the problem of autobiography, a "Striptease" of the "Shamed, autobiographical heart." Stanley made many gaffes during this period of madness, including the expression of libidinal impulses he, if not his characters, ordinarily suppressed. He was verbally offensive to his cardiologist's daughter when she answered the telephone, though no one would tell him exactly what he said or did—"must have been a heavy-breathing job"—and he called Molly, "shocking my daughter black-and-blue with my fouled thoughts." When his doctor made a house call, he placed his underclothing in the dinner dishes. In the hospital he fondled the breasts of a nurse who managed his bedpan and was rude to visitors. The problem, however, is that this is a memoir of craziness, and Elkin couldn't be positive whether he remembered these instances of misconduct or whether he'd been told them by Joan, Bernie, friends, or caregivers. All he could be sure of was that during these "most difficult, most agonizing days and nights of my life," he dealt with madness, the "disease I most despised," that he acted and thought unlike the person he believed he was, and that he couldn't recover the innocence of never having acted crazily.

"Out of One's Tree" is Elkin's most relentlessly candid essay, and the audience's reaction at Sewanee suggested some discomfort at the frankness of its confessional mode. It appeared in *Best American Essays 1994,* but some readers took issue with a perceived insensitivity in Elkin's portrayal of insanity. No one was as outraged as a reader from Georgia, who wrote a four-page complaint to editor Lewis Lapham, informing him that she'd decided against subscribing on the basis of this essay "that promotes such stigma, ignorance, and prejudice." As a caregiver, sufferer, and the daughter of a survivor, she recommended a reading list and copied national and state mental health associations, concluding indignantly, "I'm sorry you hurt their families, because that's exactly what you've done." The Illinois mother of a mentally ill child wrote a formal letter to the editor (never published), angrily noting that the January issue also contained a cartoon that could be taken as insensitive accompanying another article, "Why the Happy Are Nuts" by Richard Bentnall: "What is this—trash the mentally ill month?" By contrast, a journalist told Elkin that reading the essay caused him to relive some of the trauma of his own nervous breakdown thirty years before, one probably produced by prescriptions other than prednisone. His former editor at *Art and Antiques* mentioned that her son was helped greatly by prednisone over the summer, to which Stanley relied that "it *is* a remarkable drug." And a few correspondents thanked him for the accuracy of his describing their symptoms.[14]

The reception showed that Elkin could still, with his autobiographical candor, connect with his readers, even by challenging their most revered beliefs. But the end of his distinguished career as an essayist was upon him. He produced a piece for the *New York Times* on the 1992 Democratic convention, "A Demo of Dems," but it wasn't published. He also landed a great assignment from *Harper's*, covering the 1992 Miami trial of Panamanian dictator Manuel Noriega, a former ally of three U.S. administrations, but also one of the hemisphere's most nefarious drug traffickers and double agents. In December 1990, Elkin told Chuck Gold about his "dream assignment," five days in Florida to cover the trial. Two weeks later, *Harper's* gave him good and bad news. The magazine would pay $4,000 plus expenses, but the prosecution seemed to be moving toward a plea bargain because Noriega's lawyers petitioned to introduce several CIA documents as evidence. The trial went forward, however, in April 1992 and Noriega was sentenced to forty years in a U.S. federal prison, but Elkin never made it to Miami and the essay was never written. Molly recalls that he was delighted to get the assignment, but she's certain that the project wasn't completed.[15]

While his reputation as a familiar essayist was at its zenith, he also took advantage of a Rockefeller Foundation grant to visit Italy, where it all began in 1961 with the Zelda Elkin grant. The Elkins had traveled widely in Europe and modestly in South America since the early 1960s, but had never returned to Italy. Although Elkin often professed a desire to forget about *Boswell*, he always spoke lovingly of his months in Rome. In 1987 Dan Shea recommended him for the creative arts residency program at the Bellagio Conference and Study Center, located on the shore of Lake Como. The Elkins lived there from April 11 to May 14, 1988, celebrating Stanley's fifty-eighth birthday (like Bob Druff, the hero of the novel he worked on there) before they left. He worked productively on *The MacGuffin*, and in the dedication described his stay in "a villa for the villaless" as instrumental in moving it forward; in fact, he says he "managed to spend the five happiest weeks of my life" there. One of the reasons was a new friendship with Russell Hardin, who after the residency lamented, "I now sorely miss talking to you daily." He later nominated Charles Newman and David Milofsky.[16] But joyful as Bellagio was, his final trip to Italy was bitter. In December 1989 he accepted an invitation to deliver "The Rest of the Novel" at a conference about the novel in the twenty-first century. Almost exactly a year after the Bellagio experience, Stanley and Joan flew to Bologna and then took a train to Macerata, on Italy's eastern shore about halfway between Rome and Bologna. But his letter to Bob and Pilar Coover refers to "awful days" at the end of the conference, when he "came to feel like we were in Saigon." As the conference wound down, the organizers had invited the Coovers and a few other participants to Bologna, then onward to Venice. The Elkins weren't invited, not out of indifference, but because of the obvious incompatibility of a canal city and a wheelchair. But as soon as he got wind of the excursion, Stanley desperately wanted to go to Venice and felt exceedingly blue—the entire conference had been a disappointment because he had been so fatigued by traveling. As he wheeled in for breakfast near the conference's end, a hostess, trying to cheer him up, said, "Mr. Elkin, you look so much better today." He growled, "Better than what? Dead?" After the crowd left for Bologna, Elkin was determined to get to Venice. Coover, who stayed behind because of his friend's unhappiness, eventually talked him out of going there by reminding him of the narrow bridges and canals. But his disappointment didn't abate, so Coover searched for a place Elkin might enjoy, and they settled on Visconti, on Lake Maggiore. Bob and Pilar joined the Elkins at a wretched hotel, selected because it was the only one advertised as wheelchair accessible. But the elevator was so tiny that they had to place a dining room chair in it, help Stanley into the chair, ascend, then shift him into another chair in the hall of the floor on which his room was. Then Bob had to take the dining room chair back down and collapse the wheelchair, ascend, reassemble the wheelchair, and help Stanley into it. When Joan helped him into their room, Stanley looked out the window and groaned, "I wish I were dead." The Coovers stayed on another day, and they found a pleasant restaurant that really was wheelchair accessible. After the struggle of getting Stanley to street level, they enjoyed a splendid feast, and these were, Pilar believes, the happiest moments Stanley spent in Italy that year. The next morning the Coovers left by train and Stanley insisted on seeing them off. Inside the station they saw signs indicating the number of kilometers to various European capitals, and Stanley astonished everyone by breaking into song: "I want to go to those romantic places"—he sang the entire verse. But Coover recalls his glimpse of Stanley looking forlorn in the chair, and Joan doomed to cope alone with the hotel elevator, while the train pulled out of the station as one of "the very saddest moments of my life."[17]

At Bellagio, Elkin completed a substantial portion of *The MacGuffin*. Protagonist Bob Druff, with his many illnesses, is another Elkin doppelganger, a commissioner of city streets whose chauffeur tells him, using a line from *On the Waterfront,* that he "could have been a contender"—a serious candidate for higher office. Druff once failed in a run for mayor. His malaise has some of its basis in disappointment that, now that his life is passing him by, he realizes he missed his chance to achieve higher office, and this probably reflects Elkin's own disappointment that his public reputation diminished throughout the 1980s. He'd moved from Young Turk in the 1960s to one of America's most influential fiction writers in 1980; but his works were attracting less attention, and the sales of new novels were even more disappointing than those of past years. He was still very much in demand as a speaker and reader, but he felt his influence diminishing in the wider literary community. Like Druff, Stanley looked at the world with diminished expectations as the 1990s began. His mobility was nearly gone, and his popularity as a writer had never met his hopes. As he told an interviewer shortly after the book came out, "Druff is closer to me than any other of my characters

Elkin in 1989. Photo © 1991 by the author.

because, like him, I felt that I was losing my edge. I felt that I'd lost not only physical force, but mental force, the ability to influence those around me."[18]

Druff's story is unique among Elkin's works for several reasons. First, he called it a "vaguely political novel." He generally discouraged emphasizing the political elements in his books, though it could be argued that politics are crucial to most of his works and that the best among these, like *The Franchiser,* comment effectively on political, economic, and cultural trends in America. Longtime television writer and executive Norman Corwin playfully wrote in 1994, "You say you ain't political, but [. . .] I'd hate to get into the ring with you on polemics, you write so goddam brilliantly about the world around you, including politics."[19] But Elkin felt that political novels were limiting, with their emphasis on narrowly social agendas. So when he took up his political novel, he was careful to focus on the political process, not on the objects of that process. As he once boasted, readers can't know whether Druff is a Republican or Democrat, a progressive or a reactionary. In fact, he's coy about just which midwestern city Druff serves. Based on Elkin's descriptions of professional sports franchises, I was sure it was Indianapolis until Druff mentioned that city as a competitor.

Additionally, *MacGuffin* is in some ways a detective story, another genre Elkin despised. He included a detective story in his "Theory of the Novel" class to show how fiction isn't supposed to be done. His distaste for the genre was based on its being formulaic, emphasizing question and response. It was, he concluded, a "very limited kind of rhetoric."[20] Twice he describes Druff's quest for information as "rhetoric of Q and A." Like the postmodernist trope of the detective story as an illusion of order and coherence in Thomas Pynchon's *The Crying of Lot 49* and Jonathan Lethem's *Motherless Brooklyn,* Elkin's detective novel is unusual in several ways. Elkin keeps his amateur detective and his readers in the dark concerning whether a crime was actually committed. A Lebanese Shiite radical named Su'ad—she's also Druff's son Mikey's mistress—died in a hit-and-run accident, but it's never clear whether Druff's suspicions that she was murdered are true or part of his evolving paranoia. It's further unclear whether her death links with the unexpected affair between the old pol and a buyer named Meg Glorio. Or whether both, either, or neither is tied to apparent traffic in stolen carpets, although Glorio tells him that Su'ad supplied carpets for her flat. The goal of the traditional detective novel, absolute certainty, is exactly what Elkin withholds. Moreover, the staple of detective fiction is the retrospective narrative, usually first person, whereas Elkin's limited omniscient novel is set in "real time," with the events covering approximately the time of the narrative (there are several flashbacks, representing a mnemonic logic of association—as Druff experiences one event, it reminds him of something that happened in his past). The most dramatic variation from the detective format is, however, that *MacGuffin* is a single continuous chapter. Detective novelists generally use brief, action-filled chapters to hold reader interest, create suspense, and pace small episode climaxes, whereas in Elkin's variation, the action is internal, the narrative continuous, and the end product deconstructs the very notion of certainty.

In one small way, however, *MacGuffin* builds on a key theme of Elkin's work, the nature and effects of paranoia. He'd explored that theme in several books, especially *The Dick Gibson Show,* in which paranoia became a trope for Dick's compensating for his own fear of being inconsequential by inventing nemeses who by identifying him as an adversary would give his meager existence importance. The metafictional links between constructing identity as a signifying chain and developing a sequential narrative are manifested both in plot and pun—as Professor in "The Graduate Seminar," puts it, "The Conspiracy of Plot." The alternative, as metafictionists from Gass to Pynchon to Coover to Lethem have shown, is chaos theory, or the probability that events are linked only by our (mis) construction of them, and that the hardest thing to face is randomness, which is the true (dis)order of things. And Druff, as Elkin acknowledged while writing the book, is his most paranoid character: "[H]e finds it fascinating to have a MacGuffin, something to energize him to organize his life as a plot."[21] Because he's sick, vaguely unhappy, and disappointed that he's never been a contender, merely a moderately honest politician with a wretched relationship with his son and an unsatisfying one with his wife (his flashback to their torrid courtship and late adolescent sexual experiments is probably fueled by his elevated testosterone level when Glorio seems interested), Druff wonders what went wrong and when. As Elkin brilliantly puts it early in the story, paranoia is "the compound interest on disappointment, the wear and tear of ambition" (19). The coincidences of his day—Glorio's appearance, Su'ad's death, Mikey's possible involvement, and widespread interest in possibly contraband Oriental rugs that seem to link Su'ad and Glorio's apartment—suggest that there may be something behind these seemingly random events, and his own sense that he's been moved to the political periphery leads him to seek signification for what remains of his life. He even suspects that his drivers are spies, though he can't be sure whom they're spying for—but being spied upon proves that one isn't a nonentity. As events become increasingly entangled, Druff discovers his own Giant Rabbit, not Harvey but MacGuffin, named for the Alfred Hitchcock storytelling device that sets a plot into motion, to explain his condition and reassure him of his centrality. Although at first he's anxious about MacGuffin as a nemesis, he comes to depend on it as a "guardian angel" that is "essentially in your corner" (229) and the "Muse of his plot line" (125). Mostly MacGuffin offers an alternative to "coincidence or chaos or the scrambled random's unbroken code" (192). But we never know for sure whether MacGuffin is MacHarvey or an avatar of Druffian destiny, and we never learn whether there's a connection among all these events, or whether the only connections are that all intersect with Druff and he needs them to be some way connected.

Alice Turner of *Playboy* was excited to publish an excerpt in the December 1990 edition, but asked Elkin to trim the twenty-two magazine columns: "I'm going to hear squawks about the length anyway, but I don't care." This is exceptional for two reasons: because of Elkin's decision to write in continuous time for this work, it's very difficult to excerpt without a complete loss of context (Turner extracted a flashback describing Druff's memories of his courtship); and the contract with Simon and Schuster called for a completion date of December 1989, six months before *Playboy* accepted the section. But the book wasn't published until March 6, 1991.[22] The delay is easily explained because the sickness of 1989 wiped out much of Elkin's summer and left him weakened for some time afterward.

It came out to many good reviews, but not as many as his previous novels received. A few found it exhilarating and brilliant; many found it very good; quite a few offered qualified endorsements; but some panned it as self-indulgent and lifeless. The Aurora (Illinois) *Beacon-News* lamented the "thin plot" and the *Houston Chronicle* headlined, "Elkin's Excess Has Few Rewards." Library collection journals offered mixed recommendations, with *Publishers Weekly* very positive, *Library Journal* tending to the negative, and *Kirkus Reviews* proclaiming it "cumulatively lifeless." Although the favorable vastly outnumbered the unfavorable, these weren't the kind of reviews Elkin was used to getting. A related concern was that, although most major dailies carried reviews, the weekly news magazines, with the exception of a favorable notice in the *New Republic,* ignored it.[23] In the past, exceptional reviews might offset some of the sting of disappointing sales, but this time there were more unfavorable reviews than for any Elkin book since *Boswell.* And the sales were dismal. By the end of March 1992, his unearned balance was –$64,173.80 against a $75,000 advance; it improved to –$48,806.64 two years later, largely because of a credit for the option to publish the Viking paperback. Options were purchased by Swedish and Italian publishers, the former employing Carl Lundgren, who had successfully rendered Joseph Heller's and John Irving's works into Swedish, to translate, and an excerpt was bought for *The Penguin Book of Infidelities* (1994), edited by Stephen Brook. Elkin and Borchardt asked for relief from the provision in the contract for *MacGuffin* that gave Simon and Schuster exclusive rights on the book of essays, but Marie Arana-Ward insisted on the publisher's behalf that the contract be honored. As with many previous publishers, Stanley was "very disappointed" with the advertising efforts and Borchardt questioned the publisher's logic: "You told me that because the advance was so high there was no money left for advertising (a line of reasoning not followed by Simon for Ronald Reagan, who produced a much less interesting book)." As Elkin's agent he recognized Simon and Schuster's right to publish the essays, but questioned the decision "now that you know that the likelihood of your acquiring another Elkin work of fiction in the future is minute." Although Simon and Schuster brought out *Pieces of Soap,* disappointing sales, which he traced to lethargic advertising, led Elkin and Borchardt to switch publishers yet again for the final books he would write. In December 1992 the publisher remaindered the hardcover, offering Elkin the 3,600 copies on hand for $3.10 each.[24]

A curious note introduces the final chapter in the *MacGuffin* chronicle. Sherman Paul told Elkin the Minnesota birds are singing, and "their unmistakable message to my ears is Fuck the National Book Award, it's no big deal, the jury didn't include your peers." Elkin had a great year in 1991, winning an Elmer Holmes Bobst Award in December and being notified of his selection to receive an honorary doctorate from Bowling Green University in November (awarded in May 1992); in May he'd been inducted into the St. Louis Walk of Fame on nearby Delmar Avenue, along with baseball legend James "Cool Papa" Bell and broadcaster Jack Buck, scientific researchers Masters and Johnson, entertainer

Tina Turner, and other greater St. Louis luminaries. This recognition touched him deeply: "I accept this honor willingly, cheerfully, and with great delight." When *MacGuffin* was nominated, he was sure this was his year, that his vindication after the poor sales, the few hostile reviews, and the (in his opinion) poor marketing would be a National Book Award. He dutifully prepared the five-minute reading required of each finalist and the three-minute acceptance speech for the November 20 ceremony. But Norman Rush won for *Mating* and Elkin was furious. After all, he'd been nominated twice before, but this time he really, really expected to win. As he wrote Paul, "In the unlikely event that I'm ever nominated for another such award I will not attend unless I know in advance that the fix is in. [. . .] There's no way, I thought, there's no fucking *way* I'm going to lose this time. (I'd been up to the plate two times before.) It's in, how you say, the bag. Well, I was wrong. It seems there *was* a fucking way I could lose. And, whatever it was, though *I* never found out, the judges apparently did and I lost." To Jean Anderson he complained that the event made "me a three-time loser."[25] And his resolve was firm. His next book, *Van Gogh's Room at Arles,* was nominated for a PEN/Faulkner Award in 1994, but he refused to attend the ceremony unless the committee would assure him that he'd win. Molly, at the time practicing law in Washington, D.C., attended the Folger Shakespeare Theater ceremony and accepted his citation as runner-up. At first Elkin demurred, but he eventually told her, "Sure, go, maybe you'll sell some books." She told the audience her father couldn't attend because of illness. The audience, aware of Elkin's health problems, nodded sympathetically: "Oh, no, not the M.S., I'm talking about something far more serious in nature and far more detrimental to one's health—I'm talking about his writer's ego." She got a sympathetic laugh from everyone, including Philip Roth, who won for *Operation Shylock.*[26]

Like Druff, Elkin entered the nineties increasingly burdened by the worsening symptoms of his many diseases, and almost completely wheelchair bound, with deteriorating dexterity, breathing problems, and frailty. As he quipped, "M.S is a dumb disease. It kills you by yards but you suffer by inches."[27] His graduate seminars, like those of Professor Jack Schiff, the autobiographical protagonist of "Her Sense of Timing," met in his living room to minimize his having to travel the quarter of a mile to Duncker Hall. When he needed to be on campus, Joan got him into the car, drove to campus, and took the wheelchair to his destination, then reversed the process when the class or lecture or meeting was finished. Everybody who was interviewed for this biography sings the praises of Joan's heroic efforts as a caregiver, whose patient wasn't always the easiest person to get along with. And as is far too often the case, we sometimes take out our frustrations on the people we value the most. Quite a few of the Elkin circle felt that he could be overbearing in public, though no one I spoke to recalls Joan's ever complaining. Marilyn Teitelbaum recalls that he was "demanding," a "great burden on Joan, and he sometimes didn't treat her as well as he could have." He "obviously appreciated her efforts, but he could be very demanding, even in public. That's just the kind of person he was." While he was writing "Her Sense of Timing," he told Teitelbaum about a recurring bad dream he had, in which Joan left him and he had to cope with managing the house and his graduate seminars. He explained to the *St. Louis Post-Dispatch* that although the novella is rich in autobiographical details, it was still pure fiction; he couldn't imagine Joan ever leaving him: "It's sort of my situation pushed to the limits. [. . .] The truth is that of the two of us, the right one got sick. Joan always said that, if it had been her instead of me, I would have left a long time ago." Naomi Lebowitz agrees: "We had difficulty with him then. Joan did, really. Everybody did. But he was incredibly stubborn about getting his work done every morning." And Bernard recalls his father screaming in agony for Joan, as the MS worsened and his feet became increasingly painful. Whatever she was doing, he wouldn't stop screaming until Joan—and only Joan—came to take care of him. He gave one interview with a St. Louis paper entirely from his bed, explaining that the combination of heart disease and MS caused him to tire quickly.[28]

A gravely ill man he was. People who hadn't seen him for years were shocked to see how harshly the years had treated him. Grad school friend Jim Ballowe saw the Elkins in Chicago during the early 1990s, and "I recognized him immediately, but he wasn't the Stanley I knew. He was a homunculus [Feldman of *A Bad Man* communes with his "homunculus," or lost alternative potential] of the Stanley I knew." Pat Monaghan invited him to an extended appearance at Loyola in Chicago. When he arrived at O'Hare, she was astonished to see how his health had deteriorated. She recalled that he had tired quickly in Alaska, but was energetic and able to move around that wild land with minor problems. In O'Hare he needed a wheelchair to manage the corridors, but the extent of his illness was yet to be clear. The university housed him in a nearby hotel but he failed to show up for the class he was scheduled to visit the next morning and repeated calls to his room went unanswered. Monaghan dismissed her class and, fearing the worst, rushed to the hotel and arranged for an official to unlock the room. When they entered she saw Stanley huddled on the floor, where he had lain since falling from the bed the night before, unable to reach the telephone to call for help. When she determined that he wasn't in imminent danger, Monaghan helped him get up, but Elkin kept apologizing for the humiliating condition in which she'd found him. Although he read brilliantly from *The MacGuffin* that evening, his trip was ruined. For the rest of the visit he was "surly and often snappish," both physically and emotionally frail. He depended on a wheelchair to get around campus, and he resented the chair almost as much as the embarrassment. After that visit, he decided never again to travel alone, and for his readings or other travel ventures thereafter, Joan accompanied him.[29]

Despite the limitations his health placed on travel and the terrible events in Italy and Chicago, Stanley and Joan initiated one final "home away from home" during the 1990s. Wyatt Prunty, who had known them at Bread Loaf, asked Stanley to participate in the Sewanee Writers' Conference after he became its director. Perhaps because of its proximity to St. Louis, slightly more than 400 miles of beautiful country, and perhaps because everyone at Sewanee understood Stanley's special needs, the Elkins made their way to Tennessee during July of 1992, 1993, and 1994. At each, he gave a public reading and a lecture until 1994, with Joan ever-present to manage the wheelchair. In 1993 he appeared as an eleven-year-old in a read-through of Wendy Hammond's play *Julie Johnson* and got the biggest laughs, partly because of the incongruity of a frail man playing a potty-mouthed preadolescent, but mostly because his delivery was sharp enough to milk every ounce of mirth out of his lines. He was scheduled to return in July 1995, a few months after his death. His participation remains a conference legend. As Prunty said, "[H]e was in some ways larger than life." There's a legend that the handicapped ramp to the "Commodore," a guest suite in Rebel's Rest, the university's guest accommodation, was installed because of Stanley's handicap. A fellow participant from Boston attempted in 1993 to enlist him in a movement to pressure all writers' conferences to become more sympathetic to the needs of "mobily impaired writers." Elkin's reply echoed his feelings about activism in general: "I should say up front that while I am all for us cripples inheriting the earth, or at least that it be properly ramped, elevator'd, and bathroom'd, I am not now and never was much of an activist, even, I mean, when I could march. It's been my experience that people often go out of their way to help me. Don't get me wrong, all physical impairment sucks, but until we can repeal the laws of gravity, I don't see that there's much folks can do about us, except, of course, hold open our doors, raise up our toilets, and help with the heavy lifting." As to life at Sewanee, however, he assured her that he "found all the buildings accessible. And all of the people, too."[30]

As with most places he stayed, much of the Elkin legend at Sewanee revolves around his wit. One year Robert Olen Butler annoyed many participants by correcting their pronunciation of "Pulitzer": "When you've actually won a Pulitzer Prize, you know how it's supposed to be said." Erin McGraw confirms that Butler was irritating that summer, making it a point to steer conversations toward awards and prizes. One evening, several conferees were hanging out on the rear patio of Rebel's Rest, the cabin dating back to the university's founding, with Stanley slouched forward in his chair, leading the assault on the growing darkness. They chatted convivially of publishers, awards, writers, friends, editors, readings they'd heard, and things that had happened during the workshops. Bottles were passed and darkness gathered, and the conversation gradually came to rest, when Stanley, frail and barely visible in his wheelchair and feeling the

Anne Borchardt, Elkin, Ellen Douglas, and Francine Prose at Sewanee, July 1994.
Photo by James R. Peters, reproduced by permission.

encroaching silence, expressed the secret thoughts of many on that patio: "Let's
go beat the shit out of Robert Olen Butler."[31]

While writing *MacGuffin,* he made up his mind to undertake a third set of
novellas. His others, *Searches and Seizures* and *The Living End,* had been among
his most successful books both commercially and critically, and he was genuinely
fond of the form. He told several interviewers and friends about the project he'd
undertake after completing *The MacGuffin,* a novella based on his and Joan's
experience with MS, in which a professor of political geography has to deal
with his wife's becoming fed up and leaving. He also had a plan for a second
novella, as he put it in 1989, about the "vocation of being a princess." By 1990,
he was well into the first one and preparing to write the princess story; he had
in mind a third, about a "professional Elvis imitator who works weddings and
bar mitzvahs." Some vestiges of this plan may have evolved into his final short
story, "Golf-Ball-Size Hail," which he read at Sewanee in 1994, the year it was
published in *Playboy,* but if so the focus shifted from an Elvis impersonator to
a Las Vegas native who shares Wayne Newton's name. Borchardt sent the first
novella to the *New Yorker* but it was returned with admiration because the editors felt that it lacked the "focus and urgency" a *New Yorker* piece should have.
Tri-Quarterly eagerly brought it out in 1992.[32]

"Her Sense of Timing" is another unashamedly autobiographical story, and the fact that he changed his and Joan's names to Jack and Claire Schiff isn't going to convince anyone that this isn't Elkin's projection of a worst-case scenario, what his life might have been like if Joan hadn't stuck by him all those years after the MS got bad. Professor Schiff has Elkin's diseases, his stair-glide, his home address, his telephone number, and his sense of vulnerability. In this sense the story is a tribute to Joan's love and caring, done Elkin-style—a bizarre fantasy of what might happen if a lesser caregiver got fed up and left. Schiff's initial problem is to deal with the daily business of balancing checkbooks, arranging deliveries, and making purchases. Elkin deftly addresses end-of-century America's increased preoccupation with personal security. He negotiates an agreement to install a monitoring system, and frets throughout the story about what message he'll place on his telephone answering system. Because he has to face his dependency, the punch line from a popular television commercial for a seniors' monitoring device runs through his mind and he decides on a variation as his answering-machine message: in the commercial, an elderly lady gazes helplessly into the camera and cries out, "I've fallen and I can't get up!" The ad morbidly mirrors his Loyola of Chicago adventure. The story moreover chronicles preparations for a party for Schiff's graduate seminar; most of the students who show up are recognizable, and many, including Ethan Bumas, Mark Bautz, and Damien Wilkins, get to keep their names.

A graduate seminar in the Elkin living room, early 1990s. Photo by Herb Weitman, by permission of University Archives, Washington University in St. Louis.

Wilkins, a New Zealand writer, recalls Elkin's fiction-writing seminars from the period vividly, and his recollections provide a context for "Timing." His first Elkin class met in Mudd Hall, though it subsequently moved to Elkin's living room. After the professor was wheeled into the classroom, it became apparent that some people in the room weren't on the class list. One's name was Mudd. Elkin stared at him, then chuckled, "So your name is Mudd. Any relation to the building?" Mudd mumbled that his grandfather was the donor for whom the building was named. That didn't deter Elkin, who sent him back to get permission to attend the class, whoever his ancestors were. During that first class, Elkin shocked the students by telling them he intended to read their stories only once, no more: "Faulkner you read twice. Your stuff I don't." As a result, he occasionally made mistakes about specific details in the students' submissions. Once in a while he'd rant for several minutes about a poorly drawn character in a story. Eventually, someone would tentatively correct him, that the character he'd described was in someone else's story, or that the detail wasn't as he remembered it. Wilkins remembers that for a few moments he'd fall moodily silent: "Oh yeah, he could be grumpy." But generally he had an amazing eye for detail, and he demanded precision, seriousness, and research about all the details that went into a story. One wrote a story about a medical salesman—in itself a risky proposition, considering that Elkin's father was a supersalesman and that Elkin, a hypochondriac during his early years, was under constant and intense medical care. After the students discussed the story's merits and problems, Elkin roundly condemned it because "[n]o doctor would carry this stuff in his medical bag. Do your research." Although Wilkins and most of his fellow participants had gone into the class thinking Elkin was "larger than life, a mythic presence almost," they soon found that as a mentor he was a strict realist, someone who demanded that students be completely serious about the work they were doing. If a student wasn't serious, Elkin was verbally abrasive and lost interest in that individual.[33] The "political geography" students who come to Schiff's party, however, get rowdy, and they quite literally invade his space: playing with and breaking the stair-glide, putting him to bed, and investigating and assisting with some of the more personal hygienic details associated with MS. Some of the party's details were based, by Elkin's admission, on a party a student gave in Elkin's honor at Brown University in the 1970s, in which she overindulged and became ill on the apartment floor. She recalls shamefacedly meeting Elkin two days later, when he functioned as her literal mentor: "Do you always drink like that? Because if you do, you'll never be a writer." Looking back, she recalls these as words that "haunted me over the next few years."[34]

The second novella, "*Town Crier* Exclusive, Confessions of a Princess Manqué: 'How Royals Found Me "Unsuitable" to Marry their Larry,'" returns to a favorite theme, preoccupation with celebrity. James Boswell exhibited a pathological need for getting celebrities' attention, and the motif occurs in differing ways in *The Dick Gibson Show, The Franchiser, George Mills,* and *The Magic Kingdom,* as well as being central to "At the Academy Awards" and "Golf-Ball-Size Hail." Himself often overwhelmed, and sometimes tongue-tied, in celebrities' presence, Elkin turned this time to the more sordid element of celebrity consciousness, telling the near-princess's story via a series of installments in a gossip weekly. Each chapter is a week's installment of a series for which "Sir Sid," the tabloid owner, paid her £50,000. As the plot evolves we become aware of the extent of Sidney's role in Louise's being eliminated from her role as a princess-in-training and the real reason she wrote the exposé. A minor but humorous aspect of the story is Louise's rectitude. Parodying Victorian writers a century before, Elkin often omits vowels to s-ggest na-ghty w-rds while graphically describing risqué b-havior.

Most of the royal siblings are a paparazzo's dream—they drink, gamble, gossip, and fornicate publicly, but Prince Lawrence and his intended are expected to hold to an irreproachable standard. As the 1990s began, Britain's royal family contended with an unusually high number of scandals; Queen Elizabeth told Parliament that 1992 had been an "annus horribilis," referring to a palace fire and several misbehaviors by members of the household. Elkin's premise is that "Lulu," as the press called her, is a woman scorned, taking revenge on the family for dismissing her because the man who had her virginity (she had Lawrence's) was (at that time) a commoner. Elkin, however, downplayed the role of the tabloid press in his inspiration and complained that readers and reviewers didn't understand the plot: "My Princess manqué is a bit problematical, but not for the reasons other folks have given me—that it's not possible to satirize a Royal Family who do so much better at it themselves. I began the novella long before Diana et al. went public, and—I think it the subtlest of the novellas—it was *supposed* to be about notions of privacy, or, rather, the purposeful subverting of privacy which is pervasive. [. . .] It's about *flashing* and the privileges of power. And no one, *no* one, seems to have understood the story's ending." Like *Boswell* and "Academy Awards," this story about the public's insatiable appetite for salacious and lurid g-ssip about celebrities' private lives and the ways in which tabloid presses, paper and electronic, pander to that taste, is told in first-person central. Lulu is a charming but shameless autobiographer, who in telling her tale of being dismissed by the royal family, also tells a lurid story of being starstruck and getting her revenge on the lot of them, especially Sir Sid. The fact that Elkin privileged her voice led Norman Corwin, with whom Elkin developed a sustained correspondence during the 1990s, to complain, "There's only one thing wrong, for me, with *Town Crier:* It's that Ms. Bristol writes as well as Mr. Elkin. You have made her so damn fetching, that if the Prince won't marry her, I will."[35] The story is quite subtle, and it's great fun. But it's hard to take it terribly seriously—which isn't necessarily a bad thing.

And which isn't the case for the title novella. At one level it's a clever satire on foundations and grants, the holy grail of academia. Elkin had enjoyed the support of many prestigious grants over the years, and several of his stays as visiting professor and at conferences had stipulated that he have time to write. He'd been guest of honor at conferences in France and Germany; his Rockefeller grant in Bellagio had helped him develop *The MacGuffin*. But he was a practical man, and somewhat cynical, so he was aware of how self-indulgent and petty academics on grants can be. Part of the satire is expressed by the fact that Miller, the protagonist, is being paid to research the attitudes of professors at prestigious universities toward colleagues at community colleges; Miller feels that his fellow grant holders, from Ivy League and major research institutions, condescend to him as a professor at a community college (Jack Patterson, of *Dick Gibson's* Hartford broadcast episode, is also thin-skinned about a similar affiliation). While in Arles, he has unrestricted access to some of academia's heaviest hitters, but he sulks and fabricates evidence and quotations for the report he has to write. But, lest readers conclude that Miller's appointment to the grant is political correctness, letting in a token guy from a community college, many of the prestigious research institutions' participants are doing equally frivolous work: one tries to prove that a dozen can't exist in nature; Professor Schiff of "Her Sense of Timing" researches the notion that world-class cities aren't built on mountains; still another prepares psychological profiles of saints; one sets Broadway lyrics to a twelve-tone scale.

But satirizing the pettiness of academic prima donnas and their exotic researches, effective as it is, isn't Elkin's sole, or even principal, purpose. He focuses on the eerie transformation of Miller from researcher to one who, like Brewster Ashenden in Elkin's first novella, finds himself in art. Perhaps because he feels marginalized among the high-power researchers, and certainly because he's housed in the room Van Gogh stayed in and painted in "The Yellow House" (1888) and other works, Miller finds himself increasingly encountering scenes and images from a variety of paintings; everyone he meets seems to be descended from the model for a Van Gogh painting. One inspiration for this, Elkin's favorite story from the collection, is a postcard Molly sent him from Munich in 1992 with a reproduction of Van Gogh's "Vase with Sunflowers." Molly scribbled that she bought the reproduction in the Alte Pinakothek for her dad: "[P]ut it on the gold card. Hope you don't mind."[36]

Elkin's newest publisher, Hyperion, ironically a subsidiary of the Disney Corporation he'd sent up so mercilessly in *The Magic Kingdom*, brought out the collection in August 1993. As had often happened, the book fell far short of selling out its advance. By mid-year 1994, Hyperion reported a negative balance of $42,897.55, including payment for subsidiary paperback rights. It was also contracted for French and Italian editions. Someone named Zych inquired about

Elkin's interest in scripting *The Living End* for a televised dramatic reading, but Elkin demurred, unless Zych would substitute *Van Gogh's Room,* in which case he'd be happy to serve as narrator, but had "no interest whatsoever in preparing the script."[37] Unlike *MacGuffin,* the collection garnered enthusiastic reviews, though none quite so ecstatic as Steven Moore's comparing Elkin's linguistic virtuosity with Shakespeare's. And it was widely recommended by library journals and dailies. An alarming continuation of the *MacGuffin* trend was the absence of mentions in national weeklies: *Saturday Review* "briefly noted" it, but others, who had competed to review Elkin's books in the past, ignored this one. Only reviewers in the *New York Times* and *New York Magazine* qualified their praise, but the bottom line was that barely thirty reviews made it to press. Despite the relatively low number of notices, the book did better than anything he'd written since *Magic Kingdom* in garnering notice as a holiday season book: it was among the notable books of 1993 from the *New York Times Book Review;* declared "worth getting and giving" by the *Chicago Tribune;* labeled a volume "bound to be of interest" by the *Philadelphia Inquirer;* and made the "editor's choice" for vacation reading by the *New York Times.*[38] Unfortunately, the praise didn't translate into sales. Its contention for the PEN/Faulkner Award was an unsatisfactory recognition for the author, who was feeling increasingly marginalized.

As 1994 approached, Elkin was a very ill man. His many diseases were taking their toll, and he was sadly seeing the promise of the 1970s fail to materialize. Like Druff, he hadn't been quite the contender he'd hoped to become, and he'd sold out few advances in his career. While very much the celebrity among literary insiders, his impact on the wider literary community was diminishing, and he felt that too. But with Joan's help he planned to keep up the fight, to write another new novel for his new publisher. And his family life changed again during the 1990s.

13 "The Stanley Elkin Chair"
The Silence Descends, Posthumous Fiction, and Awards

> No country can afford to lose a writer who is one of its true prose masters, a writer able to make the language stretch and bend until it leaps into permanence. Were I to introduce Elkin today, I would compare him to a halfback weaving his way through language with a joy that none of his contemporaries matched. No subject was beyond the exuberance of his language. And he possessed a writer's true courage, absolute honesty.
>
> —Leonard Kriegel, 1995

During the early 1990s, the Elkins' home life changed once more, and some of it wasn't because of Stanley's worsening physical condition. Philip married in August 1990 and settled in suburban St. Louis. Two years later, he and Marilyn welcomed a daughter and by all accounts Stanley was a doting grandparent. Jessica delighted in the recently installed stair-glide, gleefully riding up and down with her grandfather. He enjoyed reading to her, though, Philip suspects, the books weren't always nursery rhymes. Elkin's personal correspondence from the period often celebrates the great happiness Jessica brought into the Westgate house. Two years later the extended family welcomed Jackie, and, although exceedingly frail by this time, Stanley adored her too. A third daughter, Samantha, was born after he died. The 1994 agenda also included matrimony. In October Molly married Ivan Wasserman, whom she met in law school. Stanley's wedding toast, at the Ritz-Carlton in St. Louis, was surprisingly muted, in light of his love for verbal pyrotechnics and the spotlight, and the special place Molly held in his affections. It's fewer than 200 words long, ending with a modest flourish: "So we welcome and thank you for joining us in Molly and Ivan's big sacred parade, to bask in their hope like sunbathers, in the grand glory of what is perhaps the only just cause there is."[1] Ivan and Molly's children were born after Stanley died; their third, a daughter, is named for Stanley's mother. Bernard, living near University City, set himself up in a small business, sometimes borrowing his dad's computer for business letters and advertisements.

Besides the joy of grandparenting and seeing his children launched into successful lives, Stanley maintained a vigorous correspondence. Because of his preoccupation with his deteriorating health, some letters, usually to friends like Herb
Bogart, then living in Australia, contain entropic inventories:

> By such means the world grows newer at the same time that one is aging. God
> knows *I've* aged. You could count my original, uncrowned, pre–root canalled
> teeth on the fingers of one hand. I sit in a wheelchair which I haven't the strength
> to move by myself, and I wear a 24-hour patch across my chest which shoots
> nitroglycerin up my choking arteries on a steady, time-released basis in order
> to fool my angina. I'm constipated the year round and I piss in bedside urinals.
> I'm fat and I'm bald. Still, as I say, not much has happened to me and, believe it
> or not, I don't feel a day older. I think this has something to do with my being
> as self-absorbed now as I was sixty-three and three-quarters years ago.[2]

In addition to his many longtime correspondents, Elkin's last years were cheered
by several new long-distance friendships. A few years before, an unexpected letter
from Saul Bellow brightened his week and they corresponded regularly for the
remainder of Elkin's life. Television producer, director, writer, and performer Norman Corwin wrote him in the early 1990s, initially wondering whether he'd ever
written for television or films, and theirs blossomed into an epistolary friendship
focused on two of Stanley's favorite spectator sports: politics and pop culture.
Herb Yellin, founder and CEO of Lord John Press in California, met the Elkins
at Sewanee in 1993 and they struck up a correspondence that was frequently
whimsical, but one that turned darkly serious when Yellin's wife was diagnosed
with a terminal disease. Elkin became a trusted friend, confidante, and counselor
when she decided to take a Caribbean cruise instead of undergoing another series
of chemotherapy treatments. He advised Herb to buy the tickets and they took his
advice: "I know instinctively that in this kind of bullshit you are more savvy than
anyone else. You are a good man." One of Elkin's letters succinctly expresses the
frustration we often feel when searching to find words of consolation: "Didn't I
already tell you I don't know what to say? Which only piles on more guilt because
knowing what to say is supposed to be what I do best. So the bottom line on this,
my friend, is that I was terribly sorry to hear your news about Pat. I hope she
improves. I hope she is comfortable. I wish strength for the both of you. I wish
both of you luck." Also from Sewanee, Pat Waters, whom he met in 1992 after
Howard Nemerov's recommendation that she seek Stanley's counsel, remained a
constant correspondent, writing about her work, her personal life, books, movies, and their shared concern about the direction the United States was taking
politically.[3] Amy Hempel, collaborating with Jim Shepard on *Unleashed: Poems
by Writers' Dogs* (1995), recalled Elkin's Sewanee anecdotes about his fox terrier
Bruce that used to bite him, then bit a neighbor's child and had to be put down.

Hempel hoped Elkin might write a poem in Bruce's voice, and perhaps Joan would contribute a drawing for the book. His reply suggests that his memories of Bruce weren't fond: "This dog won't hunt. I wish you luck with your project but you bark up the wrong tree. It's enough for me that Bruce lives on in your memory but I'm damned if I'll write any poems for that son of a bitch."[4]

The main concern of 1994 was, of course, Stanley's health. He'd had physical and pool therapy for some time. He stayed in touch with one of his therapists, Amy Lawrence, after she moved to Oklahoma. He was in and out of the hospital for heart and breathing problems, as well as other MS complications, several times, and remained under constant medical supervision. He was completely dependent on Joan for his eating, dressing, and hygienic functions. Travel without her was by this time unthinkable. But despite his health, or perhaps because of it, he went back to work, producing the minor story "Golf-Ball-Size Hail" for *Playboy* and one last novel, as unlike anything he'd ever written as one could imagine. As he said in "Out of One's Tree," "I'm crippled, not lazy. All I can do is work." So he worked.

He signed on the dotted line for *Mrs. Ted Bliss* in April 1993, his second contract with Hyperion, with an advance of $55,000. By July the first chapter was ready for presentation at Sewanee. Clearly struggling with his hands, manipulating the pages, he read softly and stumbled over a number of words. He announced that he was 122 pages into the book, but confessed that his audience doesn't "know these characters. Neither do I. I'm going to strut my hour on the stage, and then maybe we'll both know them." He read the early section describing the Jewish inhabitants of the Miami condo in which the principal action is set, reiterating, "they were Americans," with the old Elkin gusto; the audience was hushed and transfixed. But the reading clearly taxed him. About fifty minutes in, his speech became more slurred, and he seemed irritated over that; he stopped reading abruptly, saying his time was up. In July 1994 he told Pat Waters he was 297 pages into it, but he'd once more been in the hospital and felt "too weak to get into my stair-glide." He sent the printout to editor Pat Mulcahy in early November, with a witty note, "Defying exacerbations of his multiple sclerosis, right up in the face of his heart attack and bad breath, against the treacherous odds of all his conditions, Mr. Elkin has come through once again to give us the favor of yet another book!" He added a conciliatory sentence that seems out of character after his pugnacious rounds with previous editors: "In the interest, then, of he'll-play-ball-with-you if you'll-play-ball-with-him, he leaves himself open to suggestion and, of course, praise."[5] True to his word, he was unusually cooperative during the process, only getting his hackles up about his predilection toward two-em dashes. Then again, *Mrs. Ted Bliss* probably presented few editorial challenges because it contains fewer passages of blinding rhetoric and over-the-top plot twists than most of his recent work.

Mrs. Ted is indeed Elkin's most sedate work, and this is entirely appropriate because of the subject matter. Like "The Condominium," its setting is a complex of condos for senior citizens, mostly Jews from the Northeast and Midwest who retired to Miami. A principal plot line concerns the substantial South American population being integrated into the condo community, and Dorothy Bliss, like many of her friends, is fascinated by and fearful of the Latinos, especially after one (who looks like film star Cesar Romero) insists on paying her considerably more than book value for the late Ted's 1978 Buick LeSabre. Not coincidentally, other Latinos shower her with attention and favors. As the plot unfolds, the reason for Alcibiades Citral's excessive offer is explained by his involvement in the drug trade, a major concern of the 1990s. It's likely that some of Elkin's preparation for the essay on Panamanian dictator and drug lord Manuel Noriega's Miami trial was put to use in the Citral plot. Mrs. Bliss testifies at the trial—Citral used the LeSabre as a drug storage locker—and later visits him in jail, quite unlike the zany slammer Elkin created for *A Bad Man*. The novel also deftly satirizes trendy quack cures, something Elkin knew a lot about because friends and fans were still sending clippings about miracle cures for MS. Mrs. Bliss goes to a "recreational therapeusisist" to help her deal with the mild depression she still feels three years after Ted's death, only to find that her therapist is a nut and that her "baleboosteh" interests aren't interesting. She later makes another appointment, only to discover that her "therapeusisist" has been murdered and her new counselor is Junior Yellin, son of Herb, the name of one of Elkin's frequent correspondents. He sent Herb a set of galleys with the notation, "WARNING: CHARACTERS IN THIS BOOK ARE FICTIONAL EVEN IF THEIR NAME *IS* HERB YELLIN."[6] Junior, a scam artist, once did a number on Ted, but much of the novel concerns Dorothy's growing intimacy with him. She even contemplates joining him on a Caribbean cruise, later to discover that her son's widow, now a follower of a "holistic chiropractor," takes the cruise instead.

Ultimately *Mrs. Ted Bliss* is about gender identity and acceptance. Although Elkin was sometimes criticized for politically incorrect portrayals of women, this is a sympathetic and wise inquiry into the problems of women who identify themselves solely through the parameters their husbands provide. Hence "Mrs. Ted." Dorothy was completely dependent on him as provider and husband. Without him, she has to figure out who she is and how she fits into a patriarchic culture. Hence the Hispanics, cultures often stereotyped as macho and phallocentric. Mrs. Ted is delighted by the chivalric attentions many of the South Americans pay her. She has a vague realization that she's never been encouraged to develop her own identity separate from Ted, and to Elkin's artistic credit the reader comes to question her subordination, but Dorothy doesn't: "Because there was a trade-off. A covenant almost. Women honored the men who put the food on the table, who provided the table on which the food was put, and the men saved them. That was the trade-off. Men saved them" (75).

Elkin in front of the Olin Library portrait. Photo by Herb Weitman, by permission of University Archives, Washington University in St. Louis.

Mrs. Bliss is in many ways the anti-Elkin hero. She's passive, gentle, and forgiving. Although there is abundant suggestion that Mrs. Ted's psychological issues stem from sexual repression of which she's vaguely conscious and which she has transferred to vanity about her appearance, her journey is toward forgiveness and acceptance. She forgives Junior for scamming Ted and Citral for involving her indirectly in the drug trade. Most critically, she learns to forgive her son Marvin for dying young and his wife Ellen, whom she irrationally blamed for Marvin's leukemia; she also forgives Ellen for running off with Junior. She comes to terms with Ted's involvement as a World War II profiteer and with her son Frank's refusal to say Kaddish for either Ted or Marvin. As conscious of her diminishing future as her creator was of his—"It was awful, too awful, to live so diminished" (131)—she prepares for her death by means of rituals of forgiveness and mercy.

The novel ends in the stillness at the eye of a storm, one of Elkin's most brilliant symbols. Dorothy refuses to leave the condo during the approach of Hurricane Andrew (1992), among the worst natural disasters to strike the United States during the twentieth century. Symbolically hearing impaired, she doesn't exactly refuse to get out of harm's way; she stays out of curiosity and because leaving was "too much trouble." The novel ends with one of the most touching scenes Elkin ever wrote. A member of the condo staff finds Dorothy and they sit in her vulnerable apartment during Andrew's eye, awaiting the second, more violent, phase of the storm. As they embrace in the face of nature's worst, Dorothy arrives at her truth about the human condition: "Because everything else falls away. Family, friends, love fall away. Even madness stilled at last. Until all that's left is obligation" (292).

And those muted tones were the final published words from the great silence-shouter. He told Bogart about a plan to begin *The Freshman Novel*, which would include discussion questions "that lead the characters to alternative situations" at the end of each chapter. He planned to rest until February 1995 before taking up this project, but there's no evidence that he went further with it. In March he told Wilkins, a former graduate student writing and teaching in New Zealand, about a novel called *Third Tuesdays,* which was about ten pages complete; "it may or may not go the distance." Members of the Washington University community, including Lee Robins, heard about the project, but it's not in his archive or on his computer. It would be about Eli Robins, whose death from complications of MS had produced one of Elkin's rare uncontrolled outbursts in a letter to a childhood friend's widow: "[W]e interrupt this letter to bring you a special bulletin: my friend Al Lebowitz just called to tell me that Eli, a fellow MS'r, died last night and I no longer wish to finish this sentence."[7] Eli had been a founder of the Third Tuesday social group Elkin had so enjoyed; now, like Howard, Eli was gone too.

Mrs. Ted Bliss came out in September 1995, in a handsome edition featuring a photo of an automobile, a LeSabre one hopes, mostly covered by a tarp. The back jacket featured comments from a variety of writers: Tim O'Brien, whom Elkin knew from Bread Loaf, called him "a hero of American letters." Geoffrey Wolff: "There's no voice like his, and never has been." Kurt Vonnegut Jr.: "An important book accessible only to patient, trusting readers." Bellow: "Only an artist, the real thing, would wade so far and so deep into the commonplace in order to show us how to turn it inside out." And the reviews were amazing, better than anything since *The Magic Kingdom,* and even more uniformly, enthusiastically positive. But they were also eulogies. Maureen Howard called the novel a "brilliant end to the long career of a writer who saw the pitch of every sentence, the shape of each paragraph, as vital to the moment of his story."[8] How sad that Elkin, who loved friendly reviews much more than he admitted, never saw these. *Mrs. Ted* won Elkin's second National Book Award Critics Circle competition for 1995, edging out his friend Richard Ford's *Independence Day,* and was named as one of the *New York Times* "Best Books of 1995."

Stanley died in Barnes Memorial Hospital in St. Louis on May 31, 1995, two weeks after his sixty-fifth birthday. The cause of death, according to the Missouri papers, was "probable heart attack"; according to the *New York Times,* it was congestive heart failure, the diagnosis attributed to Molly; the Washington University *Record* listed the case as "heart failure." In view of the long history of heart and lung problems, and the exponentially increasing stress his MS placed on all his vital organs, either explanation is plausible. His medications counter-indicated the consumption of alcohol but shortly after his sixty-fifth birthday, he and Joan went out to dinner on consecutive evenings, with Yellin and then Ben Taylor. Elkin seldom drank alcohol those days, but he had a social drink or two each of those evenings. By early morning he was suffering intense abdominal cramps, but resisted Joan's and Bernard's wish to call an ambulance. Eventually the pain became so great that at his physician's insistence he agreed to let Joan take him to the hospital. That evening he told Joan and Bernie about the (as-yet undeliberated) jury verdict in the current sensation, the O. J. Simpson trial, which he'd been following closely on television. When he, in a series of short phrases, got to the "not guilty" verdict, Joan asked, "Stanley, did you just tell me a story?" He barely nodded and whispered, "The end." Fifteen minutes later he was gone.[9]

Of course the literary community knew Elkin was sick. Of course we knew his death was imminent. But it came as a shock anyway, to friends and fans alike. After all, he'd been our guy on the battlefront against pain, suffering, purposeless-ness, and death. And he knew something about suffering; Naomi Lebowitz called him the "great poet of our pain." If he could get through all this stuff, with the extra burden he had to bear, surely we could? As the truth sank in, tributes flowed from the major dailies, from readers, critics, colleagues, and literary associations. *Mrs. Ted Bliss* was selected by the Olin Library, where Elkin had written his early books, as the benchmark three-millionth acquisition; a recording of "The Coffee Room," with Elkin playing Mingus, was played to celebrate the library's milestone; and Special Collections presented an exhibit called "The Stanley Elkin Show" during 1996. In a memorial talk at the American Academy of Arts and Letters, Bill Gass compared Elkin with legendary tenor Enrique Caruso: "Stanley sang both parts during duets; he sang for the scenery; he was the boisterous crowd on the stage, and in the pit, he was the orchestra's every instrument; he was the house itself, the plush seats, the plump patrons, the young ushers; [...] for Stanley knew that voice was the soul and source of his art, that his voice was unmatched." Francine Prose, paying tribute at the 1995 Sewanee Writers' Conference, which

Elkin had been scheduled to attend, began her remarks and readings with a witticism that captures Elkin's conflicted personality, the serious artist who wanted wealth and fame. Upon hearing about his death, she put his books—that is, the ones friends hadn't failed to return when she loaned them—into a little pile on her desk: "Little? I could hear Stanley asking. His novels and stories make even the book of Job look understated, decorous, and even a little wimpy. Re-reading them I was inspired to go back and re-write a sentence I had been lazy about, and hoped nobody would notice." Prose concluded, "I can't think of another writer so willing to take upon the difficult and the dicey. In the world of fiction he was our Evel Knievel."[10]

Three memorial services were widely attended in 1995. The funeral, at Berger Memorial in St. Louis's West End, on June 11, was filled to overflowing. Remarks by Steve Teitelbaum, who was out of the country, were read by Elkin's colleague David Hadas (1931–2004), who also served as the rabbi. "His eulogy was tailored to fit the deceased, but he included the prayers of his forebears and ended with the Kaddish." Hadas also read from the book of Job—an eminently appropriate choice.[11] Dan Shea hosted a memorial at Washington University on September 24, with readings and remarks from Helen Vendler, M.F.A. student K. Anis Ahmed, Ben Taylor, W. Patrick Schuchard, Steve Teitelbaum, and Bill Gass. There was a terrible thunderstorm that day, and while Gass was eulogizing Stanley, the lights went out with a violent thunderclap. Bill improvised, "Stanley, knock it off. Can't I borrow the spotlight while I'm eulogizing you? Now put the lights back on." The third, at the Ninety-second Street Y Unterberg Poetry Center in New York on October 15, was facilitated by the Borchardt Agency. The guest list included a veritable who's who in American fiction, with readings from Elkin's works and remarks by Robert Coover, John Irving, Charles Newman, Francine Prose, and Helen Vendler. Coover recalls another "post-Stanley" moment at that memorial. The crowd was awaiting the beginning of the memorial service, and the mood was becoming increasingly serious. As the talk diminished to sotto voce whispers and greetings, a loud thud echoed from a floor above them, when something was apparently dropped. In the hush that followed, Molly, sitting in the front row, looked up and softly asked, "Dad"?[12]

Laughter. Then silence.

The early 1990s had not been kind to the Washington University Writing Center in this respect—two of the writers at the heart of that program's rise to the first tier among creative writing centers had passed away, Nemerov in 1991 and Elkin in 1995. Both endowed chair holders left a rich legacy of achievement and inspiration to students and faculty alike. Two years after Elkin's death, the university created the Stanley Elkin Professorship in the Humanities. Elkin would have been delighted that the holder is his friend Steven Zwicker, who with his family house-sat for the Elkins in the 1970s while Stanley was in London writing two of the novellas in *Searches and Seizures* and receiving the diagnosis of the disease that would define the rest of his life, while affording him a unique opportunity as an artist, to be our spokesman for Life, even a compromised Life, against the Silence.

All Stanley Elkin ever wanted was to be an uncompromising artist, to be rich and famous, and to live forever without pain. And he was uncompromising, a role model for aspiring serious writers. His work at times takes risks most writers choose not to take, and the result can be obscurity. Although everything in his books ultimately works—Peter Bailey and I have marveled about the dexterity with which Elkin could make logical the most obscure and outrageous passages— but it often doesn't work on a first, second, or even third reading. Like James and Faulkner, whom Elkin told his students you "read twice," some Elkin passages can be intimidating. And there's no question that he was self-indulgent, often to his detriment. Entire passages of nearly any of his books could be cut with no loss in plot, character development, or theme. There would, however, be a loss in rhetoric, and that's why Elkin fought with editors.

He was famous, but his fame shrank as the decades passed. He'd been an enfant terrible of American letters in the 1960s, and by 1980 he was firmly established as one of the more influential serious writers in America. Before he died, he recognized that his influence was increasingly limited to an ever-tightening circle of fierce, loyal admirers. That had to hurt. The reverence of the "fit audience though few"[13] was sustaining, but Elkin wanted everybody to adore (and buy) his books. It may be true that his absolute insistence on doing things his own way, sometimes leading to artistic indulgences, not only turned off general readers whose attention span and curiosity aren't up to *The MacGuffin,* but also eventually limited his audience even among the academic and literary communities. And there's little getting around the fact that, as Elkin put it in his South America talk "Fiction and Society," most Americans don't read serious fiction, and it's only the literary community and the academy that form the readership for most "literary" fiction. An informal sample recently indicated that fewer and fewer professors include Elkin's work on course reading lists, except for specialized classes. To compound matters even further, literature is, as T. S. Eliot argued in "Tradition and the Individual Talent," a constant competition for "place." As new writers come into play, some slip out. Elkin's, and many writers' of his generation, predicament was compounded by increased pressure to include representation by minorities and women in courses and anthologies. This again contributed to his diminishing audience. Will his stock rise in the future? One can only guess, but one purpose of this biography is to gather useful information in case that happens. When Malcolm Cowley edited the Viking Portable Faulkner in 1945, not one of Faulkner's novels was in print. We never know how literary tastes will change.

And he wanted to be rich. By the standards of most citizens, he was. He had a lovely home, a pool, more gadgets than most people acquire, much travel, and frequent dining out. But the competitive son of a spectacularly successful immigrant, Elkin kept score by advances and royalties. He once groused to Georges Borchardt that he wanted to be rich and famous like "those other Johns"—Irving and Gardner. But it was yet "other Johns" whose revenues he really envied—le Carré and Grisham, financially successful formula writers. He told me he wouldn't want to write like Stephen King, but he'd love to have King's royalties. And Elkin could have been a formula writer had his conscience let him. He knew the formulas inside out, teaching them in his "Theory of the Novel" class and imitating or parodying them in sections of novels or entire books, like *The MacGuffin*. I believe he tried to write to formula in his film script *Mudshow,* and the reason that script doesn't work is the unresolved tension between the serious artist and the commercial writer.

And he wanted to live forever without pain. Fat chance. His life was punctuated by brushes with death, not the Angel of Boswell's paranoid imagination, but the existential abyss that lurks somewhere deep in the unconscious of many a citizen of postmodernism. He fought it every way he could, with skull-and-crossbone suspenders, gestures like spitting over his shoulder, and, mostly, by writing that fear in the hearts and words of his creations. He couldn't make it bearable, for himself or his readers, but his fiction could help make it episodically manageable. And few artists have lived as long with incurable illnesses as Elkin did, making his suffering ours through his creations and exhibiting for us that although these can't be overcome, they can be endured. That's Stanley Elkin's legacy—a substantial body of work in which our common struggle against disease and death is rendered honestly, at times brilliantly, with humor, honor, and courage. He and his characters taught us what we have to do when the certainty of suffering and death overwhelm us. We can't hide, but we can't give in either. Like Elkin, but of course in a minor key, we can shout down the silence.

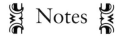 Notes

Chapter 1. *"A Sum of Private Frequencies"*

1. David Dougherty, "A Conversation with Stanley Elkin," *The Literary Review* 34 (Winter 1991): 182.

2. Singer comments, Phyllis Bernt and Joseph Bernt, "Stanley Elkin on Fiction: An Interview," *Prairie Schooner* 50 (1975): 22; black humor comments, Tom LeClair, "Stanley Elkin: The Art of Fiction LXI," *Paris Review* 17 (Summer 1976): 70. Elkin made similar professions—that he didn't know what the term *black humor* meant—in several interviews. D. Winner, *Washington University Student Life* (February 17, 1971).

3. Gass interview, 2002.

4. Elkin Archive (hereafter EA). The copy was changed slightly for the Random House publication.

Chapter 2. *When Stanley Elkin Was a Little Boy*

1. Brandwein interview, 2002.

2. "Three Meetings" (1970), *Pieces of Soap*, 314–18.

3. Stanley Elkin (hereafter SE) to Mark Eisner, March 19, 1991; "My Father's Life" (1987), *Pieces of Soap*, 246–47, 249.

4. Lebowitz interview, 2002.

5. B. Elkin interview, 2002; Jacobsen interview, 2002; SE to Morris, May 5, 1991; Doris Bargen, "Appendix: An Interview with Stanley Elkin," *The Fiction of Stanley Elkin* (Frankfurt: Peter D. Lang, 1960), 258.

6. "Sound of Distant Thunder" story, Bargen, "Interview," 224; Feine to SE, August 19, 1957. "A Sound of Distant Thunder" is collected in *Early Elkin*, 13–35. Elkin must have misremembered the title; no such transaction takes place in "A Sound of Distant Thunder"; however, Stephen Feldman from Elkin's unfinished novel *The Glass Continent* sells costume jewelry products by the gross in Des Moines: "He had made her buy a dozen necklaces that he knew the store could never sell." Whether he showed Phil the draft of this novel is uncertain. It was most likely written before Phil's death; typescript, EA.

7. Philip Elkin (Sr.) to SE, April 5, 1956.

8. Jay Clayton, "An Interview with SE," *Contemporary Literature* 24 (1983): 10.

9. Brandwein interview, 2002; *The Glass Continent* draft, EA; Don Brenwasser to SE, June 1979 (ellipsis his).

10. Spacks interview, 2002; J. Elkin interview, 2002; Siegel interview, 2006; Glen Gold (Herb's son) to SE, March 30, 1987.

11. Avedon interview, 2006; Buell interview, 2006; J. Elkin interview, 2002.

12. Gail Siegel, "Wish It Were Fiction: Stanley Elkin's Magic," November 20, 2005, http://wishitwerefiction.blogspot.com/search?q=Elkin and confirmed by email.

13. "Out of One's Tree: My Bout with Temporary Insanity," *Harper's* 286 (1993): 2. He also discusses that year in "The Future of the Novel: A View from the Eight-Seated Spaceship," *New York Times,* February 17, 1991.

14. Dougherty, "Conversation," 194.

15. J. Elkin interview, 2002.

16. "My Shirt Tale" (1989) and "The Kinsey Report" (1983), *Pieces of Soap,* 288 and 277; SE to Bellow, March 29, 1992.

17. Siegel interview, 2006; SE to M. Elkin, October 23, 1988.

18. Michael J. Farrell, "Stanley Elkin: Writing to the Rhythm of the Heart's Oom-Pa-Pa," *The Catholic Review* (May 9, 1986) (ellipses Elkin's).

19. "The Fall," unpublished typescript, EA.

20. Miriam Berkeley, "PW Interviews Stanley Elkin," *Publishers Weekly* (March 29, 1985): 74–75; Teitelbaum interview, 2002.

21. First version, Bargen, "Interview," 256; second version, LeClair, "Art of Fiction," 56.

22. "My Father's Life," *Pieces of Soap,* 248.

23. Spacks interview and email, 2002; "Memories of Cousin Stanley," an unpublished poem, quoted by permission of Barry Spacks.

Chapter 3. College, Graduate School, and the Army

1. Elizabeth G. Sayad, "Living with the Arts" *west end world* (November 1973); Carol Horowitz, review draft of copy for a University of Illinois College of Liberal Arts and Sciences newsletter piece; Horowitz to SE, December 12, 1990.

2. Bargen, "Interview," 220.

3. Novak interview, 2006; the previous three paragraphs summarize that conversation.

4. J. Elkin interview, 2002.

5. Snider interview and email, 2003; Guggenheim interview, 2002. Bill told Janis Guggenheim that at one of their camps, they woke to find a rattlesnake outside the tent; no one was hurt, but four young men were plenty scared.

6. EA; Hansen to SE, February 13, 1980.

7. Jacobsen interview, 2002 (Joan's painting hangs in his living room); J. Elkin interview, 2002.

8. J. Elkin interview, 2002.

9. "Where I Read What I Read," *Pieces of Soap,* 274; William Robertson, "Winners and Losers: A Talk with Stanley Elkin," *Miami Herald,* February 20, 1983; the professor was Harrison Hayford; "The Outlander" typescript, EA.

10. Barry Spacks to SE, June 4, 1954.

11. "The Dying," *Illini Writers* 4 (September 1950): 28.

12. "A Cup for God" typescript, EA.

13. McGraw interview, 2006; "Interview with Stanley Elkin," *AWP Newsletter* (February/March 1988): 10–11; variations occur in John Strasbaugh, "Elkin Magic," *Baltimore City Paper*, May 22, 1989, pp. 26–28 ("His coach was the brilliant, idiosyncratic and aloof Randall Jarrell"), and Jeffrey Duncan, "A Conversation with Stanley Elkin and William H. Gass," *Iowa Review* 7 (Winter 1976): 62–63.

14. Porter to SE, April 14, 1954; Leo Glassman (*The American Hebrew*) to SE, October 11, 1954; William Herskowitz (*The Jewish Horizon*) to SE, October 27, 1954.

15. Mulligans to SE, 1954; J. Elkin interview, 2004; Lebowitz interview, 2002; Jacobsen interview, 2002.

16. *Biographical Directory of the U. S. Congress*, http://bioguide.congress.gov/scripts/biodisplay.pl?index=M000315.

17. *The Dick Gibson Show*, 88; "Where I Read What I Read," *Pieces of Soap*, 269–73.

18. SE to J. Elkin [August 31], November 13, November 14, November 18, November 21, 1955; Dougherty, "Conversation," recorded interview but not included in published version. The manual is however mentioned in Berkeley, "PW Interviews," 75.

19. J. Elkin interview, 2002.

20. Kipniss interview, 2007; SE to J. Elkin, November 13, 1955 (ellipses his).

21. J. Elkin interviews, 2002 and 2005; M. Elkin confirmation, April 2006; SE to Gaddis, November 17, 1994; Kipniss interview, 2006.

22. SE to Guggenheims, January 29, 1957, courtesy of Janis Guggenheim.

23. *Virginia Quarterly Review* to SE, October 4, 1956; "Thackeray and the Well of Experience" typescript, EA; "Acquiescence and Renunciation" typescript, EA; *Views* to SE, November 22, 1956; Hathaway (*Epoch*) to SE, October 31, 1956.

24. "The Sound of Distant Thunder," *Early Elkin* (Flint, Mich.: Bamberger Books, 1985), 17.

25. J. Elkin interview, 2005; SE to Joan Greenberger, December 23, 1994.

26. Bargen, "Interview," 247.

27. Elkin's discharge (photocopy), courtesy of Joan Elkin.

Chapter 4. Family Crises, Graduate School, and a Literary Career

1. P. Elkin interview, 2002.

2. Bargen, "Interview," 224, 245; J. Elkin interview, 2002; Gold to SE, February 14, 1958; SE to Herb Yellin, November 28, 1994.

3. Reviews of *Porgy and Bess*, *The Immoral Mr. Teas*, and *The Magician* are in the EA; emphasis in the quotations are his.

4. Paul Bixler (*Antioch Review*) to SE, February 5, 1958; Thurston (*Perspective*) to SE, March 8, 1958, and October 22, 1959 (emphasis in original); Freedman (*Contact*) to SE, June 18, 1958, and June 18, 1959; Calvin Kenterfield (*Western Review*) to SE, June 16, 1959; Davidson (Atlantic–Little, Brown) to SE, July 25, 1958; Phoebe Adams (*Atlantic Monthly*) to SE, July 28, 1958; Neil Brennan (*Epoch*) to SE, September 16, 1958, and March 26, 1959; "MJB" (*Berkeley Review*) to SE, October 13, 1958.

5. Spacks interview, 2002.

6. Planning sheet and fragment, EA.

7. *The Glass Continent*, EA.

8. Robert Weaver (*Tamarack Review*) to SE, December 2, 1957; "The Last of the Go-To-Hell-God-Damn-its," EA.

9. "The Party," *Early Elkin*, 37–50.

10. A planning sheet in the EA contains two other sketches, one of which evolved into "Perlmutter at the East Pole," as discussed in chapter 5.

11. Thurston (*Perspective*) to SE, March 12 and October 22, 1959; "Cousin Poor Lesley and the Lousy People," *Criers and Kibitzers, Kibitzers and Criers*, 218–38.

12. Bargen, "Interview," 220; Ballowe interview, 2002; Gass interview, 2002; Scott Sanders, "An Interview with Stanley Elkin," *Contemporary Literature* 16 (1975): 135.

13. William Gass, "Stanley Elkin: An Anecdote," *Review of Contemporary Fiction* 15 (1975): 38–40; Gass interview, 2002; Ballowe interview, 2002.

14. Madeline Tracey Bridgen (*Mademoiselle*) to SE, April 22, 1960; Bellow to SE, May 13, 1960. Elkin told Bargen that he wrote "Criers" (the story) during the summer after he passed his prelims (the spring of 1960) (Bargen, "Interview," 221), and a story called "Wherever There's a Minion," which doesn't appear in the Elkin papers, was rejected in November by *Hudson Review* (Mary Emma Elliott to SE, November 11, 1960); it's probably an early version of "Criers and Kibitzers." Bellow story, Dougherty, "Conversation," 176–77.

15. Bellow conversation, Baltimore Public Library, 1997.

16. Ballowe interview, 2002.

17. Ballowe interview, 2002.

18. "Religious Themes and Symbols in the Novels of William Faulkner," EA, also available in *Dissertation Abstracts International*.

19. Sanders, "Interview," 132 (emphasis in original).

20. Flanagan to SE, July 18, 29, and August 31, 1960; "Religious Themes and Symbols," 155–56, 169n (emphasis in original).

21. "The Conventional Wisdom," *The Living End*, 43.

22. "Religious Themes and Symbols in the Novels of William Faulkner"; Campbell to SE, March 18, 1960; Rev. Duncan Gray to SE, March 25, 1960; Gold to the author, January 22, 2008.

23. Linda Whittemore, interview summary, EA; Ballowe interview, 2002; Dougherty, "Conversation," recorded but omitted from published versions.

Chapter 5. "Become a Strong Man"

1. Thurston interview, 2002; Gottfried interview, 2008; Demarest interview and emails, 2006.

2. Applegate to SE, April 11, 1986; Tamarkin to SE, July 29, 1986.

3. Demarest interview, 2006.

4. Demarest interview, 2006.

5. Demarest interview, 2006; Pepe, interviews, 2002 and 2005; Lebowitz interview, 2002, and Lebowitz Archive, Olin Library; Shea interviews, 2002 and 2005, and several emails; Robins interview, 2002 (in 2009 Robins disputed Elkin's account, saying Eli had only one set of parallel bars); "Why I Live Where I Live," *Pieces of Soap*, 261.

6. P. Elkin interview, 2002.

7. Pepe interview, 2002; Shea interview, 2002.

8. Gail Segal, "Stanley Elkin Plays Poker," http://wishitwerefiction.blogspot .com/2004_01_01.

9. Gottfried interview, 2008; Pepe interview, 2002; Lebowitz interview, 2002; Jacobsen interview, 2002.

10. Ballowe interview, 2002.

11. Coover to SE, March 15, April 6, May 4, 1961; Tom Payne (*Playboy*) to SE, May 24 and June 16, 1961; Harold Rosenberg (*Longview Journal*) to SE, May 24, 1961.

12. Bernt and Bernt, "Elkin on Fiction," 18.

13. Bargen, "Interview," 255; SE to Gass, January 17, 1963, William H. Gass Archive; Rust Hills (*Esquire*) to SE, October 23 and December 10, 1962, February 13, 1963; Martha Winston to SE, December 2, 1964; Nina Dorfman (Fleet) to SE, October 17, 1962; G. D. de Santillana (Houghton Mifflin) to SE, October 25, 1962; Hayden (Screen Gems) to SE, November 1, 1962.

14. Brown (*Esquire*) to SE, October 18, 1962, and August 25, 1964; Byron Lobell (*Esquire*) to SE, February 18 and April 8, 1965; Winston to SE, January 27 and February 10, 1966.

15. Inspiration story, LeClair, "Art of Fiction," 83; publication data, EA.

16. Anecdote, LeClair, "Art of Fiction," 76; University of Illinois undergraduate records.

17. Al Lebowitz to SE, September 6 and October 6, 1962; story and quotations, Richard Sale, "An Interview with Stanley Elkin in St. Louis," *Studies in the Novel* 16 (1984): 323 (variants appear in Bargen, "Interview," 221, and *AWP Newsletter* [1987]: 14); contract information, EA.

18. P. Elkin interview, 2002.

19. SE to Lebowitzes, undated, Albert and Naomi Lebowitz Archive, Olin Library.

20. SE to Winston, undated [1962]; SE to Lebowitzes, December 6, 1962, Lebowitz Archive.

21. SE to Lebowitzes, March 22, 1963, Lebowitz Archive; SE retold the story in "The Muses Are Heard," *Pieces of Soap,* 96.

22. William F. Woo, "Inward Look at an Emerging Writer," *St. Louis Post-Dispatch,* undated [1965] copy in EA.

23. Planning sheet, EA (emphasis added).

24. SE to Lebowitzes, February 22, 1963, Lebowitz Archive (emphasis in original).

25. Fox to SE, September 3, 5, and 9, 1963; SE to Fox, September 7, 1963.

26. SE handwritten to Fox, October 1963 (undated, reply to Fox of October 14); Fox to SE, October 17, November 27, and December 4, 1963.

27. Fox to SE, February 4 and 14, March 16, 1964; Macdonald to Fox, February 25, 1964; Fox to SE, March 30, 1964, quoting Southern; Friedman to Fox, April 29, 1964; Winston to SE, April 22, 1964.

28. Machell (Hamish Hamilton) to Winston, May 5 and 21, 1964.

29. J. Elkin interview, 2002; Spacks interview and emails, 2002; SE to Lebowitzes, May 13, 1962, Lebowitz Archive.

30. Bernt and Bernt, "Elkin on Fiction," 24; Robert Earlywine, "An Interview with Stanley Elkin," *Webster Review* 8 (1983): 16.

31. Harry Bowman, "Wild, Whacky World of Celebrity Hunter," *Dallas News,* July 5, 1964; Grover Lewis, "First Novel Puts Author in Top Rank," *Fort Worth Star;* unsigned,

"Sponging in Style," *London Times Literary Supplement,* October 22, 1964; Joseph Haas, "Immortality Collector," *Chicago Daily News,* September 30, 1964; John Ciardi, "Manner of Speaking," *Saturday Review* (August 15, 1964).

32. Winston to SE, March 30 and September 9, 1964; Ciardi story, *Publishers Weekly* (July 29, 1964); David Howard Bain, *Whose Woods These Are: A History of the Bread Loaf Writer's Conference 1926–1992* (Hopewell, N.Y.: Ecco Press, 1993), 95; Jerome Charyn, "On Stanley Elkin," *Review of Contemporary Fiction* 15 (1995): 42.

33. "The Endings of Novels," SE's 1964 Bread Loaf lecture, EA (emphases in original).

34. Warren Bayless (Curtis Brown) to SE, May 30, 1964; Turman to SE, June 19, 1964.

35. Schmitz to SE, October 20, 1964; SE to Schmitz, November 1 and 18, 1964; Beaty to SE, November 9 and 22, 1964, December 5, 1964; Albert Stone (Emory), December 7, 1964, January 5 and February 8, 1965.

36. D. H. Lawrence, *The Plumed Serpent* [1926] (New York: Vintage, 1955), 385.

37. Vendler interview, 2006; *New England Review* 27 (2006): 57–58.

38. Random House contract for *Criers and Kibitzers,* September 23, 1964, and memo of agreement with Anthony Blond, January 21, 1933, EA; Duker to editor, *Saturday Evening Post,* July 22, 1965; Duker to SE, August 16, 1965; Ballowe to SE, December 9 and 16, 1965; Coover to SE, April 20, August 2 and 21, October 14, 1965; Demarest to SE, May 10, 1965; Sylvan Karchmer (University of Oregon) to SE, February 10, 1965; Vendler to Robert Schmitz, October 13, 1965; Elizabeth Heide (Houghton Mifflin) to SE, April 30, 1965.

Chapter 6. *"Convicted of His Character"*

1. Discussed in chapter 3.
2. Alternative titles, EA.
3. IMDB: http://www.imdb.com/title/tt0020056/.
4. Jesse Kitching, "Fiction," *Publishers Weekly* (November 15, 1965); M. S., "In His Stories Elkin Hits Funny Bone," *National Observer* (January 10, 1966): 27; Samuel Bellman, "Nowhere to Go and No One to Know," *Saturday Review* (January 15, 1966): 41; John Thompson, "From Out of Nowhere," *New York Review of Books,* March 3, 1966; Richard P. Brickner, "Born Losers," *New York Times,* January 23, 1966, pp. 40–41; David Galloway, "Visions of Life in Recent Fiction," *Southern Review* 4 (1968): 850–60; Doris Grumbach, "Fine Print," *New Republic* (1973): 32.
5. Fox to SE, January 20 and 25, April 12, 1966; Gass to SE, December 17, 1965.
6. Spacks interview, 2002.
7. Silverberg and Rosen (Yordan's attorneys) to SE, August 3 and 28, 1967; SE's handwritten draft reply, August 30, 1967; Charles Silverberg to SE, September 12, 1969; Ornstein (Case Western Reserve) to SE, January 26, 1968.
8. Roth to SE, January 17, 1969; Crowell to SE, September 23, 1983; recordings, introduction to 1990 edition of *Criers and Kibitzers, Kibitzers and Criers,* x; Magyar contract, October 10, 1986, and Georges Borchardt to SE, October 15, 1987; playbill, Chicago Jewish Theater, March 11–April 17, 1988, in Skokie, Illinois, EA; Esmonde to SE, April 4, 1988.

9. Brown background, Douglas Martin, "Harry Joe Brown, Jr., 71, Innovative Developer, Dies," *New York Times*, November 28, 2005; Brown to SE, November 1, 1966; agreement, January 30, 1967; introduction (1987) to *The Six-Year-Old Man*.

10. Brown to SE, November 21, 1966; *The Six-Year-Old Man*, introduction and 7; "Progeria": http://www.nlm.nih.gov/medlineplus/ency/article/001657.htm#Definition.

11. Fox to SE, December 7, 1966; J. Elkin interview, 2002; Edward Loomis (UCSB) to SE, November 8, 1966; Marvin Mudrick (UCSB) to SE, December 28, 1966; loan agreement December 1, 1966, EA.

12. Pepe interview, 2005.

13. Brown to SE, March 9, 1967, and undated note; Kahn (Curtis Brown) to SE, March 21, 1967; Nellie Sukerman (Curtis Brown) to SE, October 13, 1967.

14. Elkins to SE, October 17, 1967; Brown to SE, December 26, 1967; John Gruen, "A Dynamic, Young Producer Takes Bohemian Plunge into Films," *New York World Journal Tribune*, January 31, 1967. This story was also reported in *Show Business*, December 3, 1966; *New York Times*, November 30, 1966; *Variety*, December 1 and 7, 1966; and *Hollywood Reporter*, December 1, 1966.

15. Fox to SE, January 6, May 5, and December 23, 1968; Brown to SE, August 11, 1967; Blossom Kahn to SE, August 15, 1967.

16. Secretary's message, EA.

17. Brown to SE, February 18, 1988; Roger Ebert, "Stella Stevens vs. Women's Liberation," *Chicago Sun-Times*, March 15, 1970; Stevens, emails of July and August 2008.

18. Brown to SE, February 18, 1988; introduction, *The Six-Year-Old Man*.

19. P. Elkin interview, 2002; http://www.imdb.com/title/tt0094737/.

20. Lish to SE, January 31, February 4 and 14, March 15 and 28, May 6, June 7, 1966; "A Prayer for Losers" and test questions, EA.

21. LeClair, "Art of Fiction," 79–80; corroborating comments in Sanders, "Interview," 145; Duncan, "Elkin and Gass," 68.

22. Jacket copy, 1967 Random House edition (emphasis in original); Al and Naomi Lebowitz (email 2008) can't recall who actually penned the copy.

23. Winston to SE, March 3, 1966; Gerald Freund (Rockefeller Foundation) to SE, June 30, 1967; Fox to SE, November 21, 1966.

24. Publicity campaign, EA; Mudrick to SE, March 31, 1967.

25. Winston to SE, March 9 and May 12, 1967; Susan Stanwood (*Post*) to SE, December 1 and 13, 1966; Fox to SE, May 9 and 31, June 7, November 31, and December 11, 1967.

26. Lish to SE, June 3, 1968; Maclennan Farrell (*Post*) to SE, April 7 and May 3, 1967.

27. R. Z. Sheppard, "Leo the Louse Tells Where the Money Is," *Book World* (October 22, 1967); Josh Greenfield, "The World of Leo Feldman," *New York Times Book Review*, October 15, 1967; Webster Schott, "A Comic Outburst on the Nature of Evil," *Life* (October 27, 1967); Christopher Lehman-Haupt, "Books of the Times," *New York Times*, October 7, 1967; John Weigel, "'Black Humor' Novel Shows Author's Talent," *Cincinnati Enquirer*, November 11, 1967; Bernard Bergonzi, "Catch-31," *New York Review*, January 18, 1968; Daniel Stern, "Cosmic Put-On," *Saturday Review* (November 18, 1967); Jonathan Yardley, "About Books," *Greensboro Daily News*, December 17, 1967.

28. SE to Gass, March 18, 1966, Gass Archive.

29. Fox to SE, October 25, November 7 and 9, 1967; SE's penciled response, EA.

30. J. Elkin interview, 2002.

31. Security Pictures contracts, EA; Yordan to SE, March 9, 1968; Richard Parks (Curtis Brown) to SE, January 5, 1971; Fields interview, 2002.

32. Jacques Cabau, "Un goulag américain," *L'Express* (1977): 77. "At once a documentary, social satire, and metaphysical fable, [Feldman's voyage] manifests Elkin as one of the best American novelists" [my translation].

33. "Malleus Maleficarum" has been problematic. Stephen Greenblatt, *Will in the World: How Shakespeare Became Shakespeare* (New York: W. W. Norton, 2004), 352, sheds light on the history behind the phrase. It was a "famous witchcraft manual" by Dominican inquisitors Heinrich Kramer and James Sprenger. Elkin's knowledge of Shakespeare was extensive, but he probably picked up this phrase from undisclosed sources. The Warden uses it in his call for a pogrom against bad men, cranking up his rhetoric to engage the inmates against a common enemy.

34. Terakado to SE, June 24, August 16 and 30, 1970; translator's introduction draft, EA.

35. Handwritten file copy summarizing negotiations with Thurston, September 12, 1966, EA.

36. Lebowitz interview, 2002.

37. Heller's character Bob Slocum uses this phrase in *Something Happened*.

38. Coover to SE, April 27, 1968; Yordan to SE, August 1, 1968; Yurick to SE, April 12, 1968.

39. J. Elkin interview, 2004.

40. Unpublished manuscript, EA. My transcriptions of both appear in *New England Review* 27 (2006): 41–56.

41. EA; *New England Review* 27 (2006): 48.

42. "The Purdue Speech," unpublished transcript, EA.

Chapter 7. *"Strange Displacements of the Ordinary"*

1. "Flowers at an Airport," *Stories That Could Be True: New and Collected Poems* (New York: Harper and Row, 1977), 172; Stafford mentions King and Wallace.

2. Although Elkin downplayed the importance of Nixon's call in 1989 (Dougherty, "Conversation," 180), he moved it to the novel's final moment in response to Fox's request for a stronger ending. The original typescript (EA) ends with the phrase, currently on page 334, "the scrambled I Am's of Miami beach."

3. Fox to SE, November 11, 1968; SE to Corwin, November 9, 1994 (SE's computer); SE to Fox, November 8, 1967.

4. Teitelbaum interview, 2002; Shea email, October 2006; J. Elkin interview, 2002; Pepe interviews, 2002 and 2005.

5. Pepe interview, 2002.

6. SE to Gass, February 6, 1969, Gass Archive.

7. Gass interview, 2002; Pennsylvania story, Peter Bailey email, May 2008, and "'A Hat Where There Never Was a Hat': Stanley Elkins's Fifteenth Interview," *Review of Contemporary Fiction* 15 (Summer 1995): 21–22.

8. SE to Cohen, handwritten draft January 1969; follow-up, Charles Dougherty to the author, December 4, 2006.

9. "Baseball Story," *New England Review* 27 (November 2006): 48–52; "The Mild One," *Esquire* 105 (June 1986): 113 and *Pieces of Soap*, 302–5.

10. Dougherty, "Conversation," 189.

11. Winston to SE, February 10 and April 8, 1966, March 7 and April 16, 1969; SE's handwritten response on verso of Winston's of March 7.

12. Bargen, "Interview," 247.

13. SE to Rockefeller Foundation, March 17, 1967; Leo Hamalian (CCNY) to SE, August 22, 1968. It appears that Elkin had completed at least one-third of part 1, ready for a public reading at least.

14. Lish to SE, November 8, 1967; Susan Stanwood (*Post*) to SE, September 22, 1967, January 18, February 9, and March 28, 1968; Borchardt to SE, April 10, May 28, June 25, August 20, October 31, and December 11, 1969; Fox to SE, December 28, 1969.

15. Copyedited text, EA; LeClair, "Art of Fiction," 59.

16. Legal agreements, EA; the British edition was published by George Weidenfeld and Nicolson, advancing 400 pounds at signing and 400 pounds upon printing; the Japanese edition was contracted by Hayakawa Shobo and Company, with an advance of 600 dollars (American); Pocket Books bought the paperback rights, offering $8,000 against 8 percent royalties on the first 200,000 copies, as well as a five-year exclusive option to publish the book in paperback.

17. Fox to SE, September 16 and 28, October 13 (Elkin's handwritten list on verso), November 16, December 1, 1970, March 3, 1971; Gass to Fox, November 4, 1970; *New York Times* advertisement, March 3, 1971.

18. Joseph McElroy, "Our Radio Classic?" *New York Times Book Review*, February 27, 1971; R. Z. Sheppard, "Don't Touch That Dial?" *Time* 97 (March 1, 1971): 82; Christopher Lehman-Haupt, "Listen to This One, Folks!" *New York Times*, February 27, 1971, p. D37; William Pritchard, "Stranger Than Truth," *Hudson Review* 24 (Summer 1971): 357.

19. Irving to SE, April 9, 1971.

20. Borchardt to SE, April 9, 1971, February 13, June 12, 1973.

21. Galati interview, 2002; Mohrlein interview, 2007; Novel Ventures programs and reviews courtesy of Janis Guggenheim; Novel Ventures 1979 press release, EA.

22. Lippitz contract and Chicago news clippings, EA; Lippitz to Borchardt, August 16 and October 10, 1989, January 25, 1993, and July 14, 1994; Mohrlein interview, 2007.

23. Borchardt to SE, May 14, 1969; Lisa Johnson (Doubleday) to SE, March 11 and 26, 1970; Ronnie Shusan (Doubleday) to SE, September 25, 1970; "A Preface to the Sixties (But I Am Getting Ahead of Myself)," reprinted in *Pieces of Soap*.

24. Alfred Appell (*Tri-Quarterly*) to SE, March 22 and 27, May 10, 1969; Dougherty, "Conversation," 179.

Chapter 8. "Blessèd Form"

1. B. Elkin interview, 2002; Pepe interview, 2002.

2. Sanders, "Interview," 145; Dougherty, "Conversation," 195.

3. D. Winner, *Washington University Student Life* (1971); Borchardt to SE, August 19, 1979, and January 8, 1971.

4. Lish to Borchardt, July 19, 1971; Charyn, "On Stanley Elkin"; Borchardt to SE, March 3, 17, and 31 and May 6, 1971; Fox to SE, July 5, 1971.

5. SE to Nemerov, November 1, 1971; Lebowitz to SE (undated) [January 1972]; Sayad, "Living with the Arts."

6. O'Grady to SE, May 3, 1972; the detail about Elkin's desire to "test" the story doesn't appear in any other version. Coover reiterated this in a 2006 interview. In *St. Louis Magazine* (May 1983), Elkin insists that he was unaware that the hall was a monastery and that part of the audience would be sixteen-year-old girls. Coover, however, recalls telling him about the conversion of the castle to a monastery.

7. Coover, *New England Review* 27 (2006) and interview, 2006; Gordon Burnside, "The Funniest Writer," *St. Louis* (May 1983): 28; Ballowe interview, 2002; Bargen, "Interview," 238–39; Nemerov to SE, March 31, 1972; Ken Emerson, "The Indecorous, Rabelaisian, Convoluted Righteousness of Stanley Elkin," *New York Times Magazine* (March 3, 1991): 40–41.

8. Susan Dwyer (Borchardt) to SE, July 27 and August 10, 1973; Sloan to SE, August 19, 1990; despite repeated efforts, I've been unsuccessful in locating a copy of the adaptation. Sloan died in 1995; contract, Remains Theatre, and SE, August 13, 1990.

9. Hedy Weiss, "Remains New Digs Are Just Right, but Play Misses Mark," *Chicago Sun-Times*, October 8, 1990; Scott Collins, "Changing Nightly," *Southtown Economist* (October 11, 1990); Gold to SE, November 29, 1990; Gold, note to the author, July 2008.

10. Lebowitz interview, 2002; Shea interview, 2002; Coover interview, 2006; Oates to SE, November 17, 1974; *The Journal of Joyce Carol Oates, 1973–1982*, edited by Greg Johnson (New York: Ecco Press, 2007), 50, 215, 392; Cuoco interview, 2002; Gass tells the story in *New England Review* 27 (2006): 65.

11. Demarest interview, 2006; M. Elkin interview, 2002; B. Elkin interview, 2002; J. Elkin interview, 2002; Lebowitz interview, 2002.

12. "Out of One's Tree: My Bout with Temporary Insanity"; Gass interview, 2002; Demarest interview, 2006.

13. http://www.nationalmssociety.org/about-multiple-sclerosis/index.aspx; Vendler interview, 2006, and *New England Review* 27 (2006): 58; Demarest interview, 2006; Coover interview, 2006; Dougherty, "Conversation," 186.

14. Fox to SE, April 11, February 3, and July 20, 1972; SE to Fox, March 2, 1972, Borchardt Archive; Borchardt to SE, January 6, 1972.

15. Fox to SE, February 16, 1972.

16. Rotter (*Esquire*) to Borchardt, January 19, 1972; Lish (*Esquire*) to Borchardt, January 10, 1972, Borchardt Archive; Borchardt to SE, July 23, 1972; Susan Dwyer (Borchardt) to SE, August 27 and December 31, 1975.

17. LeClair, "Art of Fiction," 67; Ellen Futterman, "Full-Tilt Elkin," *St. Louis Post-Dispatch*, April 14, 1991.

18. LeClair, "Art of Fiction"; Sanders, "Interview"; Fox to SE, September 19, 1972, November 6, 14, and 27, 1972, December 8 and 21, 1972; Duncan, "Elkin and Gass," 67.

19. Interview with SE, 1989, not included in published version of Dougherty, "Conversation."

20. Marcus anecdotes, Duncan, "Elkin and Gass," 71; financial details, copy of the Warner Brothers contract, EA; much of the information about the production is found in the publicity packet prepared by Twentieth-Century Fox, EA; details from the film, screened at the Library of Congress in February 2007.

21. Duncan, "Elkin and Gass," 71.

22. David Rosenbaum, "There Go the Points!" *Spectrum* (November 3, 1976).

23. Rosenbaum, "There Go the Points!"; Pocket Books closing balance September 30, 1978, EA.

24. Joel Thingvall, "Movies," *Mpls.* (January 1977): 52.

25. Fox to SE, September 19 and 27, 1972; SE's doodles on Fox to SE, November 6, 1972; Fox to SE, November 14 and 27, 1972, December 8 and 21, 1972, and March 2, 1973.

26. Gollancz to SE, June 7, 1973; Fox to Borchardt, January 3, 1974.

27. Reviews from clippings in EA: Marc Cogan, "The banal explodes into the exotic and magnificently funny," *Book Week*, October 4, 1973; Christopher Lehman-Haupt, "A Gag and Two Ominous Words," *New York Times*, October 9, 1973; Philip Corwin, "One for Three," *National Observer* (November 1973); Martin Seymour-Smith, "She-Bear at Large," *Financial Times*, November 7, 1974; Nina Bawden, "Recent Fiction," *London Daily Telegraph*, November 7, 1974; Wendy Monk, "New Fiction," *Birmingham Post*, November 30, 1974.

28. Borchardt to SE, August 18 and 31, 1971; Gerard Livi (for Trintignant) to SE, October 29, 1971, and SE's penciled response on same; Borchardt to SE, January 6 and 26, 1972; Lombardi (*Esquire*) to SE, February 28, 1972; Bargen, "Interview," 231–32.

29. Susan Dwyer to Pesta, June 21, 1974; SE to Borchardt, August 20, 1974; "A la Recherche du Whoopee Cushion," *Pieces of Soap*, 215–27; Pat Ryan (*Sports Illustrated*) to Borchardt, October 25, 1973; Borchardt to SE, December 15, 1973; Borchardt to SE, October 7 and November 15, 1974, Borchardt Archive; Susan Dwyer (Borchardt) to Ryan, November 6, 1974; SE to Borchardt, February 5, 1974.

Chapter 9. *"Making America Look Like America"*

1. SE to Fox, July 24, 1972, Borchardt Archive.

2. Brandwein interview, 2002; J. Elkin, however, couldn't corroborate this story.

3. SE to Borchardt, February 18 and March 8, 1972, Borchardt Archive; SE at one point decided to accept a $25,000 fee, but Schlesinger changed his mind about the offer; Borchardt to SE, February 16 and 23, 1972; SE to Ritchie, January 8, 1973; Duncan, "Elkin and Gass," 71–72.

4. Ritchie's career, IMDB.com; P. Elkin interview, 2002; Florida trip, Ritchie to SE, March 1, 1977; SE to Ritchie, January 18, 1973; Ritchie to SE, February 3, 1973.

5. http://www.pbs.org/wnet/americanmasters/episodes/robert-capa/introduction/47/; photocopies and contract between Elkin and Columbia Pictures, May 22, 1973, EA; Borchardt to Ritchie, September 25, 1973; Ritchie to SE, August 20, 1976.

6. *The Art of War,* film script, EA; Borchardt interview, 2007; Duncan, "Elkin and Gass," 70.

7. Ritchie to SE, July 6, 1973; Sayad, "Living with Arts"; Bob Keith [untitled], *Daily Iowan,* April 3, 1974; Ritchie to SE, August 20, 1980.

8. *Mudshow* typescript, EA.

9. Ritchie to SE, September 15, 1977.

10. Wendy Schacher (Borchardt) to SE, September 28, 1979.

11. Agreement, MGM, December 14, 1976; script underlined with speeches Elkin represented as his contribution, EA; Herbert S. Nusbaum (MGM) to SE, December 23, 1976, January 24 and February 14, 1977; tagline, IMDB.com.

12. 1981 introduction, EA; Irving reminiscence, *New England Review* 27 (2006): 59; M. Elkin email, July 2007.

13. Pool story, J. Elkin interview, 2007; Teitelbaum interview, 2002; Naomi Lebowitz corroborated this story in July 2007.

14. Thurston interview, 2002; Gass confirmation by email, July 2007; Pope interview, 2003, and email, January 2004; SE told a version of the Faulkner story to Clayton, "Interview," 12; Myers to SE, February 10, 1979; Earlywine, "Interview," 13.

15. Dean Ralph Morrow to SE, October 24, 1975; SE to Richard Young (Smith), November 30, 1972 ("this is an official feeler"); John Ades (Southern Illinois) to SE, November 30, 1972; Richard Holsey (Arizona) to SE, December 13, 1972; Fields interview, 2002.

16. *AWP Newsletter* (1988): 12; Roger Hahn, "The Sweet and Sour Heart of Stanley Elkin," *The Weekly* (March 8–14, 1985): 16.

17. "Short Fiction Works among 110 Contending for National Book Award," *New York Times,* March 18, 1974; Heller comment, *AWP Newsletter* (1988); SE to Howard Moss for AAAL, handwritten draft, March 5, 1974; Eloise Segal of AAAL to SE, April 1, 1974.

18. Sanders to SE, November 21, 1973, and January 4, 1974; LeClair to SE, August 15 and 21, 1974, March 21, 1975; LeClair email to the author, 2002; Guttman to SE, February 19, 1974; Bargen to SE, February 25, 1975; Doris Bargen, "The Orphan Adopted: Stanley Elkin's *The Franchiser,*" *Studies in American Jewish Literature* 2 (1982): 133; McCaffrey to SE, April 26, 1977.

19. Milofsky interview, 2007; Bain, *Whose Woods These Are,* 117–118.

20. M. Charyn to SE, July 25, 1977; J. Charyn interview, 2007; Pepe interview, 2005; Milofsky interview, 2007; Wolff to SE, November 10, 1980; P., B., and M. Elkin interviews, 2002.

21. Berkeley, "PW Interviews," 74; Marc Chenetier, "An Interview with Stanley Elkin," *Delta* 20 (February 1985): 18–19; "The Burger That Conquered the Country," *Time* (September 17, 1973).

22. Lobell to SE, April 28, 1976.

23. Clayton "Interview," 8–9; he used identical phrasing in LeClair, "Art of Fiction," 86, and Bernt and Bernt, "Elkin on Fiction," 25.

24. Elkin's response to a series of written questions, EA; he reiterated this to LeClair, "Art of Fiction," 86, mentioning an "enormous J. C. Penney catalogue" as the prominent item in his library carrel.

25. Bargen, "Interview," 223, 232; Dougherty, "Conversation," 186.

26. Peter Bailey, *Reading Stanley Elkin* (Urbana: University of Illinois Press, 1985), 132.

27. Sale, "Elkin in St. Louis," 315.

28. Bargen, "Orphan Adopted," 133. I treat the itinerary theme in *Stanley Elkin* (New York: G. K. Hall, 1991), ch. 3.

29. Bailey, *Reading Elkin,* ch. 4. See also Robert Edward Colbert, "The American Salesman as Pitchman and Poet in the Fiction of Stanley Elkin," *Critique* 21 (1980): 52–58.

30. Bargen, "Interview," 223–24; Clayton, "Interview," 10–11.

31. Nemerov to Asher, March 8, 1976; a different portion of his comment was excerpted in the publicity kit for *The Franchiser;* Coover comment, Asher to SE, April 15, 1976, quoted in full in the publicity kit.

32. *Publishers Weekly* (April 19, 1976); John Leonard, "Dreams on Credit," *Saturday Review* (May 29, 1976); Christopher Lehman-Haupt, "Books of the Times," *New York*

Times, May 21, 1976; Geoffrey Wolff, "Topping the Tank," *New York Times,* June 26, 1976; R. Z. Sheppard, "The Critics Are Saying," *New York Post,* June 6, 1976, and "A Poet of Profit and Loss," *Time* (May 24, 1976); "A Memorable Man Emerges," *Baltimore News-American,* July 4, 1976; Book-of-the-Month Club (1976).

33. Vendler to SE, July 31, 1976; Wakoski to SE, November 15, 1976; Flanagan to SE, June 6, 1976.

34. Farrar, Straus and Giroux royalty statements, June 30 and December 31, 1976, and June 30, 1977; undated English-language rights contract; Casa Editrice contract, January 31, 1977; Borchardt to SE, July 27, 1976; Godine to SE, August 6, 1979, July 29 and November 8, 1980.

35. Borchardt to SE, August 18 and 31, 1976; Asher to SE, September 22, 1976; Godine to SE, September 13, 1979.

36. Godine to SE, September 13, 1979; "deal memo" and agreement, EA; Anne Borchardt to SE, September 28, 1994; Borchardt interview, 2007; Gibson to SE, January 1, 1981.

Chapter 10. Heaven and Hell, St. Louis and Mexico, the First Crusade, and South America

1. Patricia Rice, "After Death: 'The Living End,'" *St. Louis Post-Dispatch,* July 18, 1979.

2. In "The Infinite's Jest: Stanley Elkin Imagines the Life after Life," *Harper's* (May 2004), Gass points out that the Old Testament contains many precedents, characters struck dead or punished for accidental or incidental violations of the Divine Law, and concludes, "Our author is on theologically sound ground here" (95).

3. Publishing contract for "a work known at present as *The Conventional Wisdom,*" September 8, 1978, EA; Wolff to SE, September 15, 1977; Wolitzer interview, 2007; Solotoff to SE, September 29, 1976; Ritchie to SE, August 20, 1976; Robbins to SE, November 3, 1978.

4. Coover to SE, January 19, 1977; *The Gateway* (University of Nebraska), November 8, 1978.

5. Dougherty, "Conversation," 181.

6. Robbins to SE, October 12 and 24, 1978.

7. Shea interview, 2002; Dr. Shea gave me a photocopy of the inscription and the EA contains a photocopy of the cover art for *The Bottom Line,* the title under which the triptych appears in Dutton's 1979 catalogue. See also Rice, "After Death," 3F, and Clayton, "Interview," 8; also see SE to Borchardt, January 16, 1979, quoted below.

8. Irving to Robbins, October 2, 1978; Barth to Robbins, February 14, 1979; Coover to Robbins, March 6, 1979.

9. SE to Borchardt, January 16, 1979.

10. Contracts and memos of agreement, EA.

11. Carasso to SE, November 27, 1979.

12. Jim Goldwasser to SE, June 12, 1979; Gold to SE, July 13, 1979.

13. Wilson to SE, September 21, 1981; Ledeen to SE, August 10, 1979; Leff to SE, August 16, 1979 (ellipses his); Fox to SE, August 13, 1979; Casandia Eaton (AAIAL) to SE, March 31, 1980; AAIAL citation, May 21, 1980, EA; Marjorie Can Haltern (PBS) to SE, June 6, 1981; Gregory to SE, May 11, 1989.

14. "Pearl Lee Gates" to SE, August 9, 1979 (ellipses "hers").

15. Charlotte Weiner to SE, April 5, 1980.

16. Irving, "An Exposé of Heaven and Hell," *New York Times Book Review,* June 10, 1979; LeClair, "The Living End," *Saturday Review* (October 13 1979); Wolff, "Heaven and Superhell: Elkin's Vision of the Afterlife," *Esquire* (June 19, 1979); du Pres, "To Hell and Back with Stanley Elkin," *Washington Post Book World,* July 1, 1979; Bailey, "The Quick and the Dead," *Times Literary Supplement* (U.K.), January 18, 1980; Frakes, "God Visits Hell: Hi, Hot Enough for You?" *Cleveland Plain Dealer,* July 7, 1979; Larry Collier to Frakes, July 8, 1979.

17. *Kirkus Reviews* (April 15, 1979); Evelyn Attix, *Spiritual Studies Center,* August 1979; Mary Geisheker, "Hell in Living Color," *Baltimore Sun,* July 18, 1979; David Williams, "Fiction," *London Times,* January 24, 1980; Terence deVere White, "A Merry Soul," *Irish Times,* February 2, 1980.

18. Ritchie to SE, August 20, 1976; the previous five paragraphs are a synthesis of interviews with Galati, 2002, and Wagner, 2006, and the agreement of June 26, 1980, EA.

19. Frank Galati, *Stanley Elkin's The Living End,* film script, 116, EA.

20. Earlywine, "Interview," 16.

21. Wolff to SE, February 7, 1978; "Three Meetings," *Tri-Quarterly* 17 (Winter 1970): 261–65, reprinted in *Pieces of Soap,* 313–18; U.S. Government Authorization Agreement, January 26, 1978; handwritten note by J. Elkin, EA.

22. J. Elkin interviews, 2002 and 2005; assessment by Caracas embassy, March 6, 1978; by Brasilia embassy, February 23, 1978.

23. "Address to the Hawaiians," EA.

24. Introduction to *The Best American Short Stories 1980,* reprinted in *Pieces of Soap,* 195–206.

25. Lorin Cuoco, transcript of 1995 KWMU (St. Louis) literary profile; Borchardt to SE, October 26, 1979, and January 14, 1980.

26. Coover, foreword to *Greatest Hits,* ix–x, xii.

27. Lee Milazzo, "Witty, Not-So-Witty Fiction from Charyn, Kotzwinkle, Elkin," *Dallas Morning News,* November 16, 1980.

28. Introduction to *The Coffee Room* (Louisville, Ky.: Contre Coup Press, 1987), i, iii.

29. Cuoco, "The Making of *The Coffee Room,*" program for "The Washington University Libraries Celebrate a Milestone," March 26, 1996, and interview, 2002; Lebowitz, "The Real Coffee Room," libraries program, 1996.

30. "Of Books and Authors," *John Barkham Reviews,* EA; Dougherty, "Conversation," 183–84.

31. Macrae to SE, March 9, 1982.

32. Chenetier, "Interview," 17 (ellipsis his).

33. *The First George Mills* (Dallas: Pressworks, 1980); *Antaeus* 40/41 (Winter 1981): 86–104; Wolitzer to SE, October 6, 1982.

34. Dougherty, "Conversation" 184; see also Gass, "Adventures in the Writing Life," *Washington Post Book World,* October 10, 1982.

35. Dougherty, "Conversation," 184–85; Chambers to SE, April 9, 1990.

36. The camp still exists: http://www.cassadaga.org/.

37. Dougherty, "Conversation," 184, 185, 185–86; LeClair to SE, May 26 and December 14, 1982.

38. Handwritten (not Elkin's hand) planning document, EA; J. Elkin interview, 2005.

39. J. Elkin interview, 2005; Pepe interview, 2005; Shea email, August 2005; David Gregory to SE, May 11, 1989; Gottfried interview and email, 2008.

40. Turner (*Playboy*) to Borchardt, February 12, 1982: Borchardt to SE, March 12, 1982.

41. Dougherty, "Conversation," 182–83.

42. SE to Macrae, November 11 and 17 and December 18, 1981; advertisement, *New York Times,* November 3 and 5, 1982; contract addendum, February 10, 1982, EA.

43. Leslie Marshall, "Ever Hear of Elkin? You Will Now," *USA Today,* December 10, 1982; *Publishers Weekly,* August 20, 1980; Joel Connaroe, "SE's St. Louis Everyman," *Washington Post Book World,* October 10, 1982, and *International Herald-Tribune,* October 21, 1982; Tom LeClair, "George Mills," *New Republic* (December 27, 1982); Christopher Lehman-Haupt, "Books of the Times," *New York Times,* October 20, 1982; Ken Tucker, "A Cult Offering for Elkin Fans," *Philadelphia Inquirer,* October 31, 1982; Alexander Theroux, "Quirks, Quips, Quotations: Tasteless, Topical, Tired," *Boston Globe,* October 31, 1982.

44. Nemerov to SE, October 3, 1982; Gold to SE, October 1, 1982; Ford to SE, December 22, 1982; Irving to SE, July 7, 1982.

45. Malamud to SE, January 21, 1983; Danforth to SE, January 12, 1983; Macrae quoted by Edwin Macdowell, "Publishing: Do Prizes Sell Books?" *New York Times,* April 15, 1983.

46. Contract and sales data, EA; Whitehead to SE, April 22 and May 1, 1984; Wendy Schacher (Borchardt) to SE, November 26 and December 5, 1984, and June 13, 1985.

47. Shea interview, 2002; the EA contains the diskettes and dot-matrix printouts, as well as the exam books; *AWP Newsletter* (February–March 1988).

48. Celebrity stories told to Al and Naomi Lebowitz by SE, interview, 2002; Leslie Hanscom, "How to Get Your Name above the Title," *Newsday* (March 1, 1981); Godwin to SE, May 15, 1981; Coover to SE, May 19, 1981; Coover, interview, 2006.

Chapter 11. Disney World and Alaskan Rabbis

1. Gass, "Adventures in the Writing Life."

2. Undated typescript, EA, hand-dated 1982; the allusions and theme of the broken family are consistent with that date; solid internal evidence involves the pitchers for the game Phil and Sean will see. Craig Swan was on the Mets roster in 1982, Mike Krukow's only year with the Phillies (http://mlb.mlb.com/stats/historical/_player_locator_results); Milofsky interview, 2007; "The Saturday Visit," *Colorado Review* 20, no. 2 (1993): 4–28.

3. Typescript of "The Griefs," EA; "The Griefs," *Perspective* (Spring 1982): 21–24, and *Playboy* (September 1982): 102–3, 222; *George Mills,* part 2, ch. 3.

4. SE to William Masden, April 21, 1978; Ruland to Dean Gottfried, cc: SE, May 11, 1978; Kling to SE, February 12, 1985; Shea interview, 2002.

5. P. Elkin interview, 2002.

6. B. Elkin interview, 2002; Sandra Gilligan (Churchill School) to Internal Revenue Service, August 3, 1979; SE to Bellow, March 29, 1992.

7. M. Elkin interview, 2002 and subsequent emails; Whitehead to SE, March 20, 1984; SE to Molly, June 5, 1986, excerpted by permission of M. Elkin; I've normalized some paragraph indentations and combined several to one.

8. SE to Dean Richard Rosett, January 1, 1986; Thomas Stewart (chancellor, University of Illinois) to SE, February 2, 1986; Mary Gallatin (Brandeis) to SE, March 30, 1986; Duncan to SE, February 12, 1983.

9. Lorin Cuoco, "KMWU Presents Stanley Elkin," 1985; SE offers a similar account in Chenetier, "Interview," 18; the earliest version appears in Hahn, "Sweet and Sour Heart," 17; he told the same story with minor variations in Dougherty, "Conversation," 189, and Bailey, "'A Hat,'" 25.

10. Teitelbaum interview, 2002; Elkin's representation of Mudd-Gaddis's disease echoed with Steve Homan, who asked for his help in publishing a book on Meg Casey, "the world's longest-living and best-known progeriac"; Homan to SE, November 5, 1986.

11. The effort to publish "On a Field, Rampant" is discussed in chapter 5.

12. Turner to SE, April 6, 1982; Dougherty, "Conversation," 191.

13. Dougherty, "Conversation," 190; interviews with B. and M. Elkin, 2002; Cuoco, "KMWU Presents Elkin."

14. Charlotte Whaley (*Southwest Review*) to SE, December 15, 1982; Whitehead to SE, June 10 and November 15, 1984; copy editor's copy and master galley, EA; Amy Robbins (Borchardt) to SE, August 27, 1984; *Literary Guild* announcement, August 10, 1985, EA; contract with Editions Albin Michel, May 29, 1985; Anne Dubuisson (Borchardt) to SE, November 24, 1986, and February 26, 1987; Wendy Schacher (Borchardt) to SE, August 19, 1985; contracts with Shinchosha and Thunder's Mouth, EA.

15. Kreitz contract, EA; www.imdb.com/name/nm1450389/.

16. Bailey, "'A Hat,'" 25.

17. Bailey, "'A Hat,'" 19.

18. *Kirkus Reviews* (January 15, 1985); "The Best of 1985," *Newsday* (December 8, 1985); Jeff Clark, "Stanley Elkin's Magic Kingdom," *Library Journal* (April 15, 1985); Dan Cryer, "A Genius for Making Music Out of the Macabre," *Newsday* (March 17, 1985); Max Apple, "Having Their Last Good Time," *New York Times Book Review,* March 24, 1985; Christopher Lehman-Haupt, "Books of the Times," *New York Times,* March 18, 1985, and Santa Rosa (Calif.) *Press-Democrat,* March 31, 1985; Charles Simmons, "Death Be Not Fun" *Vogue* (April 1985); Anne Tyler, "Stanley and the Horror Factory," *Detroit News,* April 14, 1985; Noel Perrin, "Stanley Elkin Meets Mickey Mouse," *USA Today,* March 22, 1985; Ted Lindberg, "Beyond Human Horror," *Washington Times,* April 22, 1985.

19. Rafelson story, Dorothy Young (Borchardt) to SE, April 12, 1984; Bob Williams (The Loft) to SE, July 25, 1984; Harry H. Sweets III (Twain Commission) to SE, December 24, 1984; Marc Chenetier to SE, January 5 and March 30, 1985.

20. Susan Welch, "Stanley Elkin Visits Minneapolis with a New Book and a Lot of Opinions," *Minneapolis Star and Tribune,* April 7, 1985; "The Contemporary Literature Speech in France," *Revue Français d'Etudes Americaines* 27–28 (February 1986): 158.

21. Dr. Murray Bornstein (Einstein College of Medicine) to SE, February 2 and April 20, 1985; Dr. Isaac Eisenberg to SE, September 30, 1985; Roberta Vaughan (Sew It Seems) to SE, September 24, 1984; Cuoco interview, 2002.

22. McHugh to SE, May 3, 1985; Eisenberg to SE, September 30, 1985.

23. Kay Boyle (PEN/Faulkner) to SE, November 21, 1985; Joe Ashby Porter (Duke) to SE, September 27, 1985; Judy Gurst (The Loft) to SE, August 3, 1985, and February 1,

1986; Borchardt to E. P. Dutton, November 8, 1985, and January 10, 1986; Ozick to SE, March 18, 1988; Allen Whitehead to SE, July 17, 1988.

24. Carver to SE, May 28, 1981; Anderson (Fireweed Press) to SE, August 13, 1983, and January 13, 1984; the source for the marijuana farm story remains confidential.

25. Anderson interview, 2006, and letters and emails; for a discussion of potlatch as trope, see my *Stanley Elkin*, ch. 6.

26. *AWP Newsletter* (1988): 12.

27. SE to Moody, November 11, 1988; Dougherty, "Conversation," 192.

28. Bailey, "'A Hat,'" 26; Whitehead to SE, February 24, 1987; Dougherty, "Conversation," 193.

29. EA.

30. Memo of agreement, SE and Mid-American Dance Company (MADCO), August 27, 1986; MADCO news release, March 15, 1987; "The Muses Are Heard," *Pieces of Soap*, 88, 100; Martha Baker, "Words to Move You," *Connoisseur* [n.d.].

31. Newman to Borchardt, October 11, 1985; Menaker to Borchardt, May 22, 1976; Robert Stewart (Scribner's) to Borchardt, March 19, 1987; jacket comments, *The Rabbi of Lud*; Irving to Scribner's, October 20, 1987.

32. Sherman to Shannon (Borchardt's), November 25, 1987.

33. Patricia Leigh Brown, "A Literate Night of Dining and Lionizing," *New York Times*, November 13, 1987.

Chapter 12. "But I Am Getting Ahead of Myself"

1. Discussed in chapter 3.

2. Bamberger to SE, September 5 and 30, 1984.

3. Kriegel, "Remembering Elkin," *Forward* 3 (November 1995).

4. Chibka to SE, September 8, 1989; SE to Chibka, Labor Day 1989 (a truncated version appears in "At the Academy Awards," *P.S.* 156–57); Solu-Medrol is prescribed for a variety of inflammatory diseases including MS. Cytoxan is ordinarily prescribed for patients with malignancies, though I've uncovered no evidence of cancer in Elkin's health history. Both Cytoxan and Solu-Medrol suppress the immune system (www.drugs.com).

5. SE to Moody, April 4, 1989.

6. Galati interview, 2002.

7. Elkin shared a similar version of this story with Al and Naomi Lebowitz, interview, 2002. Cronkite story, Teitelbaum interview, 2002, and M. Elkin email, February 4, 2003.

8. Revard to SE, January 21, 1992.

9. SE to Vendler, March 14 and 30, 1990; Vendler to SE, July 14, 1991; SE to Joe Tucker, December 20, 1992.

10. Prunty interview, 2007.

11. SE to Glennon, October 16, 1988; Updike quoted by Glennon to SE, November 30, 1990.

12. SE to Vendler, March 14 and August 18, 1990; SE, introduction, Helen Vendler, EA; Bellow to SE, July 30 and January 20, 1992; SE to Bellow, February 9, 1992 ("soul clap hands and sing" echoes William B. Yeats's "Sailing to Byzantium"); Conroy to Marie Arana-Ward, January 5, 1992.

13. SE to M. Elkin, October 23, 1988.

14. Stephanie Mayes to Lapham (*Harper's*), undated letter; Phyllis Graeser to *Harper's*, March 3, 1993; Mark Miller to SE, February 10, 1993; Lisa Solod to SE, December 15, 1992; SE to Lorraine Glennon, February 2, 1993.

15. M. Elkin email, November 9, 2007.

16. Rockefeller Foundation to SE, January 28 and July 21, 1987; Hardin to SE, June 30, 1987; dedication page, *The MacGuffin*. Elkin uses nearly identical language in a letter to Joseph Loew, December 13, 1989.

17. Coover interview, November 2006.

18. Bill Marx, "Guru of Gab," *Boston Phoenix*, April 10, 1992. Marx also announces Elkin's reading and signing at the Brattle Street Theater on April 14, 1992.

19. Corwin to SE, December 7, 1994.

20. Dougherty, "Conversation," 188, 187.

21. Dougherty, "Conversation," 187.

22. Turner (*Playboy*) to SE, May 11, 1990; contract, Borchardt to SE, April 8, 1988; press release from Linden, a Simon and Schuster subsidiary; "The MacGuffin," *Playboy* (December 1990): 118–19, 160, 232–43.

23. *Aurora Beacon-News*, February 24, 1991; Earl Dashslager, "Decline of Bobbo Druff: Elkin's Excess Has Few Rewards," *Houston Chronicle*, April 7, 1991; *Publishers Weekly* (January 28, 1991); *Library Journal* (February 1, 1991); *Kirkus Reviews* (January 1, 1991); Thomas Edwards, "Behind Gravity's Back," *New Republic* (May 20, 1991).

24. Earnings statements, EA; foreign rights, Wendy Schacher (Borchardt) to SE, February 14 and December 24, 1991; Borchardt to Arana-Ward (Simon and Schuster), May 16, 1991; Meg Hofstetter (Simon and Schuster) to SE, December 8, 1992.

25. Paul to SE, January 19, 1992; SE to Walk of Fame Committee, February 22, 1991; SE to Paul, January 1992; SE to Anderson, February 26, 1992.

26. M. Elkin email, November 9, 2007.

27. SE to Malcolm Jones, April 1985.

28. Teitelbaum interview, 2002; Ellen Futterman, "Full-Tilt Elkin," *St. Louis Post-Dispatch*, April 1991; Lebowitz interview, 2002; B. Elkin interview, 2002.

29. Ballowe interview, 2002; Monaghan, interview and emails, 2006.

30. Karen Schneiderman to SE, June 1, 1993; SE to Schniederman, June 26, 1993.

31. John Grammer interview and emails, 2007; McGraw interview, 2007.

32. Dougherty, "Conversation," 179; SE to Marc Chenetier, October 24, 1990, and to Borchardt, December 25, 1990; Daniel Menaker (*New Yorker*) to SE, February 5, 1991; Bob Perlongo (*Tri-Quarterly*) to SE, January 17, 1992; "Golf-Ball-Size Hail," *Playboy* (January 1994).

33. Wilkins, interview and emails, 2006; see Wilkins, "Opening the Bag," *Mutes and Earthquakes* (Wellington, New Zealand: Victoria University Press), 67–68; the writer was Mark Bautz.

34. Nicole Jeffords to SE, February 11, 1992; SE to Jeffords, February 27, 1992.

35. SE to Revard, June 3, 1993; Corwin to SE, September 29, 1993.

36. M. Elkin to SE, December 12, 1990

37. Contract for *Van Gogh's Room*, August 29, 1991; Italian edition contract, February 25, 1993; French edition contract, Wendy Schacher (Borchardt) to SE, August 8, 1994; SE to Zych, February 10, 1993.

38. Moore, syndicated as "Falling Down and Calling Up," *Boston Herald*, March 28, 1993; Michiko Kakutani, "People with Bad Luck and Even Worse Behavior," *New York Times*, February 23, 1993; "*Van Gogh's Room at Arles*," *New York Magazine* (March 8, 1993). Recommendations: *New York Times Book Review*, December 5, 1993; *Chicago Tribune*, December 5, 1993; *Philadelphia Inquirer*, December 12, 1993; *New York Times Book Review*, June 5, 1994.

Chapter 13. *"The Stanley Elkin Chair"*

1. P. Elkin interview, 2002; M. Elkin email, 2007; wedding toast, EA.

2. SE to Bogart, February 15, 1994.

3. Yellin to Richard (no surname), August 5, 1993; to SE, March 29, May 5, and October 6, 1994; SE to Yellin, March 23 and April 9, 1994; Waters interview, 2007.

4. Hempel to SE, April 7, 1994; SE to Hempel, undated.

5. Contract, SE and Hyperion Press, April 15, 1993; video of 1993 Sewanee reading, courtesy of Sewanee Writers' Conference; SE to Waters, July 11, 1994; SE to Mulcahy, November 5, 1994.

6. SE to Yellin, February 14, 1995.

7. SE to Bogart, December 28, 1994; SE to Wilkins, March 7, 1995; Robins interview, 2002; SE to Joan Greenberger, December 22, 1994.

8. Howard, "Sunset over Miami," *Los Angeles Times*, September 3, 1995, p. 1.

9. Obituaries, Columbia (Mo.) *Daily Tribune*, June 1, 1995; *New York Times*, June 2, 1995; Washington University *Record*, June 22, 1995; P. and B. Elkin interviews, 2002; Steve Teitelbaum email, 2008; J. Elkin, by telephone, 2008; M. Elkin emails, February and June 2008.

10. Washington University *Record*, March 14, 1996; Gass tribute, William Gaddis Archive, Olin Library; Prose, video of 1995 tribute, Sewanee Writers' Conference. Knievel was a legendary motorcycle stuntman and daredevil who jumped his cycle over buildings, automobiles, fountains, and the Snake River Canyon, often resulting in grave injuries.

11. St. Louis memorial program; Robert Duffy, "To Elkin, Farewell," *St. Louis Post-Dispatch*, June 11, 1995.

12. Program for New York memorial; Borchardt Agency fax to J. Elkin, September 9, 1995; Coover interview, 2006; M. Elkin email, February 2008.

13. John Milton, *Paradise Lost*, book 7; Bailey recalled this phrase in an email.

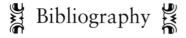 Bibliography

Works by Stanley Elkin

An online bibliography of Elkin's works is hosted at www.loyola.edu/stanleyelkin. All citations from this biography, except for personal interviews, refer to that bibliography. This version includes only original and Dalkey Archive editions, currently in print. Information about other editions and magazine publication of stories and essays that have been subsequently collected can be found in the online bibliography.

Novels

Alex and the Gypsy. New York: Pocket Books, 1976. A separate issue of "The Bailbondsman" issued in conjunction with the film.

A Bad Man. New York: Random House, 1967. Dalkey Archive, 2003.

Boswell: A Modern Comedy. New York: Random House, 1964. Dalkey Archive, 1999.

The Dick Gibson Show. New York: Random House, 1971. Dalkey Archive, 1998.

The First George Mills. Dallas: Pressworks, 1980. Limited edition of *George Mills*, part 1.

The Franchiser. New York: Farrar, Straus and Giroux, 1976. Dalkey Archive, 2001.

George Mills. New York: E. P. Dutton, 1982. Dalkey Archive, 2003.

The MacGuffin. New York: Simon and Schuster, 1991. Dalkey Archive, 1999.

Mrs. Ted Bliss. New York: Hyperion, 1995. Dalkey Archive, 2002.

The Rabbi of Lud. New York: Charles Scribner's Sons, 1987. Dalkey Archive, 2001.

Stanley Elkin's The Magic Kingdom. New York: E. P. Dutton, 1985. Dalkey Archive, 2000.

Collections of Novellas

The Living End. New York: E. P. Dutton, 1979. Dalkey Archive, 2004.

Searches and Seizures. New York: Random House, 1973. Published as *Eligible Men,* London: Gollancz, 1974.

Van Gogh's Room at Arles: Three Novellas. New York: Hyperion, 1993. Dalkey Archive, 2002.

Collections of Stories

Criers and Kibitzers, Kibitzers and Criers. New York: Random House, 1966. Dalkey Archive, 2000.

Early Elkin. Flint, Mich.: Bamberger Books, 1985.
Stanley Elkin's Greatest Hits. Foreword by Robert Coover. New York: E. P. Dutton, 1980.

Uncollected Stories

"The Dying." *Illini Writers* 4 (September 1950): 10–18.
"Alone Is Hurt Too." *Illini Writers* 4 (Spring 1951): 11–19.
"Corporate Life." *Chicago* (March 1985): 156–59.
"Golf-Ball-Size Hail." *Playboy* (January 1994): 134, 212, 250–62.
"Baseball Story." *New England Review* 27 (2006): 48–52.
"Colin Kelly's Kids." *New England Review* 27 (2006): 53–56.

Collection of Essays

Pieces of Soap. New York: Simon and Schuster, 1992.

Uncollected Essays

"Miss Taylor and Family: An Outside View." *Esquire* 62 (1964): 43–44, 46, 118–20.
"The World on $5 a Day." *Harper's* 245 (July 1972): 41–46.
"Inside Jean-Louis Trintignant." *Oui* 2 (January 1973): 84–86, 166, 168–69, 172–74.
"Representation and Performance," in *Representation and Performance in Postmodern Literature,* edited by Maurice Couturier. Montpelier, France: Delta, 1983: 181–91. Proceedings of the 1982 Conference on Postmodern Fiction, Nice.
"American Fiction and Its Reach." *Harper's* 284 (March 1992): 34–35.
"Out of One's Tree: My Bout with Temporary Insanity." *Harper's* 286 (January 1993): 69–77.

Plays

The Coffee Room. Louisville, Ky.: Contre Coup, 1987.
"The Saturday Visit." *Colorado Review* 20, no. 2 (Fall 1993): 4–28.
"The Six-Year-Old Man: A Screenplay." *Esquire* 70 (December 1968): 142–45, 226, 228, 232–33, 236–37, 240, 246–47, 251–53. Full text, *The Six-Year-Old Man.* Flint, Mich.: Bamberger Books, 1987.

Special Editions Dedicated to Elkin and His Work

Delta 20 (February 1985).
"Stanley Elkin and William H. Gass: A Special Feature." *Iowa Review* 7 (1975).
Review of Contemporary Fiction 15 (Summer 1995).
"Stanley Elkin Revisited." *New England Review* 27 (2006): 36–70.

Personal Interviews

Many people were generous with their time and memories of this extraordinary man. I want to take this opportunity to thank each one of them because many of the anecdotes originate in their stories

Anderson, Jean. Writer. Email and telephone, February 2006.
Avedon, Micki. Childhood friend. Letter and telephone, January 2006.

Bailey, Peter. Scholar, critic. Letters and emails, 2004–8.

Ballowe, James. Fellow student, lifelong friend. In person, October 2002, and emails.

Borchardt, Georges and Anne. Literary agents. In person, May 2007, and by telephone and email.

Brandwein, Diane. Sister. In person, May 2002, and by letter.

Buell, Ruth "Uncle Ruthie" Becker. Childhood friend. Telephone, January 2006.

Charyn, Jerome. Novelist, friend. Telephone, July 2007.

Coover, Robert and Pilar. Novelist, friend. In person, November 2006, and subsequent emails.

Cuoco, Lorin. Colleague, NPR interviewer. In person, June 2002.

Demarest, David. Colleague, friend. Telephone, February 2006, and subsequent emails.

Elkin, Bernard. Son. In person, June 2002.

Elkin, Joan. Spouse, caregiver, and muse. In person, June and September 2002, August 2004, August 2005, and many telephone conversations.

Elkin, Molly. Daughter. In person, December 2002, and several emails.

Elkin, Philip. Son. In person, June 2002.

Fields, Wayne. Colleague. In person, June 2002.

Galati, Frank. Screenwriter and director. In person, June 2002.

Gass, William H. Writer, colleague, close friend. In person, September 2002 and August 2006, and subsequent emails.

Gold, Charles. Colleague, long-term friend. Telephone, September 2007 and June 2008, and letters and emails.

Gottfried, Leon. Colleague. Telephone, April 2008, and subsequent emails.

Grammer, John. Sewanee colleague. In person, October 2007, and subsequent emails.

Guggenheim, Janis. Widow of childhood friend. In person, May 2002.

Jacobsen, Marshall. Brother-in-law. In person, June 2002.

Kipniss, Robert. Artist, army buddy. In person, November 2007.

Lebowitz, Al and Naomi. Lawyer, colleague, and close friends. In person, June 2002, and subsequent emails.

McGraw, Erin. Writer, former workshop student. In person, March 2006 and October 2007.

Milofsky, David. Writer, editor. Telephone, November 2007.

Mohrlein, John. Actor, theater producer. Telephone, December 2007.

Monaghan, Patricia. Writer, academic. Telephone, January 2006, and subsequent emails.

Novak, Robert. Journalist, college friend. In person, March 2006.

Pepe, George. Colleague, neighbor, close friend. In person, June 2002 and August 2005.

Pope, Nancy. Student, colleague. In person, August 2005, and email.

Prunty, Wyatt. Poet, conference director. Telephone, September 2007, and in person, October 2007.

Robins, Lee. Colleague, "Third Tuesdays," widow of Eli. Telephone, September 2002.

Shea, Dan. Colleague, close friend. In person, June 2002 and August 2005, and subsequent emails.

Siegel, Ben ("Bud"). Childhood friend. Telephone, March 2006, and subsequent emails.

Snider, Yash. High school acquaintance. Telephone, January 2003.

Spacks, Barry. Poet, cousin. Telephone and email, November 2002.

Teitelbaum, Marilyn and Steve. Colleagues, friends, "Third Tuesday." In person, June 2002, and subsequent emails.

Thurston, Jarvis (1914–February 5, 2008). Poet, editor, department chair. Telephone, September 2002.

Vendler, Helen. Critic, friend. In person, July 2006.

Wagner, Raymond. Film producer. Telephone, March 2006.

Waters, Pat. Writer, academic. Telephone, July 2007.

Wilkins, Damien. Writer, former student. Telephone, March 2006, and subsequent emails.

Wolitzer, Hilma. Writer. Telephone, July 2007.

Index

DAVID C. DOUGHERTY is a professor of English at Loyola University Maryland and the author of the critical studies *Stanley Elkin* and *James Wright* as well as the editor of two casebooks on Elkin's novels.

The University of Illinois Press
is a founding member of the
Association of American University Presses.

Composed in 9.5/13 Sabon
by Jim Proefrock
at the University of Illinois Press
Designed by Dennis Roberts
Manufactured by Thomson-Shore, Inc.

University of Illinois Press
1325 South Oak Street
Champaign, IL 61820-6903
www.press.uillinois.edu